Object-Oriented Programming in C++

Object-Oriented Programming in C++

Richard Johnsonbaugh
Martin Kalin
DEPAUL UNIVERSITY

PRENTICE HALL, Englewood Cliffs, New Jersey 07632

Cover photograph: Autograph score of Schubert's Great C major Symphony, Gesellschaft der Musikfreunde.
Used by permission

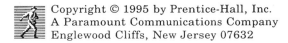

Printed in the United States of America

10   9   8   7   6   5   4

ISBN 0-02-360682-7

Prentice-Hall International (UK) Limited, *London*
Prentice-Hall of Australia Pty. Limited, *Sydney*
Prentice-Hall Canada Inc., *Toronto*
Prentice-Hall Hispanoamericana, S.A., *Mexico*
Prentice-Hall of India Private Limited, *New Delhi*
Prentice-Hall of Japan, Inc., *Tokyo*
Simon & Schuster Asia Pte. Ltd., *Singapore*
Editora Prentice-Hall do brasil, Ltda., *Rio de Janiero*

Trademark Notices

Preface

This book is based on C++ courses given by the authors at DePaul University for the last several years. The book can be used for self-study or a course on object-oriented programming in C++. We assume no prior knowledge of C++, but we do assume knowledge of C. This book is truly about C++, and *not* simply about the C subset of C++. Coverage of C at the level provided in R. Johnsonbaugh and M. Kalin, *Applications Programming in ANSI C*, 3rd ed. (New York: Macmillan, 1995) provides sufficient background for this book. In this book, as in our C books, we make extensive use of examples, figures, self-study exercises, sample applications, lists of common programming errors, and programming exercises. We strive for clarity throughout the book and also illustrate a variety of good programming style possible in C++. Our aim is to make C++ the language of choice for those who need the power of object-oriented programming.

This is the first *introductory* book on C++ that treats object-oriented design, emphasizes sound programming practices (see, e.g., Assertions and Program Correctness, Section 3.8), presents the C++ input/output class hierarchy (Chapter 7) in sufficient detail so that it can be used, and features major, useful examples (e.g., Measuring Computer Performance, Section 5.3, and A Random Access File Class, Section 7.6).

C++ is an evolving language; hence, no final standard has yet been established. The C++ presented in this book is based on the latest *Working Paper for Draft Proposed International Standard for Information Systems— Programming Language C++* developed by the X3J16 standards committee of The American National Standards Institute (ANSI). The X3J16 committee is developing a definition of C++, which eventually will evolve into a proposed standard. The *Working Paper* is available from

Standards Secretariat CBEMA
1250 Eye Street, NW
Suite 200
Washington, DC 20005

Overview

During the 1980s and 1990s, C became the language of choice for many applications and systems programmers. Most major software available for personal computers is written in C: spreadsheets, word processors, databases, communications packages, statistical software, graphics packages, and so on. Virtually all software written for the UNIX environment is likewise written in C, and many mainframe systems meant to be ported from one platform to another are also coded in C. In the early 1980s, Bjarne Stroustrup of AT&T Bell Labs developed C++ as an extension of C that supports object-oriented programming, a type of programming that is well suited to the large, complex software systems now written for all platforms, from the cheapest personal computers to the most expensive mainframes. C++ also corrects some shortcomings in C, which C++ includes as a subset, and it supports abstract data types. C++'s popularity has grown in tandem with that of object-oriented design in software. Accordingly, we cover object-oriented design and C++ programming.

C++ is a complex language. Fortunately, most C++ programmers can benefit from its power without mastering each and every one of its features. Because ours is an introductory book, we focus on the most useful aspects of the language; but we also cover all of the language's constructs. We emphasize *using* C++ to write practical applications based on sound object-oriented design.

The book includes the following features:

- Examples and exercises that cover a wide range of applications.

- Sample applications.

- A broad variety of programming exercises. The book contains 59 programming exercises.

- End-of-chapter lists of common programming errors.

- Discussion of the standard C++ input/output class library (Chapter 7).

- Self-study exercises to enable readers to check their mastery of a section. The book contains nearly 500 such exercises. Answers to the odd-numbered exercises are in the back of the book.

- Figures to facilitate the learning process.

- Major data structures, including stacks (Section 3.2), strings (Section 4.1), binary search trees (Section 4.4), and files (Section 7.6), implemented in C++.

- A number of appendixes.

- Understandable code. We opt for clarity over subtlety throughout the book.

- The latest C++ features including templates (Section 3.9), exception handling (Section 8.1), run-time type identification (Section 8.2), and namespaces (Section 8.3).

- An introduction to the object-oriented languages Smalltalk, Eiffel, and Objective C (Section 8.4).

Organization of the Book

Chapter 1 introduces key concepts associated with object-oriented design and programming: classes, abstract data types, objects, inheritance, encapsulation, polymorphism, and others. The chapter contrasts object-oriented design with top-down functional decomposition and offers examples to illustrate the difference between the approaches.

Chapter 2 discusses some important changes from C to C++. It also introduces C++ input/output so that the reader can begin using this class library right away. Chapter 7 goes into the details of C++ input/output.

Chapters 3 and 4 are devoted to classes. Chapter 3 covers the basics so that the reader can begin using classes at once. The chapter explains how to declare classes; how to write constructors, destructors, and other methods; how to overload operators; and how to write **friend** functions. Chapter 3 introduces assertions as a tool to promote correctness in object-oriented programs. Chapter 3 also introduces templates and encourages their use for constructing generic classes. We believe that assertions and templates have not received adequate coverage in other C++ books, particularly given their power to promote the goals of object-oriented design. Chapter 4 expands on Chapter 3 and introduces new material as well. Constructors are studied closely, **friend** classes are presented, and **static** data members and methods are introduced. Chapters 3 and 4 rely heavily on examples to explain how classes may be used to implement abstract data types and to meet the object-oriented goal of encapsulation.

Chapter 5 explains inheritance (including multiple inheritance) and polymorphism in depth. Through examples and sample applications (e.g., measuring computer performance, polymorphic tree traversal), the chapter illustrates basic programming techniques and also illustrates different styles of C++ programming. The chapter carefully explains the distinction between run-time and compile-time binding so that the reader is clear about the limits of polymorphism in C++.

Chapter 6 is devoted to operator overloading. The chapter first reviews earlier treatments of the topic and then offers many examples and several sample applications to highlight the power of operator overloading. The chapter shows how to overload the subscript, function, memory management, preincrement, and postincrement operators among others.

Chapter 7 serves two purposes. First, the chapter examines in detail the C++ input/output library so that the interested reader can exploit the powerful classes contained therein. This treatment culminates in a sample application that builds a random access file class through inheritance from a library file class. Second, the chapter uses the input/output library as a major, sophisticated example of object-oriented design realized in C++. Chapter 7 pays close attention to manipulators, which are powerful ways to do sophisticated input/output in C++. We believe Chapter 7 offers an unrivaled examination of C++'s input/output.

Chapter 8 covers advanced topics such as exception handling, run-time type identification, and namespaces. These topics are recent additions to C++. The chapter also contrasts C++ with other object-oriented languages such as Eiffel, Objective C, and Smalltalk. The chapter concludes with a discussion of the future of object-oriented design and programming.

This book is devoted to C++ independent of any particular operating system. However, the basic commands needed to run C++ programs are given in Appendixes C and D for the UNIX **g++** and Borland C++ compilers. In addition, Appendix C contains an extended discussion of UNIX.

We rely heavily on short examples, pictures, tables, and other figures to illustrate specific points about the syntax and semantics of C++. From our experience in teaching C++ and other languages, we are convinced that no single method is appropriate for clarifying every aspect about a language.

Most of our students agree with us that learning and using C++ is fun. We have tried to incorporate this view by using interesting examples, sample problems, programming exercises, and short slices of code.

Chapter Structure

The chapters are organized as follows:

Contents
Overview
Section
Section Exercises
Section
Section Exercises
⋮
Common Programming Errors
Programming Exercises

In Chapters 3 through 7, several sections are devoted to sample applications. Each of these sections contains a statement of a problem, a solution to the problem, and an implementation of a solution to the problem in C++. Many of these sections conclude with an extended discussion.

The sample applications include the following:

- A stack class (Section 3.2)

- A zip code class (Section 3.4)

- A complex number class (Section 3.6)

- A string class (Section 4.1)

- A binary search tree class (Section 4.4)

- Iterators (Section 4.5)

- Measuring computer performance (Section 5.3)

- An associative array (Section 6.4)

- Random access files (Section 7.6)

The *Common Programming Errors* sections highlight those aspects of the language that are easily misunderstood. The book contains 59 programming exercises drawn from a wide variety of applications.

Exercises

The book contains nearly 600 section review exercises, the answers to which are short answers, code fragments, and, in a few cases, entire programs. These exercises are suitable as homework problems or as self-tests. The answers to the odd-numbered exercises are in the back of the book, and the answers to the even-numbered exercises are in the *Instructor's Guide*. Our experience teaching C++ has convinced us of the importance of these exercises.

The applications covered in the programming exercises at the ends of the chapters include the following:

- Semaphores (Programming Exercise 3.7)

- Local area networks (Programming Exercises 4.3 and 5.2)

- Scheduling (Programming Exercise 4.7)

- Graphs (Programming Exercises 4.9 and 5.6)

- Spreadsheets (Programming Exercises 4.8 and 6.9)

- Indexed files (Programming Exercise 7.5)

Not every reader will be interested in all of these applications; however, we think that it is important to show the variety of problems that C++ can address.

Appendixes

Four appendixes are provided for reference. Appendix A contains the ASCII table. Appendix B contains a list of some of the most useful C++ functions and class methods. We describe the parameters and return values for each, the header file to include (when specified), and what the function or method does.

For those readers using C++ under UNIX, we have included Appendix C. We describe the GNU C++ compiler command **g++** in some detail. In addition to the **g++** command, we also discuss the **make** utility, the file system, commands for handling files (e.g., **ls**, **cp**), directories and several commands for navigating within directories (e.g., `pwd`, `mkdir`), pipes, `man` (the on-line help utility), the `grep` and `find` utilities, and run-time libraries.

Appendix D tells how to compile, link, and run a C++ program in Borland C++. Explanations are included for single-file and multiple-file programs.

Instructor Supplements

An *Instructor's Guide* and a program diskette are available at no cost to adopters of this book. The *Instructor's Guide* contains answers to the even-numbered section review exercises.

The program diskette contains the source code, header files, and data files for all of the book's sample applications as well as the source code for some of the longer examples. Some programming exercises ask for modifications of these programs. In any case, we assume that many readers will want to experiment with the code that we provide on the diskette. There is no charge for making copies of this diskette to distribute to students. These files also are available on Internet through anonymous ftp. The node is *kalin.depaul.edu* and the directory is */distcplus*. The directory holds standalone ASCII versions of the files as well as a compressed tar version *cpluscode.tar.Z*.

Acknowledgments

We thank the following reviewers: Kulbir Arora, SUNY at Buffalo; Rhoda Baggs, Florida Institute of Technology; Kenneth Basye, Clark University; Ed Chapin, University of Maryland, Eastern Shore; Leon Charney, Boston University; Glenn Lancaster, DePaul University; Sathis Menon, Georgia Institute of Technology; George Novacky, University of Pittsburgh; and Joe Zachary, University of Utah.

We thank our colleagues Steve Jost and Kirk Snyder for their advice on the LATEX typesetting system.

We are indebted to the Department of Computer Science and Information Systems at DePaul University and its chairman, Helmut Epp, for providing time and encouragement for the development of this book.

We are grateful to the Borland Corporation for furnishing current versions of Borland C++.

At Macmillan, we thank John Griffin and Betsy Jones, computer science editors, Bill Winschief, senior representative/field editor, and Elisabeth Belfer, production supervisor.

R.J.
M.K.

Contents

Object-Oriented Programming in C++

Chapter 1

Introduction

"Object-oriented" describes an emphasis on objects or data in a system. Accordingly, **object-oriented design** is a technique that attends first and foremost to objects or data in the design of a system, and **object-oriented programming** is an approach that attends first and foremost to objects or data in the programming of a system. In Section 1.1 we clarify these concepts in more detail.

The C++ (pronounced "C plus plus") programming language is an extension of C that supports object-oriented programming. C++ also offers improvements over C that are not specifically related to object-oriented programming. Because the "++" is C's increment operator, the name "C++" suggests that C++ is an incremental extension of C. Bjarne Stroustrup of AT&T Bell Labs developed C++ in the early 1980s. The first commercial version from Bell Labs appeared in 1985. Since then many vendors have released C++ compilers. Because C++ is an extension of standard C, *most* C programs can be compiled using a C++ compiler. (In Section 2.1, we discuss some incompatibilities between C and C++.) In this chapter, we introduce the key concepts (abstract data types, objects, classes, inheritance, and polymorphism) and show how C++ supports object-oriented programming. In the remainder of the book, we expand on these topics. Our emphasis throughout is on the use of C++ to do object-oriented programming.

1.1   Object-Oriented Design

In this section, we briefly describe and illustrate object-oriented design, contrasting this technique with top-down design. For more on object-oriented design, see J. Rumbaugh, et al., *Object-Oriented Modeling and Design*, (Englewood Cliffs, N.J.: Prentice Hall, 1991) or G. Booch, *Object Oriented Design with Applications*, (Redwood City, Calif.: Benjamin/Cummings, 1991).

Among the touted benefits of object-oriented design are:

- Increased productivity.

- Enhanced reliability.

- Improved maintenance.

- Reusable code.

- Better performance of sports teams such as the Chicago Cubs.

- Shortened recessions.

The next-to-last item is a result of the Cubs' using C++ to write some of their software. The last item results from lower costs due to increased productivity, improved reliability, and so on. With results such as these, it is no wonder that the term "object-oriented" has become ubiquitous.

Object-oriented design is characterized by

- Objects (data together with operations on the data)

Figure 1.1.1 Objects of the drawing system.

- Classes (abstract characterizations of objects)
- Inheritance (code sharing)
- Polymorphism (run-time binding of operations to objects)

We focus on objects in this section and leave classes, inheritance, and polymorphism to the remaining sections of this chapter.

Example 1.1.1. Object-oriented design emphasizes the *objects* or *data*. Consider the object-oriented design of a system to draw figures requested by a user on a graphics display terminal. The design of the system begins with the objects—the figures to be drawn. After identifying the objects, the design continues by identifying the operations to be performed on the objects and associating these operations with the objects. In this case, the objects become *figures to be drawn* (see Figure 1.1.1).

The objects exactly model the actual figures to be drawn; that is, we have *circle objects*, *line objects*, and so on. Each object has an associated operation called *draw*. The formal name for such an operation is a **method**. If *c* is a circle object, we invoke its *draw* method by *passing a message* to *c*:

   c.draw()

Similarly, if *l* is a line object, we invoke its *draw* method by passing a message to *l*:

   l.draw()

In object-oriented design the data are not static, lifeless entities. The data are objects capable of sending messages to other objects and reacting to messages received from other objects. A circle object, for example, might be empowered to create an offspring circle object and then instruct its offspring to draw itself in conformity with the parent's instructions. Data as objects are centers of message-passing and message-receiving activity. Computation occurs by passing messages among objects. The messages are invocations of methods that, in turn, are tailored to the object: a *draw* message sent to, say, a *circle* object invokes the *draw* method for *circles* rather than the *draw* method for *lines*. Indeed, an object's methods are part of it. An object's methods are **encapsulated** in it. An object thus carries within it the operations, defined as methods, that are suited to precisely that kind of object. There is no separation of an object from the operations that may be performed on it.

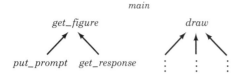

Figure 1.1.2 Top-down design.

To complete the object-oriented design of our drawing system, we would identify suitable input/output objects with methods suitable for communicating with the user and with the figure objects. For example, the user might be given methods to select an object such as a circle, to request that the object draw or erase itself, and so on. At the implementation stage, the system would require appropriate data structures to represent the objects and the appropriate routines to implement the methods.   □

A prominent design paradigm that offers an alternative to object-oriented design is **top-down design**. Object-oriented design emphasizes objects or data, whereas top-down design emphasizes operations or functions. Top-down design begins by specifying the first function to be invoked (the *top* function). The top function is frequently called *main*, as in C or C++. The designer then refines *main* into its component functions, which may in turn be refined into further functions, and so on (see Figure 1.1.2). After the top-down design is complete, the code for the functions is written. Because top-down design proceeds by refining functions, it is also known as **top-down, functional decomposition**.

Example 1.1.2. Consider the top-down design of the drawing system of Example 1.1.1. The *main* function would prompt the user for the figure to draw and then invoke a function to draw the figure. Thus *main* would be refined into functions such as *get_figure* and *draw*. A typical invocation of the function *draw* is

> *draw*(*CIR*)

where *CIR* is a flag to signal *draw* that a circle rather than some other figure is to be drawn. The function *get_figure* would be refined into functions such as *put_prompt* and *get_response*. The drawing function *draw* would similarly be refined into functions that do the actual drawing. After all of the functions are specified, the system would be completed by coding the functions.   □

The syntax of an object-oriented language emphasizes the central role of objects, whereas the syntax of a traditional language emphasizes the operations (functions). In an object-oriented language, we pass a message to a shape *c* to draw that shape:

> *c.draw*()

In a traditional language, we invoke the function *draw* and pass *CIR* as an argument to it:

draw(CIR)

Object-oriented design can provide a cleaner separation of its components than top-down design. In top-down design, modifying a function usually produces a ripple effect, and many other functions also then require modification as well. For example, if we modify a function *f* in a system created from a top-down design, we typically must also modify certain of *f*'s constituent functions, then modify their constituent functions, and so on. Moreover, it is often difficult to identify precisely all of the functions that need to be changed and exactly what changes need to be made to them.

If we want to modify the top-down version of the drawing system of Example 1.1.2 by adding an additional figure, we would have to modify almost all of the functions. We would certainly have to modify *get_figure*, *draw*, *put_prompt*, *get_response*, and many of *draw*'s component functions. We might also have to modify other less obvious functions as well. The modular separation is clearer in the object-oriented version of the drawing system (Example 1.1.1). If we add an additional figure, we could simply add an object to model that figure and modify the object that handles the input/output in fairly obvious ways. Moreover, as we will see later in this chapter, object-oriented languages provide solid support through classes, inheritance, and polymorphism for making these kinds of modifications.

Exercises

Exercises 1–4 refer to a system that responds to requests to provide all films by a particular director or to provide all films featuring a particular star.

1. What objects would you find useful in an object-oriented design of this system?

2. What methods would you find useful in an object-oriented design of this system?

3. How might a top-down design of this system proceed?

4. How would the object-oriented design of this system using the objects and methods of Exercises 1 and 2 differ from the top-down design of Exercise 3?

5. Answer Exercises 1–4 for a system that lays out the pages in the chapters of this book.

6. C++, an object-oriented programming language, is an extension of C, a traditional programming language, so C++ contains constructs that support both object-oriented and traditional features. What advantages are there in using a language that contains both object-oriented and traditional constructs? What disadvantages are there in using a language that contains both object-oriented and traditional constructs?

7. How might object-oriented design improve the reliability of software?

8. Another approach to design is *bottom-up design* in which the most primitive functions are specified first. The design continues by specifying more complex functions in terms of those already specified until all of the required functions have been laid out. Contrast this design method with top-down design and object-oriented design. What advantages does bottom-up design have over the other two paradigms? What disadvantages does bottom-up design have over the other two paradigms?

1.2   Classes and Abstract Data Types

A **class** is an abstract characterization of a set of objects; all objects in this set belong to a particular class. For example, in Section 1.1 we discussed a set of objects that consisted of figures to be drawn. The *figure class* is the class to which all of these objects belong. More formally, a class defines variables (data) and methods (operations) common to a set of objects. We can consider a class as a prototype or generator of a set of objects.

A well-designed class specifies an **abstract data type**. A data type is *abstract* if the high-level operations appropriate to the data type are isolated from the low-level implementation details associated with the data type. Suppose, for example, that we design a *circle* class that makes a circle an abstract data type. The class provides us with methods such as *draw, move, expand, contract, erase,* and so on. We can use these methods to manipulate *circle* objects in all the expected ways. The methods are all that we need to know about the *circle* class. In particular, we do not need to know exactly how a *circle* is represented. A *circle*'s underlying data structure might be an array, a record structure, a cleverly designed bit-string, and so on. Yet these details about a *circle*'s internal representation can be ignored as we create *circles*, enlarge them, move them, and the like. A *circle* as an abstract data type lets us focus exclusively on operations (methods) appropriate to *circles*; a *circle* as an abstract data type lets us ignore completely a *circle*'s internal representation.

The object-oriented environment deliberately hides implementation details about an object. This is known as **information hiding**. What is not hidden about an object is its **public interface**, which consists of the messages that may be sent to the object. The messages represent high-level

operations, such as *draw*ing a *circle*. The term **encapsulation** is also used
to emphasize a different but related aspect of abstract data types. An abstract data type combines methods (operations) and internal representation
(implementation). An object that is an instance of an abstract data type
thus **encapsulates** operations as well as representation. This encapsulation contrasts with the traditional separation of operations (functions) and
representation (data).

A C++ class supports encapsulation. The C++ syntax for declaring a
class is adapted from the C syntax for declaring a structure. Yet a C++ class,
unlike a C structure, may combine methods (functions) and data members.

Example 1.2.1. The following code declares a class **string**:

```
class string {
   char val[ 80 ];
public:
   void store( char * );
   int length();
};
```

The class **string** consists of data (the array **val**) together with methods
store and **length**. Objects in the class **string** consist of the data (characters stored in the array **val**) together with operations on this data: **store**
to store a C string (a null-terminated array of **char**) in an object belonging
to the C++ class **string** and **length** to compute the length of the string
represented by the **string** object.

C++ likewise supports information hiding. The keyword **public** makes
the methods **store** and **length** accessible to the outside world. Yet because
val is not in the **public** section of the class **string**, it is **private** by default
and therefore not accessible to the outside world. The class **string** isolates
the representation of a string, which happens to be stored in the array **val**,
from the methods **store** and **length**, which are publicly accessible. The
user need not be concerned with *how* the characters that make up the string
are represented. The user concentrates instead on the *operations* available
for manipulating objects in the class **string**.   □

A class declaration such as that of Example 1.2.1 does not create any
objects and does not allocate storage. After declaring a class and writing
the code that implements the methods, we can define objects in that class
following the C syntax for defining variables. We defer the discussion of how
to implement methods to Chapter 3.

Example 1.2.2. Given the class declaration of Example 1.2.1, the definition

```
string  s, t;
```

defines two objects **s** and **t** belonging to the class **string**. Storage is allocated for each object; s now has an array named **data** of size 80 and t also has a (distinct) array named **data** of size 80.   □

C++ borrows C's syntax for structures to reference members of a class. Suppose that **s** is an object in a class with data member **x** and method **f**. The member **x** is referenced by writing

```
s.x
```

and the method **f** is invoked by writing

```
s.f( arguments )
```

If **ptr** is a pointer to **s**, **x** is referenced by writing

```
ptr -> x
```

and the method **f** is invoked by writing

```
ptr -> f( arguments )
```

Example 1.2.3.   Given the class declaration of Example 1.2.1 and the definitions of s and t as in Example 1.2.2, we could pass a message to object s to store the C string "**Hi Mom**" in the object s by writing

```
s.store( "Hi Mom" );
```

To store the length of s in the variable **len** we could write

```
len = s.length();
```

□

Separating the operations (methods) from the implementation as in Example 1.2.1 makes it easy to change the implementation without having to change any of the code that accesses the objects.

Example 1.2.4. Suppose that we replace the class declaration of Example 1.2.1 with

```
class string {
   char data[ 80 ];
   int len;
public:
   void store( char * );
   int length();
};
```

We now represent a string by storing its characters without a null terminator. To locate the end of the string we store the index of the last character in the member **len**. We also reimplement the methods **store** and **length** to reflect this change in representation. These changes are transparent to users of this class. Code that accesses this class through its public members need not be changed at all. For example, the code of Example 1.2.3 could use the class of Example 1.2.1 or the new version of the class.   □

C has a library of functions that support various operations on strings (e.g., `strlen`, `strcat`). Nonetheless, a string is not a built-in data type in C. The C programmer implements a string as an array of `char` terminated by '\0', a nonprinting character that is easy to forget or overlook, even though the null terminator is essential for proper string handling. C thus extracts a price for use of its powerful string-handling functions: the programmer must attend to a low-level implementation detail about strings to use safely the high-level functions in the string library. By using a C++ string class, the programmer can ignore the low-level implementation details of strings and simply master the high-level methods.

It is possible to create abstract data types in languages that are not object-oriented. However, object-oriented languages provide constructs that encourage abstract data types. Classes, which can be as rich and diverse as the imagination allows, are a powerful and intuitive mechanism for creating abstract data types because they directly support information hiding and encapsulation. Inheritance, which we discuss in the next section, is a related mechanism for creating new abstract data types from already existing ones.

Exercises

1. The string class of Example 1.2.1 has two methods. List some other methods that one might expect to find in a string class.

2. In words, not in code, explain how to implement the methods `store` and `length` in the string class of Example 1.2.1.

3. In words, not in code, explain how to implement the methods `store` and `length` in the string class of Example 1.2.4. How would this implementation differ from the implementation of these methods in the string class of Example 1.2.1?

4. Suggest a way different from those of Examples 1.2.1 and 1.2.4 of representing strings. Given this representation, how would the implementation of the methods `store` and `length` differ from the implementation of these methods in the string classes of Examples 1.2.1 and 1.2.4?

5. Write a declaration for a stack class that manipulates `int`s. In words, not in code, explain how to implement the methods that push and pop `int`s on and off the stack.

6. Given the declaration of a stack class as in Exercise 5, write a line that defines two stacks. Write a line that defines an array of 100 stacks. Write a line that defines an array of 100 pointers to stack.

7. Given the declaration of a stack class as in Exercise 5, write a line that pushes the value 10 onto the stack **s**. Write a line that pops a value from the ninth stack in an array **s_arr** of 100 stacks.

1.3   Inheritance

In an object-oriented language, we can produce a new class by deriving the new class from an already existing class. The mechanism for this derivation is **inheritance** and the derived class is said to be **inherited** from the original class. In C++ the new class is called the **derived class** and the original class is called the **base class**. Following standard practice, we also call a derived class a **subclass** of the original class, which in turn is a **superclass** of the derived class. The derived class inherits all the data and methods from the existing class, but the derived class may add additional data or methods and, under certain circumstances, the derived class can redefine inherited methods so that they behave differently than they do in the original class. Deriving a class from a base class promotes code reusability and reusing already correct code promotes code robustness.

Example 1.3.1. The following declares a class pen:

```
class pen {
    int x;
    int y;
    int status;
public:
    void set_status( int );
    void set_location( int, int );
};
```

If **p** is an object of type **pen**, the message

```
p.set_location( x, y );
```

positions p at the location whose coordinates are **x,y**. The message

```
p.set_status( 1 );
```

turns the ink in the pen on, and the message

```
p.set_status( 0 );
```

turns the ink in the pen off.

Now suppose that our hardware is upgraded so that we have a colored pen. Rather than declare a brand new class to describe the colored pen, we can derive a colored pen class from the pen class:

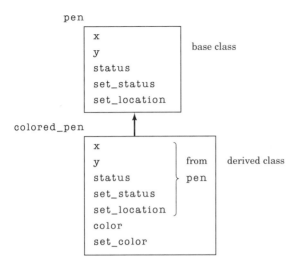

Figure 1.3.1 Deriving one class from another.

```
class colored_pen : public pen {
    int color;
public:
    void set_color( int );
};
```

The class `colored_pen` inherits all of the data and methods from the class `pen` (see Figure 1.3.1). The declaration of class `colored_pen` adds the data member `color` and the method `set_color`. Colors are coded as integers, so when the method `set_color` is invoked and a value is passed to a `colored_pen` object, the member `color` is set to this value.

The presence of the keyword `public` in the line

```
class colored_pen : public pen {
```

makes all of the base class's public members public in the derived class. (If the keyword `public` is omitted, the base class's public members become private in the derived class.) Thus the methods `set_status`, `set_location`, and `set_color` can be invoked on an object of type `colored_pen` anywhere in the program.

We could put a public method `move` in the class `pen` that would move the pen from its current position (given by members `x,y`) to a new location supplied as an argument to `move`. If the ink were on, `move` would then draw a line from the original location to the new location. In the derived class, we would need to redefine `move` so that, if the ink were on, `move` would draw a *colored* line from the original location to the new location. The color would be specified by the member `color` in the class `colored_pen`. In Chapter 5, we explain how to redefine methods in derived classes. □

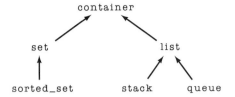

Figure 1.3.2 A class hierarchy.

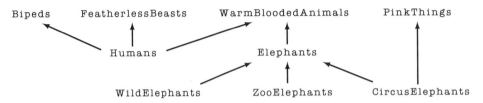

Figure 1.3.3 A class hierarchy that uses multiple inheritance.

Using inheritance, we can build a **class hierarchy**. As Figure 1.3.2 illustrates, a class hierarchy is a collection of classes obtained through inheritance. The classes `set` and `list` are derived from the base class `container`. The class `set` serves as a base class for the derived class `sorted_set`, and the class `list` serves as base class for the derived classes `stack` and `queue`. Besides any added members, the classes `stack` and `queue` have all of the members of `list` and `container`. In addition to any added members, `sorted_set` has all of the members of `container` and `set`.

C++ also permits **multiple inheritance** in which a derived class has multiple base classes.

Example 1.3.2. Figure 1.3.3 shows a class hierarchy that uses multiple inheritance. The following information is given:

- `Bipeds`, `FeatherlessBeasts`, `WarmbloodedAnimals`, and `PinkThings` are classes. None is depicted here as derived from any other class.

- `Humans` is a class that is derived through multiple inheritance from `Bipeds`, `FeatherlessBeasts`, and `WarmbloodedAnimals`.

- `Elephants` is a class that is derived from `WarmbloodedAnimals`. It has three subclasses: `WildElephants`, `ZooElephants`, and `CircusElephants`.

- `CircusElephants` is also a subclass of `PinkThings`.

□

Inheritance may be used in two broad ways to create a new class from already existing classes. Single inheritance may be used to *specialize* an existing class, whereas multiple inheritance may be used to *combine* two existing classes. We illustrate with two examples.

Figure 1.3.4 Single inheritance as specialization.

Example 1.3.3. The base class `Win`

```
// a window displayed on a video display
class Win { // base class
  ...
  int x, y;          // cartesian coordinates
  int width, height; // dimensions
  ...
};

// specialization of a Win -- add scroll bars
class ScrollWin : public Win { // derived class
  ...
};
```

has attributes such as an x-coordinate, a y-coordinate, a `width`, and a `height`. However, a `Win` does not have horizontal and vertical scroll bars. The derived class `ScrollWin` is a *specialization* of a `Win` in that a `ScrollWin` has all the attributes or properties of a `Win` and, in addition, horizontal and vertical scroll bars (see Figure 1.3.4). □

Example 1.3.4. The base classes `PopupMenu` and `ScrollWin`

```
// a PopupMenu is a menu that pops up on
// the screen in response to some user action
// such as clicking a button
class PopupMenu : public Menu {
  ...
};

// specialization of a Win -- add scroll bars
class ScrollWin : public Win { // derived class
  ...
};
```

may be combined to create a `ScrollPopupMenu`

```
class ScrollPopupMenu :
public PopupMenu, public ScrollWin {
  ...
};
```

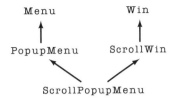

Figure 1.3.5 Combining classes using multiple inheritance.

that shares the attributes of a `PopupMenu` and a `ScrollWin`. Note that, in this example, `PopupMenu` and `ScrollWin` are both specializations through single inheritance of base classes `Menu` and `Win`, respectively (see Figure 1.3.5).   □

Classes directly support the creation of abstract data types. Inheritance extends that support by promoting the derivation of new abstract data types from already existing ones. Object-oriented languages thus provide us with the tools for programming with abstract data types. By creating abstract data types, we programmers extend the concept of *function* libraries to encompass *data type* libraries that allow the user to focus on high-level operations and to ignore low-level implementation details. Many graphics packages, such as *Windows* and *Motif*, illustrate the point. In *Motif*, for example, there is an extended class hierarchy in which each class represents an abstract data type such as various flavors of windows, fonts, geometrical drawings, and so on. The user knows only the *public interface* to such classes, where such an interface comprises the messages that may be used to create, manipulate, and destroy instances of an abstract data type. Implementation details, typically consisting of C structures and pointers, are hidden from the user, who is all the better off by being spared the very details that cause programming tedium and error. In effect, a package such as *Motif* is a library of abstract data types presented as an object-oriented graphics toolkit.

Exercises

1. Declare a class `book` with data members `title`, `author`, and `id_number`, and methods appropriate for storing information in these members.

2. Derive a class `book_loan` that includes the members and methods declared in Exercise 1, but also adds members and methods to keep track of whether someone has borrowed the book and, if so, who.

3. Declare a class `person` with data members `name` and `address`. In words, not in code, explain how you would use this class and the class `book` of

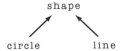

Figure 1.4.1 A class `shape` with subclasses `circle` and `line`.

Exercise 1 along with multiple inheritance to derive a class that keeps track of whether someone has borrowed a book and, if so, who.

4. Show a class hierarchy with classes that might be used to track customers and accounts at a bank.

5. What advantages are there to using multiple inheritance? What disadvantages are there to using multiple inheritance?

1.4 Polymorphism

The word *poly* comes from a Greek word meaning *many*, and *morphism* comes from a Greek word meaning *form*; thus, **polymorphism** means *many forms*. In object-oriented programming, *polymorphism* refers to identically-named methods that have different behavior depending on the type of object that they reference. For example, the classes **pen** and **colored_pen** of Section 1.3 might each have a method **move** with parameters x and y of type **int** that determines where the object moves. If the ink is on, the method **move** in class **pen** would draw a black line from its current position to the position with coordinates x,y, whereas the method **move** in class **colored_pen** would draw the line in a previously set color. When the method **move** is invoked, polymorphism assures that the appropriate operation occurs by determining at run time whether a **pen** or a **colored_pen** is the object in question. Polymorphism is useful in providing a common abstract interface to users of a class hierarchy.

The following C++ example shows why it is sometimes useful to delay until run time the decision about which object is being referenced.

Example 1.4.1. Suppose that we have a class **shape** with subclasses **circle** and **line** (see Figure 1.4.1). Suppose further that **shape** has a method **draw** that has been redefined in both subclasses so that when **circle**'s **draw** is invoked, a circle is drawn, and when **line**'s **draw** is invoked, a line is drawn. Suppose further that **composite_fig** is an array of 100 pointers to objects of type **shape**:

```
shape* composite_fig[ 100 ];
```

One of the rules in C++ is that a pointer of type "pointer to base class" can, without casting, point to any object in a derived class. Thus we assume that each cell in **composite_fig** contains the address of either a **circle** object or a `line` object. If we then step through the array and first draw the figure to which `composite_fig[ 0 ]` points, then draw the figure to which `composite_fig[ 1 ]` points, and so on, we draw the composite figure. Using polymorphism, the following loop carries out this task

```
for ( i = 0; i < 100; i++ )
   composite_fig[ i ] -> draw();
```

When this loop executes, the system determines what type of object is at address `composite_fig[ i ]`. If the object is of type `circle`, `circle`'s `draw` is invoked; if the object is of type `line`, `line`'s `draw` is invoked. Note that we can reload the array `composite_fig` with addresses of different objects, even objects from other classes derived from **shape**, and draw the new composite figure using *exactly the same* loop.   □

Object-oriented programming derives its power and elegance from the interaction of classes, objects, inheritance, and polymorphism. Classes furnish an abstract description of objects, which tie data and methods together with appropriate encapsulation; inheritance provides a way to derive new classes from old; and polymorphism binds methods to objects at run time.

Exercises

---

1. Suppose that the base class **book** has derived classes **manual** and **text**. Define an array **book_array** of 50 pointers to **book**. Suppose that **book** has a method **print** that is redefined in **manual** and **text**, and suppose that **book_array** has been initialized with the addresses of 50 objects of type **manual** or **text**. Write code that will print the books pointed to in the array **book_array**.

2. Give an example different from Example 1.4.1 which illustrates the usefulness of polymorphism.

3. The loop in Example 1.4.1 uses polymorphism to draw a composite figure. How might a similar effect be achieved in C?

Chapter 2

Basic C++

Because C++ contains standard (ANSI) C as a subset, most standard C programs are also C++ programs. In this chapter, we discuss some differences between C and C++; we introduce some extensions of C found in C++; and we introduce the C++ input/output class library. Some extensions discussed here are not directly related to object-oriented programming but rather remedy deficiencies in C or make the language more flexible.

2.1   Some Miscellaneous Extensions in C++

In this section, we list some small differences between C and C++.

Comments

Two slashes denote the beginning of a comment, which extends to the end of the line. The C-style comment /* comment */ also can be used.

Example 2.1.1. The following code illustrates the new style of comment:

```
// find largest
for ( i = 1, max = a[ 0 ]; i < end; i++ )
   if ( a[ i ] > max ) // found larger, so update
      max = a[ i ];
```

□

Casts

C++ adds an alternative notation for C casts. In the code

```
average = ( float ) hits / ( float ) at_bats;
```

the values of the int variables hits and at_bats are converted to float by using the cast operator before division. In C++, this could be written

```
average = float( hits ) / float( at_bats );
```

Enumerated Types

In C, we declare[†] an enumerated type such as

```
enum marital_status { single, married };
```

and then define variables of type enum martial_type as, for example,

```
/***** C syntax *****/
enum marital_status person1, person2;
```

[†]We use the term "define" to refer to a statement that allocates storage for a variable or to refer to the header and body of a function. We use the term "declare" to refer to the description of a data type.

In C++, by contrast, `marital_status` without the keyword `enum` is a type. Accordingly, we can define variables as in this code slice:

```
marital_status person1, person2;
```

Structures

In C++, a structure is a class in which the default status of each member is `public`. (This default status can be changed by, for example, using the keyword `private`.) Because a structure is a class, it can have member functions.

Example 2.1.2. The following declares a structure `string`:

```
struct string {
    char data[ 80 ];
    void store( char* );
};
```

By default, the members `data` and `store` are `public`. In C++, in contrast to C, `string` without the keyword `struct` is a type. Accordingly, we can define variables as in this code slice:

```
string str1, str2;
```

□

Anonymous Unions

C++ allows anonymous unions, that is, unions without tags.

Example 2.1.3. The union

```
union {
    int i;
    float x;
};
```

is anonymous. The members can be used as ordinary variables:

```
i = 10;
x = -3827.34;
```

Within the same scope, no other variables with the same names as an anonymous union's members are allowed, and no variables whose type is that of an anonymous union can be defined. □

const

The type qualifier `const` first appeared in C++ but was subsequently added to standard C. We illustrate some of its uses.

The keyword `const`, which stands for *constant*, allows the programmer to designate storage whose contents or value cannot be changed.

Example 2.1.4. The code

```
const int size = 30;
```

defines a variable `size`, which is initialized to 30. It is an error to attempt to change the value of `size`.   □

We could use the `#define` preprocessor directive to define a constant:

```
#define size 30
```

The advantage of a `const` variable over the `#define` directive is that the variable becomes a bona fide part of the program and, as such, can be referenced by name by the debugger, has storage allocated for it, has a type, and so on. On the other hand, a `#define` directive is handled by the preprocessor prior to compilation; consequently, the macro name cannot be referenced by the debugger, has no storage allocated for it, and has no type.

The type qualifier `const` applies to the type. For example, in the definition

```
char s[ ] = "Hi Mom";
const char* ptr = s;
```

`const` applies to `char*` so it is *not* legal to change what `ptr` points to, but it *is* legal to change `ptr`'s value. For example,

```
ptr[ 1 ] = 'o'; // ***** ERROR: can't change "Hi Mom"
```

is an error but

```
ptr = "Hi Dad"; // ***** OK: can change ptr
```

is legal.

To define a pointer constant (a pointer whose value cannot be changed), we would write

```
char s[ ] = "Hi Mom";
char* const ptr = s;
```

Now it is legal to change what `ptr` points to, but it is an error to change the value of `ptr` itself. For example,

```
ptr[ 1 ] = 'o'; // ***** OK: can change what ptr points to
```

is legal but

```
ptr = "Hi Dad"; // ***** ERROR: can't change ptr
```

is an error.

The following example shows how to use `const` parameters.

Example 2.1.5. The function

```
int search( const int* a, const int len, const int key )
{
    int i;

    for ( i = 0; i < len; i++ )
        if ( a[ i ] == key )
            return i; // found
    return -1; // not found
}
```

searches the array a for the value key. The parameter declaration

```
const int* a
```

states the **search** will not change any of the values in the array a. The parameter declaration

```
const int len
```

states that **search** will not change len's value; that is, after len is initialized to the value of the argument passed, **search** will not change this value. Similarly, the parameter declaration

```
const int key
```

states that **search** will not change key's value.   □

The type qualifier **const** serves as a *recommendation* to the compiler the variable be optimized. This type qualifier assures the compiler that a variable or parameter will not have its value altered. The compiler then may act on the recommendation by allocating storage in a specific partition (e.g., read-only memory) of the system's hierarchical storage system.

Defining Variables

In a C function, all variable definitions must occur at the beginning of a block. In C++, variable definitions may occur at the point at which they are first used.

Example 2.1.6. The code

```
void reverse_and_print( int a[ ], size )
{
    // fill the array
    for ( int i = 0; i < size; i++ )
        a[ i ] = 2 * i;

    // reverse the data in the array
    int temp;
    for ( i = 0; i < size / 2; i++ ) {
        temp = a[ i ];
```

```
        a[ i ] = a[ size - 1 - i ];
        a[ size - 1 - i ] = temp;
    }

    // print the array
    for ( i = 0; i < size; i++ )
        printf( "%d\n", a[ i ] );
}
```

shows how one can define variables within the block that delimits the body
of the function `reverse_and_print`.

The variable i is defined within the first `for` loop:

```
for ( int i = 0; i < size; i++ ) {
```

The scope of i extends from its definition in the first `for` loop to the end of
`reverse_and_print`.

The variable `temp` is defined just before it is needed in the second `for`
loop:

```
int temp;
for ( i = 0; i < size / 2; i++ ) {
```

         □

Exercises

---

1. Given the declaration

   ```
   enum good_jobs { tinker, tailor, soldier, spy };
   ```

   define two variables of this enumerated type.

2. Declare a **string** structure with a private member **val**, a **char** array of
   size 80, and public methods **store**, with one parameter of type **char***
   that returns no value, and **length**, with no parameters that returns an
   int.

3. Define two variables of the type declared in Exercise 2.

   In Exercises 4–9, determine whether the code is correct. If there are
   errors, tell what the problems are.

4.  ```
    int a[ ] = { 2, 4, 6 };
    int i;
    const int* p = a;
    p = &i;
    ```
    ```

5.  ```
    int a[ ] = { 2, 4, 6 };
    const int* p = a;
    p[ 1 ] = 12;
    ```

6.  ```
    int a[ ] = { 2, 4, 6 };
    int* const p = a;
    p[ 1 ] = 12;
    ```

7.  ```
    int a[ ] = { 2, 4, 6 };
    int i;
    int* const p = a;
    p = &i;
    ```

8.  ```
    char* s = "Hi Mom";
    const char* p = s;
    p[ 1 ] = 'o';
    ```

9.  ```
    char* s = "Hi Mom";
    const char* p = s;
    p = "Hi Dad";
    ```

10. Write a function **reverse** that reverses an array of **floats**. The arguments are **a**, a pointer to the first **float**, and **size**, the number of elements in the array. Declare appropriate parameters as **const**.

11. Write a complete program to read up to 100 **floats** from the standard input, compute the average of the numbers read, and then print each number and its absolute difference from the average. Use **const** to define any constants that are needed. Define variables near the point at which they are first used. Use //-style comments.

2.2   Functions

In this section, we highlight some of the ways that C++ has extended C functions.

Prototypes

Function prototype refers to the style of declaring functions and writing function headers in which the data types are included in the parentheses. In C++, prototypes are required and every function must be declared prior to being used. Standard C borrowed the function prototype syntax from C++. One difference between standard C and C++ is that, in standard C, function prototypes are optional. In C++, the function prototype is mandatory.

Example 2.2.1. The function
    ```

```
char grade( const int exam1,
            const int exam2,
            const float exam1_weight )
{
    ...
}
```

is written in prototype form.

If `grade` is invoked in a function `assign` and the definition of `grade` appears before the definition of `assign`, `grade`'s definition can also serve as its declaration:

```
// definition of grade
char grade( const int exam1,
            const int exam2,
            const float exam1_weight )
{
    ...
}

void assign( char* cl )
{
    ...
    // OK since grade's definition also serves
    // as a declaration
    c = grade( 9, 7, 0.6 );
    ...
}
```

If `grade` is defined after `assign` or in a different file, `grade` must be declared in prototype form either in or before `assign`:

```
// declaration of grade
char grade( const int exam1,
            const int exam2,
            const float exam1_weight );

void assign( char* cl )
{
    ...
    c = grade( 9, 7, 0.6 );
    ...
}
```

```
// definition of grade
char grade( const int exam1,
            const int exam2,
            const float exam1_weight )
{
   ...
}
```

The identifiers in a function declaration (`exam1`, `exam2`, `exam1_weight`, in `grade`'s declaration) are optional, but they are often included to help the user understand the meaning of the parameters. □

The compiler can use prototypes to check for matches between arguments and parameters of functions and issue appropriate warning and error messages if it detects problems. The compiler can also use prototypes to convert one type to another, if possible, when the types do not match. For example, if the prototype declaration specified a `float` parameter, but the function was called with an `int` argument, the compiler would convert the `int` argument to a `float`.

Subject to certain restrictions to be discussed in the Overloading Functions subsection, C++, unlike C, allows distinct functions with the same name. When a function `f` is invoked and there is more than one function named `f`, C++ determines which `f` to invoke by checking for a match between the types of arguments supplied and the types of parameters specified in the prototype declarations of the various `f`'s.

In C++, empty parentheses in a function prototype are interpreted as specifying no parameters. For example,

```
int print();
```

specifies that the function `print` has no parameters and returns an `int`. This is quite different from the meaning in standard C, where the specification is that no information is being supplied about `print`'s parameters and no checking of arguments and parameters is to be done when `print` is called. Thus in C++ there is really no "empty" parameter list. The declaration

```
int print();
```

is equivalent to

```
int print( void );
```

The `main` Function

Every program must contain a function called `main` where execution of the program begins. Since the system does not declare a prototype for `main`, its type is implementation dependent. However, C++ guarantees that every implementation support either

```
int main()
{
    ...
}
```

or

```
int main( int argc, char* argv[ ] )
{
    ...
}
```

As in C, in the latter form, **argc** is the number of arguments passed to the program, and **argv[0]** through **argv[argc - 1]** are the addresses of the passed arguments. Other definitions of **main** such as

```
void main()
{
    ...
}
```

may not be supported by a particular implementation.

The **return** statement

> **return** *status*;

in **main** terminates the **main** function and thus the program as a whole and returns the value *status* to the invoking process. The status values

EXIT_SUCCESS   EXIT_FAILURE

defined in *stdlib.h* are used to signal normal and abnormal termination, respectively. (Other status values may be available in a particular implementation.)

References

A **reference**, signaled by the ampersand **&**, provides an alternative name for storage.

Example 2.2.2. The code

```
int x;
int& ref = x;
```

creates one **int** cell with two names, **x** and **ref**. For example, either

```
x = 3;
```

or

```
ref = 3;
```

stores the value 3 in the int cell. □

    References operate somewhat like pointers except that no dereferencing is required. For example, we could obtain the effect of the code in Example 2.2.2 by replacing **ref** with a pointer. In this case, to store a value in the int cell using the pointer, a dereference would be required.

Example 2.2.3. If we write

```
int x;
int* int_ptr = &x;
```

two cells are created—one to store an int and one to store a pointer to int. The int cell can be accessed through its name **x** or through the pointer **int_ptr**. Either

```
x = 3;
```

or

```
*int_ptr = 3;
```

stores the value 3 in the int cell. □

    As we will see in the next subsections, references are particularly useful in passing arguments to and returning values from functions.

Pass by Reference

If we designate parameters as reference parameters using the ampersand **&**, we obtain **pass by reference** in which an argument is passed to a function by passing its address. The default parameter passing convention in C++, like C, is pass by value.

Example 2.2.4. In the program

```
#include <stdio.h>
#include <stdlib.h>

void swap( int&, int& );

int main()
{
   int i = 7, j = -3;

   swap( i, j );
   printf( "i = %d, j = %d\n", i, j );

   return EXIT_SUCCESS;
}
```

Figure 2.2.1 Passing arguments by reference.

```
void swap( int& a, int& b )
{
   int t;

   t = a;
   a = b;
   b = t;
}
```

the prototype

```
void swap( int&, int& );
```

specifies that the arguments to **swap** are passed by reference. Thus when the arguments i and j in **main** are passed to **swap**

```
swap( i, j );
```

swap receives the addresses of i and j. The ampersands in **swap**'s header

```
void swap( int& a, int& b )
```

signal that no dereferencing of the parameters **a** and **b** is required in **swap**'s body. The names **a** and **b** in **swap**'s body refer directly to the storage in **main** named i and j (see Figure 2.2.1). The function **swap** works not with copies of i and j but directly with i and j. The output of the program is

```
i = -3, j = 7
```

□

In C, we can obtain the effect of pass by reference by explicitly passing a pointer. A C version of the program of Example 2.2.4 follows.

Example 2.2.5. The program of Example 2.2.4 could be written in C in the following way:

```
#include <stdio.h>
#include <stdlib.h>

void swap_C_version( int*, int* );
```

```
int main()
{

    int i = 7, j = -3;

    swap_C_version( &i, &j );
    printf( "i = %d, j = %d\n", i, j );

    return EXIT_SUCCESS;
}

void swap_C_version( int* a, int* b )
{
    int t;

    t = *a;
    *a = *b;
    *b = t;
}
```

□

Return by Reference

The following example illustrates how a function can return a value by reference.

Example 2.2.6. The following function can be used by programmers who like arrays that begin at 1. The function takes an index i into an **int** array a, with 1 as the index of the first cell, translates it into a C++ index that begins at 0 (by subtracting 1), and returns by reference the value in the array:

```
int& new_index( const int a[ ], const int i )
{
    return a[ i - 1 ];
}
```

The return designation **int&** signals that the function is returning an **int** by reference. In effect, the address of a[i - 1] is returned, but the user need not use the dereference operator. The function **new_index** could be invoked as

```
val = new_index( a, 8 );
```

□

One advantage of using return by reference is that a function that returns a value by reference can be used on the left side of an assignment statement. For example, the following is a legal invocation of the function **new_index** of Example 2.2.6:

```
new_index( a, 8 ) = -16;
```

In this case, the value -16 would be stored in the eighth cell of a.

Inline Functions

The keyword **inline** can be used to request that a function be expanded "inline", that is, that each occurrence of a call of the function be replaced with the code that implements the function. The compiler, for various reasons, may not be able to honor the request. The situation is analogous to a macro expansion. When the preprocessor expands a macro, it replaces each occurrence of the macro with the macro's definition. When a macro is expanded or when a function is expanded inline and the program is run, the overhead of a function call is avoided so that the program may execute more efficiently. A disadvantage of using macros or inline functions is that if the expansions are large or there are many expansions, the size of the executable image can become quite large.

Unlike a macro that is expanded by the preprocessor, an inline function is expanded (i.e., translated) by the compiler. When the preprocessor expands a macro, it simply does text substitution without regard to the semantics of the code. On the other hand, when the compiler expands an inline function, it takes into account the semantics. For this reason, inline functions are generally preferable to macros.

An inline function is visible only from the point at which it is declared to the end of the file.

Example 2.2.7 shows how the program of Example 2.2.4 would be written with **swap** changed to an inline function.

Example 2.2.7. Consider the program

```
#include <stdio.h>
#include <stdlib.h>

inline void swap( int& a, int& b )
{
    int t;

    t = a;
    a = b;
    b = t;
}
```

```
int main()
{
   int i = 7, j = -3;

   swap( i, j );
   printf( "i = %d, j = %d\n", i, j );

   return EXIT_SUCCESS;
}
```

Assuming that the compiler honors the request to expand **swap** inline, no function call occurs at the line

```
swap( i, j );
```

Because **swap** is an inline function, the compiler replaces the line

```
swap( i, j );
```

with the code that implements **swap**. □

Default Arguments

C++ allows the programmer to specify default values for function parameters. If arguments are missing in the invocation of the function, the default values are used.

Example 2.2.8. The function

```
void f( int val,
        float s = 12.6,
        char t = '\n',
        char* msg = "Error" )
{
   ...
}
```

has default values for the parameters **s**, **t**, and **msg** but no default value for the parameter **val**.

Legal invocations of f are

```
f( 14, 48.3, '\t', "OK" );
f( 14, 48.3, '\t' );
f( 14, 48.3 );
f( 14 );
```

In the invocation

```
f( 14, 48.3, '\t', "OK" );
```

arguments are supplied for all of the parameters. Therefore, the initial values of the parameters are

```
val = 14,    s = 48.3   t = '\t',    msg = "OK"
```

In the invocation

```
f( 14, 48.3, '\t' );
```

no argument is supplied for the parameter **msg**. Therefore, the default value **"Error"** is used. The initial values of the parameters are

```
val = 14,    s = 48.3   t = '\t',    msg = "Error"
```

Similarly in the invocation

```
f( 14, 48.3 );
```

the initial values of the parameters are

```
val = 14,    s = 48.3   t = '\n',    msg = "Error"
```

In the invocation

```
f( 14 );
```

the initial values of the parameters are

```
val = 14,    s = 12.6   t = '\n',    msg = "Error"
```

It is an error to invoke **f** as

```
f();
```

because no default value is supplied for the first parameter.   □

Example 2.2.8 shows that it is legal to supply default values for some parameters but not for others. However, *all* the parameters without default values must come first in the parameter list and then be followed by *all* the parameters with default values.

Example 2.2.9. The header of the function

```
// ***** ERROR: Illegal mix of default
// and nondefault values ***
void g( int val = 0,
        float s,
        char t = '\n',
        char* msg = "Error" )
{
    ...
}
```

is illegal because the parameter **val** with a default value is followed by the parameter **s** without a default value.   □

Overloading Functions

C++ permits identically named functions within the same scope if they can be distinguished by number and type of parameters. If there are multiple definitions of a function f, f is said to be **overloaded**. The compiler determines which version of an overloaded function to invoke by choosing from among the identically named functions the one function whose parameters best match the arguments supplied.[†]

Example 2.2.10. The program

```
#include <stdio.h>
#include <stdlib.h>

void print( int );
void print( char* );

int main()
{
    print( 7 );
    print( "Yo. Let's rap" );

    return EXIT_SUCCESS;
}

void print( int i )
{
    printf( "%d\n", i );
}

void print( char* s )
{
    printf( "%s\n", s );
}
```

contains two distinct functions named **print**. When the line

```
print( 7 );
```

is executed, the function

```
void print( int i )
{
    printf( "%d\n", i );
}
```

[†]The precise rules for determining which function is the "best match" are complicated (see, e.g., *Working Paper for Draft Proposed International Standard for Information Systems—Programming Language C++*); however, an *exact* match is always the best match.

is invoked because the argument is of type `int`. However, when the line

```
print( "Yo. Let's rap" );
```

is executed, the function

```
void print( char* s )
{
    printf( "%s\n", s );
}
```

is invoked because the argument is of type `char*`.   □

Overloaded functions are used to give a common name to similar behavior on different data types. In Example 2.2.10, "print" is a common name for similar behavior on different data types. From the point of view of the user, there is a single function `print` that prints different data types.

Overloading Operators

When there are multiple definitions of an operator such as + or -, the operator is **overloaded**. For example, the operator + is overloaded by the system because + can refer to any numeric type. The compiler determines which version of an overloaded operator to invoke by checking the types of the arguments. For example, if i and j are `int`s, the system executes instructions appropriate for adding `int`s in evaluating i + j. If x and y are `double`s, however, the system executes instructions appropriate for adding `double`s in evaluating x + y. We now sketch restrictions on user-defined overloads of C++ operators.

Any operator except

$$. \quad .* \quad :: \quad ?: \quad \text{sizeof}$$

may be overloaded by the programmer. Some operators, such as the subscript operator [ ] and the function call operator () must be overloaded as methods. Other operators, such as + and -, either must be overloaded as methods or have at least one class object as an argument. These restrictions underscore the point that C++ operators typically are overloaded in the course of creating classes and their methods. Indeed, the only operators that may be overloaded without any reference to a class are the memory management operators `new`, `delete`, and `delete[ ]`. For this reason, we defer further discussion of operator overloading until we have examined classes in more detail. Chapter 6 is devoted entirely to operator overloading.

Exercises

---

1. Write a declaration of the function whose header is

```
        void move_arm( int arm_flag, float dir, float dist )
```

2. Find the errors and provide corrections for the following code:

```
#include <stdio.h>

const int size = 10;

main()
{
   int a[ size ];

   for ( int i = 0; i < size; i++ )
      scanf( "%d", &a[ i ] );

   reverse( a );

   for ( i = 0; i < size; i++ )
      printf( "%d\n", a[ i ] );

   return EXIT_SUCCESS;
}

void reverse( const int* a )
{
   int temp;

   for ( int i = 0; i < size / 2; i++ ) {
      temp = a[ i ];
      a[ i ] = a[ size - 1 - i ];
      a[ size - 1 - i ] = temp;
   }
}
```

Which of the definitions in Exercises 3–7 are guaranteed to be portable?

3. `int main()`
```
   {
      ...
   }
```

4. `main( int argc, char* argv[ ], char* envp[ ] )`
```
   {
      ...
   }
```

5. `main()`
```
main()
{
    ...
}
```

6. `void main()`
```
void main()
{
    ...
}
```

7. `int main( void )`
```
int main( void )
{
    ...
}
```

8. Given the declaration

```
struct string {
    char s[ 80 ];
};
```

write a function **upper** that is passed a **string** argument and converts the lowercase letters in **s** to uppercase. Characters that are not lowercase letters are unchanged. Pass the argument by reference.

9. What is the output?

```
#include <stdio.h>
#include <stdlib.h>

struct point {
    int x, y;
};

void move( point q )
{
    q.x--;
    q.y++;
}

int main()
{
    point p;

    p.x = 5;
    p.y = -12;
```

```
        move( p );
        printf( "x = %d, y = %d\n", p.x, p.y );

        return EXIT_SUCCESS;
    }
```

10. What is the output?

```
    #include <stdio.h>
    #include <stdlib.h>

    struct point {
        int x, y;
    };

    int move( point& q )
    {
        q.x--;
        q.y++;
    }

    int main()
    {
        point p;

        p.x = 5;
        p.y = -12;
        move( p );
        printf( "x = %d, y = %d\n", p.x, p.y );

        return EXIT_SUCCESS;
    }
```

11. What is the output?

```
    #include <stdio.h>
    #include <stdlib.h>

    struct point {
        int *x, *y;
    };

    void move( point q )
    {
        --*q.x;
```

```
      ++*q.y;
   }

   int main()
   {
      point p;
      int a = 5, b = -12;

      p.x = &a;
      p.y = &b;
      move( p );
      printf( "x = %d, y = %d\n", *p.x, *p.y );

      return EXIT_SUCCESS;
   }
```

12. What is the output?

```
   #include <stdio.h>
   #include <stdlib.h>

   struct point {
      int *x, *y;
   };

   void move( point& q )
   {
      --*q.x;
      ++*q.y;
   }

   int main()
   {
      point p;
      int a = 5, b = -12;

      p.x = &a;
      p.y = &b;
      move( p );
      printf( "x = %d, y = %d\n", *p.x, *p.y );

      return EXIT_SUCCESS;
   }
```

13. Write a version of the function of Example 2.2.6 in C. How would the lines

```
val = new_index( a, 8 );
new_index( a, 8 ) = -16;
```

have to be rewritten?

14. Show examples of legal invocations with different numbers of arguments of the function whose header is

```
getstr( char* buff, int size = 1, char term = '\n' )
```

15. Write a version of **print** (see Example 2.2.10) that receives a **string** (declared in Exercise 8) and prints the member **s**. Pass the argument by reference.

16. What is the error?

```
#include <stdio.h>
#include <stdlib.h>

void print( int count, int i = 0 )
{
   for ( int j = 0; j < count; j++ )
      printf( "%d\n", i );
}

void print( int count, char* s = "" )
{
   for ( int j = 0; j < count; j++ )
      printf( "%s\n", s );
}

int main()
{
   print( 10 );

   return EXIT_SUCCESS;
}
```

17. Find and correct the error:

```
void print( const FILE* fp, int i )
{
   fprintf( fp, "%d\n", i );
}
```

Description	*Operator*
Scope resolution	`::`
Value construction	*type* `()`
Storage allocation	`new`
Storage release (single cell)	`delete`
Storage release (vector)	`delete[ ]`
Member object selector	`.*`
Member pointer selector	`->*`
Throw exception	`throw`

Figure 2.3.1 New operators in C++.

2.3   C++ Operators

C++ has extended C by adding the operators shown in Figure 2.3.1. In Figure 2.3.2, we list the C++ operators, including those from C, together with their precedence and associativity rules. We discuss each of the new operators in turn.

The Scope Resolution Operator

The **scope resolution operator** `::` may be used in two ways:

```
::x     External scope
cl::m   Class scope
```

The first form `::x` is used to refer to the **extern** variable x when this variable would ordinarily be inaccessible because of a name conflict with a variable having local or class scope. The following example illustrates.

Example 2.3.1. In the code

```
float x; // extern x

void f( int n )
{
    float x; // local (auto) x

    x = 1.5;   // f's x
    ::x = 2.5; // extern x
    ...
}
```

the **extern** x would ordinarily be inaccessible within the function f because f defines an identically named variable. The scope resolution operator makes it possible to refer to the **extern** x within f.   □

Description	Operator	Associates from the	Precedence
Scope resolution	::	left	High
Function call	()	left	(Evaluated first)
Value construction	*type* ()	left	
Array subscript	[ ]	left	
Class indirection	->	left	
Class member	.	left	
Size in bytes	sizeof	right	
Incr/decr	++ --	right	
One's complement	~	right	
Unary not	!	right	
Address	&	right	
Dereference	*	right	
Cast	(*type*)	right	
Unary plus	+	right	
Unary minus	-	right	
Storage allocation	new	right	
Free storage (single cell)	delete	right	
Free storage (array)	delete[ ]	right	
Member object selector	.*	left	
Member pointer selector	->*	left	
Multiplication	*	left	
Division	/	left	
Modulus	%	left	
Addition	+	left	
Subtraction	-	left	
Left shift	<<	left	
Right shift	>>	left	
Less than	<	left	
Less than or equal	<=	left	
Greater than	>	left	
Greater than or equal	>=	left	
Equal	==	left	
Not equal	!=	left	
Bitwise and	&	left	
Bitwise exclusive or	^	left	
Bitwise inclusive or	|	left	
Logical and	&&	left	
Logical or	||	left	
Conditional	? :	right	
Assignment	= %= += -=	right	
	*= /= >>= <<=		
	&= ^= !=		
Throw exception	throw	right	(Evaluated last)
Comma	,	left	Low

Figure 2.3.2 Precedence of C++ operators (operators between horizontal lines have the same precedence).

The second form `cl::m`, which is used throughout the remainder of the book, is used to refer to member `m` in class `cl`. The subsection, The Member Selector Operators, illustrates one use of the second form of the scope resolution operator.

The Value Construction Operator

The **value construction operator**

   type ()

provides an alternative to the cast operator

   (*type*)

(see subsection Casts in Section 2.1).

The `new` and `delete` Operators

The `new`, `delete`, and `delete[ ]` operators are used to allocate and free storage dynamically. (`delete` frees a single cell, whereas `delete[ ]` frees a vector of cells.) They work much like the C library functions `malloc` and `free`. Unlike `malloc` and `free`, however, `new`, `delete`, and `delete[ ]` are built-in operators rather than library functions. Finally, `new` and `delete` are C++ keywords.

The `new` operator is used to allocate storage dynamically. The basic syntax is the keyword `new` followed by a type. For example,

```
new int
```

requests storage for one `int`. If `new` is successful in allocating the storage, the value of the expression

```
new int
```

is a pointer to the allocated storage; otherwise, the value of the expression is 0. If `int_ptr` is a pointer to `int`, a typical statement to allocate storage is

```
int_ptr = new int;
```

In the analogous C allocation statement,

```
int_ptr = ( int* ) malloc( sizeof ( int ) );
```

a cast to `int*` is required on `malloc`'s return value and `malloc` must be given, as an argument, the number of bytes to allocate. These requirements are dropped from `new`, which is therefore easier to use. The `new` operator infers the return type and the number of bytes to allocate from the type of storage requested. In sum, `new` behaves like a smart `malloc`.

The `new` operator can also be used to allocate dynamically an arbitrary number of contiguous cells, which is a **cell vector**. A cell vector is the dynamic counterpart of an array. For example, the code slice

```
int_ptr = new int[ 50 ];
```

requests a vector of 50 **int** cells. If **new** succeeds in allocating 50 contiguous cells, the first cell's address is stored in **int_ptr**. Otherwise, **new** returns 0, which is stored in **int_ptr**.

The **delete** operator is used to free storage allocated by **new**. If **int_ptr** points to a single **int** cell allocated by **new**, we can release this storage by writing

```
delete int_ptr;
```

If **int_ptr** points to a vector of **int** cells allocated by **new**, we can release this storage by writing[†]

```
delete[ ] int_ptr;
```

Example 2.3.2. The following program constructs a linked list using storage cells allocated at run time. After constructing the list, the program prints the contents of the cells and then steps through the list and frees the allocated nodes.

```
#include <stdio.h>
#include <stdlib.h>

struct elephant {
   char      name[ 10 ];
   elephant* next;
};

void      print_elephants( elephant* ptr );
elephant* get_elephants();
void      free_list( elephant* ptr );

int main()
{
   elephant* start;

   start = get_elephants();
   print_elephants( start );
   free_list( start );

   return EXIT_SUCCESS;
}

//   get_elephants dynamically allocates storage
//   for nodes. It builds the linked list and
```

[†]Some older versions of C++ require the size between the brackets, e.g., **delete[50] int_ptr;**

```
//   stores user-supplied names in the name
//   member of the nodes. It returns a pointer
//   to the first such node.

elephant* get_elephants()
{
   elephant *current, *first;
   int response;

   // allocate first node
   current = first = new elephant;

   // store name of first elephant
   printf( "\n\n\tNAME: " );
   scanf( "%s", current -> name );

   // prompt user about another elephant
   printf( "\n\n\n\tAdd another? (1 == yes, 0 == no): " );
   scanf( "%d", &response );

   // Add elephants to list until user signals halt.
   while ( response ) {
      // try to allocate another elephant node
      if ( ( current -> next = new elephant ) == 0 ) {
         printf( "Out of memory\nCan't add "
                 "more elephants\n" );
         return ( first );
      }
      current = current -> next;

      // store name of next elephant
      printf( "\n\n\tNAME: " );
      scanf( "%s", current -> name );

      // prompt user about another elephant
      printf( "\n\n\n\tAdd another? "
              "(1 == yes, 0 == no): " );
      scanf( "%d", &response );
   }

   // set link field in last node to 0
   current -> next = 0;
   return( first );
}
```

```
//    print_elephants steps through the linked
//    list pointed to by ptr and prints the name
//    member in each node as well as the position
//    of the node in the list

void  print_elephants( elephant* ptr )
{
   int count = 1;

   printf( "\n\n\n" );
   while ( ptr !=  0 ) {
      printf( "\nElephant number %d is %s.",
              count++, ptr -> name );
      ptr = ptr -> next;
   }
}

//    free_list steps through the linked list pointed
//    to by ptr and frees each node in the list

void  free_list( elephant* ptr )
{
   elephant* temp_ptr;

   while ( ptr !=  0 ) {
      temp_ptr = ptr -> next;
      delete ptr;
      ptr = temp_ptr;
   }
}
```

□

The operators **new**, **delete**, and **delete[ ]** should be used together and not intermixed with C storage management functions such as **malloc**, **calloc**, and **free**. We recommend *not* using the C storage management functions in C++ programs because the C functions, unlike **new**, **delete**, and **delete[ ]**, do not interact properly with certain important parts of C++ such as constructors and destructors (see Section 3.3).

The Member Selector Operators

C++ supports pointers that can point *only* to members of a class. The **member selector operators** .* and ->* are used to dereference such a pointer and thereby access the class member to which it points.

Example 2.3.3. The code slice

```cpp
struct C {
   int   x;
   float y;
   float z;
};

int main()
{
   // define a local float variable
   float f;

   // define a pointer to int
   int* i_ptr;

   // define two C objects
   C c1, c2;

   // define a pointer to a float
   // member of C
   float C::*f_ptr;

   // make f_ptr point to C member y
   // (Note that the assignment does not
   // specify a C object, e.g., c1 or c2.)
   f_ptr = &C::y;

   // set c1.y to 3.14
   c1.*f_ptr = 3.14;

   // set c2.y to 2.01
   c2.*f_ptr = 2.01;

   // make f_ptr point to C member z
   f_ptr = &C::z;

   // set c1.z to -999.99
   c1.*f_ptr = -999.99;

   // make f_ptr point again to C member y
   f_ptr = &C::y;

   // reset c1.y
```

```
        c1.*f_ptr = -777.77;

        // ***** ERROR: x is not a float
        //        member of C
        f_ptr = &C::x;

        // ***** ERROR: f is not a member
        //        of C, period
        f_ptr = &f;

        // ok -- i_ptr can hold the address of
        // any int and C::x is public, hence
        // visible in main
        i_ptr = &c1.x; // c1.x is an int
        ...
    }
```

illustrates the syntax for defining and using a pointer to a class member. The syntax

```
    c1.*f_ptr = 3.14;
```

says: Access the member (.) by dereferencing the pointer to the member (*). The pointer definition

```
    // define a pointer to a float
    // member of C
    float C::*f_ptr;
```

does *not* say that `f_ptr` is a pointer to a `float`, but rather that `f_ptr` is a pointer to a `float` member of C. An error thus occurs if we try to assign to `f_ptr` the address of local `float` variable `f`, which is *not* a C member:

```
    // ***** ERROR: f is not a member
    //        of C, period
    f_ptr = &f;
```

A different error occurs when we try to make `f_ptr` point to data member `x`, which is an `int` rather than a `float` member of C. Once defined, `f_ptr` may point to either `y` or `z`, as both members are `floats`.

Finally, a pointer that is *not* class specific may be used to access data members. In our example, `i_ptr` of type `int*` can be assigned the address of `c1.x` because `c1.x` is an `int`.   □

Pointers to class objects may be used in combination with pointers to class members. Such a combination requires use of the member selector operator `->*`.

Example 2.3.4. We expand Example 2.3.3 to illustrate the access to a class member through two pointers: a pointer to a class object and a pointer to its `float` data members:

```cpp
struct C {
    int   x;
    float y;
    float z;
};

int main()
{
    // define two C objects
    C c1, c2;

    // define a pointer to C
    C* c_ptr;

    // define a pointer to a float
    // member of C
    float C::*f_ptr;

    // make c_ptr point to c1
    c_ptr = &c1;

    // make f_ptr point to z
    f_ptr = &C::z;

    // set c1.z to 123.321
    c_ptr ->* f_ptr = 123.321;

    // make c_ptr point to c2
    c_ptr = &c2;

    // set c2.z to 987.789
    c_ptr ->* f_ptr = 987.789;

    // make f_ptr point to y
    f_ptr = &C::y;

    // set c2.y to -111.99
    c_ptr ->* f_ptr = -111.99;
    ...
}
```

Pointer `c_ptr` is of type `C*` and so can hold the address of either `c1` or `c2`. Pointer `f_ptr` is again of type "pointer to `float` member of `C`" and so can hold the address of either `C::y` or `C::z`. In an expression such as

```
// set c2.y to -111.99
c_ptr ->* f_ptr = -111.99;
```

the operator `->*` may be viewed as performing two tasks. First, the arrow `->` gives us access to the class object, in this case `c2`, by dereferencing `c_ptr`. Second, the star `*` gives us access to a particular data member, in this case `c2.y`, by dereferencing `f_ptr`. The syntax `->*` thus says: Access the member through the pointer to the object (`->`) by dereferencing the pointer to the member (`*`). The white space on each side of `->*` is optional. We could have written

```
// set c2.y to -111.99
c_ptr->*f_ptr = -111.99;
```

                                                    □

    A pointer to a class method follows the same syntax as that illustrated in Examples 2.3.3 and 2.3.4 for pointers to class data members.

Example 2.3.5. The following program shows how to define and use pointers to class methods:

```
struct C {
    int x;
    short f( int );
    short g( int );
};

...

int main()
{
    short s;
    C c;

    // pointer to method with one int
    // parameter that returns type short
    short ( C::*meth_ptr )( int );

    // make meth_ptr point to method f
    meth_ptr = &C::f;

    // invoke method f for object c
    s = ( c.*meth_ptr )( 8 );
```

```
// pointer to object c
C* ptr = &c;

// invoke method f for object c through ptr
s = ( ptr ->* meth_ptr )( 9 );

// make meth_ptr point to method g
meth_ptr = &C::g;

// invoke method g for object c in two ways
s = ( c.*meth_ptr )( 10 );
s = ( ptr ->* meth_ptr )( 11 );
...
}
```

□

The Throw Exception Operator

When an unexpected error, also called an **exception**, is detected in a program, the programmer can use the **throw** operator to *throw the exception.* To throw the exception is to transfer control to code, called a **handler**, which attempts to deal with the error. We defer the detailed discussion to Section 8.1.

Exercises

1. What is the output?

```
#include <stdio.h>
#include <stdlib.h>

short m = 18;

int main()
{
    short m = 4;
    printf( "%d  %d\n", ::m, m );

    return EXIT_SUCCESS;
}
```

2. Write a statement to allocate one cell of type **double** and store its address in the pointer **dbl_ptr**.

3. Write a statement to free the storage allocated in Exercise 2.

4. Write a statement to allocate 100 cells of type pointer to **char** and store the address of the first cell in the **char** pointer **str**.

5. Write a statement to free the storage allocated in Exercise 4.

6. Change Example 2.3.2 so that the user can choose to supply no names.

7. Revise Example 2.3.2 so that the function **get_elephants** checks whether the system is able to allocate storage for the first **ELEPHANT**. If the system cannot allocate the storage, **get_elephants** should return 0.

Exercises 8–17 assume the declaration

```
struct odometer {
   long miles;
   int tenths;
   void set_miles( long );
};
```

and the definition

```
odometer od1, od2;
```

8. Define a pointer to a member of type **long** in **odometer**.

9. Set the pointer of Exercise 8 to **miles**.

10. Use the pointer of Exercises 8 and 9 to set **od1**'s **miles** to 83117.

11. Use the pointer of Exercises 8 and 9 to set **od2**'s **miles** to 15004.

12. Define a pointer to **odometer**.

13. Set the pointer of Exercise 12 to **od1**.

14. Use the pointers of Exercises 8, 9, 12, and 13 to set **od1**'s **miles** to 73893.

15. Define a pointer to a method in **odometer** that takes one argument of type **long** and returns **void**.

16. Set the pointer of Exercise 15 to **set_miles**.

17. Use the pointer of Exercises 15 and 16 to invoke **od1**'s **set_miles** with argument 69402.

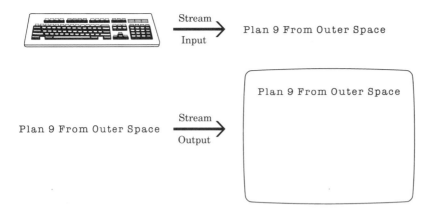

Figure 2.4.1 Stream input/output.

2.4   Introduction to C++ Input/Output

C++ provides a rich set of classes and predefined objects to support input
and output. Although the programmer still can use the C input/output
library, the new input/output classes provide an easier-to-use, extensible,
more flexible system. In this section we present sufficient basic information
so that the reader can start using certain of these features. We defer an
extended discussion of the input/output class library to Chapter 7.

In C++, input to a program is treated as a stream of consecutive bytes
from the keyboard, a disk file, or some other source. Output from a program is treated as a stream of consecutive bytes to a video display, a disk
file, or some other destination. Thus C++ input/output is called **stream
input/output** (see Figure 2.4.1).

The header file *iostream.h* must be included to use the C++ input/output
classes, predefined input/output objects, and manipulators with no arguments. The predefined objects, **cin**, **cout**, and **cerr**, are available. The
object **cin** refers to the standard input, **cout** refers to the standard output,
and **cerr** refers to the standard error. Except for the destination of the
output, **cout** and **cerr** behave similarly. The objects **cin**, **cout**, and **cerr**
in C++ are the more powerful and flexible counterparts of **stdin**, **stdout**,
and **stderr** in C.

The right shift operator **>>** is overloaded for input and the left shift
operator **<<** is overloaded for output. Both operators recognize the data
type supplied, so no format string (like that required for **printf** or **scanf**)
is necessary. The programmer can further overload the **>>** and **<<** operators
for reading and writing user-defined classes (see Section 7.3.).

Example 2.4.1. If x is a **float**, the statement

```
cin >> x;
```

reads a `float` value from the standard input and stores it in **x**. The input is converted to `float` because the variable **x** is of type `float`. If **len** is a `long`, the statement

```
cout << len;
```

writes the value of **len** to the standard output. The value is converted from `long` because the variable **len** is of type `long`.   □

The next example shows how multiple variables may be read or written in a single statement.

Example 2.4.2. The following program prompts the user for three values: an `int`, a `float`, and a string, and then writes the values to the standard output.

```
#include <iostream.h>
#include <stdlib.h>

int main()
{
    int id;
    float av;
    char name[ 20 ];

    cout << "Enter the id, the average, and the name: ";
    cin >> id >> av >> name;
    cout << "Id   " << id << '\n'
         << "Name   " << name << '\n'
         << "Average   " << av << '\n';

    return EXIT_SUCCESS;
}
```

The operators >> and << associate from the left; so in the line

```
cin >> id >> av >> name;
```

first a value is read into **id**, then a value is read into **av**, and then a value is read into **name**. Similarly, in the line

```
cout << "Id   " << id << '\n'
     << "Name   " << name << '\n'
     << "Average   " << av << '\n';
```

first Id is written, then the value of **id** is written, then the newline is written, and so on.   □

The default action of the input operator >> is to skip white space before reading the next input item. The situation is similar to that of the C library function **scanf**, except that even if the variable is of type **char**, the operator **>>** skips white space before reading the character. (It is possible to change the default action of skipping white space—see **ios::skipws** in Section 7.2.) If the variable is of type **char*** (e.g., **name** in Example 2.4.2), after skipping white space, all characters up to but not including the next white space character are read and stored.

The methods **get** and **read** may also be used with **cin** to read data. If c is a **char**

```
cin.get( c )
```

reads the next character without skipping white space and stores it in c. This version of **get** resembles the C function **getchar**.

Another version of **get** resembles the C function **fgets**. If **buff** is an array of **char**,

```
cin.get( buff, max_line )
```

reads the next line from the standard input and stores it in **buff**. The "next line" consists of

The next **max_line** − 1 characters,

or

All characters up to and but *not* including the next newline character,

or

All characters up to the end of the input,

whichever is shortest. The method **get** then stores the characters read and adds a terminating null '\0'. Notice that **get** never stores more than **max_line** characters (including '\0'). The terminating newline is *not* removed from the standard input nor is it stored in **buff**.

The variant

```
cin.get( buff, max_line, end_mark )
```

has the same behavior as **get** described in the previous paragraph except that the arbitrary character **end_mark** marks the end of the line rather than the default '\n'.

If **get** is successful in reading at least one character, it returns nonzero; otherwise, it returns zero.

Example 2.4.3. The following program produces a double-spaced version of a text file. It repeatedly reads a line from the standard input and writes it to the standard output with an extra newline added at the end of the line. Lines longer than 256 characters, including the newline, are truncated.

```
#include <iostream.h>
#include <stdlib.h>
```

```
const int line_len = 256;

int main()
{
   char c, buff[ line_len ];

   while ( cin.get( buff, line_len ) ) {
      // write line + 2 newlines
      cout << buff << "\n\n";
      // delete rest of line including newline
      for ( ; ; )
         if ( !cin.get( c ) || c == '\n' )
            break;
   }

   return EXIT_SUCCESS;
}
```

□

One way to format input or output is to use **manipulators** (see Figure 2.4.2). After a manipulator (except for **setw**) is placed into the stream, *all* subsequent input or output is formatted accordingly. For example, placing the manipulator **hex** in the output stream causes all subsequent output of **shorts**, **ints**, and **longs** to be written in hexadecimal. To use manipulators without arguments (e.g., **hex**, **endl**), the header file *iostream.h* must be included. Manipulators with arguments (e.g., **setfill**, **setw**) require the header file *iomanip.h*.

Example 2.4.4. The output of the program

```
#include <iostream.h>
#include <stdlib.h>

int main()
{
   const int i = 91;

   cout << "i = " << i << " (decimal)" << endl;
   cout << "i = " << oct << i << " (octal)" << endl;
   cout << "i = " << hex << i << " (hexadecimal)" << endl;
   cout << "i = " << dec << i << " (decimal)" << endl;

   return EXIT_SUCCESS;
}
```

Manipulator	Example	Effect
dec	cout << dec	Write output in decimal
hex	cout << hex	Write output in hexadecimal
oct	cout << oct	Write output in octal
endl	cout << endl	Write newline and flush output stream
ws	cin >> ws	Remove white space
flush	cout << flush	Flush output stream
setfill(c)	cout << setfill(c)	Make c the fill character
setprecision(n)	cout << setprecision(n)	Set floating-point precision to n
setw(n)	cout << setw(n)	Set field width to n

Figure 2.4.2 Some C++ manipulators.

is

```
i = 91 (decimal)
i = 133 (octal)
i = 5b (hexadecimal)
i = 91 (decimal)
```

If dec were omitted from the last line, the output would again be in hexadecimal because once the status of cout is changed by using a manipulator, the status remains in effect until changed again.   □

Example 2.4.5. The following program numbers lines. The line numbers are right aligned.

```
#include <iostream.h>
#include <iomanip.h>
#include <stdlib.h>

const int buffsize = 256;

int main()
{
   int line_no = 0;
   char c, buff[ buffsize ];

   while ( cin.get( buff, buffsize ) ) {
      // delete rest of line including newline
      for ( ; ; )
```

```
            if ( !cin.get( c ) || c == '\n' )
                break;
        cout << setw( 4 ) << ++line_no
                << ": " << buff << endl;
    }

    return EXIT_SUCCESS;
}
```

If the input is this source code, the output is

```
 1: #include <iostream.h>
 2: #include <iomanip.h>
 3: #include <stdlib.h>
 4:
 5: const int buffsize = 256;
 6:
 7: int main()
 8: {
 9:     int line_no = 0;
10:     char c, buff[ buffsize ];
11:
12:     while ( cin.get( buff, buffsize ) ) {
13:         // delete rest of line including newline
14:         for ( ; ; )
15:             if ( !cin.get( c ) || c == '\n' )
16:                 break;
17:         cout << setw( 4 ) << ++line_no
18:                 << ": " << buff << endl;
19:     }
20:
21:     return EXIT_SUCCESS;
22: }
```

The default field width is zero. Therefore, to right-justify the line numbers, in line 16 we first set the field width to 4 by using the manipulator **setw**. The line number is then printed in the first four columns; by default, it is right justified. After printing the line number, the field width automatically returns to its default value of zero. We then print a colon and a space, the contents of **buff**, and a newline. In C++, as in C, if the output is bigger than the field width, it is printed anyway using the minimum number of columns.   □

Using the C input/output library functions (**printf** and the like) and the C++ class library (**cout** and the like) in the same program can cause problems because reads and writes from the two libraries are not automatically synchronized. If the two libraries are mixed, the function

```
ios::sync_with_stdio();
```

should be invoked before doing any input or output. The function call does the synchronization required for intermixing C++ input/output and C input/output.

Exercises

1. Write a line that uses **cin** to read a **short** value into i, a **long double** value into x, and a string into the **char** array **str**.

2. Write a line that uses **cout** to print the values read in Exercise 1.

3. What will happen in the program of Example 2.4.3 if we delete the lines

```
for ( ; ; )
    if ( !cin.get( c ) || c == '\n' )
        break;
```

4. Write a program that prints a hexadecimal dump of the standard input. Write 25 hexadecimal values per line. Separate the values with one space. Use **setfill** to write a single digit hexadecimal value h as $0h$.

Common Programming Errors

1. It is an error to modify a **const** variable. For example, after

```
const double pi = 3.141592654;
```

it is illegal to change the value of **pi**:

```
pi = 3.0; // ***** ERROR *****
```

2. The definition of p

```
int a[ ] = { -1, -2, -3 };
const int* p = a;
```

promises not to change what p points to, although the value of p itself can be changed. Thus

```
p[ 0 ] += 2; // ***** ERROR *****
```

is an error, but

```
int b[ 4 ];
p = b; // ***** OK *****
```

is legal.

3. The definition of p

```
int a[ ] = { -1, -2, -3 };
int* const p = a;
```

promises not to change the value of p, although the value of what p points to can be changed. Thus

```
int b[ ]  = { 1, 2, 3, 4 };
p = b; // ***** ERROR *****
```

is an error, but

```
p[ 2 ]++; // ***** OK *****
```

is legal.

4. It is illegal to change the value of a **const** parameter:

```
void f( const int i )
{
    ...
    i = 8; // ***** ERROR *****
    ...
}
```

5. It is illegal to change the value to which a **const** pointer parameter points:

```
void f( const float* p )
{
    ...
    p[ 1 ] *= 2.0; // ***** ERROR *****
    ...
}
```

6. It is illegal to invoke an undeclared function:

```
#include <iostream.h>
#include <stdlib.h>
```

```cpp
int main()
{
   int i = 1, j = 3;

   // ***** ERROR: swap not declared *****
   swap( i, j );
   cout << "i = " << i << endl;

   return EXIT_SUCCESS;
}

void swap( int& a, int& b )
{
   int t;

   t = a;
   a = b;
   b = t;
}
```

This error can be corrected by defining, and implicitly declaring, swap
before main

```cpp
#include <iostream.h>
#include <stdlib.h>

void swap( int& a, int& b )
{
   int t;

   t = a;
   a = b;
   b = t;
}

int main()
{
   ...
}
```

or declaring swap before main

```cpp
#include <iostream.h>
#include <stdlib.h>
```

```
void swap( int&, int& );

int main()
{
   ...
}
```

or declaring `swap` in `main`

```
#include <iostream.h>
#include <stdlib.h>

int main()
{
   void swap( int&, int& );
   int i = 1, j = 3;
   ...
}
```

7. Since it is illegal to invoke an undeclared function, each system function must be declared. Typically, system functions are declared by including system header files such as *stdio.h* and *stdlib.h*, which contain the required function declarations. Also, all system macros must be defined by including the appropriate header files. Thus

```
int main()
{
   // ***** ERROR: printf not declared *****
   printf( "Here's lookin' at you kid.\n" );

   // ***** ERROR: EXIT_SUCCESS not defined *****
   return EXIT_SUCCESS;
}
```

is illegal since `printf` is not declared and `EXIT_SUCCESS` is not defined. These errors can be corrected by including *stdio.h*, which contains a declaration of `printf`, and *stdlib.h*, which contains the definition of EXIT_SUC-CESS:

```
#include <stdio.h>
#include <stdlib.h>

int main()
{
   // ***** CORRECT *****
   printf( "Here's lookin' at you kid.\n" );
```

```
        return EXIT_SUCCESS;
    }
```

8. It is an error to interpret the function declaration

```
    int f();
```

as giving no information about f's parameters. In fact, the declaration states that f has no parameters. For this reason, the following is an error:

```
    int f();

    int main()
    {
        ...
        // ***** ERROR: call does not match declaration *****
        i = f( 6 );
        ...
    }
```

9. The only definitions of main that are guaranteed to be portable are

```
    int main()
    {
        ...
    }
```

and

```
    int main( int argc, char* argv[ ] )
    {
        ...
    }
```

Thus definitions such as

```
    // ***** ERROR: nonportable definition of main
    void main()
    {
        ...
    }
```

may not work in some implementations.

10. Explicit dereference is *not* used when an argument is passed by reference. For this reason, the following is an error:

```
void swap( int& a, int& b )
{
    int t;

    // ***** ERROR: a and b are not pointers *****
    t = *a;
    *a = *b;
    *b = t;
}
```

A correct version is shown in Example 2.2.4.

Similarly, the following is illegal:

```
struct string {
    char s[ 80 ];
};

void copy( string& str, char* t )
{
    // ***** ERROR: str is not a pointer *****
    strcpy( str -> s, t );
}
```

The error can be corrected by changing the offending line to

```
strcpy( str.s, t );
```

11. An inline function is visible only from the point at which it is declared to the end of the file. For this reason, the following is an error:

```
#include <stdio.h>
#include <stdlib.h>

int main()
{
    int i = 9, j = 10;

    // ***** ERROR: can't find swap *****
    swap( i, j );
    printf( "i = %d, j = %d\n", i, j  );

    return EXIT_SUCCESS;
}
```

```
inline void swap( int& a, int& b )
{
   int t;

   t = a;
   a = b;
   b = t;
}
```

The error can be corrected by defining, and implicitly declaring, swap before main

```
#include <iostream.h>
#include <stdlib.h>

inline void swap( int& a, int& b )
{
   int t;

   t = a;
   a = b;
   b = t;
}

int main()
{
   ...
}
```

or declaring swap before main

```
#include <iostream.h>
#include <stdlib.h>

inline void swap( int&, int& );

int main()
{
   ...
}
```

or declaring swap in main

```
#include <iostream.h>
#include <stdlib.h>
```

```
int main()
{
    inline void swap( int&, int& );
    int i = 1, j = 3;
    ...
}
```

12. All parameters without default values must come first in the parameter list and then be followed by all the parameters with default values. For this reason, the following is an illegal function header:

```
// ***** ERROR: Illegal ordering of parameters with
//              default values *****
int f( float x = 1.3, int i, char c = '\n' )
```

The error can be corrected by omitting the default value for x or by adding a default value for i.

13. If a parameter does not have a default value, an argument must be supplied when the function is invoked. For example, if the header of f is

```
int f( float x, int i, char c = '\n' );
```

legal invocations of f are

```
// ***** LEGAL *****
f( 93.6, 0, '\t' );
f( 93.6, 0 );
```

but

```
// ***** ERROR: f must have 2 or 3 arguments *****
f( 93.6 );
```

is illegal.

14. To free a number of contiguous cells allocated by new, use delete[ ], *not* delete. As examples,

```
float_ptr = new float[ 100 ];
delete float_ptr; // ***** ERROR *****
delete[ ] float_ptr; // ***** CORRECT *****
```

15. Do not use new and delete with the C storage management functions:

```
float_ptr = new float[ 100 ];
free( float_ptr ); // ***** BAD LUCK *****
```

16. The *right* shift operator >> is overloaded for input:

```
cin >> x; // ***** CORRECT *****
cin << x; // ***** ERROR *****
```

17. The *left* shift operator << is overloaded for output:

```
cout << x; // ***** CORRECT *****
cout >> x; // ***** ERROR *****
```

18. To use the C++ classes and predefined objects for input and output, the file *iostream.h* must be included:

```
// ***** ERROR: stdio.h is the wrong .h file *****
#include <stdio.h>
#include <stdlib.h>

int main()
{
    cout << "Go Cubs!" << endl;

    return EXIT_SUCCESS;
}
```

19. The method **get**, when used in the form,

```
cin.get( buff, max_line )
```

does *not* store the terminating newline and it does *not* remove it from the standard input. For this reason, the following is an infinite loop:

```
char buff [ 80 ];

// ***** ERROR: Infinite loop *****
while ( cin.get( buff, 80 ) )
    cout << buff << endl;
```

20. After a manipulator is placed into the stream, *all* subsequent input or output is formatted accordingly except for the field width, which reverts to zero after a string or number is printed. Do *not* assume that at the end of a statement, all input/output reverts to default settings. For example, in the following code, the input is written in decimal, then in hexadecimal twice:

```
int n = 100;

cout << n << endl;
cout << hex << n << endl;
cout << n << endl; // still hex
```

21. Mixing the C and C++ input/output facilities may produce unexpected results unless the function

```
ios::sync_with_stdio
```

is invoked. As examples, the code

```
#include <stdio.h>
#include <iostream.h>
#include <stdlib.h>

int main()
{
   int a = 2, b = 5;

   // ***** RISKY *****
   printf( "%d  ", a );
   cout << b << endl;

   return EXIT_SUCCESS;
}
```

is risky; but

```
#include <stdio.h>
#include <iostream.h>
#include <stdlib.h>

int main()
{
   int a = 2, b = 5;

   // ***** OK *****
   ios::sync_with_stdio();
   printf( "%d  ", a );
   cout << b << endl;

   return EXIT_SUCCESS;
}
```

is acceptable.

Programming Exercises

In these programming exercises, use the C++ extensions discussed in this chapter wherever possible. As examples, use C++ comments (//) rather than C comments (/* */); use **const** rather than **#define**; and use the C++ input/output facilities.

2.1. Write a program that reads integers from the standard input until the end of the file and then prints the largest and smallest values.

2.2. Write a program that echoes the standard input to the standard output, except that each tab is replaced by the appropriate number of spaces. Assume that tabs are set every 8 columns, unless the user specifies a different tab setting on the command line.

2.3. Write a function **dbl** that takes an **int** argument and multiplies it by 2. Pass the argument by reference. *Example*:

```
int x = 6;
dbl( x );
cout << x; // output is 12
```

Write a **main** function that invokes **dbl** to demonstrate that **dbl** is working properly.

2.4. The structure

```
struct twodim {
    int r;
    int c;
    float* a;
};
```

represents a two-dimensional array of **floats** with **r** rows and **c** columns as a one-dimensional array **a** of **r*c floats**. Write functions **main**, **val**, **get_twodim**, and **free_twodim**.

The function **get_twodim** is passed an argument of type **twodim** by reference and **int** values **row** and **col** by value. The function **get_twodim** sets **r** to **row**, **c** to **col**, and dynamically allocates **r*c** contiguous **float** cells and stores the address of the first cell in **a**.

The function **val** receives arguments **i** and **j** by value and **x** by reference. It returns the value **x.a[i*r + j]** by reference.

The function **free_twodim** receives an argument of type **twodim** by reference and deletes the storage to which **a** points.

The function `main` invokes `get_twodim` to create a two-dimensional array of size 3×4. For all `i` and `j`, `main` then stores the value `2.5*i*j` in cell `i,j` by repeatedly invoking the function `val`. It then uses `cout` to print the values just stored by repeatedly invoking `val`. Finally, `main` invokes `free_twodim` to free the storage to which `a` points.

2.5. Write a function `print_str` that works as follows. If `print_str` is invoked with one argument `s`, a null terminated array of `char`, it prints `s` or the first 10 characters in `s`, whichever is shortest. If `print_str` is invoked with two arguments, `s`, a null terminated array of `char`, and `n`, an `int`, it prints `s` or the first `n` characters in `s`, whichever is shortest.

Write a `main` function that invokes `print_str` several times to demonstrate that `print_str` is working properly.

2.6. Given

```
struct numeric {
    long a[ 10 ];
};

struct string {
    char a[ 10 ];
};
```

write a function `print` which, when invoked with a `numeric` argument, prints the 10 `long`s in `a` one per line; but, when invoked with a `string` argument, prints all `char`s in `a` up to but not including `'\0'` on one line.

Overload `++` so that if `n` is a variable of type `numeric`,

```
n++;
```

adds 1 to each of the 10 `long` values in `a`.

Write a `main` function that invokes `print` and exercises the overloaded increment operator several times to demonstrate that `print` and the overloaded increment operator are working properly.

2.7. Add a function `reverse_elephant` to the program of Example 2.3.1, which receives a linked list, reverses the order of the nodes in the list, and returns the address of the first node in the reversed list. Modify `main` so that it invokes `reverse_elephant` several times to demonstrate that `reverse_elephant` is working properly.

2.8. This programming exercise is derived from an example originally due to Mitchell Feigenbaum and adapted by John Allen Paulos in *Beyond Numeracy* (New York: Alfred A. Knopf, 1990).

Consider the deceptively simple formula

$$\texttt{NextYr} = \texttt{Rate} * \texttt{CurrentYr} * \left(1 - \frac{\texttt{CurrentYr}}{1000000} \right)$$

which calculates next year's population of, say, waxwings on the basis of the current population and the growth rate. The variable `Rate` controls the growth rate and takes on values between 0 and 4. The variable `CurrentYr` gives the current value of the waxwing population and is assumed to have a value between 0 and 1,000,000. The variable `NextYr` gives the value of the waxwing population one year later. The formula guarantees that `NextYr` will also have a value between 0 and 1,000,000. For example, if `CurrentYr` is 100,000 and `Rate` is 2.6, `NextYr` is 234,000.

Now suppose that we initialize `CurrentYr` to 100,000 and `Rate` to 2.6 and compute the waxwing population 25 years hence by solving for `NextYr`, setting `CurrentYr` to `NextYr`, solving again for `NextYr`, and so on for 25 iterations. The waxwing population turns out to be roughly 615,385. We get the same result if we initialize `CurrentYr` to, say, 900,000 but leave `Rate` set to 2.6. In fact, the population stabilizes at roughly 615,385 for any value of `CurrentYr` so long as `Rate` is 2.6! For some values of `Rate`, the population oscillates. For example, if `Rate` is 3.14, after about 40 years the waxwing population takes on this pattern from one year to the next: 538,007 to 780,464 to 538,007 to 780,464, and so on indefinitely. For `Rate` equal to approximately 3.57, however, the population does not stabilize or oscillate but rather varies randomly from one year to the next.

Write a program that prompts the user for `Rate`, an initial `CurrentYr`, and a number of iterations. On each iteration, the program prints the year and the current waxwing population.

2.9. Simulate the Monty Hall puzzle, which gets its name from the host of the television game show *Let's Make a Deal*. The puzzle involves a game played as follows. A contestant picks one of three doors; behind one of the doors is a car, and behind the other two are goats. After the contestant picks a door, the host opens an unpicked door that hides a goat. (Because there are two goats, the host can open a door that hides a goat no matter which door the contestant first picks.) The host then gives the contestant the option of abandoning the picked door in favor of the still closed and unpicked door. The puzzle is to determine which of three strategies the contestant should follow:

- Always stay with the door initially picked.
- Randomly stay or switch (e.g., by flipping a coin to decide).
- Always switch to the unpicked and unopened door.

The user should be prompted as to which strategy he or she wishes to follow, as well as for how many times the game should be played. Use a random number generator to place the car at the start and to simulate the contestant's initial pick. If the contestant follows the second strategy, use a random number generator to determine whether the contestant stays or switches. The program should print the number of games played and the percentage of games won. (A game is won if the contestant gets the car.) Before running the simulation, try to determine whether any of the three strategies is better than the others. You then can use the simulator to test your answer. The results may surprise you. (For a technical discussion of this puzzle, see L. Gillman, "The car and the goats," *Amer. Math. Mo.* 99 (1992): 3–7.)

2.10. This programming exercise is based on Lewis Carroll's system for encoding and decoding text. We assume ASCII representation of characters. The encoding and decoding use the following table:

	bl	!	"	#	⋯	|	}	~
bl	bl	!	"	#	⋯	|	}	~
!	!	"	#	$	⋯	}	~	bl
"	"	#	$	%	⋯	~	bl	!
#	#	$	%	&	⋯	bl	!	"
⋮					⋮			
|	|	}	~	bl	⋯	y	z	{
}	}	~	bl	!	⋯	z	{	|
~	~	bl	!	"	⋯	{	|	}

Across the top and along the side we list, in order, the (printable) ASCII characters blank (bl) through ~ (see Appendix A). The first row inside the table is identical to the list across the top. Thereafter, each row is the same as the previous row, except that each character is shifted one position to the left, and the last character of a row is the first character of the preceding row.

To encode text, a string, called a *code string*, is chosen arbitrarily. To illustrate the encoding method, we assume that the code string is `Walrus` and the text to encode is

```
Meet me in St. Louis
```

Characters other than blank through ~ are not altered. We write the code string, repeated as often as necessary, on top of the text to be encoded:

```
WalrusWalrusWalrusWa
Meet me in St. Louis
```

The pairs of characters `WM`, `ae`, `le`, ..., one on top of the other, are used as indexes into the preceding table. The encoded text results from finding the entries in the table that correspond to these pairs. The entry in row `W` and column `M` is `%`, so the first character of the encoded text is `%`. The entry in row `a` and column `e` is `G`; the entry in row `l` and column `e` is `R`; and so on. Thus the text is encoded as

```
%GRgua=aVauGLol?eiAU
```

To decode text, we reverse this process.

Write a program that repeatedly prompts the user to encode text, decode text, or quit. If the user chooses to either encode or decode text, he or she is prompted for a code string, a file to encode or decode, and an output file.

Chapter 3

Classes

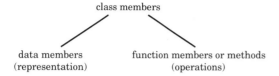

Figure 3.1.1 Class members.

Classes are at the center of object-oriented programming in C++. A C++ class can contain methods in addition to the class's internal representation, which is how C++ implements *encapsulation*. A C++ class can restrict access to its internal representation and even to its methods, which is how C++ implements *information hiding*. Classes are the natural way to implement *abstract data types* in C++. Finally, class hierarchies are the foundation for *polymorphism* in C++. Object-oriented C++ begins with classes.

A C++ **class** is a powerful extension of a C **struct**. A C++ **class**, like a C **struct**, contains member variables, which C++ calls **data members**. A C++ class, unlike a C **struct**, also may contain methods or class-specific functions that provide appropriate operations on the class's data members (see Figure 3.1.1). C++ uses **function member** as a synonym for "method." This chapter introduces classes by explaining how data members and methods are declared, defined, and used in programs. Chapters 4 and 5 expand on these explanations and introduce related material, such as inheritance.

3.1   Creating Classes

The syntax of C++ classes is close to the syntax of C **structs**. A C++ class, like a C **struct**, is a user-defined, aggregate data type whose member variables can differ among themselves in data type. We begin with a class that has no methods so that we can focus on the similarity to a C **struct**.

Example 3.1.1. The class declaration

```
// C++ code
class TestClass {
    int    integer;
    float pseudo_real;
};
```

is similar in syntax to the structure declaration

```
/* C code */
struct TestStruct {
    int    integer;
    float pseudo_real;
};
```

However, the class declaration is an implicit **typedef**. The user-defined data type is simply **TestClass** instead of **class TestClass**, whereas the data type for the C structure is **struct TestStruct**. These variable definitions underscore the difference:

```
struct TestStruct bigStructArray[ 100000 ]; /* C code */
TestClass bigClassArray[ 100000 ];          // C++ code
```

□

A typical class has several data members that provide the internal representation and several methods that define operations on the data members. A data member is defined inside the class declaration, just as a **struct** member is defined inside a **struct** declaration. A method, too, may be defined inside the class declaration, in which case the method is *inline* regardless of whether the keyword **inline** is used. However, it is legal merely to declare a method inside the class declaration and then to define the method outside the class declaration. We illustrate with an example.

Example 3.1.2. The code slice

```
// Window displayed on a screen
class Win {
    int    id;              // unique identifier
    short  x, y;            // cartesian coordinates
    short  width, height;   // dimensions in plane
    char   visible;         // 1 == yes, 0 == no
    String name;            // user-defined type
public:
    void  moveWin( short, short );
    char* getName();
    void  minWin() { width = height = 0; }
};
```

declares class **Win**. This code does not allocate storage but only describes the storage required for a variable of type **Win**. The code is a class declaration rather than a definition of a class variable. In C++ as in C, declarations describe storage requirements for a data type, whereas definitions allocate storage for variables of that type. If we define variables of type **Win**

```
// creating 100,002 objects of type Win
Win win1, win2, lots_of_wins[ 100000 ];
```

then storage is allocated in accordance with the class declaration. Variable **win1**, for example, has storage for **int** data member **id**, **short** data members **x**, **y**, **width**, and **height**, and so on. The class name or tag, in this case **Win**, serves as an implicit **typedef** identifier—the name of the class is simply **Win** rather than **class Win**. Class **Win** has data members of type **int**, **short**,

char, and String, where String is a user-defined data type. The data type
String must be visible to the declaration of class Win for a variable of type
String to be included in class Win.

The class declaration also specifies three methods: moveWin, getName,
and minWin. Method minWin is defined inside the declaration, whereas
methods moveWin and getName are only declared inside the class declaration. Functions declared but not defined inside the class declaration must
be defined outside the declaration. A function defined inside a class declaration is thereby inline, even if the keyword inline is not used. Method
minWin is thus inline. (Recall that the code for inline functions, including
methods, is substituted in place.)

The method moveWin is declared but not defined inside Win's declaration. Therefore, moveWin must be defined elsewhere. The scope resolution
operator must be used to indicate that moveWin is a Win method rather than
a method in some other class or even a toplevel function (i.e., a function that
is not a method in any class). The method's proper name is Win::moveWin.
Here is how it might be defined:

```
// define Win::moveWin
void Win::moveWin( short new_x, short new_y )
{
    x = new_x;
    y = new_y;
}
```

Whether to define a method inside or outside a class declaration is judg-
ment that should involve two considerations. First, a method defined inside
a class declaration is automatically inline. Second, defining long methods inside a class declaration may clutter the declaration. Even a method defined
outside the declaration can be made inline by using the keyword inline. We
can revise our example by moving the definition of method minWin outside
Win's declaration and keep it inline:

```
// Window displayed on a screen
class Win {
    int    id;              // unique identifier
    short  x, y;            // cartesian coordinates
    short  width, height;   // dimensions in plane
    char   visible;         // 1 == yes, 0 == no
    String name;            // user-defined type
public:
    void  moveWin( short, short );
    char* getName();
    void  minWin();         // declare minWin
};
```

```
// define minWin inline
inline void Win::minWin()
{
   width = height = 0;
}
```

In this example, the keyword **inline** occurs in **minWin**'s definition. We could have placed it in **minWin**'s declaration and omitted it from the definition or even have put the keyword in both places.

In the declaration for **Win**, the keyword **public** occurs above the methods. Its occurrence means that the three methods may be invoked from anywhere in the program where class **Win** is visible. The keyword **public** does not occur above the data members, which are therefore **private** by default. Data members that are **private** can be accessed by only two types of functions:

- Methods of the same class such as **moveWin** or **getName**.

- **friend** functions (see Section 3.7).

In C++, the keyword **private** is a mechanism for information hiding. By making a data member or method **private**, we restrict its access and, in effect, hide it from all but other methods in the same class or selected other functions known as **friends**.

We can show the difference between **private** and **public** class members by considering function **f**, which is not a **Win** method.

```
void f( Win w )
{
   // ***** ERROR: w's width and height
   // are private, not public
   cout << "width == " << w.width <<
           "height == " << w.height << endl;

   // legal -- w's minWin method is public
   w.minWin();
}
```

□

Our class declarations typically place the data members together and the methods together, and our declarations typically have the methods follow the data members. This is a matter of style. Data members and methods may occur in any order within the declaration. However, it is important to keep in mind that any class member, data member or method, defaults to **private** if a class is declared with the keyword **class**.

Example 3.1.3. The class declaration

```
class C {
    float r;     // defaults to private
public:
    int m1();    // public
    float m2();  // public
private:
    char c;      // private
public:
    void m3();   // public
    int z;       // public data member!
private:
    char cc;     // private
};
```

intermixes data members and methods.   □

Creating Classes with the Keyword struct

In C++ the keyword **struct** can be used instead of the keyword **class** to create a class.

Example 3.1.4. The code slice

```
struct Win_S {
    int    id;                 // unique identifier
    short  x, y;               // cartesian coordinates
    short  width, height;      // dimensions in plane
    char   visible;            // 1 == yes, 0 == no
    String name;               // user-defined type
    void   moveWin( short, short );
    char*  getName();
    void   minWin() { width = height = 0; }
};
Win_S main_window;
```

creates a class Win_S that has the same members as class Win from Example 3.1.2. The difference between Win and Win_S is that members are private by default in Win, which is created with the keyword class; but members are public by default in Win_S, which is created with the keyword struct. In Win we must use the keyword public to make the methods public, for otherwise they would be private by default. In Win_S we must use the keyword private to make the data members private, for otherwise they would be public by default. Classes created with the keyword struct also involve an implicit typedef. In the case of Win_S, the class's name is simply Win_S instead of struct Win_S.   □

To make data members `private` in a class created with the keyword `struct`, we must use the keyword `private`.

Example 3.1.5. The code slice

```
struct Win_DataIsPrivate {
private:
    int    id;              // unique identifier
    short  x, y;            // cartesian coordinates
    short  width, height;   // dimensions in plane
    char   visible;         // 1 == yes, 0 == no
    String name;            // user-defined type
public:
    void   moveWin( short, short );
    char*  getName();
    void   minWin() { width = height = 0; }
};
```

creates a class equivalent to class `Win` from Example 3.1.2. Note that keyword `public` must occur above the methods so that these are not caught in the scope of the `private` that introduces the data members.   □

There is no advantage in using `struct` instead of `class` to create a class. If a class's data members need to be `public`, they can be made so with the keyword `public`. Accordingly, our examples and applications usually use the keyword `class` to create classes.

Creating Classes with the Keyword union

The keyword `union` has the same effect as `struct` in creating classes: data members are `public` by default. Data members in a class created with the keyword `union` share storage, just as `union` members do in C. The storage shared is enough to accommodate the largest data member in the `union`. Classes might be created with the keyword `union` when there is a need to economize on storage.

Class Declarations and Class Scope

A class declaration may occur inside a block such as a function's body or outside all blocks. If declared inside a block, a class is visible only within that block; if declared outside all blocks, a class is visible anywhere in a file following the declaration.

Example 3.1.6. In the code slice

```
class Outside {
    ...
};
```

```
int main()
{
   class Inside {
      ...
   };
   ...
}
```

class `Outside` is visible from where its declaration occurs to the end of the file; hence, `Outside` is visible in `main`. By contrast, class `Inside` is visible only within `main`'s body because its declaration occurs only within that block. We say that class `Outside` has **file scope**, whereas class `Inside` has only **block scope**.   □

It is customary to put class declarations in a header file and then to `#include` the header file in whatever other files require access to the class. In this way, class declarations have file scope.

Example 3.1.7. Assume that our declarations for classes C1, C2, and C3 occur in the header file *classes.h* and that we need access to these classes in the file *code.cc*. We include the preprocessor directive

```
#include "classes.h"
```

in file *code.cc* to make the classes visible. The `#include` gives file scope to all the class declarations in the `#included` file.   □

Exercises

---

1. If a class is created with the keyword **class**, are its data members `private` by default and its methods `public` by default?

2. If a class is created with the keyword **struct**, are only its data members `public` by default?

3. Create a class with the keyword **union**. Make the data members `private` and the methods `public`.

4. In a class declaration, must the data members come before the methods?

5. Change the class declaration so that the data members are `private` but the methods are `public`:

```
class Dilemma {
    enum Horn { Horn1, Horn2 };
public:
    int  horn_crushed( Horn );
    void resolve_peacefully();
    char horn1[ 100 ];
    char horn2[ 100 ];
};
```

6. Is this class declaration legal?

```
class Dilemma {
    enum Horn { Horn1, Horn2 };
public:
    int  horn_crushed( Horn );
private:
    char horn1[ 100 ];
    char horn2[ 100 ];
public:
    void resolve_peacefully();
};
```

7. Explain the difference between the visibility of class members in these two class declarations:

```
// struct keyword
struct Dilemma {
    enum Horn { Horn1, Horn2 };
    int  horn_crushed( Horn );
    char horn1[ 100 ];
    char horn2[ 100 ];
    void resolve_peacefully();
};
```

```
// class keyword
class Dilemma {
    enum Horn { Horn1, Horn2 };
    int  horn_crushed( Horn );
    char horn1[ 100 ];
    char horn2[ 100 ];
    void resolve_peacefully();
};
```

8. Write a definition for a variable of type `Dilemma` (see Exercise 7).

9. Write a code slice that invokes method `horn_crushed` on the variable you defined in Exercise 8.

10. Explain the error.

```
class Dilemma {
    enum Horn { Horn1, Horn2 };
    int  horn_crushed( Horn );
    char horn1[ 100 ];
    char horn2[ 100 ];
    void resolve_peacefully();
};

int main()
{
    Dilemma d1;
    strcpy( d1.horn1, "The barber shaves himself." );
        ...
}
```

11. Write a declaration for class **Employee** that has at least six data members and at least six methods.

12. Write code slices that define **Employee** objects and invoke each of the methods.

13. If a method is defined within a class declaration, is the method thereby inline even if the keyword **inline** is not used?

14. Must a class have the same number of data members and methods?

15. May a class be declared without any methods?

16. Must the data types of a class's data members be the same?

17. Explain the error in this class declaration.

```
class C {
public:
    void write();
}
```

18. What is an alternative term for the C++ phrase "function member"?

19. Must every class method be **public**?

3.2   Sample Application: A Stack Class

Problem _____

Implement a **stack** as an abstract data type. A stack is a list of zero or more elements in which insertions and deletions occur at the same end, known as the **top**.

Solution

We create a `Stack` class with methods that allow the user to **push** an element onto the `Stack` (insertion), **pop** an element off the `Stack` (deletion), and print all the `Stack` elements top to bottom. To ensure `Stack` integrity, we first check that the `Stack` is not full before pushing and that is not empty before popping. `Stack` elements are **chars**. We practice information hiding by making a `Stack`'s internal representation **private**. We practice encapsulation by including methods within a `Stack`.

C++ Implementation

```
const int MaxStack = 10000;
const char EmptyFlag = '\0';

class Stack {
   char items[ MaxStack ];
   int  top;
public:
   enum { FullStack = MaxStack, EmptyStack = -1 };
   enum { False = 0, True = 1 };
   // methods
   void init();        // set top
   void push( char );  // add an item
   char pop();         // remove an item
   int  empty();       // no elements?
   int  full();        // too many elements?
   void dump_stack();  // top to bottom
};

void Stack::init()
{
   top = EmptyStack;
}

void Stack::push( char c )
{
   // any room left?
   if ( full() )
      return;
   // if so, move top and add item
   items[ ++top ] = c;
}
```

```
char Stack::pop()
{
   // anything to remove?
   if ( empty() )
      return EmptyFlag;
   else
      return items[ top-- ];
}

int Stack::full()
{
   // increment top, then check whether there's room
   if ( top + 1 == FullStack ) {
      cerr << "Stack full at " << MaxStack << endl;
      return True;     // full
   }
   else
      return False;    // not full
}

int Stack::empty()
{
   if ( top == EmptyStack ) {
      cerr << "Stack empty" << endl;
      return True;
   }
   else
      return False;
}

void Stack::dump_stack()
{
   for ( int i = top; i >= 0; i-- )
      cout << items[ i ] << endl;
}
```

Discussion

After class **Stack** has been declared, we can define **Stack** objects in the same way that we define, say, **int** or **float** objects: through variable definitions. A code slice such as

```
Stack s1;                 // define a Stack object
s1.init();                // invoke s1's init method
```

```
s1.push( 'a' );          // insert a
s1.push( 'b' );          // insert b
cout << s1.pop();        // remove and print b
s1.push( 'c' );          // insert c
cout << s1.pop();        // remove and print c
s1.push( 'b' );          // insert b
s1.push( 'c' );          // insert c
s1.dump_stack();         // print cba, removing none
```

illustrates how a `Stack` object can be created and then manipulated by invoking its methods.

After defining the `Stack` object `s1`, method `init` is invoked

```
s1.init();
```

to initialize member `top` to `EmptyStack`. Method `init` must be invoked before using a `Stack` so that `top` begins with the correct initial value.

A member declaration may *not* contain an initializer. For example, it is *not* possible to initialize `top` to `EmptyStack` by writing

```
class Stack {
   ...
   // ***** ERROR: Illegal initialization
   int top = EmptyStack;
   ...
};
```

If a member is to be initialized when it is created, a method *must* be used.

Normally, the programmer would access `Stack` objects through methods `push`, `pop`, and `dump_stack`. All three methods are `public`, which ensures that the programmer can invoke them wherever class `Stack` is visible in the program. There is no need for the programmer to access directly a `Stack`'s internal representation, in this case the array of `char` cells that store the `Stack`'s elements; therefore, `items` is `private`, which promotes program security through information hiding. A code slice such as

```
void f()
{
   Stack s;

   s.init();
   s.push( 'A' ); // ok

   // ***** ERROR: items private
   cout << s.items[ 0 ] << endl;
   ...
}
```

contains an error because function **f** cannot access a **private** member of
any **Stack** object, including **s**; and **s.items** is **private**. It is legal for **f** to
invoke **s.push** because **push** is **public**.

The methods **full** and **empty** normally are invoked by methods **push**
and **pop**, respectively. For example, **push** invokes **full** to determine whether
there is room on the **Stack** for another element. We could have made **full**
and **empty private** but instead made them **public**, like the other methods,
in order to give the programmer maximum flexibility. Were **full** and **empty**
private, the programmer could not invoke them directly but only indirectly
by invoking **push** and **pop**.

The two **enums**

```
class Stack {

   ...
   enum { FullStack = MaxStack, EmptyStack = -1 };
   enum { False = 0, True = 1 };
```

occur inside the class declaration and have class scope. Outside class **Stack**,
the **enums** must be referenced using the scope resolution operator, for example, **Stack::FullStack**. If the **enums** were **private**, they could be accessed
only by **Stack** methods or **friend** functions. The **enum** constant **EmptyStack**,
with value **-1**, is used to initialize data member **top**. Before a **char** is pushed
onto a **Stack**, method **push** first checks whether the **Stack** is full by invoking method **full**. If the **Stack** is not full, the preincremented **top** serves as
index into **items**, an array of **char** that represents the **Stack**:

```
void Stack::push( char c )
{
   // any room left?
   if ( full() )
      return;

   // if so, add item and move top
   items[ ++top ] = c;
}
```

Method **pop** returns the **top** element on a nonempty **Stack**. On an empty
Stack, **pop** returns **EmptyFlag**, a **char** that signals an empty condition.
Method **dump_stack** prints, from top to bottom, whatever elements are on
the **Stack** but without removing them from the **Stack**.

Exercises

---

1. Write a method **view_top** that prints the top item on the **Stack** without
   removing it from the **Stack**.

2. Write a method `reverse_stack` that inverts a `Stack`. For example, it would change `Stack` ABC to CBA.

3. Take and defend a stand for or against the proposition that methods `full` and `empty` ought to be `private` in class `Stack`.

4. Write a method `find` that takes a `char` argument and returns 1 if the `char` is currently somewhere in the `Stack` and 0 otherwise. The method must not alter the `Stack`.

5. Write a method `stack_sub` with `char` parameters c and s that substitutes the character s for every character c on a `Stack`.

3.3 A First Look at Constructors and Destructors

The programmer can specify two special types of method in a class declaration: **constructors** and **destructors**. We consider them in order.

Constructors

We begin with an example that illustrates why constructors are useful.

Example 3.3.1. The `Stack` class of Section 3.2 has an `init` method that initializes data member `top` to `EmptyStack`:

```
void Stack::init()
{
    top = EmptyStack;
}
```

Correct `Stack` manipulation through `pushes` and `pops` requires that `top` be initialized to `EmptyStack`. The problem is that the programmer is responsible for invoking `init` explicitly in a code slice such as

```
Stack s1;  // create a stack
s1.init(); // initialize the stack
...        // do pushes and pops
```

If the programmer forgets to invoke `init`, then `top` contains *junk*; that is, `top` contains, instead of `EmptyStack`, some random value that is almost sure to cause problems during `Stack` manipulation.   □

Constructors are methods that can automatically initialize a class's data members. The term "automatically" needs clarification. Although the programmer may write the code to implement a constructor, the programmer typically does not write explicit calls to a constructor. Instead, the programmer usually lets the compiler generate whatever constructor calls are appropriate. In particular, a constructor is automatically invoked whenever an object is created.

Example 3.3.2. We amend the `Stack` class by replacing `init` with a constructor that initializes `top` to `EmptyStack` when a `Stack` is created.

```
class Stack {
   char items[ MaxStack ];
   int  top;
public:
   enum { FullStack = MaxStack, EmptyStack = -1 };
   enum { False = 0, True = 1 };
   // methods
   Stack();                // set top to EmptyStack
   void push( char );      // add an item
   char pop();             // remove an item
   int  empty();           // no elements?
   int  full();            // too many elements?
   void dump_stack();      // top to bottom
};


// constructor definition
Stack::Stack()
{
   top = EmptyStack;
}


Stack s1; // object created and constructor invoked
```

Now that `Stack` has constructor `Stack::Stack`, the programmer no longer has to worry about invoking a method such as `init`. Instead, the compiler ensures that the constructor is invoked whenever a `Stack` is created. In this example, the constructor initializes `top` to `EmptyStack`. In general, a constructor can do whatever initializing work is appropriate.   □

A constructor's name is the class's name. If the constructor takes no arguments, as in Example 3.3.2, it is known as the **default constructor**. So the default constructor for the `Stack` class is named `Stack::Stack` and has an empty parameter list. No return value appears in either a declaration or the definition of a constructor. In Example 3.3.2, the header for the default constructor's definition is thus

```
// constructor definition
Stack::Stack()
```

A class may have more than one constructor, which overloads the constructor's name. Even in this case, the compiler rather than the programmer typically generates a call to whatever constructor is appropriate.

Example 3.3.3. In the following code slice, the class `Color` has two constructors.

```
class Color {
   float red;
   float green;
   float blue;
public:
   Color() { red = green = blue = 0.0; }
   Color( float, float, float ); // parameterized
};

// parameterized constructor definition
Color::Color( float r, float g, float b )
{
   red = r; green = g; blue = b;
}

// Color::Color() constructor used
Color c1;

// Color::Color( float, float, float ) constructor used
Color c2( 1.0, 0.5, 0.0 );
```

The definition of the parameterized constructor requires the scope resolution operator

```
Color::Color( ... )
```

because this definition occurs outside the declaration of class `Color`. The default constructor is defined inside the class declaration and so does not need the scope resolution operator in its name. Nonetheless, the proper name for the default constructor is `Color::Color`. It is possible that some other class, say class `Pic`, has a method named `Pic::Color` that expects no arguments or that there is a toplevel function (i.e., a function that is not some class's method) named `Color`.

When variable `c1` is defined, the default constructor

```
Color::Color()
```

initializes `c1` because `c1`'s definition does not specify any initial values. Because the default constructor is invoked when `c1` is defined, `c1.red`, `c1.green`, and `c1.blue` are all initialized to 0.0. By contrast, when `c2` is defined, parameterized constructor

```
Color::Color( float, float, float )
```

initializes `c2` because `c2`'s definition includes three initial values. The syntax of `c2`'s definition

```
Color c2( 1.0, 0.5, 0.0 );
```

makes it look as if c2 itself were a function being invoked with three arguments.   □

A constructor may have default arguments. We could amend the definition of parameterized constructor from Example 3.3.3 so that, for example, its second and third arguments default to specified values.

Example 3.3.4. If we define the parameterized constructor of Example 3.3.3 as

```
Color::Color( float r, float g = 0.5, float b = 0.0 )
{
    red = r; green = g; blue = b;
}
```

when the statement

```
Color c2( 1.0 );
```

is executed then c2.red is initialized to 1.0, whereas c2.green is initialized to 0.5 and c2.blue is initialized to 0.0. Of course, we also could define c2 with either two or three initial values:

```
Color c2( 1.0, 1.0 );  // blue defaults to 0.0
Color c2( 1.0, 0.8, 0.7 );
```

It would be an error to include more than three values in c2's definition

```
// ***** ERROR: too many args
Color c2( 0.1, 0.2, 0.3, 0.4 );
```

because Color::Color(float, float, float) expects at most three arguments.   □

Constructor Initialization

A constructor can use different styles to initialize data members.

Example 3.3.5. The three classes

```
class C1 {
  int iC1;
  float fC1;
public:
  // initialization in constructor body
  C1( int a1, float a2 ) { iC1 = a1; fC1 = a2; }
  }
};
```

```
class C2 {
  int iC2;
  float fC2;
public:
  // initialization in constructor header
  C2( int a1, float a2 ) : iC2( a1 ), fC2( a2 ) { }
};

class C3 {
  int iC3;
  float fC3;
public:
  // mixed initialization
  C3( int a1, float a2 ) : iC3( a1 ) { fC3 = a2; }
};
```

illustrate different styles of data member initialization. C1's constructor does all initialization in its body using the assignment operator. By contrast, C2's constructor initializes data members in its header rather than its body. The expression

```
iC2( a1 )
```

in C2's header initializes data member iC2 to parameter a1. Note that the two header initializations are separated by a comma and that C2's body is empty because all the work has been done already in the header. C3's constructor has a mixed style: iC3 is initialized in the header, whereas fC3 is initialized in the body.   □

Header initialization is required if a class has data members that are const or objects in some other class.

Example 3.3.6. Class C's constructor

```
class C {
  const int x; // const data member
  float y;
public:
  C( int a1, float a2 ) : x( a1 ), y( a2 ) { }
};
```

must use header initialization for x because this int data member is const. However, the constructor could use either header or body initialization for data member y, which is not const. In a similar fashion, class Y's constructor

```
class X {
  char moniker[ 20 ];
```

```
public:
    X( char* m ) { strcpy( moniker, m ); }
};

class Y {
    int num;
    X x;        // X object nested in Y
public:
    Y( int a1, char* a2 ) : num( a1 ), x( a2 ) { }
};
```

must initialize data member x in its header since x is an object in another class.   □

Copy Constructors

A class's default constructor takes no arguments. If the class has additional constructors, they take arguments. However, an argument to a constructor must not belong to the same class as the constructor: a class C constructor must not take an argument of type C.

Example 3.3.7. The code slice

```
class Color {
    float red;
    float green;
    float blue;
public:
    Color() { red = green = blue = 0.0; }
    Color( Color ); // ***** ERROR
};
```

contains an error because it attempts to create a constructor for class Color with an argument of type Color.   □

Although a class C constructor must not take an argument of type C, it may take an argument of type C&, that is, a C *reference*. Such a constructor is called a **copy constructor**.

Example 3.3.8. The code slice

```
class Color {
    float red;
    float green;
    float blue;
public:
    Color() { red = green = blue = 0.0; }
```

```
      Color( float, float, float );
      Color( Color& ); // copy
};

Color::Color( Color& c )   // copy
{
   red = c.red;
   green = c.green;
   blue = c.blue;
}
```

is legal because the copy constructor's argument is a `Color` object reference rather than a `Color` object. The copy constructor does what its name suggests: the new `Color` object is initialized as a copy of some already existing `Color` object through memberwise assignment operations—`red` is assigned `c.red`, `green` is assigned `c.green`, and `blue` is assigned `c.blue`. The compiler would invoke the copy constructor in a code slice such as

```
   Color c1( 0.1, 0.8, 0.7 );
   Color c2( c1 ); // copy constructor invoked
```

because `c2` is initialized in its definition as a copy of `Color` object `c1`. □

The programmer may provide a copy constructor, as Example 3.3.8 illustrates. If the programmer does not provide a copy constructor, the compiler automatically provides it. If we were to omit the copy constructor from Example 3.3.8, then the compiler would generate code that had the same effect as our version of `Color::Color( Color& )`: the compiler's default constructor would do a member by member assignment just as ours does.

Convert Constructors

A one-parameter (other that type `C&`) constructor for class `C` is called a **convert constructor**. If the parameter is of type *t*, the convert constructor converts type *t* to type `C`.

Example 3.3.9. Class `Clock`

```
   class Clock {
      int hour;
      int min;
      int ap; // 0 is AM, 1 is PM
   public:
      Clock() { hour = 12; min = 0; ap = 0; }
      Clock( int );
      void print_time();
   };
```

```
// time is given as 24-hour time
Clock::Clock( int time )
{
   min = time % 100;
   hour = time / 100;
   if ( hour > 12 ) {
      hour -= 12;
      ap = 1;
   }
   else
      ap = 0;
}

void Clock::print_time()
{
   cout << setfill( '0' ) << setw( 2 ) << hour
        << ':' << setw( 2 ) << min
        << setfill( ' ' );
   if ( ap )
      cout << " PM";
   else
      cout << " AM";
   cout << endl;
}
```

stores a time and has a method **print_time** to print the time in the form

   xx:xx XX

where **XX** is either **AM** or **PM**.

The default constructor

```
Clock::Clock()
```

sets the time to **12:00 AM**.

The convert constructor

```
Clock::Clock( int time )
```

converts the time, given as the **int** parameter **time**, to a **Clock** by converting **time** to the internal representation in terms of the data members **hour**, **min**, and **ap**. If c is a **Clock** object, the convert constructor may be explicitly invoked to convert an **int** to a **Clock**

```
c = Clock( 1308 ); // invoke convert constructor
c.print_time();
```

which is then copied into c. The output is **01:08 PM**.

Alternatively, an **int** may be cast to a **Clock**

```
c = ( Clock ) 123; // cast
c.print_time();
```

which is then copied into c. The difference is only syntactic. The convert constructor is invoked in this case as well. The output is 01:23 AM.

Implicit type conversion is also possible:

```
c = 1155; // implicit type conversion
c.print_time();
```

Because variable c is of type Clock, the compiler uses the convert constructor to convert the int 1155 to a Clock, which is then copied into c. The output is 11:55 AM.   □

Constructors and Dynamic Storage Allocation

A constructor's main job is to initialize a class's data members. A constructor also may dynamically allocate storage and then initialize the storage.

Example 3.3.10. The class C

```
class C {
   char* text;
   ...
public:
   C();
};

C::C()
{
   text = new char[ 20 ];  // allocate
   strcpy( text,           // initialize
           "North By Northwest" );
}

C c; // create a C object
```

has a data member text of type char*. The constructor C::C dynamically allocates storage, sets text to the address of the first cell, and then initializes the storage to a character string.   □

Classes Without Constructors

If a class has no constructor, then the class's data members are *not* initialized automatically when a class object is created.

Example 3.3.11. In the code slice

```
class C {
   int dm1;
   int dm2;
};

C c;
```

class C has no constructor. Accordingly, data members c.dm1 and c.dm2 are not initialized when c is defined. The programmer rather than the compiler now assumes responsibility for initializing the data members.   □

Constructors as Functions with No Return Value

Constructors differ from ordinary functions in that no return type is specified in their declaration or definition. This syntactic difference underscores that the programmer typically does not call a constructor explicitly and, in any case, does not expect some return value from a constructor call. A constructor's job is limited: it initializes data members and, if appropriate, dynamically allocates storage.

Constructors as Public Functions

Constructors are invoked whenever and wherever class objects are defined, which means that constructors usually should be public so that they can work correctly.

Example 3.3.12. In the code slice

```
class C {
   int x;
   C() { x = 0; }; // private!
};

int main()
{
   C c1; // ***** ERROR: C::C() not accessible!
   ...
}
```

the default constructor is private, which means that it cannot be invoked in main, which is neither a method nor a friend of C. The obvious solution is to make the constructor public.   □

Destructors

A destructor, like a constructor, is a special method that the programmer writes but typically does not call; instead, the programmer usually lets the compiler generate whatever calls to the destructor are appropriate. A destructor is automatically called whenever an object is destroyed (e.g., by going out of scope or by using the **delete** operator). A destructor's job is to free any storage that a constructor dynamically allocates before the allocated storage becomes garbage. A destructor's name consists of a tilde (~) followed by the class name. White space may occur between the tilde and the class name, but this is uncommon. For example, the destructor for class Color may be written as

```
Color::~Color()
```

or even

```
Color::~ Color();
```

Nothing but white space may occur between the ~ and the class name.

We illustrate the rationale behind destructors with an example from C.

Example 3.3.13. In the C code slice

```
typedef struct big_string {
   char* string;
   int   size;
} BigStr;

#define OneBillion    (1000000000)
void big_garbage()
{
   BigStr bs;
   bs.size = OneBillion;
   bs.string = ( char* )
      calloc( bs.size, sizeof ( char ) );

   /* process bs.string but forget to free it. */
      ...
}
```

the programmer dynamically allocates a billion **char** cells but forgets to release them (with a call to the library function **free**) before control leaves **big_garbage**. Therefore, **bs.string** becomes a dangling pointer. Because structure variable **bs** has **auto** as its default storage class, **bs** and its member variables can be accessed only within **big_garbage**. Once control leaves **big_garbage**, the billion **char** cells to which **bs.string** points remain allocated but the program has no way to access them. Each time **big_garbage** exits, it leaves behind big garbage—a billion bytes worth. □

In C++, we can equip class **BigStr** with a constructor to allocate dynamically the required storage and a destructor to ensure that this storage does not become garbage.

Example 3.3.14. In the C++ code slice

```
const long OneBillion = 1000000000;

class BigStr {
   char* string;
   long  size;
public:
   BigStr();                                  // constructor
   ~BigStr() { delete[ ] string; } // destructor
};

BigStr::BigStr()
{
   string = new char[ OneBillion + 1 ];
   for ( long i = 0; i < OneBillion; i++ )
      string[ i ] = '$';
   string[ OneBillion ] = '\0';
   size = OneBillion;
}
void no_garbage()
{
   BigStr bs;  // constructor BigStr::BigStr()
               // allocates a billion + 1 chars
   // process bs.string
      ...
   // destructor BigStr::~BigStr invoked when
   // function exits to release 1 billion + 1 chars
}
```

the constructor `BigStr::BigStr` is called automatically when variable `bs` is defined. The constructor allocates one billion contiguous `char`s, sets `bs.string` to the address of the first `char` in the billion, and copies the character $ into the `char` cells. The constructor thus allocates and initializes storage. The destructor `BigStr::~BigStr` is called automatically when control leaves function `no_garbage`. The destructor deallocates all the storage that the constructor allocated. The compiler, not the programmer, generates the call to the destructor so that the garbage generated in Example 3.3.13 does not get generated here. After writing the destructor, the programmer lets the compiler worry about releasing any storage that the constructor allocates dynamically.

Recall the syntax for freeing aggregated storage cells. We write

```
delete[ ] string;
```

instead of

```
delete string;
```

because **string** points to the first in an aggregate of cells rather than to a single, standalone cell.   □

In Example 3.3.14, destructor **BigStr::˜BigStr** is defined inside the class declaration, whereas the constructor **BigStr::BigStr** is defined outside the class declaration. This reflects our practice of defining only very short functions inside a class declaration. The destructor **BigStr::˜BigStr** could be defined outside the class declaration, in which case the scope resolution operator would have to be used.

Example 3.3.15. We revise Example 3.3.14 so that neither the constructor nor the destructor is defined inside the class declaration:

```
const long OneBillion = 1000000000;
class BigStr {
  char* string;
  long  size;
public:
  BigStr();     // constructor
  ˜BigStr();    // destructor
};

// constructor
BigStr::BigStr()
{
    string = new char[ OneBillion + 1 ];
    for ( long i = 0; i < OneBillion; i++ )
       string[ i ] = '$';
    string[ OneBillion ] = '\0';
    size = OneBillion;
}

// destructor
BigStr::˜BigStr()
{
    delete[ ] string;
}
```

□

Destructors as Functions with Neither Arguments Nor a Return Value

A destructor resembles a constructor in that the name of each includes the class's name. The difference is that the first character in a destructor's name must be the tilde (~). If a destructor is defined outside the class declaration, then its name must include the scope resolution operator, as Example 3.3.15 illustrates. A destructor never has arguments. Accordingly, the argument list must be empty in a destructor's definition or declaration.

Example 3.3.16. The code slice

```
const int MaxQueue = 5000;
class Queue {
   int   front;
   int   rear;
   int*  queue;
   unsigned int max_size;
public:
  Queue();        // constructor
  Queue( int );   // constructor
  ~Queue( int );  // ***** ERROR: no args allowed!
};
```

contains an error because the argument list in the declaration for destructor `Queue::~Queue` is not empty. The declaration must be written

```
~Queue(); // empty arg list
```

Similarly, the definition of `Queue::~Queue()` must have an empty argument list, whether the definition occurs inside or outside the class declaration. A destructor, like a constructor, has no return value—not even **void**—specified in its declaration or definition.   □

A class has only one destructor and the programmer typically writes it. Destructors are not allowed to have arguments because their job is highly specialized: a destructor simply releases any storage that a constructor dynamically allocates before such storage can become garbage. To perform this task, a destructor needs no arguments. To prevent a destructor from trying to perform any other task, C++ disallows destructors with arguments. Destructors, again like constructors, perform tasks that require no return value, especially because the programmer typically does not explicitly invoke a destructor. Invoking a destructor is normally left to the compiler.

Exercises

---

1. Does every constructor dynamically allocate storage?

2. Write the declaration for the default constructor for class **Mystery**.

3. Write the declaration for the destructor in class **Mystery**.

4. Explain the error.

```
class C {
    char* ptr;
    ...
public:
    void C();
    ...
};
```

5. Explain the error.

```
class C {
    char* ptr;
    ...
public:
    C();
    C( char* c ) {...}
    C( int c ) {...}
    C( char* c ) {...}
};
```

6. Can a class have more than one destructor? Explain why or why not.

7. Is this code legal?

```
class C {
    char* ptr;
    ...
public:
    C();
    ~        C();
};
```

8. Is this code legal?

```
class C {
    int x;
public:
    C( int x = 4, y = 6 );
    ...
};
```

9. Should a class's constructors be **private**? Explain.

10. Should a class's destructor be **private**? Explain.

11. Explain the error.

```
class C {
   int x;
      ...
public:
   C( C ); // copy constructor
      ...
};
```

How should the copy constructor be declared?

12. One destructor might free storage with the `delete` operator, whereas another might free storage with the `delete[ ]` operator. Explain the difference.

13. If the programmer does not write a default constructor for a class, does the compiler provide one?

14. If the programmer does not write a copy constructor for a class, does the compiler provide one?

15. Explain the error.

```
class C {
   int x;
public:
   int C();  // default
      ...
};
```

16. If a class does not use any dynamically allocated storage, does it need a destructor?

17. Explain how the destructor works in this code slice.

```
class C {
   char* ptr;
public:
   C() { ptr = new char[ 100 ]; }
   ~C() { delete[ ] ptr; }
};

void f()
{
   C c1, c2, c3;
      ...
}
```

18. Explain the error.

```
class C {
    char* ptr;
       . . .
public:
    void ~C();
       . . .
};
```

19. How many destructors may a class have?

20. Declare a class C that uses dynamically allocated storage and define the destructor C::~C.

21. Explain the error.

```
class C {
    int x;
    const float y;
public:
    C( int a1, float a2 ) { x = a1; y = a2; }
};
```

3.4   Sample Application: A Zip Code Class

Problem _____

Implement a zip code as an abstract data type.

Solution _____

We create class `ZipC` with methods to manipulate zip codes of different lengths (e.g., 5- or 9-digit zip codes). The class constructors allow zip codes to be generated from either character strings or integers. The class hides from the user the internal representation of a zip code, thereby allowing the user to focus on operations appropriate to a zip code. We practice information hiding by making `ZipC`'s data member **private**. We practice encapsulation by including various methods, including constructors and a destructor, in `ZipC`.

C++ Implementation _____

```
#include <stdio.h>
#include <iostream.h>
#include <string.h>
```

```
const int MinZip = 5;        // e.g., 60607
const int BigZip = 10;       // with hyphen
const int MaxZip = 32;       // let's hope not
const int InitChar = '?';
const int Hyphen = '-';
const int SuffixLen = 4;     // as in 60607-1234

class ZipC {
   char* code;               // representation
public:
   // constructors-destructor
   ZipC();                             // default
   ZipC( const char* );                // from char*
   ZipC( const unsigned long );  // from integer
   ~ZipC();                            // destructor
   void write() { cout << code << endl; }
   void expand( const char* );
};

// default constructor
ZipC::ZipC()
{
   code = new char[ MinZip + 1 ];      // +1 for terminator
   for ( int i = 0; i < MinZip; i++ )
      code[ i ] = InitChar;
   code[ i ] = '\0';
}

ZipC::ZipC( const char* zipstr )
{
   int len =
      ( strlen( zipstr ) < MaxZip ) ? strlen( zipstr ) :
                                      MaxZip;
   code = new char[ len + 1 ];
   strncpy( code, zipstr, len );
   code[ len ] = '\0';
}

ZipC::ZipC( const unsigned long zipnum )
{
   char buffer[ BigZip + 1 ];
   sprintf( buffer, "%0*ld", MinZip, zipnum );
   buffer[ MinZip ] = '\0';
```

```
      code = new char[ strlen( buffer ) + 1 ];
      strcpy( code, buffer );
}

ZipC::~ZipC()
{
   delete[ ] code;
}

void ZipC::expand( const char* suffix )
{
   char previous[ MinZip + 1 ];

   if ( strlen( code ) != MinZip ||    // 'small' size?
        strlen( suffix ) != SuffixLen ) // length ok?
      return;

   strcpy( previous, code );
   delete[ ] code;

   code = new char[ BigZip + 1 ];
   sprintf( code, "%s%c%s", previous, Hyphen, suffix );
}
```

Discussion

The class ZipC has code, a pointer to char, as its single data member. The three constructors set code to storage dynamically allocated with the new operator. How much storage is allocated depends on the constructor. For instance, the default constructor

```
// default constructor
ZipC::ZipC()
{
   code = new char[ MinZip + 1 ];  // +1 for terminator
   for ( int i = 0; i < MinZip; i++ )
      code[ i ] = InitChar;
   code[ i ] = '\0';
}
```

allocates MinZip + 1 bytes and stores InitChar, currently the character ?, in MinZip of the cells and the null terminator in the remaining cell. The compiler would have the default constructor invoked in a code slice such as

```
void f()
{
   ZipC z1;    // default constructor
       ...
}
```

because **z1**'s definition does not include an initializing value. Accordingly,
z1.code points to **MinZip + 1 chars**, each holding **InitChar**, except for
the last, which holds a **'\0'**. The constructor adds a null terminator to the
sequence of **chars** so that, for example, the user can invoke library functions
such as **strlen** or **strcpy** on the sequence. The user need not worry about
a null terminator because the constructor ensures that one is present.

The constructor

```
ZipC::ZipC( const char* zipstr )
{
   int len =
      ( strlen( zipstr ) < MaxZip ) ? strlen( zipstr ) :
                                      MaxZip;
   code = new char[ len + 1 ];
   strncpy( code, zipstr, len );
   code[ len ] = '\0';
}
```

converts a traditional C string to a **ZipC** object. The compiler would have
this constructor invoked in a code sequence such as

```
void g()
{
   ZipC z2( "60607" );  // convert constructor
       ...
}
```

because **z2**'s definition includes the initializing value 60607 given as a character string constant. In this case, the constructor would allocate six **char**
cells: five for the characters in "60607" and one for the null terminator.
This constructor ensures that the initializing value does not exceed **MaxZip**
characters in length. The constructor's single parameter, **zipstr**, has a
type qualifier of **const** to ensure that the constructor does not change the
characters to which **zipstr** points.

The last of the three constructors

```
ZipC::ZipC( const unsigned long zipnum )
{
   char buffer[ BigZip + 1 ];
   sprintf( buffer, "%0*ld", MinZip, zipnum );
   buffer[ MinZip ] = '\0';
   code = new char[ strlen( buffer ) + 1 ];
```

```
        strcpy( code, buffer );
}
```

creates a `ZipC` object from an integer. The compiler would have this constructor invoked in a code sequence such as

```
void h()
{
    ZipC z3( 60607 );  // integer constructor
        ...
}
```

The constructor uses `sprintf` to convert the integer into a null-terminated
array of `char` with length `MinZip`. For this purpose, the constructor uses an
array of `BigZip + 1 char` cells to ensure sufficient storage for the conversion. The constructor then allocates sufficient `char` cells to hold the string
that represents the `ZipC` object, including a cell for the '\0'.

Class `ZipC` has three constructors, each named `ZipC::ZipC`. Yet there
is never any question about which of the three is invoked in a particular
situation. If an object of type `ZipC` is defined without an initializing value,
then the default constructor is invoked. If such an object is defined with an
initializing string value, then the `char*` constructor is invoked. If such an
object is defined with an initializing integer value, then the `long` constructor
is invoked. In general, the compiler uses the number and type of initial values
to determine which constructor should be invoked. It is an error to have two
constructors that expect identical arguments. In our example, there can be
only one constructor that expects a single `long` argument.

The destructor for class `ZipC`

```
ZipC::~ZipC()
{
    delete[ ] code;
}
```

deallocates whatever storage a constructor allocates before such storage can
become garbage. For example, in the code slice

```
void f()
{
    ZipC zip( "60607-1312" ); // 11 bytes allocated
        ...
} // destructor invoked as control exits this block
```

the `ZipC` object `zip` has 11 bytes allocated to represent the zip code: 10
bytes for the characters in the initializing value and one byte for the null
terminator. These 11 bytes are allocated dynamically through the `new` operator. If the bytes were not freed before `f` exited, they would become garbage,
that is, dynamically allocated storage that the program cannot access. The
destructor `ZipC::~ZipC` prevents such garbage from being created in the

first place. The destructor uses the operator `delete[ ]` to free whatever storage the constructor has allocated, which in this code slice is 11 bytes. The compiler, not the programmer, takes responsibility for invoking the destructor.

Class `ZipC` also has a method, defined within the class declaration and therefore implicitly `inline`, to print the zip code. This method could be invoked as follows:

```
void f()
{
   ZipC zip( "60607-1312" );
   zip.write();              // prints 60606-1312
      ...
}
```

As `ZipC` presently stands, the only way to print `zip.code` inside function `f` is to use method `zip.write` because

- `zip.code` is `private` and therefore accessible only to `ZipC` methods or `friend` functions (see Section 3.7).

- `f` is neither a method nor a `friend` function of `ZipC`.

By contrast, method `zip.write` is accessible in `f` because all of `ZipC`'s methods are `public`.

Finally, method `expand` takes a zip code suffix, such as 1234, and appends it to a standard zip code such as 60607, inserting a hyphen between the code and the suffix. Of course, many other methods may be appropriate to support zip code operations. All such methods should provide users with desired functionality without requiring users to know the underlying representation of a `ZipC`. In short, `ZipC` is an abstract data type.

Exercises

---

1. Write a method `shorten` that shortens a 9-digit zip code such as 60607-1234 to a 5-digit zip code. The 5-digit zip code then becomes the official zip code.

2. Write a method `sameZip` that checks whether two `ZipC`s are identical.

3. Write a method `getMainZip` that extracts a 5-digit `ZipC` from a 9-digit `ZipC`. However, the 9-digit zip code is still the official zip code.

3.5   A First Look At Class Operator Overloading

Arithmetic operators such as + and / are overloaded even in C. For example, the / operator means integer division in the expression

```
2 / 3    // divide 2 by 3 ==> 0
```

and floating-point division in the expression

```
2.0 / 3.0    // divide 2.0 by 3.0 ==> 0.666667
```

It would be clumsy to have separate operators for integer division and floating-point division. Instead, we have a single overloaded operator, that is, an operator with more than one meaning.

The convenience of operator overloading extends to classes. By overloading operators for class objects, we can ease the manipulation of such objects and thereby provide the programmer with a higher level interface.

Example 3.5.1. Consider the class

```
class String {
    char* string;
public:
    ...
};
```

in which **string** points to dynamically allocated storage that can hold null-terminated **chars**. Now suppose that we store "bob" in **String** object **s1** and "carol" in **String** object **s2**. We would like the expression

```
s1 + s2    // String concatenation
```

to represent **String** concatenation. We therefore overload the + operator, the built-in version of which expects numeric rather than **String** operands. Here is a sketch:

```
class String {
    char* string;
public:
    String& operator+( const String ) const;
    ...
};

String& String::operator+( const String s ) const
{
    ...    // code that defines operator+ for Strings
}
```

(For now, ignore the **const**s that occur in the example. We clarify them in the next section.) The overloaded operator's name is **String::operator+**. It expects a single **const** argument of type **String** and returns a **String&**, that is, a **String** reference. Once the + operator has been overloaded for the **String** class, it can be used in expressions with **String** operands. □

An operator is overloaded by defining it as an **operator function**. The keyword **operator** occurs in the definition.

Example 3.5.2. We expand Example 3.5.1 by overloading the > operator so that it can be used to compare two **String** objects on the basis of their lexicographical order.

```
class String {
   char* string;
public:
   int operator>( const String s ) const; // declaration
   . . .
};

// definition
int String::operator>( const String s ) const
{
   return strcmp( string, s.string ) > 0;
}
```

Suppose that s1.string points to "lettuce" and that s2.string points to "lattice", where s1 and s2 are **String** objects. The expression

```
s1 > s2
```

would evaluate to 1 because "lettuce" is lexicographically greater than "lattice." The overloaded > operator could be used in code slices such as

```
if ( s1 > s2 )
   . . .
else
   . . .
```

The overloading extends an operator originally defined for numeric types such as **int**s and **float**s to **String**s.   □

An overloaded operator such as > may be used in syntactically distinct ways, which we characterize as *operator* and *method syntax*. For example, the code

```
if ( s1.operator>( s2 ) ) // method syntax
   . . .
```

has the same meaning as

```
if ( s1 > s2 )    // operator syntax
   . . .
```

Because method syntax for operators is clumsy, we typically use operator syntax. Indeed, ease of use is the very motivation behind operator overloading for a class.

C++ does not permit the overloading of these five operators:

```
.        // class member operator
.*       // class member dereference operator
::       // scope resolution operator
?:       // conditional operator
sizeof   // size in bytes operator
```

All other operators—including even the comma operator (,)—may be overloaded.

Exercises

---

1. Explain the error.

```
class Dict {
   char word[ 100 ];
   char definition[ 1000 ];
public:
   void write();
   int operator>( const Dict ) const; // declaration
   ...
};

// definition
int Dict::>( const Dict d ) const
{
   return strcmp( word, d.word ) > 0;
}
```

2. Overload the < operator for class Dict.

3. For the overloaded operator in Exercise 1, give code slices in which the operator is invoked using method syntax.

4. For the overloaded operator in Exercise 1, give code slices in which the operator is invoked using operator syntax.

5. Can you envision any use for an overloaded comma operator?

6. Explain the difference between operator and method syntax for an overloaded class operator. Give an example of each.

7. Declare a class C that includes a pointer. Overload the == operator for C.

8. Do you see any potential danger in operator overloading?

9. Explain the error.

```
class Dict {
   char word[ 100 ];
   char definition[ 1000 ];
public:
   void write();
   int operator.( const Dict ) const; // declaration
   ...
};

// definition
int Dict::operator.( const Dict d ) const
{
   ...
}
```

10. Which C++ operators, if any, may not be overloaded?

3.6   Sample Application: A Complex Number Class

Problem _____

Implement complex numbers as an abstract data type that supports standard binary operations such as addition and multiplication of objects in the class.

Solution _____

We create class `Complex` with two `double` data members to represent the real and imaginary components of a complex number. We extend the standard arithmetic operators such as + and * to `Complex` objects. We practice information hiding by making a `Complex`'s data members `private`. We practice encapsulation by including methods, including constructors and overloaded operators, in `Complex`.

C++ Implementation _____

```
#include <iostream.h>

class Complex {
   double real;
   double imag;
public:
   // constructors
   Complex();                 // default
   Complex( double );         // real given
   Complex( double, double ); // both given
```

```cpp
      // other methods
      void write()
      {
         cout << "real == " << real <<
                 "imaginary == " << imag << endl;
      }
      // operator methods
      Complex operator+( const Complex ) const;
      Complex operator-( const Complex ) const;
      Complex operator*( const Complex ) const;
      Complex operator/( const Complex ) const;
};

// default constructor
Complex::Complex()
{
   real = imag = 0.0;
}

// constructor -- real given but not imag
Complex::Complex( double r )
{
   real = r; imag = 0.0;
}

// constructor -- real and imag given
Complex::Complex( double r, double i )
{
   real = r; imag = i;
}

// Complex + as binary operator
Complex Complex::operator+( const Complex c ) const
{
   return Complex( real + c.real,
                   imag + c.imag );
}

// Complex - as binary operator
Complex Complex::operator-( const Complex c ) const
{
   return Complex( real - c.real,
                   imag - c.imag );
}
```

```
Complex Complex::operator*( const Complex c ) const
{
   return Complex( real * c.real - imag * c.imag,
                      imag * c.real + real * c.imag );
}

Complex Complex::operator/( const Complex c ) const
{
   double abs_sq = c.real * c.real + c.imag * c.imag;

   return Complex(
         ( real * c.real + imag * c.imag ) / abs_sq,
         ( imag * c.real - real * c.imag ) / abs_sq );
}
```

Discussion

The class **Complex** has three constructors but no destructor because it does not use dynamically allocated storage. The default constructor initializes data members **real** and **imag** to 0.0. The one-argument constructor initializes **real** to the **double** parameter and **imag** to 0.0. The two-argument constructor initializes the data members to the respective parameter values. The three constructors could be combined into one as:

```
Complex::Complex( double r = 0.0, double i = 0.0 )
{
   real = r; imag = i;
}
```

Our main interest lies in the arithmetic operators overloaded for the class. The purpose of the overloading is to extend the standard arithmetic operators to **Complex** numbers, thus allowing code such as

```
int main()
{
  Complex c1( 7.7, 5.5 );
  Complex c2( 4.4, 3.3 );
  Complex c3;

  c3 = c1 + c2; // + for Complex variables
  ...
}
```

In the declarations and definitions for the overloaded arithmetic operators, the keyword **const** occurs twice, once in the formal parameter list and then at the end:

```
Complex operator+( const Complex ) const; // declaration
```

The **const** in the parameter list ensures that the argument's value will not be altered during the addition, and the **const** at the end ensures that the method's invoker—the **Complex** object whose **operator+** is invoked on the argument—will not be altered during the addition. The operator returns the **Complex** result of the addition but does alter the objects involved in the addition.

Exercises

---

1. Overload the **+=** operator for class **Complex** and show a code slice that uses the overloaded operator.

2. Overload the **-=** operator for class **Complex** and show a code slice that uses the overloaded operator.

3. Overload the **/=** operator for class **Complex** and show a code slice that uses the overloaded operator.

4. Overload the ***=** operator for class **Complex** and show a code slice that uses the overloaded operator.

5. In the declaration

   ```
   Complex operator*( const Complex ) const; // declaration
   ```

   explain what each of **const**s means.

6. Explain the error.

   ```
   int main()
   {
     Complex c1( 1.1, 2.2 );
     Complex c2( 2.2, 3.3 );
     Complex c3;
     c3 = c1.+( c2 );
     ...
   }
   ```

7. Give code slices in which **Complex::operator-** is used with operator syntax and method syntax.

3.7   Friend Functions

A class's `private` members, which typically are its data members, are accessible to its methods and to its `friend` functions. To make function `f` a friend of class `C`, we declare `f` within `C`'s declaration using the keyword `friend`:

```
class C {
   int x;
public:
   friend int f(); // friend function
   ...
};
```

Except for being able to access one or more class's private members, a `friend` function is no different from any other function.

There are three main reasons to use `friend` functions:

- To allow selected functions access to the private members of a class.

- To allow a function to access the private members of two or more classes. (If a function needs access to the private members of only one class, it should be a method.)

- To allow more flexible operator overloading.

Because a `friend` function is *not* a method and still has access to `private` class members, a `friend` function violates a strict interpretation of object-oriented principles. Accordingly, `friend` functions are controversial and open to misuse. We recommend using `friend` functions only when absolutely necessary. We illustrate each use of `friend` functions.

Selected Function Access to private Members

Consider the class `C` that has a `private` data member of type `char*`:

```
class C {
   char* string;
public:
   C( char* s )
   {
     string = new char[ strlen( s ) + 1 ];
     strcpy( string, s );
   }
};

int sel()
{
   C c1( "tcp/ip" );
```

```
         // ***** ERROR: string is private
         int len = strlen( c1.string );
         ...
   }
```

The function **sel** cannot access **string** because **string** is **private**. One way around the problem is to make **sel** a **friend** so that it can access a private data member such as **string**:

```
   class C {
      char* string;
   public:
      C( char* s )
      {
        string = new char[ strlen( s ) + 1 ];
        strcpy( string, s );
      }
      friend int sel();
   };

   int sel()
   {
      C c1( "tcp/ip" );
      int len = strlen( c1.string ); // ok
      ...
   }
```

friends of Two or More Classes

Example 3.7.1. Consider a version of the **Stack** class (see Section 3.2) designed for **Complex** objects rather than **chars**:

```
   class Complex; // makes class Complex
                  // visible to ComplexStack

   class ComplexStack {
      ...
      Complex items[ MaxStack ];
   public:
      ...
      friend void dump_stack( ComplexStack );
   };

   class Complex {
      double real;
```

```
        double imag;
   public:
        ...
        friend void dump_stack( ComplexStack );
   };

   // note: dump_stack is not a method
   void dump_stack( ComplexStack s )
   {
      for ( int i = top; i >= 0; i-- )
         cout << s.items[ i ].real
              << ' ' << s.items[ i ].imag;

      cout << endl;
   }
```

In the original Stack class, dump_stack is a method. Here dump_stack is a **friend** of ComplexStack and a **friend** of Complex because dump_stack needs access to ComplexStack's private member **items** and to Complex's **private** members **real** and **imag**. In the original Stack class, dump_stack needs access only to **private** member **items** in Stack itself and so is best implemented as a method.

   Note that we declare Complex

```
   class Complex; // makes class Complex
                  // visible to ComplexStack

   class ComplexStack {
        ...
```

before declaring ComplexStack because ComplexStack references Complex.   □

Using friends in Operator Overloading

Example 3.7.2. Operator functions in class Complex could have been implemented as **friends** rather than as methods. For example,

```
   class Complex {
      double real;
      double imag;
   public:
      // constructors
      Complex();                    // default
         ...
```

```
      // friends
      friend Complex operator+( const Complex, const Complex );
         ...
};

Complex operator+( const Complex c1, const Complex c2 )
{
   return Complex( c1.real + c2.real,
                   c1.imag + c2.imag );
}
```

The declaration of **operator+** contains the keyword **friend**, but the operator's definition does not. Note, too, that the operator's name is simply **operator+** rather than **Complex::operator+**. Whether **operator+** is a method or a **friend**, its invocation looks exactly like the method's invocation when operator syntax is in use:

```
int main()
{
  Complex c1( 1.0, 1.0 );
  Complex c2( 2.0, 2.0 );
  Complex c3;

  c3 = c1 + c2; // either friend or operator syntax
  ...
}
```

If **operator+** is a **friend** rather than a method, however, then method syntax cannot be used. This code is illegal for the **friend** version

```
   c3 = c1.operator+( c2 );   // ***** ILLEGAL for friend
```

because **operator+** is not a **c1** method. However, the code

```
   c3 = operator+( c1, c2 ); // legal for friend
```

is legal.   □

The code slice

```
int main()
{
  Complex c1( 2.0, 2.0 );
  Complex c2;

  c2 = c1 + 99.0;  // c2 = c1.operator+( 99.0 );
  ...
}
```

is legal because, if `operator+` is a method or a **friend**, `Complex` object `c1` invokes its `operator+` with `99.0` as its argument. Although `99.0` is *not* a `Complex` object, the compiler can convert `99.0` to a `Complex` type by invoking the convert constructor `Complex::Complex( double )` so that the addition can proceed. However, the code slice

```
c2 = 99.0 + c1; // ***** ERROR: 99.0 not Complex
```

is in error if `operator+` is a method because `99.0` is not a `Complex` object with an `operator+` that can be invoked with `c1` as its argument. If we implement `operator+` as **friend** that expects two `Complex` objects as arguments, then either

```
c2 = c1 + 99.0; //ok
```

or

```
c2 = 99.0 + c1; // ok
```

is legal.   □

One class's method may be another class's **friend**, or classes may share a function as a **friend**. Yet these and related uses of **friend** functions strain the style of object-oriented programming in C++. Some object-oriented languages allow only methods to access data members as a way of enforcing information hiding. C++ gives the programmer flexibility by allowing **friend** functions as well as methods to access a class's **private** members, but we recommend that **friend** functions be used sparingly. The normal access to a class's **private** members should be through its methods.

Exercises

---

1. Create a class and test whether you can make **main** a **friend** function of this class.

2. Overload all the operators for class `Complex` as **friend** functions rather than as methods.

3. Explain why the extensive use of **friend** functions may compromise the spirit of object-oriented programming.

4. On your system, find the header file *complex.h*. (On UNIX systems, it is likely in the directory */usr/include* and in Borland C++ it is likely in the *INCLUDE* subdirectory.) Check whether the arithmetic operators have been overloaded as **friend** functions or as methods.

5. When does it seem useful to have **friend** functions?

6. If we overload * for class `Complex` as a method rather than as a `friend`, which of these expressions is legal and which illegal? Explain why in each case.

```
int main()
{
  Complex c1( 111.0, 999.0 );
  Complex c2;
  c2 = c1 + 777.0;
  c2 = 888.0 + c1;
  c2 = 777.0 + 888.0;
  ...
}
```

7. Assuming + is overloaded as a `friend` for `Complex`, explain the error(s).

```
int main()
{
  Complex c1( 1.0, 1.0 );
  Complex c2( 3.0, 3.0 );
  Complex c3;

  c3 = c1 + c2;
  c3 = c1.operator+( c2 );
  c3 = +( c2, c1 );
  c3 = operator+( c1, c2 );
  ...
}
```

3.8 Assertions and Program Correctness

A goal of any software development environment is to produce quality software. In particular, software should confirm to the specifications. An **assertion** in a program is a condition that must always be true at some particular point of the program's execution. Assertions, which formally represent the specifications and are embedded in the code, are checked for correctness when the program is running. When an assertion fails, the system detects and reports the error. Much attention has been given to formal methods of producing correct software, especially by developers of object-oriented languages. C++ and standard C support assertions through macros. Other object-oriented languages (e.g., Eiffel) support assertions directly in the language. In this section, we discuss **preconditions** and **postconditions** (assertions that must be true at entrance and exit from methods) and **class invariants** (assertions that must be satisfied by the class as a whole). Using preconditions, postconditions, and class invariants, it is possible to give a formal definition of what it means for a class to be correct [see B. Meyer, *Object-oriented Software Construction*, (Englewood Cliffs, N.J.: Prentice Hall, 1988), Chapter 7].

Consider the following variant of the stack class of Section 3.2:

```
const int MaxStack = 3;

class Stack {
    char items[ MaxStack ];
    int top;
public:
    enum { FullStack = MaxStack, EmptyStack = -1 };
    Stack();
    void push( char );
    char pop();
    int empty();
    int full();
};

Stack::Stack()
{
    top = EmptyStack;
}

void Stack::push( char c )
{
    items[ ++top ] = c;
}

char Stack::pop()
{
    int val;

    val = items[ top-- ];
    return val;
}

int Stack::full()
{
    return top + 1 == FullStack;
}
```

```
int Stack::empty()
{
    return top == EmptyStack;
}
```

In this version of the stack class, the user is responsible for checking for a full stack before pushing an item on the stack and for checking for an empty stack before popping an item off the stack.

Consider the method **push**. Because it is an error to push an item onto a full stack, we *assert* that, when **push** is entered, the stack is not full. A *precondition* for **push** is that the stack is not full. When **push** is exited, the stack is not empty. A *postcondition* for **push** is that the stack is not empty. Formally, we write

```
void Stack::push( char c )
{
    // precondition: true--OK; false--error
    assert( !full() );

    items[ ++top ] = c;

    // postcondition: true--OK; false--error
    assert( !empty() );
}
```

When **push** is invoked, the statement

```
assert( !full() );
```

is executed. The expression between the parentheses, !full() in this case, is evaluated. If this expression is true, execution proceeds normally to the next statement; but, if the expression is false, the program terminates with a message such as

```
Assertion failed: !full(), file ASSERT.CPP, line 29
Abnormal program termination
```

Similarly, after the statement

```
items[ ++top ] = c;
```

is executed, the statement

```
assert( !empty() );
```

is executed. If the expression !empty() is true, execution proceeds normally with a return from **push**; but, if the expression is false, the program terminates with a message.

We must include the system header file *assert.h* to use the **assert** macro. The following example shows the stack class with preconditions and postconditions added to **push** and **pop** and some sample output.

Example 3.8.1. We show two sample runs of the following program:

```cpp
#include <iostream.h>
#include <assert.h>
#include <stdlib.h>

const int MaxStack = 3;

class Stack {
   char items[ MaxStack ];
   int top;
public:
   enum { FullStack = MaxStack, EmptyStack = -1 };
   Stack();
   void push( char );
   char pop();
   int empty();
   int full();
};

Stack::Stack()
{
   top = EmptyStack;
}

void Stack::push( char c )
{
   // precondition: true--OK; false--error
   assert( !full() );

   items[ ++top ] = c;

   // postcondition: true--OK; false--error
   assert( !empty() );
}

char Stack::pop()
{
   int val;

   // precondition: true--OK; false--error
   assert( !empty() );

   val = items[ top-- ];
```

```
      // postcondition: true--OK; false--error
      assert( !full() );

      return val;
}

int Stack::full()
{
   return top + 1 == FullStack;
}

int Stack::empty()
{
   return top == EmptyStack;
}

int main()
{
   char resp, val;
   Stack s;

   for ( ; ; ) {
      cout << "Push (2), Pop (1), Quit (0): ";
      cin >> resp;
      switch ( resp ) {
      case '2':
         cout << "Push what value? ";
         cin >> val;
         s.push( val );
         break;
      case '1':
         cout << "Pop val = " << s.pop() << endl;
         break;
      case '0':
         return EXIT_SUCCESS;
      }
   }
}
```

The following is the output of a session in which a push fails:

```
Push (2), Pop (1), Quit (0): 2
Push what value? a
Push (2), Pop (1), Quit (0): 2
```

```
Push what value? b
Push (2), Pop (1), Quit (0): 2
Push what value? c
Push (2), Pop (1), Quit (0): 2
Push what value? d
Assertion failed: !full(), file ASSERT.CPP, line 29
Abnormal program termination
```

The following is the output of a session in which a pop fails:

```
Push (2), Pop (1), Quit (0): 2
Push what value? a
Push (2), Pop (1), Quit (0): 1
Pop val = a
Push (2), Pop (1), Quit (0): 1
Assertion failed: !empty(), file ASSERT.CPP, line 42
Abnormal program termination
```

□

Because a certain amount of overhead is associated with checking assertions, C++ makes it possible to disable the assertions by defining the macro NDEBUG (No DEBUG). The following example illustrates.

Example 3.8.2. If we insert the line

```
#define NDEBUG
```

just before the line

```
#include <assert.h>
```

the assertions will not be checked, as the following output from a sample session illustrates:

```
Push (2), Pop (1), Quit (0): 2
Push what value? a
Push (2), Pop (1), Quit (0): 2
Push what value? b
Push (2), Pop (1), Quit (0): 2
Push what value? c
Push (2), Pop (1), Quit (0): 2
Push what value? d
Push (2), Pop (1), Quit (0): 0
```

□

A *class invariant* is an assertion that must be satisfied by the class as a whole. To be more precise, a class invariant must be satisfied after any constructor is invoked and it must be satisfied at entrance and exit from each public method. For example, in the stack class, top must always be greater than or equal to EmptyStack, and top must always be less than FullStack. Thus the condition

```
top >= EmptyStack && top < FullStack
```

is a class invariant for the class Stack.

The following example shows the stack class with preconditions, post-conditions, and a class invariant.

Example 3.8.3. The class

```
const int MaxStack = 3;

class Stack {
   char items[ MaxStack ];
   int top;
public:
   enum { FullStack = MaxStack, EmptyStack = -1 };
   Stack();
   void push( char );
   char pop();
   int empty();
   int full();
};

// the class invariant
#define Stack_inv ( top >= EmptyStack && top < FullStack )

Stack::Stack()
{
   top = EmptyStack;
   assert( Stack_inv );
}

void Stack::push( char c )
{
   assert( !full() && Stack_inv );
   items[ ++top ] = c;
   assert( !empty() && Stack_inv );
}
```

```
char Stack::pop()
{
    int val;

    assert( !empty() && Stack_inv );
    val = items[ top-- ];
    assert( !full() && Stack_inv );
    return val;
}

int Stack::full()
{
    assert( Stack_inv );
    return top + 1 == FullStack;
}

int Stack::empty()
{
    assert( Stack_inv );
    return top == EmptyStack;
}
```

contains preconditions, postconditions, and a class invariant. If we deliberately insert the erroneous statement

```
top--;
```

just before the line

```
assert( Stack_inv );
```

in the constructor and run the program with the main function of Example 3.8.1 added, the output is

```
Assertion failed: Stack_inv, file ASSERT.CPP, line 28
Abnormal program termination
```

□

Exercises

1. Supply preconditions, postconditions, and class invariants for the zip code class of Section 3.4.

3.9 Generic Classes Using Templates

In Section 3.2, we constructed a stack class that pushed and popped **chars** on and off the stack. If we need a stack class that pushes and pops **ints**, we could modify our **char** stack by replacing **char** by **int**, but otherwise the code would remain the same. If we use this technique, every time we want a stack to manipulate a different data type, we would have to modify the code, replacing one data type by another. C++ provides a better way. By using **templates**, we can construct a stack class once and for all, and then construct stack classes for particular data types as needed. Thus templates directly support code reusability and promote code correctness.

When we use a template to construct a class, particular data types (such as **char** in the stack example) are replaced by symbolic names called **parameters**. Types constructed using parameters are called **parameterized types**. When the programmer requests a class from a parameterized class by providing arguments for the parameters, the system replaces the parameters by the given arguments and produces an actual class. A class that uses parameters for data types is also known as a **generic class**. Such a class is "generic" in the sense that the parameters are merely placeholders for specific data types. The parameters are not themselves actual data types.

The following example shows a version of the stack class of Section 3.2 rewritten as a generic class using templates.

Example 3.9.1. The code

```
template< class Typ, int MaxStack >
class Stack {
   Typ items[ MaxStack ];
   int top;
public:
   enum { FullStack = MaxStack, EmptyStack = -1 };
   Stack();
   void push( Typ );
   Typ pop();
   int empty();
   int full();
};

template< class Typ, int MaxStack >
Stack< Typ, MaxStack >::Stack()
{
   top = EmptyStack;
}
```

```
template< class Typ, int MaxStack >
void Stack< Typ, MaxStack >::push( Typ c )
{
    items[ ++top ] = c;
}


template< class Typ, int MaxStack >
Typ Stack< Typ, MaxStack >::pop()
{
    return items[ top-- ];
}


template< class Typ, int MaxStack >
int Stack< Typ, MaxStack >::full()
{
    return top + 1 == FullStack;
}


template< class Typ, int MaxStack >
int Stack< Typ, MaxStack >::empty()
{
    return top == EmptyStack;
}
```

constructs a generic stack class.

The line

```
template< class Typ, int MaxStack >
```

must be followed by a declaration or definition of a class or function. The statement makes the parameters given between the angle brackets (Typ and MaxStack in this case) available to the class or function that follows. The line

```
template< class Typ, int MaxStack >
```

serves somewhat the same purpose for parameterized types as does a function header for functions.

Each parameter listed between the angle brackets must be either a *type parameter* or a *function-style parameter*. A type parameter, which is preceded by the keyword class, is replaced by an actual type when a particular class is constructed. In our example, Typ is a type parameter that could be replaced by either a built-in data type such as int or by a user-defined data type such as a class. A function-style parameter, which follows the same syntax as function parameters, is replaced by a value when a particular class is constructed. In our example, MaxStack is a function-style parameter.

To construct a particular stack class and define an object, we could write

```
Stack< int, 1000 > s;
```

This code creates the class Stack< int, 1000 > and defines an object **s** of this type. The system obtains a declaration of Stack< int, 1000 > by replacing the type parameter Typ by int and the function-style parameter MaxStack by 1000 in the code

```
class Stack {
    Typ items[ MaxStack ];
    int top;
public:
    enum { FullStack = MaxStack, EmtpyStack = -1 };
    Stack();
    void push( Typ );
    Typ pop();
    int empty();
    int full();
};
```

Note that the expression

```
Stack< int, 1000 >
```

resembles a function call in which parameters receive arguments.

To define the methods, we must also use the keyword **template** since the methods are parameterized functions. For example, to define the method push, we write

```
template< class Typ, int MaxStack >
void Stack< Typ, MaxStack >::push( Typ c )
{
    items[ ++top ] = c;
}
```

The line

```
template< class Typ, int MaxStack >
```

makes the parameters Typ and MaxStack available to the function

```
Stack< Typ, MaxStack >::push
```

which follows. As shown, the method must be scoped to the parameterized class

```
Stack< Typ, MaxStack >
```

$\square$

Templates are similar to parameterized macros and serve the same general purpose. Indeed, early versions of C++ did not support templates and so generic classes had to be constructed using parameterized macros. Templates are far superior to parameterized macros because templates are part

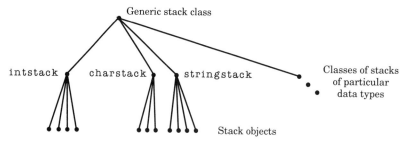

Figure 3.9.1 Levels of abstraction for stacks.

of the language and are not handled by the preprocessor, as are parameterized macros. Templates are easier to write than parameterized macros, and they are also easier to debug.

Generic classes provide yet another level of abstraction for the programmer. Just as a class is an abstraction of an object, so a generic class is an abstraction of a class (see Figure 3.9.1).

Exercises

---

1. Find the error.

```
template< class Typ >
class C {
    ...
public:
    C();
    ...
};

template< class Typ >
C::C()
{
    ...
}
```

2. Write a line that constructs a stack class using the generic class of Example 3.9.1 for a maximum stack size of 500 elements of type **char**.

3. Write a line that constructs a class stack class using the generic class of Example 3.9.1 for a maximum stack size of 2000 elements of type **String***.

4. Show the changes to the stack class of Example 3.9.1 if we add a method **top** that returns, but does not remove, the item at the top of the stack.

5. Revise the stack class of Example 3.9.1 so that it has one type parameter Typ. Provide a constructor with an **int** parameter **size** that dynamically allocates an array of **size** elements. Provide a default constructor that dynamically allocates an array of 100 elements. Also provide an appropriate destructor.

6. Write a line that constructs a stack class using the generic class of Exercise 5 to a maximum stack size of 100 elements of type **float**.

7. Write a line that constructs a stack class using the generic class of Exercise 5 to a maximum stack size of 1000 elements of type **Complex***.

Common Programming Errors

---

1. It is an error to declare a class without using exactly one of the keywords **class**, **struct**, or **union** in the declaration.

2. The keyword **class** is not needed to create class objects. For example, we write

```
class C {
   ...
};

C c1, c2; // object definitions
```

instead of

```
class C c1, c2; // keyword class not needed
```

3. If a class member is **private**, it can be accessed only by class methods and **friend** functions. For example, this code is in error

```
class C {
   int x;
   ...
public:
   C() { x = -999; }
};

void f()
{
   C c;
   cout << c.x;  // ***** ERROR
}
```

because x is `private` in class C and function `f` is neither a method nor a `friend` of C.

4. It is illegal to specify a return type, including `void`, for a constructor or a destructor in either its declaration or its definition. If C is a class, for example, then

```
void C::~C()      // ***** ERROR: void not allowed here
{
   ...
}
```

is illegal.

5. It is illegal to specify any argument, including `void`, in either the declaration or definition of a class's default constructor. In class C, for example, the default constructor

```
C::C( void ) // ***** ERROR
{
   ...
}
```

cannot be defined with any argument.

6. It is illegal to specify any argument, including `void`, in either the declaration or definition of a class's destructor.

7. It is illegal to have two constructors for the same class with exactly the same argument types because there is then no way for the compiler to determine which version of the constructor should be invoked.

8. It is illegal for a constructor for class C to have an argument of type C. However, such a constructor can have an argument of type C&, that is, a C *reference*. Such a constructor is called the copy constructor.

9. It is illegal for a member declaration to have an initializer:

```
class C {
   // ***** ERROR: illegal initialization
   int x = 1;
};
```

Initialization must be done by a method, typically, a constructor:

```
class C {
   int x;
   ...
```

```
public:
  // correct initialization
  C() { x = 1; }
};
```

10. It is illegal to initialize a `const` data member in a constructor's body. The initialization must occur in the constructor's header:

```
class C {
  const int x;
public:
  // ***** ERROR: const initialized in body
  C( int a ) { x = a; }
};

class Z {
  const int x;
public:
  // ok
  Z( int a ) : x( a ) { }
};
```

11. Initialization of an object in another class must be done in a constructor's header. The code

```
class N {
    int x;
public:
    N( int a ) { x = a; }
};

class C {
    int y;
    // ***** ERROR: illegal initialization
    N n( 0 );
public:
    C() { y = 0; }
};
```

contains an error because a member declaration cannot have an initializer. The correct way to initialize n is through C's constructor:

```
class C {
    int y;
    N n;
public:
```

```
      // correct
      C() : n( 0 ) { y = 0; }
};
```

12. It is illegal to declare or define a function operator without the keyword
`operator`. For example, the overloaded + operator for class `Complex` must
be declared

```
Complex Complex::operator+( const Complex ) const;
```

rather than

```
Complex Complex::+( const Complex ) const; / ***** ERROR
```

13. It is illegal to use method syntax on an overloaded `friend` operator.
Instead, operator syntax must be used. If + is overloaded as a `friend` for
class `Complex`, it must be invoked as

```
c1 + c2              // OK
operator+( c1, c2 ) // OK
```

rather than as

```
   c1.operator+( c2 ) // ***** ERROR: method syntax
```

14. It is illegal to overload any of these operators:

```
   .        // class member
   .*       // class member dereference
   ::       // scope resolution
   ?:       // conditional
   sizeof  // size in bytes
```

15. A method in a parameterized class such as

```
template< class Typ >
class C {
   ...
   int f( char );
   ...
};
```

is a parameterized function and therefore requires a template. For this
reason,

```
// ***** ERROR: template required
int C< Typ >::f( char c )
{
   ...
}
```

is an error.

Also, the class is C< Typ > rather than C. Accordingly, the following is an error:

```
// ***** ERROR: the class is C< Typ >, not C
template< class Typ >
int C::f( char c )
{
    ...
}
```

The correct syntax is

```
// correct
template< class Typ >
int C< Typ >::f( char c )
{
    ...
}
```

Programming Exercises

3.1. Implement a **Calendar** class. The public interface consists of methods that enable the user to

- Specify a start year such as 1776 or 1900.
- Specify a duration such as 1 year or 100 years.
- Specify generic holidays such as Tuesdays.
- Specify specific holidays such as the third Thursday in November.
- Specify a month-year such as July-1776, which results in a display of the calendar for the specified month-year.

To simplify matters, you may ignore leap years. Holidays should be marked so that they can be readily recognized as such whenever the calendar for a month-year is displayed.

3.2. Implement a **CollegeStudent** class with appropriate data members such as **name**, **year**, **expectedGrad**, **major**, **minor**, **GPA**, **coursesAndGrades**, **maritalStatus**, and the like. The class should have at least a half-dozen methods in its public interface. For example, there should be a method to compute **GPA** from **coursesAndGrades** and to determine whether the **GPA** merits honors or probation. There also should be methods to display a **CollegeStudent**'s current course load and to print remaining required courses.

3.3. Implement a `Deck` class that represents a deck of 52 cards. The public interface should include methods to shuffle, deal, display hands, do pairwise comparisons of cards (e.g., a Queen beats a Jack), and the like. To simulate shuffling, you can use a random number generator such as the library function `rand`.

3.4. Implement a `Profession` class with data members such as `name`, `title`, `credentials`, `education`, `avgIncome`, and the like. The public interface should include methods that compare `Professions` across the data members. The class should have at least a dozen data members and a dozen methods.

3.5. A **queue** is a list of zero or more members. A member is added to a queue at its **rear**; a member is removed from a queue at its **front**. If a queue is **empty**, then a removal operation is illegal. If a queue is **full**, then an add operation is illegal. Implement a generic `Queue` class with preconditions, postconditions, and class invariants.

3.6. A **deque** is a list of none or more members. It is a generalization of a stack and a queue in that members may be added or removed from either end. Implement a generic `Deque` class with preconditions, postconditions, and class invariants.

3.7. A **semaphore** is a mechanism widely used in computer systems to enforce synchronization constraints on shared resources. For example, a semaphore might be used to ensure that two processes cannot use a printer at the same time. The semaphore mechanism first grants exclusive access to one process and then to the other so that the printer does not receive a garbled mix from the two processes. Implement a `Semaphore` class that enforces synchronization on files so that a process is ensured exclusive access to a file. The public interface consists of methods that *set* semaphore for a specified file, that *release* a semaphore protecting a specified file, and that *test* to determine whether a semaphore is currently protecting a specified file.

3.8. Implement an interactive `Calculator` class that accepts as input an arithmetic expression such as

    25 / 5 + 4

and then evaluates the expression, printing the value. In this example, the output would be

    9

There should be methods to validate the input expression. For example, if the user inputs

```
25 / 5 +
```

then the output should be an error message such as

```
ERROR: operator-operand imbalance.
```

3.9. Implement a `Set` class, where a **set** is an unordered collection of none or more elements with no duplicates. For this exercise, the elements should be `ints`. The public interface consists of methods to

- Create a `Set`.
- Add a new element to a `Set`.
- Remove an element from a `Set`.
- Enumerate the elements in the `Set`.
- Compute the **intersection** of two `Sets` S1 and S2, that is, the set of elements that belong both to S1 and to S2.
- Compute the **union** of two `Sets` S1 and S2, that is, the set of elements that belong to S1 or to S2 or to both.
- Compute the **difference** of two `Sets` S1 and S2, that is, the set of elements that belong to S1 but not to S2.

3.10. Implement a generic `Set` class (see Programming Exercise 3.9).

3.11. Implement a `Bag` class. A **bag** is like a set except that a bag may have duplicates. For this exercise, the bag's elements should be `ints`. The public interface should support the counterpart operations given in Programming Exercise 3.9.

3.12. Implement a generic `Bag` class (see Programming Exercise 3.11).

3.13. Create a `Spaceship` class suitable for simulation. One of the constructors should allow us to specify the `Spaceship`'s initial position in 3-dimensional space, its trajectory, its velocity, its rate of acceleration, and its target, which is another `Spaceship`. The simulation should track a `Spaceship`'s movement every clock tick (e.g., every second), printing such relevant data as the `Spaceship`'s identity, its trajectory, and so forth. If you have access to a graphics package such as UNIX *curses* or Borland C++ Graphics, you can add graphics to the simulation.

3.14. Implement a `Database` class where a `Database` is a collection of *tables*, which in turn are made up of *rows* and *columns*. For example, the employee table

	Social Security Number	Last Name	Department	Boss
1	111-11-1234	Cruz	Accounting	Werdel
2	213-44-5649	Johnstone	InfoSystems	Michaels
3	321-88-7895	Elders	Marketing	Bierski
	. . .			

has numbered records, each of which has four fields (Social Security Number, Last Name, Department, and Boss). The public interface should allow a user to

- Create a table.
- Change a table's structure by adding or removing fields.
- Delete a table.
- Add records to a table.
- Remove records from a table.
- Retrieve information from one or more tables at a time using a suitable query language.

3.15. This exercise requires access to a basic graphics package such as UNIX *curses* or the Borland C++ graphics library. Implement a `GeoFig` class with methods that allow the user to draw on the screen geometric figures such as lines, squares, circles, and the like. The public interface also should include methods for creating, moving, enlarging, shrinking, and destroying such objects. The idea behind this exercise is to take operations already available in a package such as UNIX *curses* and to encapsulate them with a class so that they enjoy the ease-of-use associated with object-oriented programming.

Chapter 4

More On Classes

This chapter begins with a sample application, a `String` class, that introduces important and subtle issues with respect to constructors, destructors, and assignment operators. We use the sample application to clarify these issues in subsequent sections and to introduce related material.

4.1   Sample Application: A String Class

Problem ⸻

Implement a string as an abstract data type.

Solution ⸻

We create a `String` class with constructors and a destructor that allows the user to focus on the manipulation of `Strings` without concern for their internal representation. For example, the constructors ensure that the array of `char` used in the internal representation is null-terminated and that all dynamically allocated storage is freed before it can become garbage. We practice information hiding by making a `String`'s internal representation `private`. We practice encapsulation by including methods (including constructors, a destructor, and overloaded operators) in a `String`.

C++ Implementation ⸻

```
// header file: strings.h

// Use an #ifndef to guard against the
// case in which this header file is
// inadvertently #included more than once
// in some other file
#ifndef StringHeaderLoaded_Version_1_0
#define StringHeaderLoaded_Version_1_0

class String {
    char* str;      // data member -- private
    int   len;      // actual
  public:
    enum SortOrder { Asc, Desc };
    enum ErrorsIO { ReadFail, WriteFail };
    // constructors-destructor
    String();                    // default constructor
    String( const String& );  // copy constructor
    String( const int );       // string initialized to blanks
    String( const char* );     // from a C string, char*
```

```cpp
    ~String();                    // destructor
    // other methods as functions
    int write();
    int write( FILE* );
    int read();
    int read( FILE* );
    // operators
    String operator+( const String& ) const;
    int operator<( const String ) const;
    int operator>( const String ) const;
    String& operator=( const String& );
    // friends
    friend void sort( String*, int, int ); // selection sort
};

#endif   // StringHeaderLoaded_Version_1_0

// end of header file: strings.h

// source code file: strings.cpp

#include <iostream.h>
#include <stdio.h>
#include <string.h>
#include <stdlib.h>
#include "strings.h"

// default constructor -- create empty string
String::String()
{
   str = new char[ 1 ];  // allocate
   *str = '\0';          // initialize to null string
   len = 0;
}

// convert constructor
String::String( const char* cstr )
{
   // +1 to ensure room for null terminator
   str = new char[ strlen( cstr ) + 1 ];
   strcpy( str, cstr );
   len = strlen( str );
}
```

```
// copy constructor -- String ==> String
String::String( const String& strarg )
{
  // copy an existing String.str into a new
  // one after first allocating sufficient storage
  strcpy( str = new char[ strarg.len + 1 ],
          strarg.str );
  len = strarg.len;
}

// blank string constructor
String::String( const int lenarg )
{
   str = new char[ lenarg + 1 ];
   len = lenarg;
   char* ptr = str;

   for ( int i = 0; i < len; i++ )
      *ptr++ = ' ';
   *ptr = '\0';     // null terminate
}

// destructor -- deallocate storage
String::~String()
{
   delete[ ] str;
}

// write String to standard output
// with a terminating newline
int String::write()
{
   return printf( "%s\n", str );
}

// write String to specified file
int String::write( FILE* outfile )
{
   if ( !outfile )
      return WriteFail;
   else
      return fprintf( outfile, "%s\n", str );
}
```

```
// read String from standard input
int String::read()
{
    scanf( "%s", str );

    return len = strlen( str );
}

// read String from designated file
int String::read( FILE* infile )
{
    if ( !infile )
        return ReadFail;
    else {
        fscanf( infile, "%s", str );
        return len = strlen( str );
    }
}

// assignment operator
String& String::operator=( const String& strarg )
{
    // check whether String assigned to itself
    if ( this != &strarg ) {
        delete[ ] str;                // free current storage
        len = strarg.len;
        str = new char[ len + 1 ];    // allocate new storage
        strcpy( str, strarg.str );    // copy contents
    }
    return *this;
}

// < operator for less than comparisons
int String::operator<( const String strarg ) const
{
    return strcmp( str, strarg.str ) < 0;
}

// > operator for greater than comparisons
int String::operator>( const String strarg ) const
{
    return strcmp( str, strarg.str ) > 0;
}
```

```
// + operator for concatenations
String String::operator+( const String& strarg ) const
{
   // allocate enough storage for 2 strings + '\0'
   char* temp = new char[ len + strarg.len + 1 ];

   // copy 1st string and concatenate second
   strcpy( temp, str );
   strcat( temp, strarg.str );

   // define a variable of type String to be
   // used as a return value
   String retval( temp );

   // free temporary storage
   delete[ ] temp;

   return retval;
}

// selection sort an array of String
void sort( String a[ ], int size, int order  )
{
   int next;

   // set comparison operator based on order parm
   int ( String::*compare_op )( const String ) const;
   compare_op =
      ( order == String::Asc ) ? String::operator< :
                                 String::operator>;

   // loop thru array, picking biggest or smallest
   // element each time, depending on sort order
   for ( int i = 0; i < size - 1; i++ ) {
      next = i;   // assume ith String smallest-biggest

      // compare against remaining elements
      for ( int j = i + 1; j < size; j++ )
         if ( ( a[ j ].*compare_op )( a[ next ] ) )
            next = j;

      // put smallest-biggest at position i
      if ( i != next ) {
         String temp = a[ i ];
```

```
                        a[ i ] = a[ next ];
                        a[ next ] = temp;
                }
        }
}
```

Discussion

The class **String** has two data members: an **int** variable **len** that stores the **String**'s length and a pointer **str** to the **char** cells that hold the **String**'s value. The **char** cells include a cell for a **'\0'**, which means that the total number of cells is the **String**'s length + 1. The data members are **private** by default and so accessible only to a **String**'s four constructors, its destructor, the other four member functions, the four member operators, and the **friend** function **sort**, which does a selection sort on an array of **Strings**. The sort may be done in either ascending or descending order. The data member **len** is included as a convenience for defining the constructors. The class **String** could be created without the **len** member, as we request in an exercise. We now examine how the methods and **friend** function work.

The default constructor

```
// default constructor -- create empty string
String::String()
{
    str = new char[ 1 ];  // allocate
    *str = '\0';          // initialize to empty
    len = 0;
}
```

expects no argument and so is invoked whenever a variable of type **String** is defined without any initializing value. For example, in a definition such as

```
String string1;
```

the default constructor is invoked. This constructor dynamically allocates a single **char** cell, sets its value to the null terminator, and sets its length to 0. Because class member **str** now points to a null-terminated array of **char**, **string1.str** is an ordinary C string and so can be passed as an argument to library functions such as **strlen**, **strcmp**, **strcat**, and the like.

The convert constructor

```
// convert constructor
String::String( const char* cstr )
{
    // +1 to ensure room for null terminator
    str = new char[ strlen( cstr ) + 1 ];
    strcpy( str, cstr );
```

```
        len = strlen( str );
    }
```

is invoked whenever a `String` object is defined with an ordinary C string as
its initializing value. For example, in the definition

```
    String string2( "mercy!" );
```

this constructor is invoked. The constructor allocates `strlen(cstr) +
1 char` cells so that there are enough cells to hold the C string and the
`'\0'`. The constructor then copies the argument into the cells and sets data
member `len` to `strlen( cstr )`. The argument to this constructor is `const`
to ensure that the constructor does not alter the value of the C string while
initializing `str`.

   The copy constructor

```
    // copy constructor -- String ==> String
    String::String( const String& strarg )
    {
        // copy an existing String.str into a new
        // one after first allocating sufficient storage
        strcpy( str = new char[ strarg.len + 1 ],
                strarg.str );
        len = strarg.len;
    }
```

initializes a newly created `String` to an already existing `String`. For example, in the code slice

```
    String string2( "foo " );
    String string3( string2 );
```

the copy constructor is invoked to initialize `string3` from the previously
defined `string2`, which in turn is initialized from an ordinary C string.
Had we not provided our own copy constructor, the compiler would have
provided one for us; but the compiler's copy constructor would not have
worked properly because a `String` object includes a pointer to dynamically
allocated storage. Figures 4.1.1 and 4.1.2 contrast the compiler's default
copy constructor and our own.

   The problem with the compiler's copy constructor is that it does memberwise assignment:

```
    string3.len = string2.len;
    string3.str = string2.str;
```

The memberwise assignment is proper for the `len` data member but not for
the `str` data member. After the assignment

```
    string2.str = string3.str;
```

the two pointers point to exactly the same storage! Our intent is to have
`string3.str` and `string2.str` point to *different* storage cells but to have

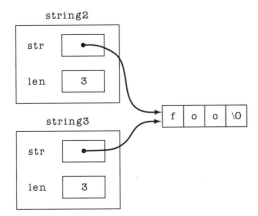

Figure 4.1.1 The compiler's default copy constructor for a **String**.

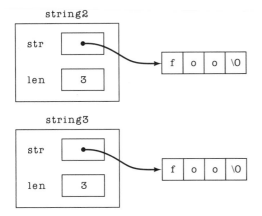

Figure 4.1.2 Our copy constructor for a **String**.

Constructor	Type	Sample Invocation
String::String()	Default	String s1;
String::String(char*)	Convert	String s2("foo");
String::String(int)	Convert	String s3(1000);
String::String(String&)	Copy	String s4(s2);

Figure 4.1.3 Constructor summary for String.

the same chars in these cells. Our copy constructor achieves this goal, but the compiler's does not. Our copy constructor first allocates separate storage for string3 and then uses strcpy to copy string2.str into string3.str. The constructor finishes its work by setting string3.len to string2.len.

Whenever we create a class with a pointer as a data member, we typically provide our own copy constructor. If we create a class without any pointers as data members, we typically let the compiler generate the copy constructor for us. Our copy constructor's single argument is const because the copy constructor does not alter it.

The convert constructor

```
// blank string constructor
String::String( const int lenarg )
{
    str = new char[ lenarg + 1 ];
    len = lenarg;
    char* ptr = str;

    for ( int i = 0; i < len; i++ )
        *ptr++ = ' ';
    *ptr = '\0';    // null terminate
}
```

creates a blank string of length len and provides an extra char cell to hold a null terminator. This constructor would be invoked in a definition such as

```
String string3( 100 ); // 100 blanks + null terminator
```

Figure 4.1.3 summarizes the different types of constructor, using the String constructors as examples.

The destructor

```
// destructor -- deallocate storage
String::~String()
{
    delete[ ] str;
}
```

deallocates however much storage has been allocated by a constructor. For example, in the case of

```
String string1;
```

the destructor would free the single cell that the default constructor allocates for `string1.str2`. In the case of

```
String string2( "bar foo bar" );
```

the destructor would deallocate 12 cells for `string2.str`—11 for "bar foo bar" and one for the null terminator. In a code slice such as

```
void f()
{
   String s( "War and Peace" );
   ...
} // s's destructor fires as control exits f
```

the constructor

```
String::String( char* )
```

is automatically invoked when f is invoked and the object is created. The destructor

```
String::~String()
```

is automatically invoked when f terminates and the object s is destroyed.

There are four other methods: two versions of **write** and two versions of **read**. The following code slice illustrates how each might be used:

```
int main()
{
   // variable definitions
   FILE* out = fopen( "DiskOut", "w" );
   FILE* in = fopen( "DiskIn", "r" );
   String s( "Once upon a midnight dreary..." );
   s.write();        // writes to standard output
   s.write( out );   // writes to disk file DiskOut
   s.read();         // reads from standard input
   s.read( in );     // reads from disk file DiskIn
   ...
}
```

Calls to `s.write()` and `s.write( out )` print `s.str` to the standard output and *DiskOut*, respectively. The calls `s.read()` and `s.read( in )` read a string from the standard input and *DiskIn*, respectively, storing the string in the cells to which `s.str` points. These member functions rely upon **fprintf** and **fscanf**.

The class **String** overloads four operators: >, <, +, and =. The operator < is overloaded by the code

```
// < operator for less than comparisons
int String::operator<( const String strarg ) const
{
    return strcmp( str, strarg.str ) < 0;
}
```

to simplify the syntax of **String** comparison. The code slice

```
int main()
{
  String string1( "bonnie" );
  String string2( "clyde" );
  if ( string1 < string2 )
     cout << "bonnie" << " < " << "clyde" << endl;
  else
     cout << "clyde" << " <= " << "bonnie" << endl;
  ...
}
```

illustrates how the operator might be used. The output is

```
bonnie < clyde
```

The single argument to the overloaded operator is **const** because the comparison does not alter the argument.

The overloaded operator +

```
// + operator for concatenations
String String::operator+( const String& strarg ) const
{
    // allocate enough storage for 2 strings + '\0'
    char* temp = new char[ len + strarg.len + 1 ];

    // copy 1st string and concatenate second
    strcpy( temp, str );
    strcat( temp, strarg.str );

    // define a variable of type String to be
    // used as a return value
    String retval( temp );

    // free temporary storage
    delete[ ] temp;

    return retval;
}
```

is more complex. Here is a code slice to illustrate its use:

```
int main()
{
   String s1( "Get a life, George" );
   String s2( " and Martha!" );
   String s3;
   s3 = s1 + s2; // Get a life, George and Martha!
   s3.write();   // prints s3.str to standard output
   ...
}
```

The overloaded + is used for string concatentation. Because the operator returns a value of type String, the line

```
String retval( temp );
```

is needed to convert the C string temp into a String. When retval is defined, temp (which points to the concatenation of s1.str and s2.str) provides the initializing value stored at retval.str. The constructor

```
// C string to String constructor
String::String( const char* cstr )
{
    // +1 to ensure room for null terminator
    str = new char[ strlen( cstr ) + 1 ];
    strcpy( str, cstr );
    len = strlen( str );
}
```

is invoked to initialize retval. Before the + operator function returns, it frees the storage to which temp points so that no garbage is left behind. The operator then returns the required value of type String:

```
return retval;
```

The class String also overloads the assignment operator = and thereby gives us a first look at the C++ keyword this. The compiler sets the value of this to the address of the object whose function or operator member is invoked. We illustrate with a simple example before looking at the body of the = operator.

The method write with no arguments could be changed from the original

```
// write String to standard output
// with a terminating newline
int String::write()
{
    return printf( "%s\n", str );
}
```

to

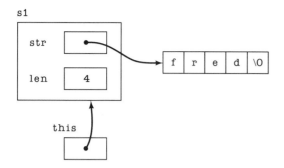

Figure 4.1.4 The pointer `this`.

```
// write String to standard output
int String::write()
{
    return printf( "%s\n", this -> str );   // this
}
```

The two code slices do the same thing. In the code slice

```
int main()
{
  String s1( "fred" );
  s1.write();
  ...
}
```

`this` points to `String s1` (see Figure 4.1.4). The pointer variable `this` has type qualifier `const` so that it would be an error to use `this` as the target of an assignment expression. Any statement of the form

```
this = ...;   // ***** ERROR
```

is wrong. Also, `this` is a C++ keyword, which rules out a user-defined variable or parameter of the same name.

In the case of the = operator,

```
// assignment operator
String& String::operator=( const String& strarg )
{
    // test whether object assigned to itself
    if ( this !=  &strarg ) {
       delete[ ] str;
       len = strarg.len;
       str = new char[ len + 1 ];
       strcpy( str, strarg.str );
    }
    return *this;
}
```

this is needed to check, in the **if** statement, whether a **String** object is being assigned to itself. For example, in the code slice

```
int main()
{
   String s1( "fred" );
   s1 = s1;    // pointless assignment of s1 to s1
   ...
}
```

the body of the **if** statement is not executed because the test

```
if ( this != &str ) {
```

fails. (Exercise 6 asks you to investigate the result of removing the **if** test from the operator.) If the **String** object is not being assigned to itself, the body of the **if** statement frees the current storage to which **str** points, allocates new storage to hold **strarg.len + 1** bytes, and copies the string into this new storage. The operator uses the statement

```
return *this;
```

to return the current object, that is, the object to which **this** points. It is important that **String::operator=** return a **String** reference to enable constructs such as

```
int main()
{
   String s1( "hello, world" );
   String s2;
   String s3;
   s3 = ( s2 = s1 );  // parentheses optional
   ...
}
```

Recall that the assignment operator is, technically, an operator *function*, that is, a function that permits operator syntax. So **String::operator=** may be used with the syntax of a binary operator

```
s2 = s1;              // operator syntax
```

or the syntax of a method

```
s2.operator=( s1 ); // method syntax
```

The point is that **String::operator=** expects a **String** reference as an argument. Therefore, the statement

```
s3 = ( s2 = s1 ); // parentheses optional
```

should be understood as

```
s3.operator=( s2.operator=( s1 ) ); // method syntax
```

For this to work, the expression

```
s2 = s1
```

must evaluate to a String reference—the argument to s3's operator=.

The friend function sort uses one of the overloaded comparison operators (either > or <), the overloaded assignment operator =, and the copy constructor. The code slice

```
int ( String::*compare_op )( const String ) const;
compare_op =
    ( order == String::Asc ) ? String::operator< :
                               String::operator>;
```

defines the variable compare_op as a pointer to a String method that expects a const argument of type String and returns an int (see Section 2.3). The assignment statement sets compare_op to either operator< or operator>, depending on the value of parameter order. Once compare_op has been set, we can use it to compare values during the sort:

```
if ( ( a[ j ].*compare_op )( a[ next ] ) )
    next = j;
```

For example, if compare_op is operator>, the if condition tests whether a[j].str is lexicographically greater than a[next].str.

The code

```
// put smallest-biggest at position i
if ( i != next ) {
    String temp = a[ i ];
    a[ i ] = a[ next ];
    a[ next ] = temp;
}
```

swaps two Strings so that they are in the correct lexicographical order. In the next section, we illustrate how the assignment operator and the copy constructor are both at work in this code.

Exercises

---

1. Explain which constructor is invoked in each of the object definitions:

```
int main()
{
    String s1;
    String s2( 1000 );
    String s3( "fred" );
    String s4( s3 );
    ...
}
```

2. Rewrite the `String` class without data member `len`.

3. Explain why the programmer should provide a copy constructor for a class with a data member that is a pointer.

4. Rewrite the `String` class without null-terminating the `chars` to which `str` points.

5. Rewrite the `read` and `write` methods so that they use functions such as `puts`, `gets`, `fputs`, and `fgets`.

6. Why would it be dangerous to remove the test

   ```
   if ( this !=  &str ) {
   ```

   from `String::operator=`? If you do not see any danger, remove the test and do a sample run.

7. Write a method `substitute` that substitutes `len` `chars` for the blanks used in the constructor

   ```
   String::String( const int lenarg )
   ```

   Recall that this constructor initializes a newly created `String` to `lenarg` blanks.

8. Overload the `==` operator for class `String`.

9. Overload the `!=` operator for class `String`.

10. The method `String::write( FILE* )` does not make its `FILE*` argument a `const`. Explain why not. If the reason is not clear, make the argument `const` and do a sample run that invokes the method.

11. Express in words the data type of `compare_op` in `friend` function `sort`.

12. What is the scope of `enum SortOrder`?

13. Change the `String` class so that `enum ErrorsIO` has file rather than class scope.

14. The `String` method `operator+` uses local variable `retval` of type `String` to hold the operator's return value. Is this local variable necessary? That is, could you rewrite the operator so that it uses no local variable of type `String`?

15. Explain in words how the expression

    ```
    ( a[ j ].*compare_op )( a[ next ] )
    ```

    works in the `sort` function. In particular, is there a function call here?

16. Would the sort still work if **sort** were a method rather than a **friend**? Explain your answer.

17. Why does the **String** destructor use the **delete[ ]** operator rather than the **delete** operator?

18. Illustrate how **this** behaves by rewriting the **read** and **write** methods so they all explicitly use **this**.

19. What is the data type of **this** in any of the **String** methods?

20. In which **String** methods, if any, must **this** be explicitly used?

21. Explain the error:

```
this = ...;
```

22. Write a **String** method that replaces, in the internal representation, one specified character by another. For example, this method would replace every blank character by, say, the character '!' in the **String**'s internal representation.

23. Explain what each of the **consts** means in the definition of **String::operator+**.

4.2   More on the Copy Constructor

A copy constructor for class C has the header

```
C::C( const C& )
```

The compiler provides such a constructor if the programmer does not, and the programmer typically provides one if class C contains a pointer among its data members. The copy constructor expects a reference as its argument and, like all constructors, does not return a value. The compiler invokes the copy constructor in three contexts, regardless of whether the user or the compiler furnishes the copy constructor. We consider each context separately and use the **String** class of Section 4.1 to illustrate.

Object Definition with Copy Initialization

At times C++ syntax hides rather than reveals underlying operations. This is particularly true with respect to object initialization, which may appear to use the assignment operator rather than one of the class's constructors.

Example 4.2.1. In the code slice

```
int main()
{
  // code slice 1
  String s1( "RISC versus CISC" ); // convert constructor
  String s2( s1 );                 // copy constructor
  String s3 = s1;                  // copy, not assignment!
  ...
}
```

s2 is initialized through the copy constructor because s1 is a String. Object s3 also is initialized through the copy constructor, even though the assignment operator seems to be at work. In C++, *the assignment operator is never at work when a variable is initialized in its definition.* The reason can be seen by reviewing the String assignment operator:

```
// assignment operator
String& String::operator=( const String& strarg )
{
   // test whether object assigned to itself
   if ( this != &strarg ) {
      delete[ ] str;
      len = strarg.len;
      str = new char[ len + 1 ];
      strcpy( str, strarg.str );
   }
   return *this;
}
```

Note that the assignment operator uses the delete[ ] operator to free the previously allocated storage to which str points. However, when a String such as s3 is initialized in its definition, s3.str does not yet point to dynamically allocated storage. Instead, s3.str contains some random value that, as luck usually has it, constitutes an illegal address. The delete[ ] operator within the assignment operator thus could cause an access violation on the spot or even more subtle mischief later on. (The prudent programmer assumes that an uninitialized pointer points to an illegal address.) A copy constructor, which is designed precisely for variable initialization, usually does not contain a delete[ ] operator because there is no previously allocated storage to delete. Accordingly, the copy constructor is the appropriate way to initialize s3.

The code slice

```
int main()
{
  // code slice 2
  String s1( "RISC versus CISC" );  // convert
  String s2;                        // default
```

```
    s2 = s1;                              // assignment
    ...
}
```

is altogether different from code slice 1. Here the default constructor is used to initialize s2. Afterwards, s1 is assigned to s2. The copy constructor is *not* involved in code slice 2. The delete[ ] operator within the assignment operator is not a problem because the default constructor does dynamically allocate a single cell and does set s2.str to this cell's address. The assignment operator deletes the cell before allocating new storage of size

```
    strlen( s1.str ) + 1
```

to store the String.   □

It bears repeating that the assignment operator is never at work in C++ when objects are initialized in their definition.

Example 4.2.2. In the code slice

```
    int main()
    {
      String s1 = String( "judy" );   // no assignment
      String s2 = ( String ) "judy";  // no assignment
      ...
    }
```

neither the copy constructor nor the assignment operator is at work. The two statements are equivalent. They are syntactic variants of

```
    String s1( "judy" );  // convert constructor
```

                                                                            □

Just as an individual object may be initialized in its definition, so may an array of objects. Initial values are enclosed in braces, just as they would be in initializing an array in C.

Example 4.2.3. The code

```
    char* Cstrs[ ] = { "black holes",
                       "white dwarfs",
                       "supernovas",
                       "neutron stars",
                       "warped spacetime" };

    String s( Cstrs[ 4 ] );          // convert

    String Sstrs[ ] = { Cstrs[ 0 ],   // convert
                        Cstrs[ 1 ],   // convert
```

```
                    String(),      // default
                    s,             // copy
                    Cstrs[ 2 ] }; // convert
```

illustrates how an array of `String` might be initialized. Array `Sstrs` has five members because the compiler allocates one `String` for every initial value. The initializations include an explicit call to the default constructor to signal that the third element, `Sstrs[ 2 ]`, should be initialized with the default constructor. If we left out the default constructor, the compiler would have allocated only four `String` cells for `Sstrs` because, in that case, only four initial values would have been provided. However, we could specify an array size and provide fewer initial values:

```
String strs[ 5 ] = { Cstrs[ 0 ],   // convert
                     Cstrs[ 1 ] }; // convert
```

Because there are only two initial values, `strs[ 2 ]`, `strs[ 3 ]`, and `strs[ 4 ]` are all initialized with the default constructor.   □

Class storage allocated with the **new** statement is always initialized with the default constructor. It is an error to try to provide initial values for such storage.

Example 4.2.4. In the code slice

```
String* strings = new String[ 100 ]; // default all 100

// ***** ERROR: can't initialize storage allocated with new
String* bad = new String[ 2 ] = { "fred", "frieda" };
```

`strings` is set to the address of the first of 100 contiguous `String` cells, each initialized with the default constructor. In the case of pointer `bad`, an error occurs because it is illegal to provide initial values for cells allocated by the **new** operator.   □

Objects Passed by Value to a Function

If an object is passed by value to a function, the compiler invokes the copy constructor to initialize the temporary storage.

Example 4.2.5. The code

```
#include <stdio.h>
#include "strings.h"

void func( String s )
{
    ...
}
```

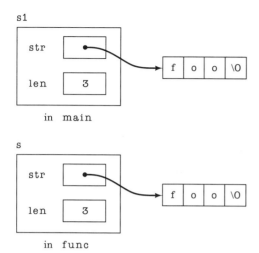

Figure 4.2.1 Role of copy constructor in call by value.

```
int main()
{
    String s1( "foo" );
    func( s1 );
    ...
}
```

passes **String** variable **s1** by value to function **func**. The copy constructor is invoked to initialize the storage cells that hold the copy of **s1** that is passed to **func** (see Figure 4.2.1).   □

Objects Returned by Value from a Function

Whenever a class object is returned by value by a function, the compiler calls the copy constructor to initialize the receiving storage. Recall the code

```
// + operator for concatenations
String String::operator+( const String& strarg ) const
{
    // allocate enough storage for 2 strings + '\0'
    char* temp = new char[ len + strarg.len + 1 ];

    // copy 1st string and concatenate second
    strcpy( temp, str );
    strcat( temp, strarg.str );

    // define String variable for return value
    String retval( temp );
```

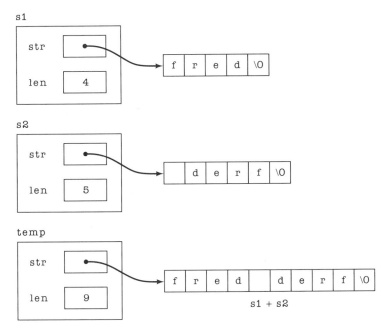

Figure 4.2.2 Result of copy construction in return by value.

```
        // free temporary storage
        delete[ ] temp;

        return retval;   // return String value
    }
```

that overloads the + operator so that it can be used for **String** concatenation. Here is a sample use:

```
    int main()
    {
      String s1( "fred " );
      String s2( " derf" );
      s1 + s2;      // value ==> fred derf
      s1.write();   // prints fred
      s2.write();   // prints derf
      ...
    }
```

The concatenation changes neither **s1** nor **s2**, as the calls **s1.write()** and **s2.write()** illustrate. The concatentation operator does return a **String** value, which is stored in a temporary **String** cell initialized with the copy constructor (see Figure 4.2.2).

In a code slice such as

```
int main()
{
  String s1( "Galileo was lucky." );
  String s2( " Bruno was not." );
  String s3;
  s3 = s1 + s2; // s3: Galileo was lucky. Bruno was not.
  ...
}
```

the contents of the temporary String cell that holds s1 + s2 are assigned
to s3. The assignment operator returns a String reference rather than a
String value, which explains why the copy constructor is *not* invoked in the
assignment operation. For example, the copy constructor is *not* invoked in
this code slice:

```
int main()
{
  String s1( "Mick Jagger is older than the Pres!" );
  String s2;
  s2 = s1;    // operator= returns String reference
  ...
}
```

Overloading the Assignment Operator for Classes

If the user does not overload the assignment operator when creating a class,
then the compiler does so. The compiler's assignment operator, which does
a member by member copy, is likely to cause problems if the class contains
a pointer as a data member.

Example 4.2.6. The code slice

```
class C {
   char* ptr;   // points to dynamically allocated storage
public:
   C();                    // default
   C( const char* );       // convert
   ~C() { delete[ ] ptr; }
   void write() { cout << ptr << endl; }
   friend void setValue( C, char* );
};

C::C()
{
   ptr = new char[ 1 ];
   *ptr = '\0';
}
```

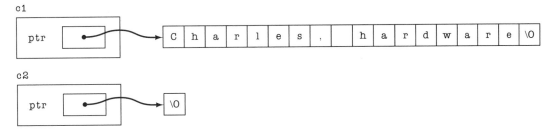

Figure 4.2.3 After initialization.

```
C::C( const char* cstr )
{
   ptr = new char[ strlen( cstr ) + 1 ];
   strcpy( ptr, cstr );
}

void setValue( C object, char* cstr )
{
   if ( strlen( object.ptr ) >= strlen( cstr ) )
      strcpy( object.ptr, cstr );
}

int main()
{
   C c1( "Charles, hardware" );  // convert
   C c2;                         // default

   c2 = c1;    // c2.ptr == c1.ptr
   setValue( c2, "Ada, software" );

   c2.write();  // Ada, software
   c1.write();  // Ada, software
   return EXIT_SUCCESS;
}
```

defines two objects c1 and c2 of type C. After initialization, c1.ptr points
to the string

Charles, hardware

and c2.ptr points to the null string (see Figure 4.2.3). The assignment
statement

c2 = c1;

sets pointer c2.ptr to the same address as pointer c1.ptr (see Figure 4.2.4).
After the call to setValue, c2.ptr points to the string

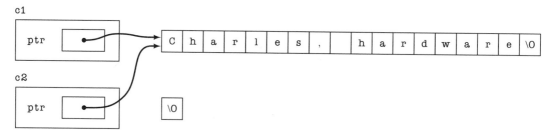

Figure 4.2.4 After the assignment statement c2 = c1;

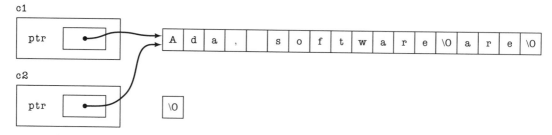

Figure 4.2.5 After the call to setValue.

Ada, software

However, c1.ptr also points to this string because it points to the *same* cell to which c2.ptr points (see Figure 4.2.5)! This is not what we want. We want c1.ptr and c2.ptr to point to different cells that hold different strings. We can achieve this goal by overloading the assignment operator:

```
C& C::operator=( const C& c )
{
   // check whether c is to be assigned to itself
   if ( this != &c ) {
      delete[ ] ptr;
      ptr = new char[ strlen( c.ptr ) + 1 ];
      strcpy( ptr, c.ptr ); // copy contents, NOT address
   }
   return *this;
}
```

With our own copy constructor in place, after

   c2 = c1;

we have the situation in Figure 4.2.6. After the call to setValue, c1.ptr and c2.ptr point to different cells that hold different strings (see Figure 4.2.7).   □

c1

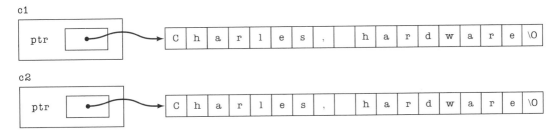

c2

Figure 4.2.6   After the assignment statement with the assignment operator overloaded.

c1

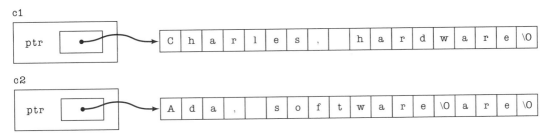

c2

Figure 4.2.7   After the call to `setValue`.

Overloading the Equality and Inequality Operators for Classes

It makes sense to overload the equality (==) and inequality (!=) operators whenever it makes sense to overload the assignment operator. The equality and inequality operators are overloaded so they test for equality as defined by the assignment operator.

Example 4.2.7.   For the class of Example 4.2.6 with the assignment operator overloaded, we could overload the equality and inequality operators as

```
int C::operator==( const C& c )
{
   return strcmp( ptr, c.ptr ) == 0;
}

int C::operator!=( const C& c )
{
   return strcmp( ptr, c.ptr ) != 0;
}
```

Now for the situation in either Figure 4.2.4 or Figure 4.2.6, the expression

```
c1 == c2
```

evaluates to 1 (true).   □

A Sample Program Run

We conclude this section with a program slice that defines **Strings**, passes them by value and by reference to functions, returns them by value and by reference, assigns them to other **Strings**, and so on. We add print statements to the constructors, destructor, and **String** assignment operator to trace the program's run. We also have print statements at function entry and exit points. The sample run's output illustrates how the constructors, destructor, and assignment operator behave for **Strings**.

```
// ************ code
int main()
{
   cout << "\n\tInto main()..." << endl;

   void f( String );
   String s1;
   String strings[ ] =
      { "moe", "curly", "larry" };
   String s2( strings[ 0 ] );
   String s3;
   s3 = ( String ) "natasha";
   f( s3 );

   cout << "\n\tOut of main()..." << endl;

   return EXIT_SUCCESS;
}

void f( String s )
{
   cout << "\n\tInto f( String )..." << endl;

   void g( String );
   String local;
   g( s );
   g( local );

   cout << "\n\tOut of f( String )..." << endl;
}

void g( String s )
{
   cout << "\n\tInto g( String )..." << endl;
```

```
            String h( String );
            String local;
            local = h( s );

            cout << "\n\tOut of g( String )..." << endl;
        }

        String h( String s )
        {
            cout << "\n\tInto h( String )..." << endl;

            String k( String& );
            String local;
            local = k( s );

            cout << "\n\tOut of h( String )..." << endl;

            return s;
        }

        String& k( String s )
        {
            cout << "\n\tInto k( String )..." << endl;
            cout << "\n\tOut of k( String )..." << endl;

            return s;
        }

        // ************ sample run
        Into main()...
        Default -- String::String() ***
        Convert -- String::String( const char* ) *** moe
        Convert -- String::String( const char* ) *** curly
        Convert -- String::String( const char* ) *** larry
        Copy -- String::String( const String& ) *** moe
        Default -- String::String() ***
        Convert -- String::String( int ) ***
        Convert -- String::String( const char* ) *** natasha
        Assignment -- String::operator=( const String& ) *** natasha
        Destructor -- String::~String() *** natasha
        Copy -- String::String( const String& ) *** natasha

        Into f( String )...
        Default -- String::String() ***
```

```
Copy -- String::String( const String& ) *** natasha

Into g( String )...
Default -- String::String() ***
Copy -- String::String( const String& ) *** natasha

Into h( String )...
Default -- String::String() ***

Into k( String& )...

Out of k( String& )...
Assignment -- String::operator=( const String& ) *** natasha

Out of h( String )...
Copy -- String::String( const String& str ) *** natasha
Destructor -- String::~String() *** natasha
Destructor -- String::~String() *** natasha
Assignment -- String::operator=( const String& ) *** natasha
Destructor -- String::~String() *** natasha

Out of g( String )...
Destructor -- String::~String() *** natasha
Destructor -- String::~String() *** natasha
Copy -- String::String( const String& ) ***

Into g( String )...
Default -- String::String() ***
Copy -- String::String( const String& ) ***

Into h( String )...
Default -- String::String() ***

Into k( String& )...

Out of k( String& )...
Assignment -- String::operator=( const String& ) ***

Out of h( String )...
Copy -- String::String( const String& ) ***
Destructor -- String::~String() ***
Destructor -- String::~String() ***
Assignment -- String::operator=( const String& ) ***
Destructor -- String::~String() ***
```

```
Out of g( String )...
Destructor -- String::~String() ***
Destructor -- String::~String() ***

Out of f( String )...
Destructor -- String::~String() ***
Destructor -- String::~String() *** natasha

Out of main()...
Destructor -- String::~String() ***
Destructor -- String::~String() *** natasha
Destructor -- String::~String() *** moe
Destructor -- String::~String() *** larry
Destructor -- String::~String() *** curly
Destructor -- String::~String() *** moe
Destructor -- String::~String() ***
```

Exercises

These exercises refer to the **String** class of Section 4.1.

1. Next to each expression, indicate which constructor or operator is used.

```
int main()
{
  String s1;
  String s2 = s1;
  String s3;
  s3 = s1;
  String s4( "glory days by bs" );
  String s5;
  s5 = s4;
  String s6 = s5;
  String s7 = String( "judy blue eyes" );
  ...
}
```

2. Define an array of **Strings** and initialize every other element to "widget." Elements not initialized to "widget" should be initialized by the default constructor.

3. Explain the error:

```
String* strptr = new String[ 10 ] = { "a", "b" };
```

4. Which constructor is at work in this code slice?

```
String* s = new String;
```

5. If the programmer does not write his or her own copy constructor, is the compiler's copy constructor still at work during call by value?

6. Illustrate with pictures how the copy constructor works during a call by value with a `String` object.

7. Why should you not rely on the compiler to overload the assignment operator for class `String`?

8. Illustrate with pictures how the copy constructor works during return by value with a `String` object.

9. Why does `String::operator=` check whether a `String` object is being assigned to itself? What problem would arise if this check were absent?

10. Illustrate with pictures a problem that could arise if we did not provide `String::operator=` for class `String`.

11. Can you imagine a situation in which it would be a good idea to write your own copy constructor but not your own assignment operator?

12. Is the copy constructor at work in return by reference? Explain.

13. Is the copy constructor at work in call by reference? Explain.

14. Explain why the `==` operator should be overloaded for class `String`.

15. Explain why the `!=` operator should be overloaded for class `String`.

4.3   Friend Classes

A class's `private` members, typically its data members, are accessible only to its methods and whatever other functions are designated as `friends`. A `friend` function may be either a toplevel function (i.e., a function that is not a method) or a method in some other class.

Example 4.3.1. Class C

```
class F {
  int adm; // data member
public:
  int f();
};
```

```
class C {
  int cdm; // data member
public:
  int m();              // method
  friend int t();       // toplevel friend
  friend int F::f();    // method friend
};
```

has two **friend** functions, t and F::f. As the scope resolution operator makes clear, F::f is a method in class F. By contrast, t is a toplevel function. The two **friend** functions have the same access to C's **private** members, however. Either **friend** can access C::cdm.   □

Making a method in class F a **friend** of class C is a piecemeal approach to granting F access to C. Suppose, however, that F has 20 or so methods, each of which is to be a **friend** to C. We could take the piecemeal approach and make each of F's methods a **friend**. A wholesale approach is to make F a **friend** class.

Example 4.3.2. The code

```
class F {
  int adm; // data member
public:
  int f();
  ...             // other methods
};

class C {
  friend F;    // class F a friend
  int cdm;     // data member
public:
  int m();              // method
  friend int t();       // toplevel friend
};
```

makes F a **friend** class of C. As a result, any method in F has full access to all members of C, even **private** ones. For instance, F::f can access **private** data member C::cdm.   □

The **friend** relationship between F and C is not symmetric. Class F is a **friend** to C, which means that all F's methods have access to all C's members. By contrast, class C is *not* a **friend** to F, which means that C's methods have no access to F's **private** members. Of course, F's **public** members (in this case, its methods) are accessible to C's methods as they

are to any other functions. Two classes can befriend each other so that the
relationship is symmetrical.

Example 4.3.3. The code

```
class C; // forward declaration

class F {
  friend C; // C a friend to F
  int adm;  // data member
public:
  ...              // other methods
};

class C {
  friend F;    // F a friend to C
  int cdm;     // data member
public:
  ...
};
```

makes F a `friend` to C, and C a `friend` to F. Note that class C is declared in
abbreviated form above F's declaration so that its name is visible in F when
C is designated a `friend`.   □

    The `friend` relationship among classes is not transitive. If class P is a
`friend` of class Q, which in turn is a `friend` of class R, it does not thereby
follow that P is a `friend` of R. If we want P to be a `friend` of R, then we
must explicitly declare P to be so.

    A `friend` class, like a `friend` function, is a C++ convenience that strains
the spirit of object-oriented programming because it compromises the principle that a class's `private` members should be hidden except within the
class. Nonetheless, as we shall see in Section 4.4, there are situations in
which a `friend` class, like a `friend` function, makes programming easier.

Exercises

1. Write class declarations for C1, C2, and C3 so that C1 is a `friend` to C2,
   which in turn is `friend` to C3.

2. If C1 is a `friend` of C2, which in turn is a `friend` of C3, is C1 automatically
   a `friend` of C3 as well?

3. If class C is a `friend` of class D, is there any difference in the access rights
   of C's methods and D's methods with respect to D's `private` members?

4. Give an example in which it makes more sense to have C and D be mutual `friends` instead of combining them into a single class.

5. Is the `friend` relationship symmetric? Explain.

6. Does it make sense for a class to be a `friend` to itself? Explain.

4.4   Sample Application: A Binary Search Tree Class

Problem

Implement a **binary search tree** as a class. A binary search tree is a binary tree in which each node contains data. The data are arranged so that, for any node N in binary search tree T, any data item in N's left subtree is less than or equal to the data item in N; and any data item in N's right subtree is greater than the data item in N.

Solution

We use two classes, Node and BST, with BST a `friend` to Node. The class BST consists of Nodes ordered as described previously. We practice information hiding by having only **private** data members in BST and Node. Making BST a `friend` to Node eases the programming but does compromise information hiding. We practice encapsulation by including methods in both classes.

C++ Implementation

```
#include <iostream.h>

const char None = ' ';

class BST; // forward declaration

class Node {
  friend BST;  // friend class
  char val;    // value == contents
  Node* lc;    // left child
  Node* rc;    // right child
public:
  Node();      // default constructor
  int empty(); // val == None
  void write();
};
```

```
class BST {
  Node* root;
  Node* tree;
  void addNodeAux( const char );
  void inorderAux( Node* );
public:
  BST();
  void addNode( const char );
  void inorder();
};

Node::Node()
{
  lc = rc = 0;
  val = None;
}

int Node::empty()
{
  return val == None;
}

void Node::write()
{
  cout << val;
}

BST::BST()
{
  root = tree = new Node;
}

void BST::addNode( const char v )
{
  tree = root;      // start at root
  addNodeAux( v );
}

void BST::addNodeAux( const char v )
{
  // if root of current subtree is
  // empty,
  //   -- store v there
  //   -- create a left and right subtree
```

```
      //    -- return
      if ( tree -> empty() ) {
        tree -> val = v;
        tree -> lc = new Node;
        tree -> rc = new Node;
        return;
      }

      // otherwise, search either left or right
      // subtree for Node to store v
      if ( v <= tree -> val )
        tree = tree -> lc;
      else
        tree = tree -> rc;

      addNodeAux( v );
    }

    void BST::inorder()
    {
      inorderAux( root );
    }

    void BST::inorderAux( Node* n )
    {
      // if current subtree is empty,
      // return as there are no nodes
      // to traverse in it
      if ( n -> empty() )
        return;

      inorderAux( n -> lc );   // traverse left subtree
      n -> write();            // visit Node
      inorderAux( n -> rc );   // traverse right subtree
    }
```

Discussion

Classes Node and BST are interdependent: Node has BST as a **friend**, whereas BST has two data members of type Node*. To make BST visible to Node's declaration, we place the forward declaration

```
    class BST; // forward declaration
```

above Node's declaration, which in turn occurs above the declaration for BST. We make BST a **friend** of Node so that BST methods such as addNodeAux and `inorderAux` can access `Node`'s `private` data members `lc` and `rc`. As we add other BST methods, they too will have access to `private` data members in `Node` objects. Making individual BST methods into `friends` of `Node` would be less convenient, especially as we add to these methods.

The default BST constructor

```
BST::BST()
{
  root = tree = new Node;
}
```

dynamically allocates a `Node` object and has `root` and `tree` point to it. The default constructor for `Node`

```
Node::Node()
{
  lc = rc = 0;
  val = None;
}
```

sets pointers `lc` and `rc` to null address 0 before setting `val` to value `None`, which is used to identify an "empty" `Node`. Pointer `root` always points to the root of the entire binary search tree, whereas `tree` points to the current subtree. Initially, the entire tree is the current subtree. This approach lets us write BST methods `addNode` and `addNodeAux` with only one argument, the `val` to be stored in a `Node`:

```
void BST::addNode( const char v )
{
  tree = root;     // start at root
  addNodeAux( v );
}

void BST::addNodeAux( const char v )
{
  // if root of current subtree is
  // empty,
  //   -- store v there
  //   -- create a left and right subtree
  //   -- return
  if ( tree -> empty() ) {
    tree -> val = v;
    tree -> lc = new Node;
    tree -> rc = new Node;
    return;
  }
}
```

```
  // otherwise, search either left or right
  // subtree for Node to store v
  if ( v <= tree -> val )
    tree = tree -> lc;
  else
    tree = tree -> rc;

  addNodeAux( v );
}
```

The BST method `addNode` sets `tree` to `root` to ensure that the search always starts at the root of the entire tree. Method `addNodeAux` does the work. If the current `Node` (i.e., the `root` of the current subtree) is empty, then `addNodeAux` stores the value there and creates a left and a right child before returning. Otherwise, the method sets `tree` to the current `Node`'s left or right subtree before invoking itself. Note that `addNodeAux` is `private` in BST but that `addNode` is `public`. There is a similar relationship between `inorderAux`, which is `private`, and `inorder`, which is `public`. The two `public` methods are the BST's public interface, whereas the `private` methods represent a functional decomposition of the `public` methods. A user adds a `Node` to a BST by invoking the `public` method only, which then turns the task over to a `private` method.

Once a BST has been built, method `inorder` is invoked to perform an inorder traversal of the tree. The method traverses `Node`'s left subtree, prints `Node`'s `val`, and then traverses `Node`'s right subtree. The recursive method starts at the tree's `root` so that the traversal visits every `Node`.

The BST methods `addNodeAux` and `inorderAux` illustrate two styles of recursion. Before each recursive call, `addNodeAux` sets `tree` to its left subtree (`lc`) or its right subtree (`rc`), thereby determining the direction of the search for an empty `Node`. The only argument passed is `v`, the data item to be stored in the appropriate empty `Node`. By contrast, `inorderAux` changes its parameter to either the left or the right subtree of the current `Node`. Each recursive method is `private` so that the user can remain oblivious to this dreaded programming technique while benefiting from its power.

Finally, here is a code slice that illustrates the BST methods:

```
int main()
{
  BST bst;                // create binary search tree
  bst.addNode( 'K' ); // add K node
  bst.addNode( 'G' ); // etc.
  bst.addNode( 'F' );
  bst.addNode( 'I' );
  bst.addNode( 'H' );
  bst.addNode( 'R' );
```

```
bst.addNode( 'P' );
bst.addNode( 'X' );
bst.addNode( 'S' );
bst.addNode( 'A' );
bst.inorder();          // prints: AFGHIKPRSX

return EXIT_SUCCESS;
}
```

Exercises

1. If we restrict BST::val to letters, will the inorder traversal print them in alphabetical order no matter what the order in which they are addNoded?

2. Write a BST method to perform a preorder traversal.

3. Write a BST method to perform a postorder traversal.

4. Rewrite BST using root as the only data member of type Node*.

5. In general, when should a method be made private rather than public?

6. Write BST::~BST() so that it systematically deletes all Nodes in the binary tree. *Hint*: The destructor should delete the left and right subtrees before deleting the root.

7. Explain why

   ```
   class BST {
     const Node* root;  // changed from Node* root
     ...
   };
   ```

   will not work in the current implementation of BST.

8. Do a hand trace of

   ```
   bst.addNode( 'T' );
   ```

   Assume the statement occurs at the end of the code slice immediately preceding these exercises.

9. Explain why BST needs to be a friend to Node.

10. Explain why Node does not need to be a friend to BST.

11. Write a code slice that creates a BST object.

12. Write a copy constructor for a BST.

4.5 Sample Application: An Iterator Class

Problem ────────────────────────────────

An **iterator class** or **cursor class** is a class whose objects can scan an aggregate one element at a time and, in this sense, *iterate* through the aggregate. The problem here is to implement an iterator class for the BST class of Section 4.4. An object in this iterator class iterates through the nodes of a binary search tree. The iteration is to be nondestructive; that is, the iteration must not alter the binary search tree.

Solution ────────────────────────────────

We implement an iterator class IterBST as a **friend** to class BST and class Node from Section 4.4. The class IterBST treats a BST as a list of Nodes through which it steps one Node at a time. We practice information hiding by making all data members **private**, although the use of **friend** classes BST and IterBST does compromise information hiding in the case of Node. We practice encapsulation by including methods in all three classes.

C++ Implementation ────────────────────────────

```
#include <iostream.h>

const char None = ' ';

class BST;
class IterBST;

class Node {
   friend BST;       // friend class
   friend IterBST;   // friend class
   char  val;        // value == contents
   Node* lc;         // left child
   Node* rc;         // right child
public:
   Node();                // constructor
   int empty();   // val == None
   void write();
};

class IterBST {
   Node** nodeStack;   // list of Nodes in BST
   int nextNode;       // index into list
   int nodeCount;      // total Nodes in BST
```

```
      void stackNodes( BST* );
      void stackNodesAux( Node* );
   public:
      IterBST( BST* );
      ~IterBST() { delete[ ] nodeStack; }
      Node* getNextNode();
   };

   class BST {
      friend IterBST;
      int count;
      Node* root;
      Node* tree;
      void addNodeAux( const char );
      void inorderAux( Node* );
   public:
      BST();
      void addNode( const char );
      void inorder();
   };

   IterBST::IterBST( BST* bst )
   {
      nodeCount = bst -> count;
      nodeStack = new Node*[ nodeCount ];
      nextNode = 0;
      stackNodes( bst );
      nextNode = 0;
   }

   void IterBST::stackNodes( BST* bst )
   {
      stackNodesAux( bst -> root );
   }

   // inorder traversal
   void IterBST::stackNodesAux( Node* n )
   {
      if ( n -> empty() )
        return;
      stackNodesAux( n -> lc );
      nodeStack[ nextNode++ ] = n;
      stackNodesAux( n -> rc );
   }
```

```
Node* IterBST::getNextNode()
{
   Node* retval = nodeStack[ nextNode ];
   nextNode = ( nextNode + 1 ) % nodeCount;
   return retval;
}

Node::Node()
{
   lc = rc = 0;
   val = None;
}

int Node::empty()
{
   return val == None;
}

void Node::write()
{
   cout << val;
}

BST::BST()
{
   root = tree = new Node;
   count = 0;   // no nodes yet
}

void BST::addNode( const char v )
{
   tree = root;       // start at root
   addNodeAux( v );
}

void BST::addNodeAux( const char v )
{
   if ( tree -> empty() ) {
      tree -> val = v;
      count++;  // increment count
      tree -> lc = new Node;
      tree -> rc = new Node;
      return;
   }
```

```
      if ( v <= tree -> val )
         tree = tree -> lc;
      else
         tree = tree -> rc;
      addNodeAux( v );
   }

   void BST::inorder()
   {
      tree = root;
      inorderAux( root );
   }

   void BST::inorderAux( Node* n )
   {
      if ( n -> empty() )
         return;
      inorderAux( n -> lc );
      n -> write();
      inorderAux( n -> rc );
   }
```

Discussion

An IterBST has a convert constructor that expects a single argument, a BST. The code slice

```
   Node* n;
   BST bst;                  // create a BST
   bst.addNode( 'K' );   // add a Node...
   bst.addNode( 'G' );   // and another...
   bst.addNode( 'F' );   // and another
   IterBST iter( bst );     // create inorder iterator
   n = iter.getNextNode(); // get 1st Node -- F
   n -> write();            //    write it
   n = iter.getNextNode(); // get 2nd Node -- G
   n -> write();            //    write it
   n = iter.getNextNode(); // get 3rd Node -- K
   n -> write();            //    write it
```

illustrates how an IterBST might be created and used to iterate through the Nodes in a BST. This particular IterBST steps through the Nodes *in-order*, although it could be modified to step through them *preorder* or *pos-torder* as well (see Exercises 1 and 2). Accordingly, F is the first Node that getNextNode returns.

The iterator's constructor

```
IterBST::IterBST( BST* bst )
{
    nodeCount = bst -> count;
    nodeStack = new Node*[ nodeCount ];
    nextNode = 0;
    stackNodes( bst );
    nextNode = 0;
}
```

takes advantage of a change made to the BST class; namely, a BST keeps a count of how many Nodes it has. Because IterBST is a **friend** class of BST, IterBST can use this count to allocate a nodeStack that stores a pointer to each Node in the BST. The IterBST data member nextNode, an index into nodeStack, is initialized to zero so that it references the first Node in the iterator list. Each time the iterator accesses a Node, nextNode is updated so that the subsequent call to getNextNode returns the next Node in the iterator list:

```
Node* IterBST::getNextNode()
{
    Node* retval = nodeStack[ nextNode ];
    nextNode = ( nextNode + 1 ) % nodeCount;
    return retval;
}
```

The modulus operator % is used so that the iterator steps from the last Node in the iterator list back to the first.

An IterBST must be a **friend** to a BST in order to access BST data members such as root and count. An IterBST also must be a **friend** to a Node. To build the iterator list, an IterBST traverses a BST. The traversal requires access to Node data members lc and rc, which point to a Node's left and right subtrees, respectively.

Exercises

---

1. Change IterBST so that the iterator list reflects a preorder traversal.

2. Change IterBST so that the iterator list reflects a postorder traversal.

3. Explain why IterBST is a **friend** to BST and Node.

4. Consider the code slice:

```
int main()
{
  Node* n;
  BST bst;              // create a BST
  bst.addNode( 'K' );   // add a Node...
  bst.addNode( 'G' );   // and another...
  bst.addNode( 'F' );   // and another
  ...
  IterBST iter( bst ); // create an iterator
  bst.addNode( 'Z' );   // add another node
  ...
}
```

Our `IterBST` would not see a `Node` such as Z that is added to the BST *after* the BST is created and initialized. Change `IterBST` so that it would see `Nodes` added to the BST after the `IterBST` is created. *Hint*: Data member `BST::count` counts every `Node` added to a BST.

5. Explain why `IterBST` does not need `friends`.

6. Overload the assignment operator for `IterBST`.

7. Rewrite `IterBST::getNextNode` so that it returns 0 if there are no more `Nodes`. This change would allow code such as

```
while ( n = iter.getNextNode() )  // loop until 0
  n -> write();
```

4.6   Static Data Members and Methods

A class may have `static` data members and methods. We look first at `static` data members and then at `static` methods.

Static Data Members

A `static` data member belongs to a *class* as a whole, not to any particular object within the class. Storage for a `static` data member is allocated once—in its definition—and this storage is shared by all of the class's objects. A nonstatic data member, by contrast, belongs to a particular *object* in the class. A `static` data member is declared with the keyword `static` inside the class declaration and is then defined *without* the keyword `static` outside all blocks. In particular, a `static` data member must be defined *outside* the class declaration. In its definition, a `static` data member is referenced with the scope resolution operator as `C::sdm`, where `sdm` is a `static` data member in class `C`. A `public static` data member `sdm` in class `C` can be referenced outside the class as `C::sdm` or `obj::sdm` if `obj` is an object in class C. Except for its definition, a **private** **static** data member cannot be accessed outside the class.

Example 4.6.1. The declaration for class C

```
class C {
  static int sdm;  // static data member
  ...
};
```

includes a declaration for **static** data member **sdm**. The declaration does not allocate storage. Accordingly, C::sdm must be defined elsewhere as, for example:

```
int C::sdm = -999;  // define static C::sdm and initialize
                    // keyword static NOT used!
int main()
{
  ...
}
```

Note that C::sdm's definition includes the scope resolution operator. If the scope resolution operator were omitted

```
int sdm = -999;  // define an extern variable named sdm
                 // that is NOT the same as C::sdm
```

then we would be defining an **extern** variable named **sdm** (i.e., ::sdm) rather than C::sdm.

A **static** data member must be defined outside all blocks. It would be an error, for example, to try to define C::sdm inside **main**:

```
int main()
{
  // ***** ERROR: static data member can't be
  // defined inside a block
  int C::sdm = -999;
  ...
}
```

                                                                              □

Because a **static** data member belongs to the class as a whole, not to any particular object within the class, no constructor is invoked to initialize a **static** data member, and the destructor never destroys a **static** data member. After all, constructors and destructors deal with particular class objects. We can approach the same point from a different angle. Each object in a class has its own copies of the class's data members, which have an **auto** storage class by default; an object's data members come into existence and go out of existence as the object does.

Example 4.6.2. Data members for object **s**

```
// f's body is the containing block for
// String s's definition so that s is
// visible only within f
void f()
{
    String s;   // define String object s with
                // data members string and length
    ...
}               // s goes out of existence when f exits
```

come into existence when **s** is defined in **f**. Data members **s.str** and **s.len** likewise go out of existence when **s** does: when control leaves **f**. Because the scope of object **s** is the body of **f**, the scope of **s**'s data members is also the body of **f**.   □

A class's **static** data members do not depend upon particular class objects. Indeed, a **static** data member can be defined before any object belonging to the class is defined.

Example 4.6.3. In the code slice

```
class C {
    char* name;
    int id;
    static int sdm;
    ...
}

int C::sdm;   // C::sdm is defined
              // no object in C exists yet
int main()
{
    void f();
    f();
    ...
}

void f()
{
    C s;        // 1st C object exits
    C r;        // 2nd C object exists
    ...
}
```

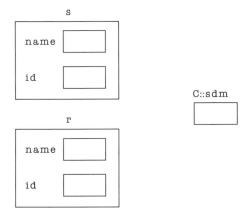

Figure 4.6.1 static data member shared by two class objects.

the static data member C::sdm is defined before the first class object s is defined. Objects s and r have their own copies of data members name and id, but the two share the static data member sdm (see Figure 4.6.1). If a static data member is defined without an initial value, then the compiler initializes it to zero. So, for example, given this definition of C::sdm

```
int C::sdm;    // initialized by compiler to 0
```

the compiler initializes C::sdm to zero. □

A static data member is useful when we need to track information about the class as a whole. It is appropriate that such information should not be stored in any particular class object. It is also appropriate that such information should be associated with the class and not stored in, say, an independent global variable.

Example 4.6.4. We amend the declaration for class String to include a static data member:

```
class String {
    char* str;   // data member -- private
    int len;     // actual
    static int count; // static data member
public:
    ...
    friend void print_count(); // access count
};

void print_count()
{
    cout << "Total strings ==> " << String::count << endl;
}
```

Data member `count` is `static` and tracks the total number of `String` objects created in the program. Function `print_count` is a `friend` that can access this data member in order to print its value. We make `count` a `static` data member rather than, say, an `extern` variable in order to associate `count` with class `String`. For `count` to reflect the current number of `String` objects, the `String` constructors should be amended to include the statement

```
count++;
```

and the `String` destructor should be amended to include the statement

```
count--;
```

□

If a `static` data member is `private`, then it is visible only to function members and `friend` functions. If a `static` data member is `public`, then it may be accessed using its full class name.

Example 4.6.5. Data member `sdm` is a `static` yet `public` data member in class C

```
class C {
public:
    static int sdm;  // declare
    ...
}


C::sdm = -999;  // define
```

and so can be accessed anywhere in the program using its full name as, for example, in this code slice:

```
void f()
{
    while ( C::sdm < 0 ) {  // C::sdm is public
      ...
    }
    ...
}
```

Of course, class C must be visible to `f`.   □

Static Methods

Although a class's methods (including the constructors and the destructor) and `friend` functions have access to `static` data members, these members may be accessed in another and more restrictive way: through `static` methods. A `static` method, like a `static` data member, belongs to the class as a whole and not to any particular object in the class. A `static` method may access *only* static data members. An attempt to access nonstatic data members is illegal and, indeed, impossible because a static method does not have a this pointer to any particular class object.

Example 4.6.6. In the code slice

```
class C {
    int id;          // nonstatic data member
    static int count; // static data member
public:
    static void count_up();
};

int C::count = 0;    // define static data member

void C::count_up() // define static method
{
    count++;    // legal -- count static
    id = 999;   // ***** ERROR: id nonstatic
}
```

C has two data members, the nonstatic member id and the static member count. The static method C::count_up is declared inside C's class declaration and then defined, like C::count, outside C's declaration. However, C::count_up could have been defined inside C's declaration. The error in this example occurs because C::count_up, as a static method, can access only static data members and id is not static.   □

A class's constructors and destructor cannot be static. If they could be, they would be unable to initialize and clean up storage for nonstatic data members and, in this sense, would be worthless. A static method is highly specialized in that its sole task is to manipulate whatever static data members a class may have.

Example 4.6.7. We amend the String class so that it has a static method to increment the static data member count:

```
class String {
    char* str;        // data member -- private
    int len;          // actual
    static int count; // count declared here
public:
    ...
    // static functions
    static void count_up() { count++ };
    ...
};
```

```
void print_count()
{
   cout << "Total strings ==> " << String::count << endl;
}
```

The constructor such as `String::( char* )` is then changed from

```
// char* constructor
String::String( const char* cstr )
{
   // +1 to ensure room for null terminator
   str = new char[ strlen( cstr ) + 1 ];
   strcpy( str, cstr );
   len = strlen( str );
   count++;    // another String created
}
```

to

```
// char* constructor
String::String( const char* cstr )
{
   // +1 to ensure room for null terminator
   str = new char[ strlen( cstr ) + 1 ];
   strcpy( str, cstr );
   len = strlen( str );
   count_up();  // increment static data member count
}
```

□

As Example 4.6.7 illustrates, nonstatic methods such as constructors and destructors may manipulate static data members. The constructor in Example 4.6.7 increments the static data member count.

Exercises

1. Can a static data member be defined as well as declared within a class declaration?

2. Can a static method be defined as well as declared within a class declaration?

3. Explain the error.

```
class X {
   int x;
   static int sX;
   ...
};

int main()
{
  X::sX = -999;
  ...
}
```

4. Explain the error.

```
class X {
   int x;
   static int sX;
   ...
};
sX = -999; // definition of X::sX
```

5. Explain the error.

```
class X {
   int x;
   static int sX;
   ...
};
static int X::sX = -999;
```

6. Must a **static** data member be **private**?

7. Is this code legal?

```
class Z {
   int z;
public:
   static int sZ;
};
int Z::sZ = 10;

int main()
{
   if ( Z::sZ < 10 )
      ...
}
```

8. Explain the error.

```
class C {
   int c;
   static int sC;
public:
   static void fC() { count << c; }
   ...
};
```

9. Explain the difference in access rights between a **static** method and a **friend** function.

10. Can a constructor be **static**? Explain.

11. Can a destructor be **static**? Explain.

12. Explain the error.

```
class C {
   int c;
   static int sC;
public:
   static void fC()
      { cout << this -> sC; }
   ...
};
```

13. Explain the advantage of using a **static** data member instead of a global variable.

Common Programming Errors

---

1. Although the programmer is never obligated to write a copy constructor or to overload the assignment operator, it is usually a mistake not to do so for a class that contains a pointer as a data member. It also is a good idea to overload == and != for any class with a pointer as a data member.

2. It is an error to have a parameter named **this**, which is a C++ keyword.

3. It is an error to use **this** as the target of an assignment expression such as

```
this = ...;    // ***** ERROR: this is const
```

because **this** is a constant.

4. It is an error for class C to have a constructor that expects an argument of type C. However, a constructor may take a C *reference* as an argument:

```
class C {
   ...
};

C::C( C c )    // ***** ERROR
{
   ...
}

C::C( C& c )   // ok
{
   ...
}
```

5. It is an error to provide more initializing values than there are cells in an array:

```
// ***** ERROR: 2 cells, 3 initializing values
String strings[ 2 ] = { "good", "bad", "ugly" };
```

However, it is legal to provide fewer initializing values than there are cells in an array:

```
// ok
String strings[ 12 ] =
     { "good", "bad", "ugly" }; // only 3 values
```

6. It is an error to provide initializing values for an object created with the **new** operator:

```
String* strings = new String[ 3 ] =
     { "good", "bad", "ugly" }; // ***** ERROR
```

The default constructor, if present, is invoked automatically to initialize the array elements.

7. It is an error to attempt to *define* a **static** data member within a class declaration, although a **static** data member must be *declared* within the class declaration. Note the difference:

```
class C {
    static int sdm = 6; // ***** ERROR
    ...
};
```

```
class D {
   static int sdm; // ok -- declaration
   ...
};

// ok -- definition with initialization
D::sdm = 6;
```

8. It is an error to define a static data member inside a block:

```
class D {
   static int sdm; // ok -- declaration
   ...
};

void f()
{
  // ***** ERROR: definition in a block!
  D::sdm = 6;
  ...
}
```

9. It is an error to *define* a static data member with the keyword static. However, the data member must be *declared* with the keyword static:

```
class D {
   static int sdm; // ok -- declaration
   ...
};

// ***** ERROR: no keyword static
static D::sdm = 6;
```

10. It is illegal to attempt to reference a public static data member without the scope resolution operator:

```
class C {
   ...
public:
   static int sdm; // declaration
   ...
};

C::sdm = 6;  // definition + initialization
```

```
void f()
{
  if ( sdm > 0 ) // ***** ERROR: name is C::sdm
    ...
}
```

11. It is an error to make a constructor or destructor `static`.

12. It is an error to use the keyword `this` within a `static` method.

13. It is an error for a `static` method to reference a data member that is not `static`.

Programming Exercises

4.1. Applications in fields such as cryptography and number theory require integers that are too big or too small to be stored as `ints` or `longs`. Create a `BigInt` class that can handle signed integers that exceed the storage limitations of C++ built-in integer types. Provide methods that support the standard integer operations of +, -, *, /, and % together with relational operations such as >, ==, and the like. (Recall that operators may be overloaded as methods.) `BigInt` should be implemented as an abstract data type so that the user needs to know only the class's public interface and not its internal representation.

4.2. Implement a `BankTransaction` class that allows the user to

- Open an account.
- Close an account.
- Add funds to an already open account.
- Remove funds from an already open account.
- Transfer funds from one open account to another.
- Request a report on one or more open accounts.

There should be no upper bound on the number of accounts that a user may open. The class also should contain a method that automatically issues a warning if an account is overdrawn.

4.3. Introduce appropriate classes to simulate the behavior of a **local area network**, hereafter **LAN**. The network consists of **nodes**, which may be devices such as personal computers, workstations, FAX machines, telecommunications switches, and so forth. A LAN's principal job is to support data communications among its nodes. The user of the simulation should, at a minimum, be able to

- Enumerate the nodes currently on the LAN.

- Add a new node to the LAN.

- Remove a node from the LAN.

- Configure a LAN by giving it, for example, a **star** or a **bus** topology.

- Specify packet size, which is the size in bytes of message that goes from one node to another.

- Send a packet from one specified node to another.

- Broadcast a packet from one node to all others.

- Track LAN statistics such as the average time it takes a packet to reach the most distant node on the LAN.

4.4. Implement a memory-resident `HashTable` class, where a **hash table** is a structure that supports **constant-time** access to any of its entries. An entry may be any object whatever: an integer, a string, an array, a list, or even another `HashTable`. The access is constant-time in that it takes the same time to access any item in the table. By contrast, a linked-list supports only **sequential-time** access because, for example, it takes longer to access the last entry than it does to access the first entry. The `HashTable` should make use of a **hash function** that maps an object into the `HashTable`. To handle the case in which two or more objects hash to the same slot in the `HashTable`, the class must provide a **conflict-resolution policy**. The public interface supports operations such as

- Creating a hash table.

- Destroying a hash table.

- Adding an object to a hash table.

- Removing an object from a hash table.

- Accessing an object from a hash table but without removing it.

- Copying a hash table.

4.5. Implement a **list** as an abstract data type `List`, where a list is an ordered collection of none or more elements. In a traditional programming language such as C, a list typically is implemented either as an array or as a linked-list, with shortcomings in either implementation: an array's size must be fixed at definition time, and a linked-list usually requires that the user manipulate pointers. By contrast, the user of a `List` should need to know only the public interface, which supports the following operations:

- Create a list of none or more elements.

- Destroy a list.

- Insert an item into a specified spot in the list.

- Remove one or more items from a list.

- Concatentate two or more lists to create a new list.

- Divide a list into two or more sublists.

- Copy a list.

4.6. Implement a `ListIterator` class that iterates through `List` elements (see Programming Exercise 4.5). The `ListIterator` should be nondestructive; that is, it should not change any `List` element in the course of its iteration.

4.7. Implement a `Schedule` class that produces an optimal conflict-free subset of activities given an input set of activities together with the start and finish time for each activity. The conflict-free subset, together with the start and finish times, is a schedule. The schedule is conflict-free because, given any two distinct activities, one finishes before the other starts. For example, given the input set

Activity	Start	Finish
A1	6	10
A2	1	5
A3	1	6
A4	9	12
A5	5	7
A6	6	14
A7	3	7
A8	10	14
A9	13	16

the `Schedule` would be

Activity	Start	Finish
A2	1	5
A5	5	7
A4	9	12
A9	13	16

Given the input set, it is impossible to produce a `Schedule` of five or more nonconflicting activities. The public interface should include methods for creating, destroying, revising, and combining `Schedules`. There also should be a method that explains exactly why the produced `Schedule` cannot be expanded to include any more of the input activities. *Hint*: Iterate through the activities, picking in each iteration the activity with the minimal finish time that does not conflict with any previously selected activity for the `Schedule`.

4.8. Implement a `SpreadSheet` class. A `SpreadSheet` consists of **cells** that can be accessed through row-column indexes. For example, `cell(11,44)` is at row 11 and column 44. A cell may hold a numeric value or a formula. For example, `cell(11,44)` might hold the value `3.14`, whereas `cell(34,989)` holds the formula

> `cell(11,44) * cell(14,23)`

The **value** of `cell(11,44)` is `3.14`, but the value of `cell(34,989)` is `cell(11,44)` multiplied by `cell(14,23)`. The public interface allows the user to create, destroy, copy, and compute `SpreadSheet`s. To **compute** a `SpreadSheet` is to compute the value of each of its **cells**. The user also must be able to specify a **cell**'s value, of course.

4.9. Implement a `Graph` class, where a **graph** is a set of vertices *V* and a set of edges *E* such that each edge in *E* is associated with an unordered pair of distinct vertices in *V*. The following figure

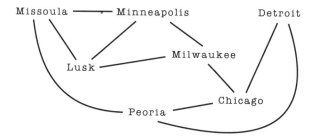

shows a graph in which the vertices represent cities and the edges represent airline routes between pairs of cities. A graph **search** is the counterpart of a tree *traversal* (see Section 4.3) in that the search visits every vertex in the graph. Two general-purpose graph searches are **depth-first search** and **breadth-first search**, which can be sketched as follows:

```
// depth-first search
1. Designate a vertex as the START. Let V = START.
2. Visit V and mark it as visited.
3. Choose an unvisited vertex W that is adjacent to V.
   Do a depth-first search from W.
4. When you reach a vertex U that has no unvisited
   adjacent vertices, back up to the most recently
   visited vertex W that does have an unvisited vertex X.
   If there is no such vertex W, terminate the search;
   otherwise, do a depth-first search from X.

// breadth-first search
1. Designate a vertex as the START. Let V = START.
2. Visit V and mark it as visited.
```

>   3. Let W be the most recently visited vertex. Visit and
>   mark as visited each unvisited vertex adjacent to W.
>   4. If all vertices have been visited, terminate the
>   search; otherwise, repeat step 3.

For the graph in the preceding figure, one depth-first search with Chicago as START is

Chicago Milwaukee Minneapolis Lusk Missoula Peoria Detroit

One breadth-first search with Lusk as START is

Lusk Missoula Minneapolis Peoria Milwaukee Chicago Detroit

The public interface should include methods to

- Add a vertex to a graph.

- Remove a vertex from a graph.

- Depth-first search the graph.

- Breadth-first search the graph.

- Iterate through the graph, one vertex at a time.

4.10. Implement a `Polynomial` class to represent polynomial expressions. A polynomial expression may have any number of terms. Class methods should support the standard operations such as addition, subtraction, multiplication, and division. The user should be able to create arbitrary polynomial expressions such as

    2a**10 + b**5 + c**3 + 2

where a**b means a^b. Also, there should be a method that allows the user to encode a polynomial as a bit-string. For example, the bit-string

    1101

represents the polynomial expression

    x**3 + x**2 + x**0 = x**3 + x**2 + 1

because the bit-string contains a 1 in positions 0, 2, and 3.

4.11. Implement a `SymbolTable` class. A **symbol table** lists all identifiers (i.e., function and variable names) in a program's source code together with pertinent information such as the identifier's data type, its role within the program (e.g., whether the identifier is a function name, variable name, or a label), and its position in a source code file (e.g., a line number designating the source code line in which the identifier occurs). The public interface should allow the user to specify one or more source files from which the `SymbolTable` is to be built. There also should be methods for displaying and editing a `SymbolTable`.

4.12. Implement a `RegExp` class to represent **regular expressions**, which are used in pattern matching. A regular expression is a character string that consists of ordinary and special characters. For example, the regular expression

   aRgT

matches only other strings with exactly these four characters in this order. Use the following special characters:

Special Character	*What It Matches*
.	Any character.
[<list>]	Any character in <list>.
	For instance, [aBc] matches
	a, B, or c.
[^<list>]	Any character not in <list>.
[<X>-<Y>]]	Any character in range <X> to <Y>.
	For instance, [a-c] matches a, b,
	or c.
*	Zero or more occurrences of the
	preceding `RegExp`.
	For instance, ab* matches ab,
	abab, ababab, and so on.

The public interface consists of methods to create and destroy `RegExps` as well as to match `RegExps` against other strings.

Chapter 5

Inheritance

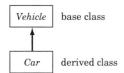

Figure 5.1.1 A base class and a derived class.

A class can occur in an **inheritance hierarchy**, which plays two roles in C++ as an object-oriented language. First, an inheritance hierarchy allows code to be reused. Code written for one class—data members and methods—can be used by other classes in the hierarchy. If the code is written correctly for a class, then it remains correct in the classes that inherit the code, thus promoting system robustness. Second, an inheritance hierarchy supports polymorphism—the run-time binding of a function reference to a particular body of code—in the form of virtual methods. We begin by clarifying basic concepts and syntax.

5.1   Basic Concepts and Syntax

Base and Derived Classes

Classes in an inheritance hierarchy stand in **superclass/subclass** relationships. The C++ name for superclass is **base class** and the C++ name for subclass is **derived class**. Whenever an existing class can be modified to produce a new class, we can derive the new class from the base class rather than declare a whole new class, thus promoting reusable code.

Example 5.1.1. Classes *Car* and *Vehicle* are related such that every *Car* is a *Vehicle* as well (see Figure 5.1.1). *Car* is thus a *subclass* or *derived class* of *Vehicle*, and *Vehicle* is a *superclass* or *base class* of *Car*. Our figures use an arrow to point from a derived class back to a base class.

Inheritance relationships are either **direct** or **indirect**. Suppose that *Coupe* is a subclass of *Car* (see Figure 5.1.2). Because there is no intermediate superclass between *Coupe* and *Car*, *Car* is a *direct superclass* or a *direct base class* of *Coupe*. Conversely, *Coupe* is a *direct subclass* or *direct derived class* of *Car*. By contrast, *Vehicle* is an *indirect superclass* or *indirect base class* of *Coupe*, and *Coupe* is an *indirect subclass* or *indirect derived class* of *Vehicle*. Note that *Car* is a derived class with respect to *Vehicle* but a base class with respect to *Coupe*.

The terms *direct* and *indirect* also apply to inheritance links. For example, *Coupe* inherits directly from *Car* but only indirectly from *Vehicle*. There is a direct inheritance link from *Vehicle* to *Car* but only an indirect inheritance link from *Vehicle* to *Coupe*.

C++ supports **multiple inheritance** in which a subclass has multiple superclasses. For example, *Car* also might be a subclass of *ExpensiveToy* (see

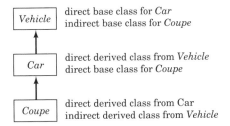

Figure 5.1.2 Direct inheritance.

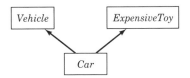

Figure 5.1.3 Multiple inheritance.

Figure 5.1.3). Section 5.7 is devoted to multiple inheritance. Conversely, a superclass may have multiple subclasses. For example, *Vehicle* may have *HugeSemiTruck* as another subclass (see Figure 5.1.4).   □

Member Accessibility

Among object-oriented languages, C++ offers the programmer the richest control over access to class members within an inheritance hierarchy. The type of inheritance between a base class and a derived class affects access to data members and methods inherited by a derived class from a base class. We begin with the three types of inheritance supported in C++.

Each member of a class is either

private   **protected**   **public**

(We discussed **private** and **public** members in Section 3.1.) A **private** member may be accessed only by methods within its class or by **friend** functions. A **protected** member may be accessed only by methods within its class hierarchy (i.e., within its class and within certain classes directly and indirectly derived from its own class) or by **friend** functions. A **public** member is globally accessible.

Example 5.1.2. In the code

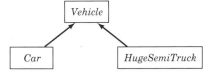

Figure 5.1.4 Multiple subclasses.

```
class Pen {
public:
   move_pen( int a, int b ) { x += a; y += b; }
   set_pen( int a, int b ) ( x = a; y = b; }
   Pen() { initial_pen(); }
protected:
   void initial_pen();
private:
   int x;
   int y;
};

int main()
{
   Pen p;
   p.set_pen( 0, 0 ); // OK -- set_pen is public
   p.initial_pen();   // *** ERROR: initial_pen is protected
   p.x = 0;           // *** ERROR: x is private
   ...
}
```

move_pen and set_pen can access x and y because x and y are members
of the class Pen. Because x and y are private members, they cannot be
accessed outside Pen; thus,

```
   p.x = 0; // ***** ERROR: x is private
```

is an error.

Similarly, the constructor can access initial_pen because initial_pen
is a member of the class Pen. Because initial_pen is a protected member,
it cannot be accessed outside Pen or classes directly or indirectly derived from
Pen; thus,

```
   p.initial_pen(); // ***** ERROR: initial_pen is protected
```

is an error.

Because set_pen is a public member, it can be accessed globally. Accordingly,

```
   p.set_pen( 0, 0 ); // OK -- set_pen is public
```

is legal.   □

By making a member of a class private, we restrict its visibility to that
class. Except for a friend class, no class—derived or otherwise—can access
a private member of another class. A protected member is like a private
member except that it is visible in a derived class. By making a member of
a class public, we make the member visible wherever the class is visible.

In C++, *all* data members and methods of the base class, except for constructors, the destructor, and the overloaded assignment operator, are *always* automatically included in the derived class. In this sense, the derived class *inherits* from the base class. Although the derived class inherits members from the base class, the accessibility of an inherited member can change. For example, a `public` member in the base class can become `private` in the derived class. The C++ programmer has considerable flexibility, not only in constructing new classes from old through inheritance, but also in controlling the accessibility of the inherited members. In the remainder of this section, we explain the syntax and semantics of inheritance and accessibility of members.

Syntax for Deriving a Class

To derive the class D from the class B, we write

```
class B { // base class
   ...
};


class D : access-specifier B { // derived class
   ...
};
```

where optional *access-specifier* is one of `private`, `protected`, or `public`.

The *access-specifier* controls the type of *access* provided to the data members and methods inherited by the derived class from the base class. (We use the phrase *inheritance link* interchangeably with *access-specifier*.) If *access-specifier* is omitted, it defaults to `private`. (If `class` is replaced by `struct` and *access-specifier* is omitted, *access-specifier* defaults to `public`.)

Although a derived class cannot prohibit any of its base class's data members or methods from being inherited, the derived class may specify additional data members or methods.

Example 5.1.3. In the code slice

```
class Vehicle {  // base class
public:
    float mph;      // meters per hour
    float cpmph;    // cost per mph
    float weight;   // in kilograms
};

class Car : public Vehicle { // derived class
public:
    char brand_name[ 100 ];
};
```

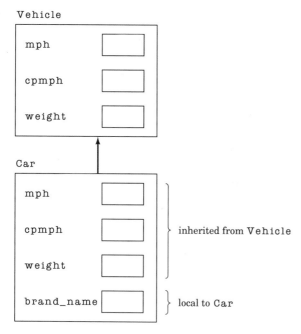

Figure 5.1.5 Class `Car` is derived from class `Vehicle`.

class `Car` is derived from the base class `Vehicle`. The *access-specifier* is
`public`. Derived class `Car` inherits the members `mph`, `cpmph`, and `weight`
from superclass `Vehicle` and adds a fourth member `brand_name` (see Figure
5.1.5).   □

public **Inheritance**

The most important type of *access-specifier* is `public`. In a `public` derivation

- Each `public` member in the base class is `public` in the derived class.

- Each `protected` member in the base class is `protected` in the derived
  class.

- Each `private` member in the base class remains `private` in the base
  class and so is visible only in the base class.

Example 5.1.4. In the code slice

```
class B { // base class
public:
    int x;
protected:
    int w;
private:
```

```
        int z;
};

class D : public B { // public derived class
public:
    int y;
    void set_w( int a ) { w = a; }
};
```

class D is derived from the base class B. The *access-specifier* is `public`. The members of the derived class D are

Member	Access Status in D	How Obtained
x	public	From class B
w	protected	From class B
z	Not accessible	From class B
y	public	Added by class D
set_w	public	Added by class D

In the code

```
int main()
{
    D d1;
    d1.x = 33; // ok -- x is public
    d1.y = 99; // ok -- y is public
    d1.w = 77; // ***** ERROR: w is protected
    d1.z = 88; // ***** ERROR: z is accessible only within B
    ...
}
```

we may access the `public` members x and y of D but not the `protected` member w, which is visible only within the class hierarchy. Within class D, it is legal to access w:

```
void set_w( int a ) { w = a; } // ok
```

It is an error to try to access z outside of B. In particular, z cannot be accessed even in D:

```
class D : public B {
    ...
    // ***** ERROR: z is accessible only within B
    void set_z( int a ) { z = a; }
    ...
};
```

□

In Example 5.1.4, **z** is inherited by **D** from **B** even though **z** is *not* visible in **D**. Whenever a **D** object is created, storage for **z** is allocated. Although a `private` member of a base class is not visible in a derived class and, therefore, may not be directly accessed, it might be indirectly accessed through a derived method as the following example shows.

Example 5.1.5. Given the class declarations

```
class Point {
    int x;
    int y;
public:
    void set_x( int x1 ) { x = x1; }
    void set_y( int y1 ) { y = y1; }
    int get_x() { return x; }
    int get_y() { return y; }
};


class IntensePoint : public Point {
    int intensity;
public:
    void set_intensity( int i ) { intensity = i; }
    int get_intensity() { return intensity; }
};
```

the members of the derived class `IntensePoint` are

Member	Access Status in IntensePoint	How Obtained
x	Not accessible	From class Point
y	Not accessible	From class Point
set_x	public	From class Point
set_y	public	From class Point
get_x	public	From class Point
get_y	public	From class Point
intensity	private	Added by class IntensePoint
set_intensity	public	Added by class IntensePoint
get_intensity	public	Added by class IntensePoint

Class `IntensePoint` inherits data members **x** and **y**, which are visible only in class `Point`. Nevertheless, class `IntensePoint` can indirectly access these data members through the methods `set_x`, `set_y`, `get_x`, and `get_y`, which *are* visible in `IntensePoint`.   □

A derived class may access `protected` members that it *inherits* from a base class. A derived class may access these `protected` members precisely because, once inherited, they belong to the derived class. Yet a derived class may *not* access `protected` members of a base class *object*, that is, an object that belongs to the base class but *not* to the derived class.

Example 5.1.6. In the code slice

```
class B { // base class
protected:
    int w;
};


class D : public B { // derived class
public:
    // w belongs to D because it is inherited from B
    void set_w( int a ) { w = a; }

    // ***** ERROR: b.w not visible in D since b.w is
    // member of B, not D
    void base_w( B b ) { b.w = 0; }
};
```

the reference to `w` in class D

```
void set_w( int a ) { w = a; } // OK
```

is legal because this `w` is D's member, which is inherited from B. It is visible in D because it is `protected` in B. The reference to `b.w` in class D

```
void base_w( B b ) { b.w = 0; }
```

is illegal because this `w` is B's member and it is visible only in B. In other words, `b.w` is the data member of a B object that is *not* a D object. □

A class may be derived from more than one base class. In this case, its base classes are separated by commas in the derived class's declaration.

Example 5.1.7. In the code slice

```
class B1 { // base class 1
protected:
    int x1;
};


class B2 { // base class 2
protected:
    int x2;
};
```

```
class D : public B1, public B2 { // derived class
  int d;
};
```

class D is derived directly from two independent base classes, B1 and B2. D inherits x1 from B1 and x2 from B2. Because both *access-specifiers* are public, the members x1 and x2 are protected. (The added member d is private.).   □

Example 5.1.7 illustrates **multiple inheritance**, a topic to which we devote an entire section (Section 5.7). For now, though, our examples use only single inheritance, that is, inheritance to a derived class from a single base class.

protected Inheritance

In a protected derivation

- Each public member in the base class is protected in the derived class.

- Each protected member in the base class is protected in the derived class.

- Each private member in the base class remains private in the base class and so is visible only in the base class.

Example 5.1.8. In the code slice

```
class B { // base class
public:
    int x;
protected:
    int w;
private:
    int z;
};

class D : protected B { // protected derived class
public:
    int y;
};
```

class D is derived from the base class B. The *access-specifier* is protected. The members of the derived class D are

Member	Access Status in D	How Obtained
x	protected	From class B
w	protected	From class B
z	Not accessible	From class B
y	public	Added by class D

□

private Inheritance

In a `private` derivation

- Each `public` member in the base class is `private` in the derived class.
- Each `protected` member in the base class is `private` in the derived class.
- Each `private` member in the base class remains `private` in the base class and so is visible only in the base class.

Example 5.1.9. In the code slice

```
class B { // base class
public:
    int x;
protected:
    int w;
private:
    int z;
};

class D : private B { // private derived class
public:
    int y;
};
```

class D is derived from the base class B. The *access-specifier* is `private`. The members of the derived class D are

Member	Access Status in D	How Obtained
x	private	From class B
w	private	From class B
z	Not accessible	From class B
y	public	Added by class D

□

Example 5.1.10. Because `private` is the default value for *access-specifier*, the declaration of class D in Example 5.1.9 is equivalent to

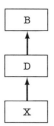

Figure 5.1.6 Indirect inheritance.

```
class D : B { // private (default) derived class
public:
    int y;
};
```

□

Indirect Inheritance

Data members and methods may traverse several inheritance links as they are included from a base to a derived class. For example, suppose that B is D's base class and that D is X's base class (see Figure 5.1.6). In this case, X inherits D's data members and methods—including whatever data members or methods D inherits from B. Inheritance thus may be either direct (to a derived class from a direct base class) or indirect (to a derived class from an indirect base class).

Example 5.1.11. In the code slice

```
// direct base class for Cat,
// indirect base class for HouseCat
class Animal {
protected:
    char  speciesInLatin[ 100 ];
    float lifeExpectancy;
    int   warmBlooded_P;    // 0 == False, 1 == True
};

// direct derived class from Animal,
// direct base class for HouseCat
class Cat : public Animal {
protected:
    char  range[ 100 ][ 100 ];
    float favoritePrey[ 100 ][ 100 ];
};
```

```
// indirect derived class from Animal,
// direct derived class from Cat
class HouseCat : public Cat {
    char toys[ 10000 ][ 100 ];
    char catPsychiatrist[ 50 ];
    char catDentist[ 50 ];
    char catDoctor[ 50 ];
    char apparentOwner[ 50 ];
};
```

HouseCat has 10 data members: five are added, two are inherited directly from Cat, and three are inherited indirectly from Animal by way of Cat. The inherited data members remain **protected** in HouseCat.   □

Access Declarations

Access to an inherited member may be **adjusted** to that of the base class by declaring it **public** or **protected** in the derived class.

Example 5.1.12. In the code slice

```
class BC { // base class
protected:
    int x;
    int y;
public:
    int z;
};

class DC : private BC { // private inheritance
protected:
    BC::x;
public:
    BC::z;
    int w;
};
```

the declaration

```
BC::x;
```

adjusts x in DC to the same **protected** status that this data member has in base class BC. The adjustment is done by placing the declaration

```
BC::x;
```

in the **protected** section of DC. Without the declaration, x would be **private** in DC because the inheritance link from BC to DC is **private**. Similarly, the declaration

```
BC::z;
```

adjusts z to its public status in the base class BC by declaring it in the public section of the derived class DC. Inherited member y is private in DC because DC is obtained by private inheritance from BC and y's status was not adjusted. Added member w is public.   □

It is an error to try to use an access declaration to change the status of a base class member.

Example 5.1.13. In the code slice

```
class BC { // base class
private:
   int y;
protected:
   int x;
public:
   int z;
};
class DC : private BC { // private inheritance
protected:
   BC::y; // ***** ERROR: can't change private to protected
   BC::z; // ***** ERROR: can't change public to protected
};
```

the statement

```
BC::y; // ***** ERROR: can't change private to protected
```

is an error because private member y in BC cannot have its status changed. (In fact, y is *not* even visible in DC.) The statement

```
BC::z; // ***** ERROR: can't change public to protected
```

is an error because public member z in BC cannot have its status changed through a declaration. (z is public if it is declared public in DC, and z is private if it is not declared in DC.)   □

Name Hiding

If a derived class adds a data member with the same name as a data member in the base class, the local data member **hides** the inherited data member.

Example 5.1.14. In the code slice

```
class B { // base class
public:
   int x;  // B::x
};
```

```
class D : public B { // derived class
public:
   int x;  // ***** DANGER: hides B::x
};

int main()
{
   D d1;

   d1.x = 999;  // D::x, not B::x
   d1.B::x = 4; // ok -- but clumsy!
   ...
}
```

class D inherits x from B. However, D also has a local data member named x, which means that the local data member hides the inherited data member in the sense that B::x is not in class D's scope. The only way to access B::x in D is by using the scope resolution operator, as in the second assignment statement. □

Similarly, if a derived class adds a method with the same name in the base class, the added method hides the base class's method.

Example 5.1.15. In the code slice

```
class B { // base class
public:
   void h( float ); // B::h
};

class D : public B { // derived class
public:
   void h( char* );  // ***** DANGER: hides B::h
};

int main()
{
   D d1;

   d1.h( "Boffo!" ); // D::h, not B::h
   d1.h( 707.7 );    // ***** ERROR: D::h hides B::h
   d1.B::h( 707.7 ); // OK: invokes B::h
   ...
}
```

The error occurs because method D::h expects a **char*** argument rather than a **float** argument. The inherited B::h, which does expect a **char*** argument, is hidden in **d** by D::h and so must be invoked with the scope resolution operator.   □

Exercises

---

1. Draw a class hierarchy in which a base class has multiple derived classes.

2. Draw a class hierarchy in which a derived class has multiple base classes.

3. Draw a class hierarchy in which a base class has multiple derived classes, at least one of which has a second base class.

4. Draw a class hierarchy that illustrates the distinction between direct and indirect inheritance.

5. Explain the relationship among the terms *superclass, subclass, base class,* and *derived class.*

6. Is it possible for class **C** to be both a base class and a derived class? If so, draw a figure to illustrate. If not, explain why not.

7. Draw a class hierarchy that is at least five deep. List the directly and indirectly derived classes of the top class in the hierarchy.

8. In the code slice

   ```
   class A {
      int x;
   };

   class B : A {
      int y;
   };

   B b1;
   ```

   how many data members does **b1** have?

9. Explain the error.

   ```
   class A {
      int x;
   };
   ```

```
class B : A {
    int y;
    void f() { y = x; }
};
```

10. Is the inheritance link from **A** to **B** **private** or **public**?

```
class A {
    ...
};


class B : A {
    ...
};
```

11. Explain the error.

```
class A {
protected:
    float f1, f2;
private:
    int x;
};

int main()
{
    A a1;
    A* ptr = &a1;

    ptr -> f1 = 3.14;
    ...
}
```

12. Explain the difference between **private** and **protected** with respect to a class's data members and methods.

13. Write the code for a class hierarchy in which there is **public** inheritance from base class **B** to derived class **D**.

14. Change the inheritance link from **A** to **B** from **private** to **public**.

```
class A {
    ...
};
```

```
class B : A {
   ...
};
```

15. Draw an inheritance hierarchy in which P has a direct inheritance link to base class Q and an indirect inheritance link to base class R.

16. Explain the advantage of `protected` over `private` data members or methods.

17. Explain the advantage of `protected` over `public` data members or methods.

18. Suppose that data member `B::x` is `public`. Use an inheritance link from B to D to deny `public` access to `D::x`.

19. Explain the error.

```
class A {
protected:
   float f1, f2;
public:
   int x;
};

class B : private A {
public:
   void pf1() { cout << f1 << endl; }
};

int main()
{
   B b1;
   b1.f1 = 3.14;
   b1.pf1();
   b1.x = ( int ) b1.f1;
   ...
}
```

20. Explain the error.

```
class A {
protected:
   int x;
};
```

```
class B : public A {
    int y;
    void f( A a ) { y = a.x; }
};
```

21. Explain the error.

```
class A {
protected:
    int x;
};

class B : public A {
public:
    int y;
};

int main()
{
    B b1;
    b1.x = 8;
    b1.y = 9;
    ...
}
```

22. In the code slice

```
class B {      // base class
protected:
    int num1;
    int num2;
};
class D : public B { // derived class
    int num3;
};
D d1;
```

how many data members does **d1** have?

23. Write the body of **init**, which initializes D's members.

```
class B {      // base class
protected:
    int num1;
    int num2;
};
```

obj

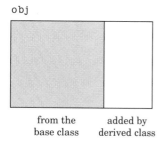

from the   added by
base class   derived class

Figure 5.2.1 A derived class as a specialization of a base class.

```
class D : public B { // derived class
    int num3;
public:
    void init( int, int, int );
};
void D::init( int n1, int n2, int n3 )
{

}
```

24. Explain the difference between inheritance and access. Write rules that summarize the difference.

25. Explain the error.

```
class A {
protected:
    int x;
};
class B : public A {
public:
    void f1() { x = 6; }
    void f2( A a ) { a.x = 1; }
};
```

5.2   Constructors Under Inheritance

A derived class is a specialization of a base class. An object in a derived class inherits characteristics from the base class but also has characteristics that are specific to the derived class (see Figure 5.2.1). For this reason, a base class constructor (if any) is invoked when a derived class object is created. The base class constructor handles initialization, dynamic storage allocation, and the like for the "from the base class" part of the object. If the derived class has a constructor of its own, then this constructor can handle the "added by the derived class" part of the object.

Example 5.2.1. In the code slice

```
class B {  // base class
protected:
   int x;
   int y;
public:
   B() { x = y = -1; } // base constructor
};

class D : public B { // derived class
public:
   void write() { cout << x * y << endl; }
};

int main()
{
   D d1;        // B::B() invoked
   d1.write(); // 1 written to standard output
   ...
}
```

B's default constructor is invoked when **d1** is defined because D is derived from B. The constructor initializes **d1.x** and **d1.y** to -1. Note that **d1** inherits its only data members from B. □

Base class constructors are often sufficient for the derived class. Sometimes, however, it makes sense for a derived class to have its own constructors. A constructor specific to a derived class may invoke a base class constructor, if one exists.

Example 5.2.2. The code slice

```
const int MaxName = 100;

class Animal {
protected:
   char species[ MaxName + 1 ];
public:
   Animal() { strcpy( species, "Animal" ); }
   Animal( char* s ) { strcpy( species, s ); }
};

class Primate: public Animal {
   int heart_cham;
public:
```

```
      Primate() : Animal( "Primate" ) { }
      Primate( int n ) : Animal( "Primate" )
         { heart_cham = n; }
};


Animal slug;                  // Animal()
Animal tweety( "canary" );    // Animal( char* )

Primate godzilla;             // Primate()
Primate human( 4 );           // Primate( int )
```

has four constructors: two for base class **Animal** and two for derived class **Primate**.

The two **Primate** constructors invoke a base class **Animal** constructor in their headers:

```
Primate() : Animal( "Primate" ) { }
Primate( int n ) : Animal( "Primate" )
   { heart_cham = n; }
```

The syntax indicates that each **Primate** constructor invokes an **Animal** constructor *before* executing its own body. For instance, the default **Primate** constructor invokes the base class constructor **Animal(char*)** before executing its own body, which happens to be empty. In the case of the **Primate** constructor with one argument, the body contains an assignment of n to **heart_cham**.   □

In a deep inheritance hierarchy, creation of an object belonging to a derived class may have a domino effect with respect to constructor invocation.

Example 5.2.3. In the code slice

```
const int MaxName = 100;

class Animal {
protected:
   char species[ MaxName + 1 ];
public:
   Animal() { strcpy( species, "Animal" ); }
   Animal( char* s ) { strcpy( species, s ); }
};

class Primate: public Animal {
protected:
   int heart_cham;
public:
   Primate() : Animal( "Primate" ) { }
```

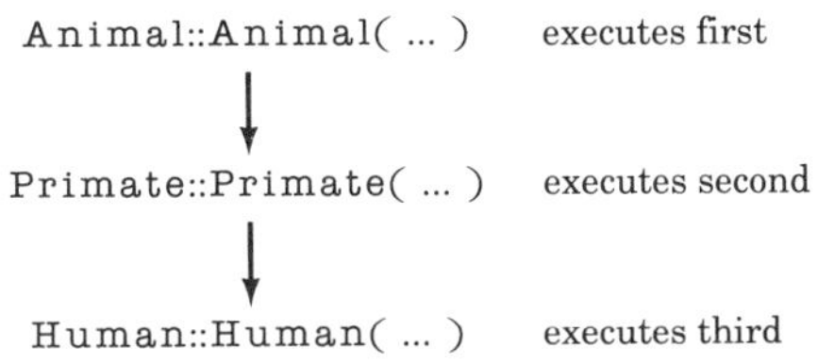

```
Animal::Animal( ... )    executes first

        │
        ▼

Primate::Primate( ... )    executes second

        │
        ▼

 Human::Human( ... )    executes third
```

Figure 5.2.2 Constructor firing in `Animal-Primate-Human` hierarchy.

```
            Primate( int n ) : Animal( "Primate" )
                { heart_cham = n; }
        };

        class Human : public Primate {
        public:
            Human() : Primate() { };
            Human( int c ) : Primate( c ) { }
        };

        Human jill();      // Human()
        Human fred( 4 ); // Human( int )
```

the inheritance hierarchy is now three deep. `Human` inherits `heart_cham` directly from `Primate` and `species` indirectly from `Animal` by way of `Primate`. Each of the `Human` constructors invokes the direct base class constructor `Primate` before executing an empty body. The `Primate` constructor, in turn, invokes the `Animal` constructor before executing its own body. The effect is that the constructors are executed in a top-down order, where `Animal` is at the top, `Primate` in the middle, and `Human` at the bottom of the inheritance hierarchy (see Figure 5.2.2). □

Derived Class Constructor Rules

If a base class has constructors *but no default constructor*, then a derived class constructor *must* explicitly invoke some base class constructor.

Example 5.2.4. The code slice

```
// B has constructors but no
// default constructor
class B { // base class
    int x;
    int y;
public:
    B( int a ) { x = a; y = 999; }
    B( int a1, int a2 ) { x = a1; y = a2; }
};
```

```
// D has a constructor (any constructor
// will do for the example)
class D : public B { // derived class
  int z;
public:
  // ***** ERROR: D( int ) must explicitly
  //       invoke a B constructor
  D( int n ) { z = n; }
};
```

is in error because B does not have a *default* constructor and D's constructor
does *not* explicitly invoke a B constructor. We can avoid the error in two
ways: by having D's constructor explicitly invoke, in its header, one of B's
constructors or by giving B a default constructor. We amend the code slice
to illustrate the two approaches:

```
// approach 1: have D's constructor explicitly
// invoke one of B's constructors

class B { // base class
  int x;
  int y;
public:
  B( int a ) { x = a; y = 999; }
  B( int a1, int a2 ) { x = a1; y = a2; }
};

// D's constructor explicitly invokes a
// B constructor in its header
class D : public B { // derived class
  int z;
public:
  // ok: D( int ) explicitly invokes B( int, int )
  D( int n ) : B( n, n + 1 ) { z = n; }
};

// approach 2: give B a default constructor

class B { // base class
  int x;
  int y;
public:
  B() { x = 1; y = 2; } // default
  B( int a ) { x = a; y = 999; }
```

```
   B( int a1, int a2 ) { x = a1; y = a2; }
};

// D's constructor need not invoke a B
// constructor because B how has a
// default constructor
class D : public B { // derived class
  int z;
public:
  // ok: B has a default constructor
  D( int n ) { z = n; }
};
```

There is rarely a good reason for a base class not to have a default constructor. Giving a base class a default constructor avoids the problem and still allows a derived class constructor to invoke any base class constructor. Accordingly, we recommend that every base class have a default constructor.

□

Suppose that a base class has a default constructor and that a derived class has constructors, none of which explicitly invokes a base class constructor. In this case, the base class default constructor is invoked automatically whenever a derived class object is created.

Example 5.2.5. The output for the code slice

```
class B { // base class
  int x;
public:
  B() { cout << "B::B() fires..." << endl; }
};

class D : public B { // derived class
  int y;
public:
  D() { cout << "D::D() fires..." << endl; }
};

int main()
{
  D d;
  ...
}
```

is

```
B::B() fires...
```

```
D::D() fires...
```

It is legal but unnecessary for D's constructor to invoke B's default constructor explicitly:

```
// legal but unnecessary
D() : B() {...}
```

□

We now summarize the rules, using D as a class derived from B.

- If D has constructors but B has no constructors, then the appropriate D constructor fires automatically whenever a D object is created.

- If D has no constructors but B has constructors, then B must have a default constructor so that B's default constructor can fire automatically whenever a D object is created.

- If D has constructors and B has a default constructor, then B's default constructor fires automatically whenever a D object is created unless the appropriate D constructor *explicitly* invokes, in its header, some other B constructor.

- If D and B have constructors but B has no default constructor, then each D constructor must explicitly invoke, in its header, a B constructor, which then fires when a D object is created.

It makes sense that the creation of a derived class object should cause some base class constructor, if any, to fire. A derived class constructor may depend upon actions from a base class constructor. For example, the derived class may assume storage dynamically allocated by the base class constructor or data member initializations performed by the base class constructor. Also, a derived class object is a specialization of a base class object, which means that a base class constructor, if present, should execute *first* when a derived class object is created. The more specialized constructor, which is the local derived class constructor, then can handle any special details.

Example 5.2.6. In the code slice

```
const int MaxLen = 100;

class B {  // base class
protected:
   char* name;
   int   maxlen;
public:
   B()
   {
      maxlen = MaxLen;
```

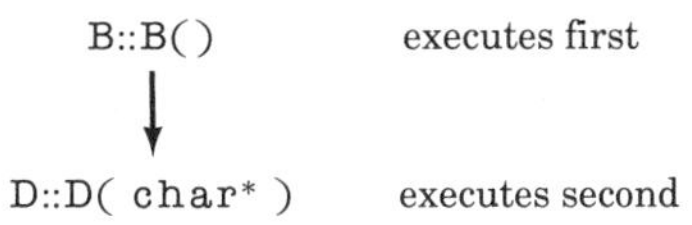

B::B( )   executes first

↓

D::D(char*)   executes second

Figure 5.2.3 Firing of base class and derived class constructors.

```
        name = new char[ maxlen ];
    }
};

class D : public B { // derived class
public:
    D( char* n ) : B() { strcpy( name, n ); }
};

D foo( "foo" );
```

D's constructor is called when **foo** is defined with the initializing value "foo", which is copied into the dynamically allocated storage to which **name** points. The copy occurs in D's body. The dynamically allocated storage consists of **maxlen char** cells. It is B's default constructor, not D's parameterized constructor, that initializes **maxlen** and dynamically allocates the storage. Therefore, B's default constructor must be invoked before the body of D's parameterized constructor executes. D's parameterized constructor does invoke B::B() and, as a result, **foo**'s creation and initialization work properly (see Figure 5.2.3).   □

Exercises

---

1. Explain the error.

```
class B {
    int x;
public:
    B( int a ) { x = a; }
};

class D : public B {
    ...
public:
    D() {...}
};
```

2. In Example 5.2.3, the default constructor for `Human` explicitly invokes the default constructor for `Primate` but does not explicitly invoke the default constructor for `Animal`. Why not?

3. Create a class hierarchy at least three deep and write constructors for each class. The constructors should contain print statements so that you can trace their firing. Create objects that belong to each class and trace the constructor firings.

4. What is the output?

```
class B {
  ...
public:
  B() { cout << "B" << endl; }
};

class D1 : public B {
  ...
public:
  D1() : B() { cout << "D1" << endl; };
};

class D2 : public D1 {
  ...
public:
  D2() : D1() { cout << "D2" << endl; };
};

D2 d2;
```

5. Is it mandatory that a derived class have a constructor?

6. Is it mandatory that a base class have a constructor? Write and compile sample code to confirm your answer.

7. Is it possible for a derived class to have a constructor but its base class not to have a constructor? Write and compile sample code to confirm your answer.

8. Suppose that base class B has two constructors, the default constructor `B::B()` and the constructor `B::B( int )`. D is derived from B and has a single constructor, `D::D( int )`. Must D invoke *both* of B's constructors before executing its own body?

9. C++ requires that when a derived class object is created, a base class constructor, if one exists, be invoked. Explain the reasoning behind this rule.

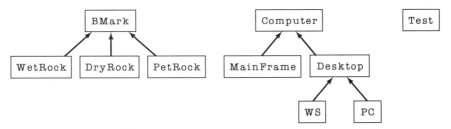

Figure 5.3.1 Hierarchies for measuring computer performance.

10. Extend the class hierarchy of Example 5.2.3 at least two more levels, writing constructors for each of the additional classes.

5.3 Sample Application: Measuring Computer Performance

Problem _____

Simulate the measurement of computer performance.

Solution _____

We use three inheritance hierarchies anchored on base classes **BMark** (benchmark program), **Computer**, and **Test**. **BMark** has **WetRock**, **DryRock**, and **PetRock** as derived classes. **Computer** has **Desktop** and **Mainframe** as derived classes, and **Desktop** has **WS** (workstation) and **PC** (personal computer) as derived classes. **Test** does not occur in an inheritance hierarchy. Figure 5.3.1 illustrates.

A **Test** consists of a **Computer** running a **BMark**, the results of which are printed to the standard output. **Test** is a **friend** to **BMark** and **Computer** so that **Test** can access relevant attributes of **BMark** and **Computer** in order to measure a **Computer**'s performance in executing a **BMark**.

C++ Implementation _____

```
#include <iostream.h>
#include <string.h>
#include <math.h>

const int MaxName = 100;
const float Tolerance = 0.01;

class Test;
```

```cpp
class BMark {    // benchmark
friend Test;
protected:
   // instruction breakdown by
   // categories -- in percentages
   float alP; // arithmetic-logic
   float mP;  // memory
   float cP;  // control
   float ioP; // io
   float tlP; // tight-loop
   float ic;  // executed instruction count
   char name[ MaxName + 1 ];
public:
   BMark() // base class constructor
   {
      init();
      strcpy( name, "???" );
   }

   BMark( char* n )
   {
      init();

      if ( strlen( n ) < MaxName )
         strcpy( name, n );
      else
         strncpy( name, n, MaxName );
   }

   void report()
   {
      cout << "Benchmark "
           << name << endl;
      cout << "Total instructions executed == "
           << ic << endl;
      cout << "   Arithmetic-logic == "
           << alP << endl;
      cout << "   Memory == "
           << mP << endl;
      cout << "   Control == "
           << cP << endl;
      cout << "   Input/Output == "
           << ioP << endl;
   }
```

```
      // Check whether percentages sum within
      // Tolerance to 1.0.
      int ok()
      {
         return fabs( 1.0 - ( alP + mP + cP + ioP ) )
                <= Tolerance;
      }

      // Print error message in case percentages
      // do not sum within Tolerance to 1.0.
      void init_error()
      {
         cout << name << " -- init error!" << endl;
      }

   private:
      // Initialize percentages to 0.0.
      void init()
      {
         alP = cP = mP = ioP = ic = 0.0;
      }
   };

   // Benchmark emphasizes arith-logic and
   // control statements with moderate
   // memory traffic and low i/o.
   class WetRock : public BMark {
   public:
      WetRock() : BMark( "WetRock" ) // WetRock constructor
      {
         alP = 0.50;
         cP =  0.20;
         mP =  0.20;
         ioP = 0.10;
         ic = ( float ) 4500301;

         if ( !ok() )
            init_error();
      }
   };

   // Benchmark emphasizes arith-logic and
   // control with light memory traffic and
```

```
// no i/o.
class DryRock : public BMark {
public:
   DryRock() : BMark( "DryRock" ) // DryRock constructor
   {
      alP = 77.0;
      cP = 16.6;
      ioP = 0.0;
      mP = 1.0 - alP - cP - ioP;
      ic = ( float ) 6700909;

      if ( !ok() )
         init_error();
   }
};


// Benchmark emphasizes memory traffic
// with moderate i/o and low arith-logic
// and control.
class  PetRock : public BMark {
public:
   PetRock() : BMark( "PetRock" ) // PetRock constructor
   {
      alP = 12.2;
      mP = 57.7;
      ioP = 23.9;
      cP = 1.0 - mP - ioP - alP;
      ic = ( float ) 10400500;

      if ( !ok() )
         init_error();
   }
};

class Computer {
friend Test;
protected:
   // cpi = cycles per instruction
   float alcpi;   // arithmetic-logic cpi
   float ccpi;    // control cpi
   float iocpi;   // input-output cpi
   float mcpi;    // memory cpi
   float ct;      // cycle time (nanoseconds)
   char name[ MaxName + 1 ];
```

```cpp
      // cost range: upper - lower
      float costU;
      float costL;

   protected:
      Computer( float al, float c, float io,
                float m, float t,
                char* n, float l, float u )
      {
         alcpi = al;
         ccpi = c;
         iocpi = io;
         mcpi = m;
         ct = t;
         if ( strlen( n ) < MaxName )
            strcpy( name, n );
         else
            strncpy( name, n, MaxName );
         costU = u;
         costL = l;
      }

      void report()
      {
         cout << "Computer " << name
              << " at cost ranging from $" << costL
              << " to $" << costU << "." << endl;
         cout << "   Clock cycle (nanoseconds): "
              << ct << endl;
         cout << "   CPIs: " << endl;
         cout << "      Arith-Logic: " << alcpi << endl;
         cout << "      Control:     " << ccpi << endl;
         cout << "      Memory:      " << mcpi << endl;
         cout << "      I/O:         " << iocpi << endl;
      }
};

// Desktop machines comprise workstations and
// personal computers.
class Desktop : public Computer {
protected:
   Desktop( float al,   // arith-logic
            float c,    // control
            float m,    // memory
```

```
           float io,   // io
           float t,    // ct
           char* n,    // name
           float l,    // lower bound
           float u )   // upper bound
      : Computer( al, c, m, io, t, n, l, u ) { }
};

class PC : public Desktop {  // personal computer
public:
   PC( float al = 1.8,        // arith-logic
       float c = 2.3,         // control
       float m = 5.6,         // memory
       float io = 9.2,        // io
       float t = 230,         // ct
       char* n = "PC",        // name
       float l = 800.00,      // lower bound
       float u = 14500.00 )   // upper bound
         : Desktop( al, c, m, io, t, n, l, u ) { }
};

class WS : public Desktop { // workstation
public:
   WS( float al = 1.3,        // arith-logic
       float c = 1.7,         // control
       float m = 2.1,         // memory
       float io = 5.8,        // io
       float t = 15,          // ct
       char* n = "WS",        // name
       float l = 4500.00,     // lower bound
       float u = 78900.00 )   // upper bound
         : Desktop( al, c, m, io, t, n, l, u ) { }
};

class Mainframe : public Computer {     // mainframe
public:
   Mainframe( float al = 1.2,            // arith-logic
              float c = 1.5,             // control
              float m = 3.6,             // memory
              float io = 3.2,            // io
              float t = 50,              // ct
              char* n = "$$",            // name
```

```
                    float l = 310000.00,     // lower bound
                    float u = 20000000.00 )  // upper bound
                : Computer( al, c, m, io, t, n, l, u ) { }
};

class Test {
    float rt; // response time in nanoseconds
    void results( Computer c, BMark b );
public:
    Test( Computer c, BMark b );
};

// Compute response time of running benchmark b
// on computer c, where
//   rt  = response time
//   ct  = clock cycle time
//   ic  = instruction count
//   cpi = clock cycles per instruction
// Then rt = ic * cpi * ct
// The response time is given in nanoseconds.
Test::Test( Computer c, BMark b )
{
    // instruction counts by type
    float al_rt, c_rt, m_rt, io_rt;
    // compute response times per type
    al_rt = b.alP * b.ic * c.alcpi * c.ct;
    c_rt =  b.cP  * b.ic * c.ccpi  * c.ct;
    m_rt =  b.mP  * b.ic * c.mcpi  * c.ct;
    io_rt = b.ioP * b.ic * c.iocpi * c.ct;
    rt = al_rt + c_rt + m_rt + io_rt;
    results( c, b );
}

void Test::results( Computer c, BMark b )
{
    cout << "\nBenchmark results:\n" << endl;
    cout << "  RT (ns) for " << c.name
        << " running " << b.name
        << " = " << rt <<  endl;
    cout << "\nBenchmark and computer details follow.\n"
        << endl;
    b.report();
    c.report();
}
```

Discussion

A `Test` simulates the measurement of **response time** for a `Computer` running a `BMark`. Response time is the time that it takes a computer to run a program from start to finish. A benchmark is a special program designed to measure computer performance. For a discussion of performance in general and the pitfalls of using benchmarks to measure it, see John L. Hennessy and David A. Patterson *Computer Architecture: A Quantitative Approach* (San Mateo, CA: Morgan Kaufmann Publishers, Inc., 1992).

Computer designers define response time as the product

$$RT = IC * CPI * CT$$

where

Metric	Definition
RT	Response time
IC	Instruction count, the number of instructions executed
CPI	Average clock cycles per instruction
CT	Clock cycle time, usually in nanoseconds

Viewing RT in this way allows designers to focus on different strategies for lowering RT and thereby improving the computer's performance. For example, improvements in compiler technology can lower IC and, therefore, RT as well. Improvements in instruction set design together with acceleration techniques such as pipelining and cache memory can lower CPI. RT is generally measured in nanoseconds, as this is the unit typically used for CT.

`BMark` has data members to store the benchmark's IC as well as the instruction breakdown by category. Four categories of instruction are used:

- Arithmetic/logic instructions such as *add, multiply, test for equality,* and *logical or.*

- Control instructions such as *if-then-else* and *jump.*

- Memory instructions such as *read* and *write.*

- Input/output instructions such as *print.*

Data members `alP`, `cP`, `mP`, and `ioP` store the breakdown of IC by percentage into the four categories. For example, a `cP` value of `0.40` means that 40 percent of the benchmark's instructions fall into category *Control*. `Computer` has data members to store the machine's average CPI for each instruction category. For example, a `ccpi` value of `1.8` means that the machine's average CPI for control instructions is `1.8`; that is, the machine averages `1.8` clock cycles to execute a control instruction such as *if-then-else*. Given a `BMark` and a `Computer`, a `Test` simulates running the benchmark on the computer to measure RT, which `Test` stores in data member `rt`.

Test is a friend to Computer and BMark. Test accesses the Computer's data members alcpi, ccpi, mcpi, and iocpi to get the cycles per instruction for each type of instruction. Test accesses the BMark's data member ic to get the benchmark's instruction count and data members alP, cP, mP, and ioP to get the breakdown of benchmark instructions for each instruction category. Test then computes separately the response time for the arithmetic-logic, the control, the memory, and the input-output instructions. By summing these, Test computes the run time for the entire benchmark. Test prints its own report to the standard output and then invokes BMark and Computer methods, each named report, to print reports on the benchmark and the computer particulars.

The inheritance hierarchy with BMark as its base class has WetRock, DryRock, and PetRock as derived classes. The constructor BMark::BMark initializes data member name for each benchmark. Constructors for the derived classes initialize data members such as alP, which are inherited from the base class. Each derived constructor invokes the base class constructor before executing its own nonempty body, as we see in the PetRock example:

```
class  PetRock : public BMark {
public:
    PetRock() : BMark( "PetRock" ) // PetRock constructor
    {
        alP = 12.2;
        mP = 57.7;
        ioP = 23.9;
        cP = 1.0 - mP - ioP - alP;
        ic = ( float ) 10400500;

        if ( !ok() )
            init_error();
    }
};
```

Inherited method BMark::ok checks whether the percentages sum within Tolerance to 1.0, and inherited method BMark::init_error prints an error message if they do not. Inheritance from BMark to each derived class is public. BMark's data members are all protected and all of its methods but one are public. The exception is method init, which is meant to be invoked only by the constructor and so is private. The derived classes thus have access to all the base class data members and to all the methods except one, which is invoked within the accessible base class constructor.

The inheritance hierarchy with Computer as its base class differs in organization from the BMark hierarchy. In the case of the Computer hierarchy, the derived classes have no data members except the ones inherited from the base class; and each derived class has only one constructor among its local methods. For example, the declaration for `Desktop` is:

```
class Desktop : public Computer {
protected:
   Desktop( float al,  // arith-logic
            float c,   // control
            float m,   // memory
            float io,  // io
            float t,   // ct
            char* n,   // name
            float l,   // lower bound
            float u )  // upper bound
      : Computer( al, c, m, io, t, n, l, u ) { }
};
```

The declaration for PC, which is derived from `Desktop`, follows the pattern:

```
class PC : public Desktop {  // personal computer
public:
   PC( float al = 1.8,          // arith-logic
       float c = 2.3,           // control
       float m = 5.6,           // memory
       float io = 9.2,          // io
       float t = 230,           // ct
       char* n = "PC",          // name
       float l = 800.00,        // lower bound
       float u = 14500.00 )     // upper bound
         : Desktop( al, c, m, io, t, n, l, u ) { }
};
```

The local constructor's body is empty, which means that its base class's constructor does all the work. Defining a PC object

```
PC my_pc;
```

invokes the PC constructor, which immediately invokes the `Desktop` constructor before executing its own body; and the `Desktop` constructor immediately invokes the `Computer` constructor before executing its own body. As a result, the constructors complete in the left-to-right order

```
Computer Desktop PC
```

Technically, the PC constructor is invoked first, `Desktop` constructor is invoked second, and the `Computer` constructor is invoked third. Yet the calling sequence behaves as if the `Computer` constructor were invoked first, the `Desktop` constructor were invoked second, and the PC constructor were invoked third (see Figure 5.3.2). Note that a low-level constructor such as `PC::PC` has default values for its arguments. These can be overwritten, of course, in a call such as

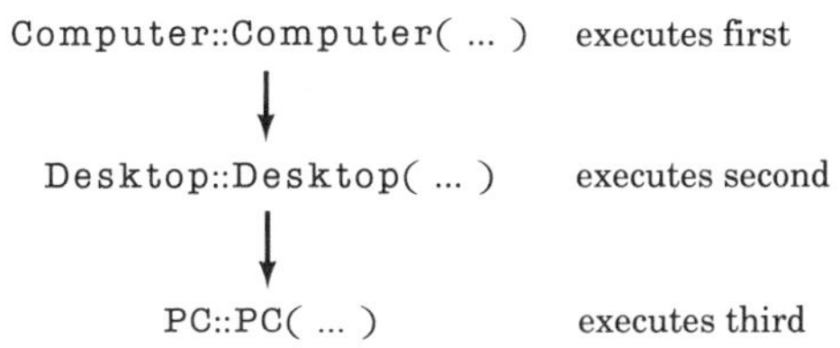

```
Computer::Computer( ... )    executes first
         │
         ▼
 Desktop::Desktop( ... )      executes second
         │
         ▼
     PC::PC( ... )            executes third
```

Figure 5.3.2   Order of constructor invocation.

```
PC pc1( 1.9,        // arithmetic-logic cpi
         2.3,       // control cpi
         3.8,       // memory cpi
         6.5,       // i/o cpi
         160,       // clock cycle time
     "Secret",      // name
      850.00,       // low-end price
      850.00 );     // high-end price
```

The constructors for **PC**, **WS**, and **Mainframe** are **public** so that they may be invoked anywhere in the program where their respective classes are visible. By contrast, the constructors **Computer** and **Desktop** are **protected** rather than **public** so that they cannot be invoked except from within the inheritance hierarchy anchored on base class **Computer**. A **public** constructor such as **PC** invokes a **protected** constructor such as **Desktop**.

The program generates an output report that summarizes the computer's response time when running the benchmark. A code slice such as

```
int main()
{
  WetRock wr;
  PC pc;                 // use default values
  Test test( pc, wr );   // test pc running wr
  ...
}
```

generates the report

```
Benchmark results:

  RT (ns) in for PC running WetRock = 4.254135e+09

Benchmark and computer details follow.

Benchmark WetRock
Total instructions executed == 4500301
  Arithmetic-logic == 0.5
  Memory == 0.2
  Control == 0.2
```

```
Input/Output == 0.1
Computer PC at cost ranging from $800 to $14500.
  Clock cycle (nanoseconds): 230
  CPIs:
    Arith-Logic: 2.5
    Control:     2.3
    Memory:      9.2
    I/O:         5.6
```

Exercises

1. Is `Desktop` a base or a derived class? Explain.

2. Add `Minicomputer` as a derived class of `Computer`. Be sure to write a constructor for it.

3. Add data member `superscalar` to `Desktop`. The data member has value true (1) if the machine is superscalar and false (0) otherwise. A computer is **superscalar** if

   ```
   average CPI < 1
   ```

   Some workstations achieve superscalar status by executing integer and floating-point instructions in parallel.

4. Add `protected` data members or methods to each of `Computer`'s derived classes. For example, derived class `Desktop` might have a data member `footprint` that indicates how much desk space is required for the machine.

5. Computer technology changes so fast that the default clock cycle time and *CPI* values listed in a constructor such as `PC::PC` may already be out of date and, in any case, soon will be. Determine accurate values for an actual machine and change the default values.

6. Throughput—work done per unit of time—is a second measure of computer performance. Extend the sample application so that `Test` can test either throughput or response time.

7. Throughput varies inversely with response time. For example, if response time goes down, then throughput goes up. This means that an improvement in response time entails an improvement in throughput. Is the converse true? Does an improvement in throughput automatically bring an improvement in response time?

8. Add a method `balanced` to `BMark`. Its value is true (1) if the percentages of the four instruction categories are approximately equal and false (0) otherwise. For example, `balanced` would be true if

   ```
   alP = 25.0;
   cP = 25.0;
   mP = 26.0;
   ioP = 24.0;
   ```

   Be sure to define "approximately equal."

9. For the code slice

   ```
   WS workstation;
   ```

   trace the order in which the relevant constructors are invoked and the order in which they complete.

10. Computer vendors often are selective in making public how their machines run different benchmarks. Explain why a given machine might fare far better running, say, `PetRock` than `WetRock`.

11. **MIPS** is a commonly used indicator of computer performance that stands for **Millions** of **Instructions** **Per** **Second**. Add data member `mips` to `Test` and have a `Test` method that sets its value.

12. MIPS is a very suspicious measure of computer performance for various reasons. For one thing, it is possible that a drop in a computer's response time when running a given program may bring a drop in its MIPS rating as well! In order words, the MIPS rating gets worse as the machine's performance gets better. How is this possible? *Hint*: MIPS is highly sensitive to a program's instruction mix.

5.4 Polymorphism and Virtual Methods

Polymorphism refers to the run-time binding of a pointer to a method. For example, suppose that classes `Circle` and `Rectangle` are both derived from base class `Figure`. Suppose further that the two derived classes redefine method `draw`. Finally, assume that pointer `ptr` may point to either a `Circle` object or a `Rectangle` object. Under polymorphism, the statement

```
// draw a Circle or Rectangle
// depending on the type of object
// to which ptr points
ptr -> draw();
```

executes differently depending on whether `ptr` currently points to a `Circle` object or a `Rectangle` object. Polymorphism delays until run-time the determination of whether a `Circle`'s `draw` or a `Rectangle`'s `draw` is invoked. Accordingly, the programmer can use the same code

```
ptr -> draw();
```

to invoke different `draw` methods simply by having `ptr` point to different types of objects such as `Circles` and `Rectangles`.

C++ supports polymorphism through `virtual` methods and pointers. In the previous example, `draw` would be a `virtual` method and `ptr` would be a pointer to a `Figure` (`Figure*`), which means that `ptr` could point to both `Circles` and `Rectangles`. There is a sharp difference between `virtual` methods such as `draw` and nonvirtual functions (including nonvirtual methods) that happen to have the same name. For nonvirtual functions with the same name, the system determines at *compile-time* which of the functions to invoke. For `virtual` methods with the same name, the system determines at *run-time* which of the methods to invoke. The invoked method is determined by the type of object to which a pointer points. For example, if `ptr` currently points to a `Circle` object, then a `Circle`'s `virtual` method `draw` is invoked by

```
ptr -> draw();
```

If `ptr` currently points to a `Rectangle` object, then a `Rectangle`'s `virtual` method `draw` is invoked by the same statement.

"Pure" object-oriented languages such as Smalltalk have only run-time binding. C++ inherits compile-time binding from C and then adds run-time binding. In this sense, C++ is a hybrid language. Run-time binding in C++ is restricted to `virtual` functions and C++ allows only methods to be `virtual`. Pointers are also central to polymorphism in C++. To enable polymorphism, C++ allows a pointer to a base class (e.g., a pointer of type `Figure*`) to point to either a base class object (e.g., a `Figure`) or to any derived class object (e.g., a `Circle` or a `Rectangle`). No explicit cast is required to have the pointer point to a derived class object; and, of course, the derived class may be either directly or indirectly derived. The code slice

```
int main()
{
  Figure* ptr; // pointer to Figure
  Circle  c;   // Circle derived from Figure
  ptr = &c;    // ptr points to a Circle
  ...
}
```

illustrates. By contrast, a pointer to a derived class object (e.g., a pointer of type `Circle*`) may *not* point to a base class object without explicit casting. The code slice

```
int main()
{
  Figure fig;
  Circle* ptr;
  ptr = &fig;   // ***** ERROR: derived class pointer can't
                //       point to base class object
  ...
}
```

is illegal. It would be legal if a cast were included:

```
ptr = ( Circle* ) &fig;
```

We review these points with another example.

Example 5.4.1. Given

```
class B {
  ...
};

class D : public B {
  ...
};

B b;
D d;
B* ptr;
```

each of these assignment statements

```
ptr = &b;
ptr = &d;
```

is legal.

Given

```
class B {
  ...
};

class D : public B {
  ...
};

B b;
D d;
D* ptr;
```

the assignment

```
ptr = &d; // OK
```

is legal, but the assignment

```
// ***** ERROR: derived class pointer can't
//              point to base class object
ptr = &b;
```

is illegal.   □

A method to be bound at run-time must be flagged using the keyword
virtual; otherwise, compile-time binding is in effect as usual. After a
virtual method is defined for a base class, derived classes may tailor the
virtual method to their own needs by redefining it.

Example 5.4.2. In the code slice

```
class B {
public:
   virtual void g();
   int h();
};

class D : public B {
public:
   void g();
   int h();
};

int main()
{
   D d;
   B* ptr = &d;

   ptr -> h();     // B::h invoked
   ptr -> g();     // D::g invoked
   ...
}
```

the base class B contains a **virtual** method g, which derived class D then
redefines, and a nonvirtual method h. Since h is nonvirtual, compile-time
binding is in effect in the statement

```
ptr -> h();
```

Because ptr is of type B*, B's h is invoked. On the other hand, because g is
virtual, run-time binding is in effect in the statement

```
ptr -> g();
```

Because `ptr` points to an object of type D, D's **g** is invoked. It is legal for `ptr` to point to a D object even though `ptr` is of type B* because D is derived from B.

In compile-time binding, the data type of the pointer resolves which method is invoked. In run-time binding, the type of the object pointed to resolves which method is invoked. □

A derived class need not redefine a `virtual` method in the base class. If the `virtual` method is not redefined, it is simply inherited in the usual way by the derived class.

Example 5.4.3. In the code slice

```
class B {
public:
   virtual void g();
};

class D : public B {
public:
   int f( char );
};

int main()
{
   D d;
   d.g();  // D::g (inherited from B) is invoked
   ...
}
```

method **g** in class B is inherited by D in the usual way. □

If a derived class redefines a `virtual` method in the base class, the redefined method must have exactly the same prototype as the base class method; otherwise, the derived class method hides (see Example 5.1.15) the `virtual` method in the base class and compile-time binding is used.

Example 5.4.4. In the code slice

```
class B {
public:
   virtual void f( int );
};
```

```
class D : public B {
public:
    void f( float ); // hides B's f
};

int main()
{
    D d;
    B* ptr = &d;
    ptr -> f( 3.3 ); // B::f invoked
    ...
}
```

the parameter types of B::f and D::f differ; hence, D does *not* redefine f, but rather defines a *new* f that hides B's f. Furthermore, compile-time binding is used. Because ptr is of type B*, B::f is invoked in the statement

```
ptr -> f( 3.3 );
```

Because B::f expects an int argument, 3.3 is converted to the int value 3 by dropping the fractional part and 3 becomes the argument to B::f.   □

It is a compile-time error to attempt to redefine a **virtual** method and change the return type.

Example 5.4.5. In the code slice

```
class B {
public:
    virtual void f( int );
};

class D : public B {
public:
    // ***** ERROR: Can't change the return type
    int f( int );
};
```

D's attempt to change the return type of f from **void** to **int** results in an error.   □

Example 5.4.6. Consider the class hierarchy

```
class One {
public:
    void whoami() { cout << "One" << endl; }
};
```

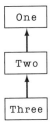

Figure 5.4.1 The One-Two-Three hierarchy.

```
class Two : public One {
public:
  void whoami { cout << "Two" << endl; }
};

class Three : public Two {
public:
  void whoami() { cout << "Three" << endl; }
};
```

(see Figure 5.4.1). Each class has a method whoami that prints its name to the standard output. When main executes

```
int main()
{
  // define three objects
  One one;
  Two two;
  Three three;

  // define an array of pointers to One
  One* array[ 3 ];

  // initialize array
  array[ 0 ] = &one;
  array[ 1 ] = &two;
  array[ 2 ] = &three;

  // have each object print its name
  for ( int i = 0; i < 3; i++ )
    array[ i ] -> whoami();

  return EXIT_SUCCESS;
}
```

the output is

```
One
One
One
```

It would be nice if the output were

```
One
Two
Three
```

instead. However, the system determines at *compile-time* which of the
whoami methods to invoke. Because the array elements are of type pointer
to One (One*), the system invokes One::whoami in each loop iteration despite the fact that array[1] points to a Two and array[2] points to a
Three.   □

Example 5.4.7. We slightly amend the code of Example 5.4.6 to get sig-
nificantly different behavior:

```
// This time, make whoami a virtual method.
class One {
public:
  virtual void whoami() { cout << "One" << endl; }
};

class Two : public One {
public:
  virtual void whoami { cout << "Two" << endl; }
};

class Three : public Two {
public:
  virtual void whoami() { cout << "Three" << endl; }
};

int main()
{
   // define three objects
   One one;
   Two two;
   Three three;

   // define an array of pointers to One
   One* array[ 3 ];

   // initialize array
```

```
      array[ 0 ] = &one;
      array[ 1 ] = &two;
      array[ 2 ] = &three;

      // have each object print its name
      for ( int i = 0; i < 3; i++ )
         array[ i ] -> whoami();

      return EXIT_SUCCESS;
   }
```

This time the output is

```
One
Two
Three
```

The only difference is that `whoami` is now a `virtual` method, which means that the system determines at *run-time*—not at compile-time—which of the three `whoami` to invoke. Because `array[ 0 ]` points to a `One`, the system invokes `One::whoami` for it. Because `array[ 1 ]` points to a `Two`, the system invokes `Two::whoami` for it. Because `array[ 2 ]` points to a `Three`, the system invokes `Three::whoami` for it.

The output in this example would be the same if the keyword `virtual` were omitted in the definitions of `Two::whoami` and `Three::whoami`. C++ adheres to the principle

- Once virtual, always virtual!

for `virtual` methods.   □

The next example shows the usefulness of polymorphism.

Example 5.4.8. Suppose that we have a database of books that is supported by the class hierarchy

```
class Book {
public:
   virtual void print();
   ...
};

class Textbook : public Book {
public:
   virtual void print();
   ...
};
```

```
class Referencebook : public Book {
public:
    virtual void print();
    ...
};
```

Each class derived from `Book` specializes `virtual` method `print` for its class. For example, `Textbook`'s `print` prints information about the book as well as courses for which the book is appropriate, the level of the book (e.g., elementary, high school, college), and so on. Similarly, `Referencebook`'s `print` prints information about the book as well as subject areas to which it is relevant, type of reference book (e.g., dictionary, journal), and so on.

Periodically, output is produced that lists all of the books in order together with information about each, which is supplied through the `print` methods. To facilitate the sort, the array

```
Book* list[ NoBooks ];
```

is defined and initialized to the various objects from the classes `Textbook` and `Referencebook` representing the books. After sorting, the output is produced by the loop

```
for ( int i = 0; i < NoBooks; i++ )
    list[ i ] -> print();
```

Because method `print` is `virtual`, if `list[ i ]` points to a `Textbook` object, `Textbook`'s `print` is invoked. If `list[ i ]` points to a `Referencebook` object, `Referencebook`'s `print` is invoked.

If the kinds of books are expanded by deriving additional classes from `Book`, the code for producing the output need not be changed. An added class would require only code for its version of `print`.

Sorting also could be supported through polymorphism. For example, if each class contained a `virtual` method `key` that returned the key on which to sort, the array `list` could be sorted by accessing the sort key as

```
list[ i ] -> key()
```

Now if the kinds of books are expanded by deriving additional classes from `Book`, the code for sorting would not have to be changed. An added class would require only code for its version of `key`.   □

Pure `virtual` Methods and Abstract Classes

An **abstract class** is a base class that is *required* to have a derived class. An abstract class is also called a **partial class**. The mechanism for declaring a class to be abstract is, however, subtle: we declare a **pure virtual method** in the abstract class's declaration.

Example 5.4.9. The code slice

```
class AC { // abstract class
   ...
public:
   virtual void f( int ) = 0; // pure virtual method
};
```

declares AC to be an abstract class, namely, a base class that must have a derived class. AC is made abstract by declaring f as a *pure virtual method*. This is done through the assignment statement

```
virtual void f( int ) = 0;  // f == 0
```

As a pure `virtual` method, f must be defined in a class derived from AC. For example, the code slice

```
class D : public AC {
   ...
public:
   virtual void f( int i ) {...}
};
```

satisfies the requirement that f be defined in a class derived from AC. □

Objects may *not* be created for an abstract class. Further, it is an error to invoke a pure `virtual` method if it has not been defined in a derived class.

Example 5.4.10. The code slice

```
class AC { // abstract class
public:
   virtual void f() = 0; // pure virtual method
   ...
};

class D : public AC {
public:
   virtual void f() {...} // f defined
   ...
};

AC ac;  // ***** ERROR: AC is abstract
D d;    // ok
```

contains an error because it defines ac as an object in an abstract class AC. Object d is defined legally. □

Abstract classes are a means of expressing program design requirements within C++. For example, suppose that a team of programmers is working

on a project. The manager partitions the project, giving each programmer a part of the system to code. The manager further specifies the project
requirements by declaring abstract classes, which is a way of forcing the programmers to code at least one derived class for each abstract class. Further,
the programmers are required to define, somewhere in the derived classes,
the pure virtual methods that make a base class abstract in the first place.

An abstract class may have its own definition for the pure virtual
method that makes it abstract, although this would be pointless because
an abstract class is not allowed to have objects that belong directly to it.
Nonetheless, a code slice such as

```
class AC {
public:
  virtual void f() = 0; // declare f pure
  ...
};

class D : public AC {
public:
  virtual void f() {...} // define f
  ...
};

void AC::f() // legal but pointless
{
  ...
}
```

is legal.

Miscellany

A virtual method may not be static because a virtual method is always
a member of a particular object in a class rather than a member of the class
as a whole. So a virtual method is nonstatic by its very nature.

To make a method virtual, we use the keyword virtual in the method's
declaration but not in its *definition* if this occurs outside the class declaration.

Example 5.4.11. In the code slice

```
class X {
public:
  virtual int f();      // declare
  virtual int g() {...} // define inline
};
```

```
int X::f() // virtual does NOT occur
{
   ...
}
```

f and g are both virtual. Technically, g is declared *and* defined inside X's declaration; but the keyword virtual is part of g's declaration, not its inline definition. In the case of f, the declaration and definition are separated: the keyword virtual occurs in the declaration but not in the definition, which occurs outside X's declaration. It would be an error for the keyword virtual to occur in X::f's definition.   □

Exercises

1. What is the output?

```
class A {
public:
   void f() { cout << "A!" << endl; }
};

class Z : public A {
public:
   void f() { cout << "Z!" << endl; }
};

int main()
{
   A* ptr;
   Z z;
   ptr = &z;
   ptr -> f();
   return EXIT_SUCCESS;
}
```

2. What is the output?

```
class A {
public:
   void f( int i ) { cout << "A!" << endl; }
};
```

```
class Z : public A {
public:
   void f( double x ) { cout << "Z!" << endl; }
};

int main()
{
   A* ptr;
   Z z;
   ptr = &z;
   ptr -> f( 9999999.9999 );
   return EXIT_SUCCESS;
}
```

3. What is the output?

```
class A {
public:
   virtual void f() { cout << "A!" << endl; }
};

class Z : public A {
public:
   virtual void f() { cout << "Z!" << endl; }
};

int main()
{
   A* ptr;
   Z z;
   ptr = &z;
   ptr -> f();
   return EXIT_SUCCESS;
}
```

4. What is the output?

```
class A {
public:
   virtual void f( int i ) { cout << "A!" << endl; }
};
class Z : public A {
public:
   virtual void f( double x ) { cout << "Z!" << endl; }
};
```

```
int main()
{
    A* ptr;
    Z z;
    ptr = &z;
    ptr -> f( 27 );
    return EXIT_SUCCESS;
}
```

5. What is the error?

```
class A {
public:
    void f() { cout << "A!" << endl; }
};

class Z : public A {
public:
    void f() { cout << "Z!" << endl; }
};

int main()
{
    A* ptr;
    Z z;
    ptr = &z;
    ptr -> f();
    ptr -> Z::f();
    return EXIT_SUCCESS;
}
```

6. Explain the difference between compile-time and run-time binding.

7. Is compile-time or run-time binding at work in this code slice?

```
class B {
public:
  int f( int );
};

class D : public B {
public:
  int f( float );
};
```

```
int main()
{
   D d1;
   B* ptr = &d1;

   ptr -> f();   // run-time or compile-time?
   ...
}
```

8. Explain why it does not make sense for a **virtual** method to be **static**.

9. Explain the error. (**g** and **f** are not methods.)

```
void g( int, int, double );
virtual int f( double );
```

10. Explain the error.

```
class A {
public:
   static virtual void f() {...}
};
```

11. What is an abstract class? Write code to illustrate.

12. What is a pure **virtual** method? Write code to illustrate.

13. Explain the relationship between an abstract class and a pure **virtual** method.

14. Explain the error.

```
class A {
public:
   virtual void f() = 0;
};

A a1, a2, a3;
```

15. Is this code legal?

```
class A {
   ...         // no virtual methods here
};
class B : public A {
public:
   virtual void f();
};
```

```
class C : public B {
public:
  virtual void f();
};
```

16. Is Z::f a virtual method?

```
class A {
public:
  virtual void f();
};
```

```
class Z : public A {
public:
  void f();
};
```

17. What is the error?

```
class A {
public:
    virtual void g();
};
```

```
virtual void A::g()
{
  ...
}
```

18. What is the error?

```
class A {
public:
    void virtual h();
};
```

```
void A::h()
{
  ...
}
```

5.5   Sample Application: Virtual Tree Traversal

Problem ──

Implement the standard binary tree traversals (inorder, preorder, and postorder) as `virtual` functions.

Solution ──

We revise the **binary search tree** of Section 4.4 so that class BST is now an abstract or partial class that declares `traverse` as a pure `virtual` function. There are three derived classes that then define `traverse`: InBST, PreBST, and PostBST. The BST methods that create a binary search tree and add Nodes to it remain unchanged.

C++ Implementation ────────────────────────────────

```
#include <iostream.h>

const char None = ' ';

class BST; class InBST; class PreBST; class PostBST;

class Node {
   friend BST;        // abstract class
   friend InBST;      // derived from BST
   friend PreBST;     // derived from BST
   friend PostBST;    // derived from BST
   char  val;  // value == contents
   Node* lc;   // left child
   Node* rc;   // right child
public:
   Node();                  // constructor
   int empty();   // val == None
   void write();
};

class BST {  // abstract class
protected:
   int count;
   Node* root;
   Node* tree;
   void addNodeAux( const char );
public:
   BST();
```

```
        BST( BST& );                    // copy constructor
        void addNode( const char );
        virtual void traverse() = 0; // pure virtual
    };

    class InBST : public BST {
        void inorderAux( Node* );
    public:
        void inorder();
        virtual void traverse(); // declaration
        InBST() : BST() { }
        InBST( BST& bst ) : BST( bst ) { }
    };

    void InBST::traverse()
    {
        inorder();
    }

    void InBST::inorder()
    {
        tree = root;
        inorderAux( root );
    }

    void InBST::inorderAux( Node* n )
    {
        if ( n -> empty() )
            return;
        inorderAux( n -> lc );
        n -> write();
        inorderAux( n -> rc );
    }

    class PreBST : public BST {
        void preorderAux( Node* );
    public:
        void preorder();
        virtual void traverse(); // declaration
        PreBST() : BST() { }
        PreBST( BST& bst ) : BST( bst ) { }
    };
```

```
void PreBST::traverse()
{
   preorder();
}
void PreBST::preorder()
{
   tree = root;
   preorderAux( root );
}

void PreBST::preorderAux( Node* n )
{
   if ( n -> empty() )
      return;
   n -> write();
   preorderAux( n -> lc );
   preorderAux( n -> rc );
}

class PostBST : public BST {
   void postorderAux( Node* );
public:
   void postorder();
   virtual void traverse( Node* ); // declaration
   PostBST() : BST() { }
   PostBST( BST& bst ) : BST( bst ) { }
};

void PostBST::postorder()
{
   // stub function
}

void PostBST::postorderAux( Node* n )
{
   // stub function
}

BST::BST()
{
   root = tree = new Node;
   count = 0;
}
```

```cpp
BST::BST( BST& bst )
{
   root = bst.root;
   tree = bst.tree;
   count = bst.count;
}

void BST::addNode( const char v )
{
   tree = root;        // start at root
   addNodeAux( v );
}

void BST::addNodeAux( const char v )
{
   if ( tree -> empty() ) {
      tree -> val = v;
      count++;
      tree -> lc = new Node;
      tree -> rc = new Node;
      return;
   }
   if ( v <= tree -> val )
      tree = tree -> lc;
   else
      tree = tree -> rc;
   addNodeAux( v );
}

Node::Node()
{
   lc = rc = 0;
   val = None;
}

int Node::empty( void )
{
   return val == None;
}

void Node::write( void )
{
   cout << val;
}
```

Discussion _____

There are moderate changes to the original code (see Section 4.4). The most significant is that BST is now an abstract class with **traverse** as its pure **virtual** method. BST has InBST, PreBST, and PostBST as three derived classes, each of which defines **traverse**. For example, InBST defines **traverse** to perform an inorder traversal of the BST

```
void InBST::traverse()
{
   inorder();
}
```

by invoking local method **inorder**. PreBST has a comparable local method **preorder** that produces a preorder traversal of the BST.

BST now has a copy constructor in addition to the default constructor. The code for copy constructor is straightforward:

```
BST::BST( BST& bst )
{
   root = bst.root;
   tree = bst.tree;
   count = bst.count;
}
```

Each derived class also has a default and a copy constructor with empty bodies. The constructors merely invoke their BST counterpart. Here is the InBST copy constructor:

```
InBST( BST& bst ) : BST( bst ) { }
```

The copy constructors have been added to allow code slices such as this:

```
int  main()
{
  BST* ptr;              // pointer to BST
  InBST in;              // create InBST object
  ...                    // add Nodes to the InBST
  ptr = &in;             // set pointer
  ptr -> traverse();     // invoke virtual function
                         //   InBST::traverse called to
                         //   perform inorder traversal
  PreBST pre( in );      // create PreBST object as a copy
                         //   of InBST object
  ptr = &pre;            // set pointer
  ptr -> traverse();     // invoke virtual function
  ...
}
```

The new program is more "object driven" than the original. In the original program, we build a BST and then *explicitly* invoke method `inorder` to perform an inorder traversal. If we want a preorder traversal instead, then we must *explicitly* invoke `preorder`. In the new program, we can invoke the virtual function `traverse` through a pointer, as in the code slice

```
int main()
{
   BST* ptr;            // pointer to BST
   ...                  // build a BST of one flavor
                        //   or another, e.g., PostBST
   ptr -> traverse();   // object determines what sort
                        //   of traversal is performed
   ...
}
```

The object to which `ptr` points determines what sort of traversal is performed. The programmer simply invokes `traverse` and lets the system determine at run-time the appropriate `virtual` function to call.

Exercises

---

1. The new code makes BST, InBST, PreBST, and PostBST all `friends` of Node. Why must BST still be a `friend`?

2. Name a major consequence of our decision to make BST an abstract class.

3. What is the mechanism by which BST is made an abstract class?

4. Must the keyword `virtual` be used in declaring `InBST::traverse` in order for the function to be `virtual`?

5. Is the keyword `virtual` used in the *definition* of `PreBST::traverse`?

6. Write the code for `PostBST::postorder`.

7. Write the code for `PostBST::postorderAux`.

8. Why does the new code have a copy constructor for BST?

9. Explain why the default and the copy constructor for `PreBST` have empty bodies.

10. How many definitions of `traverse` are required so that the pure `virtual` function requirement is met?

11. Summarize the difference in approach between the original BST program and the new one. Which strikes you as more object-oriented in design? Justify your answer.

5.6   Destructors Under Inheritance

Constructors in an inheritance hierarchy fire in a

- base class to derived class

order. Destructors in an inheritance hierarchy fire in a

- derived class to base class

order. So the destructors fire in the reverse order of the constructors.

Example 5.6.1. The output for the code slice

```
class A {
public:
   A() { cout << "A's constructor"; }
   ~A() { cout << "A's destructor"; }
};

class B : public A {
public:
   B() : A() { cout << "B's constructor"; }
   ~B() { cout << "B's destructor"; }
};

int main()
{
   void f();

   f();

   return EXIT_SUCCESS;
}

void f()
{
   B b;
}
```

is

```
A's constructor
B's constructor
B's destructor
A's destructor
```

□

A destructor's main job is to free storage that a constructor dynamically allocates. By firing in the reverse order of constructors, destructors ensure that the most recently allocated storage is the first storage to be freed.

Example 5.6.2. The output for the code slice

```
class B { // base class
  char* sB;
public:
  B()
  {
    sB = new char[ 3 ];
    cout << "B allocates 3 bytes" << endl;
  }

  ~B()
  {
    delete[ ] sB;
    cout << "B frees 3 bytes" << endl;
  }
};

class D : public B { // derived class
  char* sD;
public:
  D() : B()
  {
    sD = new char[ 5 ];
    cout << "D allocates 5 bytes" << endl;
  }

  ~D()
  {
    delete[ ] sD;
    cout << "D frees 5 bytes" << endl;
  }
};

int main()
{
  D d1;

  return EXIT_SUCCESS;
}
```

is

```
B allocates 3 bytes
D allocates 5 bytes
D frees 5 bytes
B frees 3 bytes
```

D's five bytes are allocated *after* B's three bytes, and D's five bytes are freed *before* B's three bytes. Note that the storage allocated by B's constructor is freed by B's destructor and that the storage allocated by D's constructor is freed by D's destructor.   □

Virtual Destructors

Constructors may *not* be `virtual` but destructors may be. The need for `virtual` destructors is best explained through an example.

Example 5.6.3. The output for the code slice

```cpp
class B {  // base class
  char* ptrB;
public:
  B()
  {
    ptrB = new char[ 5 ];
    cout << "B allocates 5 bytes" << endl;
  }

  ~B() // base class destructor
  {
    delete[ ] ptrB;
    cout << "B frees 5 bytes" << endl;
  }
};

class D : public B { // derived class
  char* ptrD;
public:
  D() : B()
  {
    ptrD = new char[ 1000 ];
    cout << "D allocates 1000 bytes" << endl;
  }

  ~D() // derived class destructor
  {
    delete[ ] ptrD;
```

```
            cout << "D frees 1000 bytes" << endl;
      }
};

int main()
{
      const int Forever = 1;
      void f();

      // generate lots of garbage
      while ( Forever ) {
        f();
      }

      return EXIT_SUCCESS;
}

void f()
{
      B* p = new D; // p points to a D object
      ...
      delete p;
}
```

is

```
B allocates 5 bytes
D allocates 1000 bytes
B frees 5 bytes
```

for each iteration of the **while** loop. On each entry to **f**, B's constructor
allocates five bytes and D's constructor allocates a thousand bytes. When **f**
exits, the thousand bytes allocated by D's constructor are not freed; instead,
only the five bytes allocated by B's constructor are freed.

The problem is that B's destructor is nonvirtual, which means that the
system must bind **p** at compile-time. Because **p** is of type B*, **p** is bound
to B's data members and methods, including constructors and destructors,
rather than to D's data members and methods. When **f** exits, B::~B frees
the five bytes. Yet D::~D fails to fire, thus leaving behind another thousand
bytes of garbage.

The solution is to make B::~B a **virtual** destructor:

```
class B {
  char* ptrB;
public:
```

```
B()
{
  ptrB = new char[ 5 ];
  cout << "B allocates 5 bytes" << endl;
}

virtual ~B() // virtual destructor
{
  delete[ ] ptrB;
  cout << "B frees 5 bytes" << endl;
}
};
```

In this case, p is bound at *run-time* to the data members and methods of the object to which it currently points. So if p points to a D object, as in f, then D::~D fires when control exits. B::~B also still fires when f exits because the D object to which p points is, by virtue of inheritance, a B object as well. With B::~B as a **virtual** destructor, our output becomes

```
B allocates 5 bytes
D allocates 1000 bytes
D frees 1000 bytes
B frees 5 bytes
```

□

The rule of thumb is that a destructor should be **virtual** whenever two conditions are met:

- Constructors for the base and the derived class dynamically allocate *separate* storage. In Example 5.6.3, for instance, B's constructor allocates storage to which ptrB points and D's constructor allocates separate storage to which ptrD points.

- The program dynamically allocates a class object. In Example 5.6.3, for instance, f dynamically allocates a D object.

Exercises

1. What is the output?

```
class X {
public:
  X() { cout << "X::X" << endl; }
  ~X() { cout << "X::~X" << endl; }
};
```

```
class Y : public X {
public:
  Y() : X() { cout << "Y::Y" << endl; }
  ~Y() { cout << "Y::~Y" << endl; }
};

class Z : public Y {
public:
  Z() : Y() { cout << "Z::Z" << endl; }
  ~Z() { cout << "Z::~Z" << endl; }
};

int main()
{
  Y y;
  Z z;

  return EXIT_SUCCESS;
}
```

2. In Exercise 1, make all the destructors **virtual**. Does the code run any differently than before?

3. For Exercise 1, list all the methods that Z has.

4. Must a derived class constructor invoke a base class constructor if one exists?

5. Must a derived class destructor invoke a base class destructor if one exists?

6. Can a constructor be **virtual**?

7. Give an example where a **virtual** destructor is required.

8. Must every destructor in an inheritance hierarchy be **virtual**?

9. What is the rule of thumb about whether a destructor should be made virtual?

10. Explain the connection between run-time binding and **virtual** destructors.

5.7 Multiple Inheritance

In **single inheritance**, a derived class has a single base class. In **multiple inheritance**, a derived class has multiple base classes (see Figure 5.7.1). In

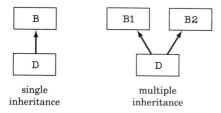

single   multiple
inheritance   inheritance

Figure 5.7.1 Single versus multiple inheritance.

technical jargon, a hierarchy with only single inheritance is a **tree**, whereas
a hierarchy with multiple inheritance is a **graph**.

In a single inheritance hierarchy, a derived class typically represents a
specialization of its base class. Because classes are user-defined data types
in C++, such a derived class is a specialization or refinement of the more
general data type that its base class represents. In a multiple inheritance hierarchy, a derived class typically represents a *combination* of its base classes.

Example 5.7.1. In the single inheritance hierarchy

```
// Window base class -- no scroll bars
class Win { // base class
protected:
   ...
};


// Scrolled window derived class -- scroll bars
class ScrollWin : public Win {
  Widget horizontalSB;
  Widget verticalSB;
   ...
};
```

a `ScrollWin` is a specialization of a `Win`. In particular, a `ScrollWin` has a
horizontal and a vertical scrollbar, which are not present in a `Win`.   □

Example 5.7.2. In the multiple inheritance hierarchy

```
// Popup menu class -- no scroll bars
class PopupMenu {
protected:
   int  menuChoices;
   Win* menuSubWins;
   ...
};
```

```
// Scrolled window class -- not a popup
class ScrollWin : public Win {
  Widget horizontalSB;
  Widget verticalSB;
  ...
};
```

```
// Combination of popup and scrolled
class ScrollPopupMenu :
    public PopupMenu, public ScrollWin {
  ...
};
```

a `ScrollPopupMenu` combines a `PopupMenu` and a `ScrollWin` to form a new class that inherits features from each of its base classes. □

Example 5.7.3. In the multiple inheritance hierarchy

```
class istream { // input
  ...
};
```

```
class ostream { // output
  ...
};
```

```
class iostream :
    public istream, public ostream { // input-output
  ...
};
```

an `iostream` is a class that supports input and output operations. It combines `istream`, which supports only input operations, and `ostream`, which supports only output operations. These classes and others are declared in the C++ header file *iostream.h*. Chapter 7 looks closely at the multiple inheritance hierarchy that C++ provides for input/output. □

Inheritance and Access

The rules of inheritance and access do *not* change from a single to a multiple inheritance hierarchy. A derived class inherits data members and methods from *all* its bases classes, regardless of whether the inheritance links are `private`, `protected`, or `public`.

Example 5.7.4. The code slice

```
// all public
class B1 { // base class 1
  ...
};

class B2 { // base class 2
  ...
};

class B3 { // base class 3
  ...
};

class D :
  public B1, public B2, public B3 { // derived class
 ...
};

// all private
class BB1 { // base class 1
  ...
};

class BB2 { // base class 2
  ...
};

class BB3 { // base class 3
  ...
};

class DD :
  private BB1, private BB2, private BB3 { // derived class
 ...
};

// mixed
class BBB1 { // base class 1
  ...
};

class BBB2 { // base class 2
  ...
};
```

```
class BBB3 { // base class 3
  ...
};

class DD :
    private BBB1, public BBB2, public BBB3 { // derived class
  ...
};
```

illustrates three possible combinations of inheritance. □

With multiple inheritance comes increased opportunities for name conflicts. The conflict can occur between the derived class and one of the base classes or between the base classes themselves. It is up to the programmer to resolve the conflict.

Example 5.7.5. In the code slice

```
class B1 { // base class 1
protected:
  int x;
};

class B2 { // base class 2
protected:
  int x;
};

class D : public B1, public B2 { // derived class
protected:
  int x;
public:
  friend void tester();
};

void tester()
{
  D d1;
  d1.x = 999;    // local x
  d1.B1::x = 111; // inherited from B1
  d1.B2::x = 222; // inherited from B2
  ...
}
```

the local x hides the inherited B1::x and B2::x. Further, B1 and B2 each
has a data member named x. The only way to resolve these conflicts is to
use the scope resolution operator in referencing either of the inherited x's. □

Virtual Base Classes

Multiple inheritance hierarchies can be complex, which may lead to the
situation in which a derived class inherits multiple times from the *same*
indirect base class.

Example 5.7.6. In the code slice

```
class B { // base class
protected:
  int x;
  ...
};

class D1 : public B { // path 1 through D1
protected:
  ...
};

class D2 : public B { // path 2 through D2
protected:
  ...
};

class Z : public D1, public D2 { // x comes twice
  ...
};
```

Z inherits x twice from B: once through D1 and again through D2 (see Figure
5.7.2). This is wasteful and confusing. We correct the problem by changing
D1 and D2 into virtual base classes for Z:

```
class B { // base class
protected:
  int x;
  ...
};

class D1 : public virtual B { // path 1 through D1
protected:
  ...
};
```

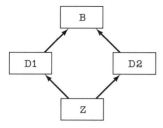

Figure 5.7.2 The need for `virtual` inheritance.

```
class D2 : public virtual B { // path 2 through D2
protected:
   ...
};

class Z : public D1, public D2 { // x comes once
   ...
};
```

There is now a single copy of x in Z. By making D1 and D2 into `virtual` base classes for Z, we tell them in effect to send to Z only one copy of whatever they inherit from their own common ancestor B. □

Exercises

---

1. Explain the difference between using inheritance (1) to *specialize* or *refine* a class or data type and (2) to *combine* classes or data types. Which type of C++ inheritance is best suited for each of (1) and (2)?

2. Change the code so that multiple rather than single inheritance is at work.

```
class A {
   ...
};

class B : public A {
   ...
};
```

3. How many data members does R have?

```
class P {
protected:
  int x;
  int y;
};

class Q {
protected:
  float a;
  float b;
};

class R : public P, public Q {
public:
  void f() {...}
};
```

4. Can an inheritance link be **private** under multiple inheritance? If so, illustrate with an example. If not, explain why not.

5. Write code to assign values to each of R's data members.

```
class P {
protected:
  int x;
  int y;
};
class Q {
protected:
  float a;
  float b;
};
class R : public P, public Q {
public:
  void f() {...}
};
```

6. Under multiple inheritance, can derived class D have a **public** inheritance link to one base class and a **private** inheritance link to another base class?

7. How many copies of x does D inherit?

```
class B {
protected:
  int x;
};
```

```
class B1 : public B {
protected:
  float y;
};

class B2 : public B {
  float z;
};

class D : public B1, public B2 {
  ...
};
```

8. How many copies of x does D inherit?

```
class B {
protected:
  int x;
};

class B1 : virtual public B {
protected:
  float y;
};

class B2 : virtual public B {
protected:
  float z;
};

class D : public B1, public B2 {
  ...
};
```

Common Programming Errors

1. It is an error to access a **private** data member outside its class except through a **friend** function. For example, the code slice

```
class C {
    int x;
};
```

```
int main()
{
  C c1;
  c1.x = 6; // ***** ERROR: x is private in C
  ...
}
```

contains an error because x is `private` in C and, therefore, accessible only to C's methods or `friends`.

2. It is an error to access a `protected` data member outside its class hierarchy except through a `friend` function. For example,

```
class C { // base class
protected:
    int x;
};

class D : public C { // derived class
    ...
};

int main()
{
  C c1;
  c1.x = 9; // ***** ERROR: x is protected in C
  ...
}
```

contains an error because x is accessible only to C's methods and `friends` and to methods and `friends` of certain classes, such as D, that are derived from C.

3. It is an error for a derived class to have more than one access-specifier per base class. The code slice

```
class BC { // base class
    ...
};

// ***** ERROR: only one access-specifier for
// each base class
class DC : public, private BC { // derived class
    ...
};
```

contains an error because DC's access to BC must be *either* `private` *or* `protected` *or* `public`. However, a derived class may have different access-specifiers for different base classes:

```
class BC1 { // base class 1
   ...
};

class BC2 { // base class 2
   ...
};

// ok
class DC : protected BC1, public BC2 {
   ...
};
```

4. If a base class has constructors but no default constructor, then a derived class constructor *must* explicitly invoke a base class constructor in its header:

```
class B {
   int x;
   int z;
public:
   // constructors -- but no default constructor
   B( int a ) { x = a; z = -1; }
   B( int a1, int a2 ) { x = a1; z = a2; }
};

class D1 : public B {
   int y;
public:
   // ***** ERROR: D( int ) must explicitly invoke
   //       one of B's constructors
   D1( int a ) { y = a; }
};

class D2 : public B {
   int y;
public:
   // ok -- D2 explicitly invokes a B
   // constructor in its header
   D2( int a ) : B( a ) { y = a; }
};
```

5. If a derived class has more than one base class, then it is an error to omit a comma that separates the access-specifiers for the base classes. Here are two examples:

```
class BC1 { // base class 1
   ...
};
class BC2 { // base class 2
   ...
};


// ***** ERROR: access-specifiers must be
// separated by commas
class DC1 : public BC1 public BC2 {
   ...
};


// correct
class DC2 : public BC1, public BC2 {
   ...
};
```

6. It is an error to use an access declaration to change the status of a base class member. The code slice

```
class BC { // base class
private:
   int y; // private in BC
public:
   int z; // public in BC
};
class DC : public BC { // derived class
protected:
   BC::y; // ***** ERROR: can't change to protected
   BC::z; // ***** ERROR: can't change to protected
};
```

7. If a derived class has a method with the same name as a base class method, then the derived class's method *hides* the base class method. It is therefore an error to invoke the base class method:

```
class BC { // base class
   ...
public:
   void f( double ); // method f
};
```

```
class DC : public BC { // derived class
   ...
public:
   void f( char* ); // CAUTION -- hides BC::f
};

int main()
{
   DC d;

   // ***** ERROR: DC::f, which hides BC::f,
   // expects a char* and not a double
   d.f( 3.14 );
   ...
}
```

8. It is an error to declare a nonmethod **virtual**. Only methods may be virtual. For example, the code slice

```
// ***** ERROR: f not a method
virtual int f( int, int );
```

contains an error because **f** is not a method.

9. A **virtual** method in a base class can only be redefined in a derived class if the derived class declares the method with the same prototype as the base class method. If the arguments are changed, the result is a *new* method that hides the **virtual** method in the base class. Furthermore, run-time binding is disabled. For example, in the code slice

```
class BC { // base class
public:
   virtual int f( char*, double );
};

class DC : public BC { // derived class
public:
   virtual int f( int ); // DC's f hides BC's f
};
```

BC::f is not in the scope of class DC. BC::f can only be accessed within class DC by using the scope resolution operator. Furthermore, compile-time binding will be used.

10. It is an error to declare a method in a derived class with the same parameter types as a `virtual` method in the base class but with a different return type:

```
class BC { // base class
public:
   virtual int f( char*, double );
};

class DC : public BC { // derived class
public:
   // ***** ERROR: different return type
   virtual double f( char*, double );
};
```

11. It is an error for a `virtual` method to be declared `static`.

12. It is an error to include the keyword `virtual` in a `virtual` method's *definition* if the definition occurs outside the class declaration. The code slice

```
class C {
public:
   virtual int f(); // declaration -- ok
   virtual int g() {...} inline definition -- ok
};

// ***** ERROR: virtual must not appear in
// definition outside class declaration
virtual int C::f()
{
   ...
}
```

13. It is an error to make a constructor `virtual`. However, a destructor may be `virtual`.

14. It is an error for an abstract or partial class not to have a derived class.

15. It is an error to define an object in an abstract class. However, objects may belong to a class derived from the abstract class. In the code slice

```
class AC { // abstract class
public:
   virtual int f() = 0; // pure virtual function
   ...
};
```

```
class DC : public AC { // derived class
   ...
};

// ***** ERROR: can't define AC objects
AC ac1;

DC dc1; // ok -- DC derived from AC
```

the attempted definition of `ac1` is thus illegal, whereas the definition of `dc1` is legal.

Programming Exercises

5.1. Implement a `Library` hierarchy with at least a dozen classes. For purposes of the exercise, consider a *library* to be a collection of literary or artistic materials that are not for sale. In addition to the constructors and destructors, classes should include methods that describe the class much in the way that a human librarian might describe a class or subclass of materials among library's holdings.

5.2. Implement a `LAN` (local area network) hierarchy by using the `LAN` class of Programming Exercise 4.3 as a base class. Subclasses may be derived to represent different topologies such as *star*, *ring*, *bus*, and *hub*. Data members should represent properties such as *transmission medium, access control method, data frame format, standards, data rate*, and the like. For at least one subclass, simulate the activity of nodes in such a `LAN`.

5.3. Implement an `Employee` hierarchy for any type of business with which you are familiar. The hierarchy should have at least four levels, with inheritance of data members and methods. There should be methods for hiring, firing, promoting, demoting, transferring, and retiring `Employees`. Also, there should be methods for calculating raises and bonuses for `Employees` in keeping with both their category (e.g., hourly-wage versus salaried) and their performance. The inheritance hierarchy also should be used to provide different types of access to `Employees`. For example, the type of access granted the general public presumably would differ from the type of access provided to an `Employee`'s supervisor, to the payroll department, or to the FBI. Use inheritance to distinguish among at least four different types of access to `Employee` information.

5.4. Implement a `ProgLang` hierarchy in which classes represent types of programming language. The hierarchy should begin with an abstract class that has a `virtual` method to place a sample language in the hierarchy. For example, given C++ as a sample language, the method would identify it as an object-oriented language; given LISP as a sample language, the method would identify it as a functional or applicative language. The hierarchy also should include a method that identifies code slices. For example, given the code slice

```
for ( i = 0; i < n; i++ ) {
   ...
}
```

the method would identify the language as `C_Type`, where `C_Type` is a base class with `C` and `CPlusPlus` as derived classes. Given the code slice

```
for ( int i = 0; i < n; i++ ) {
   ...
}
```

the method would identify the language as `CPlusPlus`. The hierarchy should include at least six classes in addition to the abstract class `ProgLang`.

5.5. Implement an `Automobile` within a multiple inheritance hierarchy. In addition to being a `Vehicle`, an `Automobile` is also a `Commodity`, a `StatusSymbol`, a `ModeOfTransport`, and so on. `Automobile` should be have at least three base classes and at least three derived classes. Use `virtual` inheritance wherever appropriate.

5.6. Implement a `Graph` hierarchy with `Graph` as the base class (see Programming Exercise 4.9). Sample derived classes are

- `UndirectedGraph` in which each edge is associated with an *unordered* pair of vertices.

- `DiGraph` (*Di*rected *Graph*) in which each edge is associated with a an *ordered* pair of vertices.

- `WeightedGraph` in which each edge is labelled with a number that represents its weight, which is the cost of the edge.

- `CompleteGraph` in which there is an edge between each distinct pair of vertices.

- `AcyclicGraph` in which there are no cycles.

- `ConnectedGraph` in which there is a path between each pair of distinct vertices.

The hierarchy should have methods appropriate to all graphs (e.g., search methods) as well as methods particular to a specific type of graph (e.g., methods to compute the cost of a path in a `WeightedGraph`).

5.7. Implement a hierarchy of numeric data types that extends the fundamental data types such as `int` and `float` available in C++. You could begin with classes such as `BigInt` (see Programming Exercise 4.1) and `Complex` (see Section 3.6). Other candidate classes include `Fraction`, `Vector`, and `Matrix`. Each class in the hierarchy should have methods that extend, where appropriate, the built-in arithmetic operators to the class.

5.8. Implement a `GeoFig` class that represents geometrical figures such as *point*, *line*, *rectangle*, *triangle*, and the like. Provide `virtual` methods to draw, enlarge, move, and destroy such objects. The hierarchy should consists of at least a dozen classes.

5.9. Implement a `Task` hierarchy that provides classes suitable for simulation. A `Task` has basic temporal properties such as

- Earliest start time.
- Latest start time.
- Earliest finish time.
- Latest finish time.
- Duration.

A `Task` also requires one or more **resources**. For example, the `Task` of mowing the lawn requires a lawn mower, trimming shears, and so on. So a `Task` should have data members to reflect *resource requirements*. A `Task` also has temporal constraints with respect to other `Tasks`. For example, in steel making, the `Task` of casting the steel into a bar cannot begin until the `Task` of heating the steel has finished. Temporal constraints on `Tasks` can be implemented as relations such as

- Start-before-start (e.g., T_i must start before T_j starts).
- Start-after-finish (e.g., T_i must start after T_j finishes).
- Finish-after-finish (e.g., T_i must finish after T_j finishes).

Provide at least half a dozen temporal relations by which the user can constrain `Tasks`. Document the methods that define a `Task`'s public interface and include a graphical depiction of the class hierarchy.

5.10. Implement a `Sequence` hierarchy where a **sequence** is an ordered collection of none or more items. Vectors, character strings, linked-lists, stacks, queues, and dequeues then can be derived directly or indirectly from `Sequence`. The hierarchy should contain a rich assortment of methods to handle operations such as creating and destroying `Sequences`, adding objects and removing them from `Sequences`, and so forth. Wherever possible, `virtual` methods should be used so that the user has the same public interface whatever the particular type of `Sequence`. For instance, a method such as `insert` should be `virtual` so that the user invokes `insert` regardless of the particular `Sequence` type (e.g., `StackSeq` or `QueueSeq`).

5.11. Zoology offers rich examples of inheritance hierarchies from phyla to species to levels of subspecies (see Example 5.2.2). Implement a zoological hierarchy that has at least six levels of derivation and twelve classes.

5.12. Implement an `ErrorCode` hierarchy. Error codes are used in data communications to detect and to correct errors that occur when digital information is transmitted over a channel from a sender to a receiver. Two broad classes are `ForwardErr` and `BackwardErr` codes: the former codes include sufficient information so that the receiver can fix a detected error in place, whereas the latter codes provide only enough information so that the receiver can detect an error and "fix" it by requesting retransmission of the data. Subclasses of `ErrorCode` include *parity, block sum, Hamming,* and *cyclic redundancy codes.* For further details, consult a text in data communications such as Fred Halsall, *Data Communications, Computer Networks, and Open Systems* (New York: Addison-Wesley, 1993).

Chapter 6

Operator Overloading

In C++, built-in operators such as + and [ ] may be overloaded so that they extend beyond primitive built-in data types to apply to classes as well. For example, the + operator can be extended beyond `ints` and `floats` so that it applies to `Strings` for concatenation (see Section 4.1). In this chapter, we cover the basics of operator overloading and then illustrate more advanced uses that make it easier to write applications in C++.

6.1   Basic Operator Overloading

C++ allows any operator to be overloaded except for these five:

```
.        // class member operator
.*       // class member dereference operator
::       // scope resolution operator
?:       // conditional operator
sizeof   // size in bytes operator
```

Every overloaded operator in a base class, except the assignment operator (=), is inherited in a derived class.

An overloaded operator is a user-defined *function* that retains the convenience of *operator syntax*. The technical name for an overloaded operator, **operator function**, underscores the point. In general, an overloaded operator must be either a method or include a class object among its arguments. The exceptions are the memory-management operators, that is, the `new`, `delete`, and `delete[ ]` operators. These three operators may be overloaded as toplevel operator functions that need not take class objects as arguments. Particular operators such as the subscript operator [ ] and function call operator () must be implemented as methods.

Example 6.1.1. The code slice

```
// ***** ERROR: neither a method nor a
// a function that takes a class argument
void operator%( const float f1, const float f2 )
{
   ...
}
```

contains an error because an overloaded operator must be either a class method or take a class object as an argument.   □

It makes sense for C++ to require that an integer operator such as % either be overloaded as a method or take at least one class object as an argument. Otherwise, in an expression such as

```
int x = 11, y = 3, z;
z = x % y;
```

the system could not distinguish between the built-in % and some user-defined %. If % is overloaded either as a method or as an operator function that takes a class object as an argument, then the system can determine which % operator to invoke in a particular context.

Example 6.1.2. The code slice

```
// ***** ERROR: [ ] must be overloaded as a method
void operator[ ]( String s ) {...}
```

contains an error because the subscript operator [ ] must be overloaded as a method rather than as a toplevel function. The same holds for the function call operator (). If these operators could be overloaded as nonmethods, then the system could not determine in a particular context whether to invoke the built-in or some user-defined version.   □

Example 6.1.3. The code slice

```
Complex Complex::operator-( const Complex c ) const
{
    return Complex( real - c.real,
                    imag - c.imag );
}
```

comes from the `Complex` class (see Section 3.6). The example meets both requirements for overloading an operator because `operator-` is a method in the `Complex` class and also takes a `Complex` object as an argument.   □

Example 6.1.4. Because code slice

```
String& operator+( const String s1, const String s2 ) const
{
    ...
}
```

has a class object—a `String`—as an argument, it does not contain an error even though `operator+` is overloaded as a toplevel function rather than a method. One `String` argument would be sufficient to meet the requirement.   □

Operator Precedence and Syntax

Operator precedence and syntax cannot be changed through overloading. For example, the binary operator || always occurs *between* its two arguments, whether built-in or overloaded; and || retains its original precedence even when overloaded.

Example 6.1.5. In the code slice

```
int main()
{
  Complex c1( 1, 1.1 );
  Complex c2( 2, 2.2 );
  Complex c3( 3, 3.3 );
  Complex ans;

  ans = c1 + c2 * c3;
  ...
}
```

the expression

```
ans = c1 + c2 * c3;
```

is equivalent to

```
ans = c1 + ( c2 * c3 );
```

There is no way to change the precedence of the built-in operators + and *
so that, for example, `Complex::+` had higher precedence than `Complex::*`.
Also, the *binary* operator + always occurs *between* its two arguments. There
is no way to overload the binary + so that it occurred either before or after
its two arguments. In similar fashion, the unary + in C++ always occurs
before its argument, even if the operator is overloaded.   □

Operator Arity

If a built-in operator is unary, then all overloads remain unary. If a built-in
operator is binary, then all overloads remain binary. In technical terms, overloading an operator cannot change its **arity**. Operator arity can be tricky
because overloaded operators have two different syntactic forms: *method
syntax* and *operator syntax*. We illustrate with a series of examples.

Example 6.1.6. The code slice

```
// ***** ERROR: overloaded + must be binary
Complex Complex::operator+ ( const Complex c1,
                             const Complex c2 )
{
  ...
}
```

overloads `operator+` as a *method* in class `Complex`. The code contains an
error because the built-in addition operator + is *binary*, not ternary. Therefore, the overloaded `Complex::operator+` also must be binary, which means
that it must take *one* rather than two arguments. Recall that an expression
such as

```
c3 = c2 + c1; // operator syntax
```

is a convenient alternative to

```
c3 = c2.operator+( c1 ); // method syntax
```

In order to be a binary operator, the overloaded `Complex::operator+` thus needs a *single* argument because the other operand is a class object such as c2.

If we overloaded `operator+` as a `friend` to `Complex` rather than as a `Complex` method, then the operator would take two arguments:

```
class Complex {
  ...
friend:
  void operator+( Complex c1, Complex c2 )
  {
    ...
  }
  ...
};
```

Note that the + operator is binary as either a method or a toplevel `friend`. The issue is one of *syntax* only.   □

Example 6.1.7. The code slice

```
void Complex::operator%()
{
  ...
}
```

contains an error because the built-in modulus operator % is *binary*, not unary. Therefore, the overloaded `Complex::operator%` must be binary as well, which means that `Complex::operator%`—a method—needs exactly one argument. We can correct the error as follows

```
void Complex::operator%( Complex c )
{
  ...
}
```

□

As these examples illustrate, care must be taken in distinguishing between operators defined as class methods and operators defined as toplevel functions (for instance, as `friends`) that expect class objects as arguments. The point to keep in mind is that a binary operator overloaded as a class method takes *one* argument, as the other argument is the class object itself. A binary operator overloaded as a a toplevel function takes *two* arguments.

A unary argument overloaded as a class method takes *no* arguments, whereas a unary operator overloaded as a toplevel function takes *one* argument.

Example 6.1.8. Here is an overload of the binary operator && as a class method:

```
// && overloaded as a class method
class C {
public:
  // method -- 1 argument
  int operator&&( C c )
  {
    ...
  }
  ...
};

int main()
{
  C c1;
  C c2;

  if ( c1 && c2 ) // same as: if ( c1.operator&&(c2 ) )
  ...
}
```

The operator function takes a single argument, as the other argument is the class object itself—in this case, c1. Here is the same operator overloaded as a friend to C, but implemented as a toplevel function:

```
class C {
  ...
friend:
  // not a method -- 2 arguments
  int operator&&( C comp1, C comp2 )
  {
    ...
  }
};

int main()
{
  C c1, c2;
  if ( c1 && c2 ) // same as: if ( operator&&( c1, c2 ) )
  ...
}
```

Now the operator function takes two arguments, as it is *not* a method but a toplevel function.   □

The increment ++ and decrement operators -- are among those that can be overloaded in C++. Recall that each operator comes in a *prefix* and a *postfix* flavor:

```
int x = 6;
++x;        // prefix ++
x++;        // postfix ++
```

Accordingly, we can overload the prefix ++, the postfix ++, the prefix --, and the postfix --. Such overloads can be used to ensure, for example, that pointers to array cells always point to a cell within the array's bounds. We begin with an example that overloads the prefix increment operator. We give the code and then explain it:

```
#include <iostream.h>
#include <string.h>
#include <stdlib.h>

// safe string -- ptr can't fall off the end
// when incremented with the SafeStr::operator++
class SafeStr {
   char* str;
   int size;
public:
   char* ptr;
   SafeStr();
   SafeStr( char* );
   ~SafeStr();
   char* operator++();
};

char* SafeStr::operator++()
{
   if ( *ptr != '\0' )   // bounds check
      return ++ptr;      // ok to increment
   else
      return  ptr;       // not ok to increment
}

SafeStr::SafeStr()
{
   str = ptr = new char[ 1 ];
   *str = '\0';
```

```
      size = 0;
   }

   SafeStr::SafeStr( char* s )
   {
      size = strlen( s );
      str = ptr = new char[ size + 1 ];
      strcpy( str, s );
   }

   SafeStr::~SafeStr()
   {
      delete[ ] str;
   }
```

SafeStr has two variables of type char*: str is a **private** data member that always points to the first **char** in a character string, whereas ptr is a **public** data member that may point to any **char** in the string. The code slice

```
   int main()
   {
     SafeStr s1( "foo" ); // length is 3

     // ***** NOTE: 100 increments for a
     // string of length 3
     for ( int i = 0; i < 100; i++ ) {
        cout << s1.ptr << endl;
        ++s1;   // increment ptr
     }
     ...
   }
```

produces the output

```
   foo
   oo
   o
   ... // empty strings with line feeds
```

After the loop's third iteration, s1.ptr points to the cell that holds the null terminator. The if test in the overloaded ++ operator

```
   char* SafeStr::operator++()
   {
      if ( *ptr != '\0' )   // bounds check
         return ++ptr;      // ok to increment
      else
```

```
        return ptr;        // not ok to increment
  }
```

therefore fails because the value of *ptr is indeed the null terminator. Accordingly, s1.ptr is not incremented during the remaining loop iterations as this would result in its pointing to cells beyond those allocated to hold foo and a null terminator. □

We now give an example that overloads both prefix and postfix versions of the increment operator ++. The declaration

```
    operator++();
```

with no parameters describes the prefix operator and the declaration

```
    operator++( int );
```

with a single int parameter describes the postfix operator. (Similar comments apply to the decrement operator.) The int parameter in the postfix form serves to distinguish this form from the prefix form. The parameter itself may be but need not be used.

If class C overloads the prefix increment operator and obj is an object in class C, the expression

```
    ++obj
```

is equivalent to

```
    obj.operator++()
```

Either expression may be used.

If class C overloads the postfix increment operator and obj is an object in class C, the expression

```
    obj++
```

is equivalent to

```
    obj.operator++( 0 )
```

Either expression may be used. The method may also be invoked with an arbitrary argument n:

```
    obj.operator++( n )
```

Example 6.1.9. Class Clock overloads both the prefix and postfix ++ operator:

```
    class Clock {
       int hour;
       int min;
       int ap; // 0 is AM, 1 is PM
    public:
       Clock( int, int, int );
```

```
     Clock tick();
     void print_time();
     Clock operator++();      // ++c
     Clock operator++( int ); // c++
};

Clock::Clock( int h = 12, int m = 0, int ap_flag = 0 )
{
   hour = h;
   min = m;
   ap = ap_flag;
}

Clock Clock::tick()
{
   ++min;
   if ( min == 60 ) {
      hour++;
      min = 0;
   }

   if ( hour == 13 )
      hour = 1;

   if ( hour == 12 && min == 0 )
      ap = !ap;

   return *this;
}

Clock Clock::operator++()
{
   return tick();
}

Clock Clock::operator++( int n )
{
   Clock c = *this;
   tick();
   return c;
}
```

```
void Clock::print_time()
{
   cout << setfill( '0' ) << setw( 2 ) << hour
        << ':' << setw( 2 ) << min
        << setfill( ' ' );
   if ( ap )
      cout << " PM";
   else
      cout << " AM";
   cout << endl;
}
```

The prefix and postfix increment operators are overloaded so as to act on Clocks just as the built-in prefix and postfix increment operators act on numeric types such as ints. If c is a Clock, c++ advances the time one second. The value of the *expression* c++ is the *original* Clock. Executing ++c also advances the time one second, but the value of the expression ++c is the *updated* Clock.

The default constructor sets the clock to 12:00 AM. Method tick adds one second to the Clock and then returns it. Method operator++() overloads the prefix increment operator. It advances the time one second by invoking tick and returns the updated Clock.

Method operator++(int) serves to overload the postfix increment operator. It saves the current Clock, referenced as *this, in c. It then advances the time one second by invoking tick and returns c, the (unchanged) original Clock. The parameter n is not used.

The method print_time prints the time in the form

xx:xx XX

where XX is either AM or PM.

The output of the code

```
int main()
{
   Clock c, d;
   c = d++;
   cout << "Clock c: ";
   c.print_time();
   cout << "Clock d: ";
   d.print_time();
   ...
}
```

is

```
Clock c: 12:00 AM
Clock d: 12:01 AM
```

The output of the code

```
int main()
{
  Clock c, d;
  c = ++d;
  cout << "Clock c: ";
  c.print_time();
  cout << "Clock d: ";
  d.print_time();
  ...
}
```

is

```
Clock c: 12:01 AM
Clock d: 12:01 AM
```

□

Exercises

---

1. Explain the error.

```
class C {
  void operator.( C c1, C c2 );
  ...
};
```

2. Explain the error.

```
int operator,( int i1, int i2, int i3 )
{
  ...
}
```

3. Explain the error.

```
class C {
  int operator||( C c1, C c2, C c3 );
  ...
};
```

4. For class C, write code that overloads the unary + as a method.

5. Overload the && operator as a toplevel **friend** to C.

6. For class C, write code that overloads the binary + as a method.

7. Overload the binary + operator as a toplevel **friend** to C.

8. Overload the /= operator for class **Complex**. Implement the overloaded operator as a method.

9. Does this code slice

```
class C {
public:
  void operator->*( const char* a ) {...}
  ...
};
```

contain an error?

10. List the C++ operators that cannot be overloaded.

11. Must an overloaded operator always be either a class method or take at least one class object as an argument?

12. Define a class **Odd** that consists of odd integers. Overload the ++ operator so that it increments the integer by two.

13. Take a stand for or against the C++ policy that the **sizeof** operator cannot be overloaded.

14. If an operator is binary, must an operator function that overloads it take two arguments? Explain.

15. For class C, write code that overloads the comma operator.

16. Add to class **SafeStr** an overload of the postfix increment operator.

6.2 Sample Application: Bounds Checking

Problem _____

Implement **bounds checking** that detects illegal array subscripts.

Solution _____

We create a **Matrix** class, where a **matrix** is a two-dimensional array with the same number of rows and columns. We overload the function call operator () to act as subscript operator that checks whether indexes into a **Matrix** fall within bounds. If indexes are out of bounds, then an error message is printed.

C++ Implementation _____

```cpp
#include <iostream.h>
#include <stdlib.h>

const int MaxSide = 1000;
int OverflowFlag = -999;

class Matrix {
   int* cells;
   int side;
   void toobig( int );
   void overflow( int, int );
public:
   Matrix( int );  // constructor
  ~Matrix();       // destructor
   void dump();    // print contents
   int& operator()( int, int ); // row-col access
};

Matrix::Matrix( int s )
{
   // allowable size?
   if ( s > MaxSide )  {
      toobig( s );
      return;
   }

   // allocate s * s matrix cells
   cells = new int[ s * s ];
   side = s;
}

Matrix::~Matrix()
{
   // deallocate storage from constructor
   delete[ ] cells;
}

void Matrix::toobig( int s )
{
   cout << s << " exceeds MaxSide of "
        << MaxSide << "." << endl;
}
```

```
void Matrix::overflow( int r, int c )
{
   cout << "\n\tRow-Col reference "  << r
       << "-" << c << " is out of bounds."
       << endl;
}

// overload () for use as bounds-checking
// subscript operator
int& Matrix::operator()( int r, int c )
{
   // row-col reference in bounds?
   if ( r < 0       ||
        c < 0       ||
        r >= side  ||
        c >= side ) {
      overflow( r, c );
      return OverflowFlag;
   }
   else
      return cells[ r * side + c ];
}
```

Discussion

The user creates a bounds-checked **Matrix** through code such as

```
Matrix m1( 8 );   // 8 by 8 matrix
```

and manipulates it through code such as

```
m1( 1, 1 ) = 26; // m1[ 1 ][ 1 ] = 26

// store i * j in each matrix cell
for ( int i = 0; i < 8; i++ )
  for ( int j = 0; j < 8; j++ )
    m1( i, j ) = i * j;

cout << m1( 4, 6 ); // cout << m1[ 4 ][ 6 ]
```

Because **m1** is an 8×8 **Matrix**, the legal indexes for either a row or a column range between 0 and 7. An expression such as

```
m1( 8, 4 ) = -999; // 8 is illegal index
```

causes the warning message

```
Row-Col reference 8-4 is out of bounds.
```

to be printed to the standard output. The definition of the overloaded ()
operator

```
// overload () for use as bounds-checking
// subscript operator
int& Matrix::operator()( int r, int c )
{
   // row-col reference in bounds?
   if ( r < 0      ||
        c < 0      ||
        r >= side  ||
        c >= side ) {
      overflow( r, c );
      return OverflowFlag;
   }
   else
      return cells[ r * side + c ];
}
```

includes a test to ensure that the row and the column index (parameters
r and c, respectively) fall within bounds, which means that the index can
take values between 0 and side - 1. The operator function returns an int
reference rather than an int value so that a Matrix can occur on either side
of an assignment expression:

```
int num;
Matrix m1( 8 );
m1( 4, 4 ) = 1234; // left side
num = m1( 4, 4 );  // right side
```

If Matrix::operator() returned a value rather than a reference, then a
Matrix such as m1 could occur only on the right side of an assignment expression, which would not be very useful.

A Matrix's internal representation is hidden from the user, who sees
a Matrix as a two-dimensional object with the same number of rows as
columns. In its internal implementation, a Matrix is one-dimensional: cells
points to the first of side * side dynamically allocated int cells. An assignment expression such as

```
m1( 4, 3 ) = 77; //
```

causes 77 to be stored in int cell

```
4 * side + 3
```

Assuming side is 8, then 77 is stored at position 35:

```
4 * 8 + 3  // cells[ 35 ] = 77
```

The Matrix class also has a destructor to deallocate the storage to which
cells points. The public method dump prints to the standard output each

cell's value. The `private` method `toobig` ensures that a `Matrix`'s `side` does not exceed `MaxSide`, and `private` method `overflow` produces the error message for out-of-bounds references.

Exercises

1. Write the code to implement `Matrix::dump`.

2. Change the appropriate `Matrix` methods so that, in case of overflow, the offending index is highlighted. For example, if `m1` is an 8×8 `Matrix`, then an expression such as

   ```
   m1( 3, 9 ) = 88;
   ```

   should single out 9 as the offending index. The index 3 is within bounds.

3. Write the `Matrix` method `copy` that copies one `Matrix`'s cells to the other's. The method must ensure that the two `Matrix`es are of the same size.

4. Write the method `Matrix::change_dim` that changes a `Matrix`'s dimensions:

   ```
   Matrix m1( 8 );        // 8-by-8
   ...
   m1.change_dim( 12 );   // 12-by-12
   ...
   m1.change_dim( 3 );    // 3-by-3
   ```

   It is understood that data may be lost when a `Matrix` changes its dimensions.

5. Explain why `Matrix::operator()` returns an `int` reference rather than an `int` value.

6. The method `Matrix::operator()` returns a reference to `OverflowFlag` in case a `Matrix` reference is out-of-bounds. Why is anything returned at all? Take out the `return` statement in the if-body and test your compiler's reaction.

7. Could `OverflowFlag` be made `const` as the implementation now stands? Explain.

8. Why do you suppose that we overloaded the function call operator () instead of the subscript operator [ ] in this application? Could we have overloaded the subscript operator instead? Explain.

9. Is there any other C++ operator that we could have overloaded to serve
    as a bounds-checking subscript operator for a **Matrix**?

10. Modify the **Matrix** class so that the user can specify, as optional **int**
    arguments to the constructor, the range of legal indexes. For example,
    code such as

    ```
    Matrix m1( 8, 1, 8 );
    ```

    means that **m1** is an 8×8 **Matrix** with legal indexes that range between
    1 and 8 instead of between 0 and 7.

6.3   Sample Application: An Associative Array

Problem _____

Implement an **associative array**, that is, an array that accepts as indexes
noninteger expressions such as character strings.

Solution _____

We create a *dictionary* class implemented as an array of *word-definition* pairs
together with appropriate methods. In particular, one method overloads the
subscript operator [ ] so that a word (character string) may be used as an
index into the array. The overloaded operator prints the word's definition if
the word occurs in the dictionary. We also overload the function call operator
() for use as an iterator (see Section 4.5). Our implementation is inspired
by an example in Bjarne Stroustrup, *The C++ Programming Language*, 2nd
ed., (Reading, Mass.: Addison-Wesley, 1992).

C++ Implementation _____

```
#include <iostream.h>
#include <string.h>

const int MaxWord = 100;
const int MaxDef = 1000;
const int MaxEntries = 100000;

class Entry {
   char word[ MaxWord + 1 ];
   char def[ MaxDef + 1 ];
public:
```

```
   Entry()
   {
      strcpy( word, "" );
      strcpy( def, "" );
   }

   void write() const;
   void add( const char*, const char* );
   int match( const char* ) const;
};

void Entry::write() const
{
   cout << word << " defined as "
        << def << "." << endl;
}

void Entry::add( const char* w, const char* d )
{
   strcpy( word, w );
   strcpy( def, d );
}

int Entry::match( const char* key ) const
{
   return strcmp( key, word ) == 0;
}

class DictIter;

class Dict {
friend class DictIter;
   Entry entries[ MaxEntries + 1 ];
   int count;      // how many entries
public:
   Dict() { count = 0; }
   void dump();
   void add( const char*, const char* );
   void operator[ ]( const char* ) const;
};
```

```cpp
void Dict::dump()
{
   for ( int i = 0; i < count; i++ )
      entries[ i ].write();
}

void Dict::add( const char* w, const char* d )
{
   if ( count < MaxEntries )
      entries[ count++ ].add( w, d );
   else
      cout << count << " exceeds MaxEntries." <<
      endl;
}

void Dict::operator[ ]( const char* k ) const
{
   int i = 0;

   // sequential search -- inefficient
   while ( i < count )
      if ( entries[ i ].match( k ) ) {
         entries[ i ].write();
         break;
      }
      else
         i++;
   if ( i == count )
      cout << k << " not in dictionary." << endl;
}

class DictIter {
   int current;
   Dict* dict;
public:
   DictIter( Dict& d )
   {
      dict = &d;
      current = 0;
   }
   Entry* operator()();
};
```

```
Entry* DictIter::operator()()
{
    if ( current >= dict -> count )  // at end?
        return 0;
    return &dict -> entries[ current++ ];
}
```

Discussion

Class `Dict` contains as data members an array of `Entry` objects, where `Entry` is itself a class, and an `int` variable `count` that tracks how many entries (up to a maximum of `MaxEntries`) are currently in the dictionary. An `Entry` consists of a `word` and its `definition`, each implemented as a character string. `Dict` and `Entry` have identically named methods called `add`, each expecting a `word` and its `def`. A typical code sequence for adding pairs and then printing them is:

```
int main()
{
    // Create a dictionary of MaxEntry word-definition pairs
    Dict d;

    // Add some pairs
    d.add( "residual fm", "incidental fm" );
    d.add( "diode", "two-element solid-state device" );
    d.add( "pixel",  "picture element" );
    d.add( "incidental fm", "residual fm" );
    d.add( "recursion", "See recursion" );
    ...
    // Print all pairs in the dictionary.
    d.dump();
    ...
}
```

Method `Dict::add` simply invokes `Entry::add` on the first open slot in the dictionary. This slot is indexed by `Dict::count`, which is incremented after each `add` operation:

```
void Dict::add( const char* w, const char* d )
{
    if ( count < MaxEntries )
        entries[ count++ ].add( w, d );
    else
        cout << count << " exceeds MaxEntries." <<
        endl;
}
```

`Dict` overloads the [ ] operator so that character strings can be used as indexes. A code slice such as

```
d[ "diode" ];  // what's the definition of diode?
```

initiates a search of `Dict::entries` for a word that matches `diode`. If there is a match, the word's definition is printed. If not, a failure message is printed.

`DictIter` is the iterator class for `Dict`. A code slice such as

```
int main()
{
  Dict d;              // create a dictionary
  DictIter di( d );    // create an iterator for d
  Entry* e;            // return value of di.operator()
  ...                  // add items to dictionary
  while ( e = di() )   // loop thru dictionary elements
    e -> write();      //    equivalent to d.dump()
  ...
}
```

shows how `DictIter::operator()` may be used to iterate through the dictionary `entries`. The loop condition works because `DictIter::operator()` returns 0 when it reaches the end of `entries`.

The syntax

```
Entry* DictIter::operator()()
{
  ...
}
```

may look peculiar in that there are two pairs of parentheses right next to each other. The first pair represents the operator that we are overloading, which is the function call operator (). The second pair of parentheses is the argument list for our overloaded function call operator. The list is empty because our overload of () does not expect any arguments.

Overloading the [ ] and () operators provides the applications programmer with convenient, intuitive tools for manipulating a dictionary. Such overloading coats the C++ language with a layer of syntactic sugar so as to make the language more palatable to its programmers.

Exercises

1. Change class `Entry` so that its data members are of type `String` (see Section 4.1) rather than `char*`.

2. Change the appropriate methods so that each new `Entry` preserves sorted order among the `Dict` entries.

3. Why must `DictIter` be a `friend` to `Dict`?

4. Why does `DictIter` not have to be a `friend` to `Entry`?

5. Explain the syntax

```
Entry* DictIter::operator()()
{
    ...
}
```

In particular, explain what each pair of `()` means in the operator function's header.

6. If we overload `operator[ ]`, how many arguments must the overloaded operator take?

7. If we overload `operator()`, how many arguments must the overloaded operator take?

8. Implement

```
void Dict::remove( char* w )
```

which removes word `w` from the dictionary if `w` occurs there.

9. Implement

```
void Dict::append( char* w, char* d )
```

which appends `d` to `w`'s definition if `w` occurs in the dictionary.

10. Implement

```
void Dict::change( char* w, char* d )
```

which changes `w`'s definition to `d` if `w` occurs in the dictionary.

6.4 Type Conversions

Recall the `String` class of Section 4.1, which implements a string as an abstract data type. A `String`'s internal representation includes a pointer of type `char*`, which is a suitable argument for library functions such as `strlen`, `strstr`, `strtok`, and the like. However, a `String` itself is *not* a suitable argument to such a library function.

Example 6.4.1. The code slice

```
String s1( "foo bar" );
int len = strlen( s1 ); // ***** ERROR: s1 is wrong type
```

contains an error because `strlen` expects an argument of type `char*`, not
of type `String`.   □

Of course, we could write `String` methods that mimic `strlen` and the
other library functions, but this would be tedious and wasteful. Library
functions are meant to be used, not reinvented. A solution is to overload a
type conversion operator so that a `String` behaves as if it were `char*`
in contexts that require `char*`.

Example 6.4.2. We amend the `String` class to include a type conversion
operator so that a `String` may be passed to a library function such as
`strlen`:

```
class String {
   char* str;      // data member -- private
   int   len;      // actual
 public:
   enum SortOrder { Asc, Desc };
   enum ErrorsIO { ReadFail, WriteFail };
   ...
   operator const char*() const; // declaration
   ...
};


// type conversion operator: String to char*
String::operator const char*() const
{
   return str;
};
```

Note that neither the declaration nor the definition of the overloaded operator shows a return value, not even `void`, although the function operator's
body contains the `return` statement

```
return str;
```

It is illegal to give a return value, even `void`, in either the declaration or the
definition of a type conversion operator.

The first `const` in the type conversion operator signals that code outside
the `String` class should not modify the storage to which data member `str`
points. The second `const` signals that the type conversion operator itself
does not change this storage. The operator returns `str`, which points to a
null-terminated vector of `char`. In short, `str` is of type `char*`. This means
that `str` is a suitable argument to library functions such as `strlen`. Code
such as

```
String s1;          // s1 is String, not char*
int len;
len = strlen( s1 ); // s1 converted to char*
```

is legal with the type conversion operator. Because **strlen** expects a **char***
rather than a **String**, the compiler issues a call to the type conversion operator, which returns **s1.str**—of type **char***—to **strlen**. Note that the user
does not explicitly invoke the type conversion operator, leaving that task to
the compiler. The user thus enjoys the benefits of type conversion without
the associated work.   □

The syntax of a type conversion operator indicates the conversion that
it performs. For example,

```
String::operator const char*() const
{
   return str;
}
```

indicates a conversion from a **String** to a **char*** (technically, to a **const char***).
Had we a reason to convert **String**s to **int**s, our type conversion operator
would look like this:

```
String::operator int()
{
   ...
}
```

Type conversion operators occur in built-in and user-defined classes.
We take an example from the **iostream** class (see the system header file
iostream.h and Chapter 7).

Example 6.4.3. This code slice

```
char next;

while ( cin >> next ) // read from standard input
    cout << next;      // write to standard output
```

copies the standard input to the standard output until end-of-file is encountered. The **while** condition must evaluate to an integer or pointer value: a
value of zero means *false* and any nonzero value means *true*. However, the
input expression

```
cin >> next
```

evaluates to an **istream**, where **istream** is a class from the *iostream* library.
A type conversion operator handles the conversion from **istream** to **void***,
thus supporting the convenience of the **while** construct.   □

Despite their convenience, type conversion operators should be used with caution because the compiler, not the programmer, typically invokes a type conversion operator. The normal call to a type conversion operator is thus *hidden* from the programmer, who may not have anticipated all the situations in which such an operator would be invoked.

Exercises

---

1. Explain the error.

   ```
   // type conversion operator
   char* String::operator const char*() const
   {
       return str; // type char*
   }
   ```

2. Assume that we would like to use code such as

   ```
   String s1( "O sole mio" );
   ...
   if ( s1 ) {   // if ( strlen( s1.str ) )
   ...
   }
   ```

   The problem is that an `if` condition must evaluate to an integer or pointer expression, not to a `String` expression. Write a type conversion operator that allows this programming construct for `Strings`.

3. Explain the meaning of each `const` in the function header

   ```
   String::operator const char*() const
   {
     ...
   }
   ```

4. Does the compiler or the programmer normally invoke a type conversion operator?

5. Explain how the compiler determines whether to invoke a type conversion operator in a particular context.

6. A type conversion operator's definition and declaration must not give a return value, even `void`. What do you think is the point of this rule?

7. Why should type conversion operators be used cautiously, despite their convenience?

8. If we had not provided a type conversion operator that converts a `String` to a `const char*`, then a code slice such as

```
String s1( "agnes" );
int len = strlen( s1 );
```

would cause the compiler to issue a type violation warning. With the type conversion operator in place, the compiler is silent. Explain the disadvantages of silencing such compiler warnings.

6.5 Sample Application: File Subscripts

Problem ⎯⎯⎯⎯⎯⎯⎯⎯⎯⎯⎯⎯⎯⎯⎯⎯⎯⎯⎯⎯⎯⎯⎯⎯⎯⎯⎯⎯

Extend array syntax to files so that the user can access a file for reading and writing as if the file were an indeterminately large, one-dimensional array of `char`. In other words, implement a **file subscript** that behaves as if it were an array subscript.

Solution ⎯⎯⎯⎯⎯⎯⎯⎯⎯⎯⎯⎯⎯⎯⎯⎯⎯⎯⎯⎯⎯⎯⎯⎯⎯⎯⎯⎯

We create a `File` class that supports the standard operations of opening, closing, reading, and writing a file. The `friend` class `FileRef` handles some implementation details. Together the two classes overload the subscript operator `[ ]` and the assignment operator `=`, and define a type conversion operator to convert a `FileRef&` to a `char`. The overall result is an extension of array syntax to files. The example is adapted from James O. Coplien, *Advanced C++* (Reading, Mass.: Addison-Wesley, 1992).

C++ Implementation ⎯⎯⎯⎯⎯⎯⎯⎯⎯⎯⎯⎯⎯⎯⎯⎯⎯⎯⎯⎯⎯

```cpp
#include <stdio.h>
#include <iostream.h>

class File;
class FileRef {
   File& file;
   char buffer;
   unsigned long index;
public:
   FileRef( File& f, unsigned long i ) :
      file( f ), index( i ) { }
   FileRef& operator=( char c );
   operator char();
};
```

```
class File {
   friend class FileRef;
private:
   FILE* fptr;
public:
   File( const char* name ) { fptr = fopen( name, "wb+" ); }
   ~File() { fclose( fptr ); }
   FileRef operator[ ]( unsigned long );
};

FileRef File::operator[ ]( unsigned long index )
{
   return FileRef( *this, index );
}

FileRef& FileRef::operator=( char c )
{
   fseek( file.fptr, index, SEEK_SET );
   fputc( ( int ) c, file.fptr );
   return *this;
}

FileRef::operator char()
{
   fseek( file.fptr, index, SEEK_SET );
   buffer = fgetc( file.fptr );
   return buffer;
}
```

Discussion

Here is a code sequence that illustrates file subscripts:

```
int main()
{
   char c = 'A';
   File f1( "foo" );              // create and open file
   File f2( "bar" );              // create and open another

   for ( int i = 0; i < 26; i++ )
      f1[ i ] = c++;             // write next character

   c = f1[ 23 ];                 // read 'X' from f1
   cout << f1[ 24 ] << endl;     // read 'Y'
```

```
    f1[ 23 ] = 'x';                 // overwrite 'X' with 'x'
    f1[ 5 ] = f2[ 99 ] = 'Z';       // write 'Z' to two files
    ...
}
```

At the syntax level, a `File` now looks like an array of indeterminate
size. A `File` is written or read as if it were an array of `char`. The C++
implementation is compact and contains some subtle features.We begin with
a straightforward feature.

The `File` constructor opens the named file in mode `wb+`, which means
that the file is created if it does not already exist and may be read as well
as written. The `File` destructor closes the file. Once created, a `File` may
be treated as if it were an indeterminately long one-dimensional array. The
file's actual size is system-dependent, of course. In any case, the file may be
read or written using array syntax. The index must be an integer expression,
however, as the overload of the subscript operator makes no provision for,
say, `Strings` as indexes. Expressions such as

```
    int x = 10;
    int y = 20;
    char c;

    f1[ 6 ] = 'A';
    f1[ x + y ] = 'Z';
    c = f1[ y - x ];
```

are all legal.

The overloaded subscript and assignment operators together with the
type conversion operator serve one purpose: to handle situations in which
a subscripted `File` occurs as the *source* and as the *target* in an assignment
expression. As a source, a subscripted `File` occurs on the *left* side of an
assignment; as a target, a subscripted `File` occurs on the *right* side of an
assignment:

```
    c = f1[ 23 ];   // File as source
    f1[ 23 ] = c;   // File as target
```

We begin with a subscripted `File` as a target.

In the expression

```
    f1[ 10 ] = 'Q'; // File as target
```

the subscript operator

```
    FileRef File::operator[ ]( unsigned long index )
    {
        return FileRef( *this, index );
    }
```

returns the value of the constructor call

```
FileRef( *this, index )
```

Recall that *this evaluates to f1. The FileRef constructor thus creates a *dummy* FileRef object, sets its data member file to the first argument (in this case f1), and sets its data member index to the second argument (in this case 10). The dummy FileRef object is returned. It is this dummy FileRef object whose assignment operator is invoked. Note that the overloaded assignment operator is a *method* in class FileRef and therefore requires a FileRef object. The overloaded assignment operator treats the index, in this example 10, as an offset into the File. An fseek is done to the specified position, after which the character Q is written. The overloaded assignment operator returns a FileRef&, which enables such constructs as

```
File f1( "foo" );
File f2( "bar" );
f1[ 6 ] = f2[ 978 ] = 'B';
```

When a File occurs as the source or right side of an assignment and the target is a char variable, then the type conversion operator comes into play. In the assignment

```
char c;
c = f1[ 23 ];
```

the subscript operator once again evaluates to a FileRef. However, the context now requires a char value because c is of type char, not FileRef. The compiler thus invokes the type conversion operator

```
FileRef::operator char()
{
    fseek( file.fptr, index, SEEK_SET );
    buffer = fgetc( file.fptr );
    return buffer;
}
```

so that a char is stored in c. The type conversion operator also does the required fseek and fgetc to read the char at index 23.

The example has instructive subtleties at the implementation level. The point worth noting, in the spirit of object-oriented programming, is that the user can ignore these subtleties and manipulate files as if they were arrays of indeterminate size.

Exercises

---

1. Explain why FileRef is a friend to File.

2. Explain why File is not a friend to FileRef.

3. The body of the overloaded assignment operator ends with

   ```
   return *this;
   ```

   instead of with

   ```
   return this;
   ```

   Explain why *this is returned.

4. Explain how the assignment expression

   ```
   f1[ 2 ] = f2[ 3 ] = 'A';
   ```

   works, where f1 and f2 are Files.

5. The assignment operator is overloaded as a FileRef method, whereas the subscript operator is overloaded as a File method. Explain why the overloads are done this way.

6. Does the type conversion operator come into play when a subscripted File occurs as the target or right side of an assignment expression? Explain.

7. Does the overloaded assignment operator come into play during File reads and writes? Explain.

8. Explain the error.

   ```
   char FileRef::operator char()
   {
      fseek( file.fptr, index, SEEK_SET );
      buffer = fgetc( file.fptr );
      return buffer;
   }
   ```

9. In this section, we talk about a *dummy* FileRef being returned by the overloaded subscript operator. Explain the sense in which this FileRef object is a dummy or intermediate value.

10. Implement bounds checking for the overloaded subscript operator. An index value should not be less than zero or greater than MaxFileSize, a const variable that you should set to some appropriate value.

6.6   Memory Management Operators

The memory management operators **new**, **delete**, and **delete[ ]** may be
overloaded as either methods or toplevel operator functions. Such overloading is useful when an application needs to take control of its own memory
management. An embedded system (for example, a microprocessor system
that regulates a refrigerator or an automobile engine) may have very limited
memory resources that the application needs to manage directly. Some environments, such as Microsoft Windows, have memory management schemes
that application programs are advised to follow, thus requiring direct memory management.

Example 6.6.1. The code slices

```
// overloaded as method in class C
void* C::operator new( size_t size )
{
   ...
}
```

and

```
// overloaded as toplevel operator function
void* operator new( size_t size )
{
   ...
}
```

illustrate two overloads of the operator **new**. The overloaded **new** operators
both return a **void***, just as the built-in **new** operator does. In this example,
each overloaded operator function expects a single argument of type **size_t**.
A typical invocation of C::**new** would be

```
C* c1 = new C; // allocate a C object
```

The system uses the overloaded C::**new** operator. If such an operator were
not defined, then the system would use the built-in **new** operator.   □

The initial parameter in the overloaded **new** operator must be of type
size_t. The value of this parameter is equal to the size in bytes of the
object being created. Other parameters are optional and depend on the
body of the overloaded **new**. In any case, an overload such as

```
void* C::new( void* ptr ) // ***** ERROR: no size_t
{
   ...
}
```

contains an error because the first parameter is not of type **size_t**.

Example 6.6.2. The code slices

```
// overloaded as method
void C::operator delete( void* objPtr )
{
   ...
}
```

and

```
// overloaded as toplevel function operator
void operator delete( void* objPtr )
{
   ...
}
```

illustrate two overloads of the **delete** operator. The operator returns **void**
and expects an argument of type **void***, which points to the storage to be
freed. A typical invocation of **C::delete** would be

```
C* c1 = new C;    // allocate
...
delete c1;        // free
```

The system again uses the overloaded **delete** if one is present and the built-
in **delete** otherwise.   □

   The initial parameter in the overloaded **delete** or **delete[ ]** must be
of type **void***. Other parameters are optional.
   Next we take a longer example to illustrate an overload of **new** as a
method. The overloaded **new** allocates storage from a fixed pool available to
the program.

Example 6.6.3. We define a **Frame** class, which represents data frames to
be transmitted in a data communications application:

```
#include <iostream.h>
#include <stdio.h>
#include <string.h>

const int MaxFrames = 48;
const int DataSize = 128;
const int NameSize = 4;

class Frame {
   static Frame* allFrames;
   Frame* nextFrame;
   char name[ NameSize ];
   char data[ DataSize ];
public:
```

```
      Frame();
      Frame( const char* );
      Frame( const char*, const char* );
      void print();
      void* operator new( size_t );
};

Frame* Frame::allFrames = 0;   // no Frames yet
unsigned char framePool[ MaxFrames * sizeof ( Frame ) ];
const unsigned char* poolEnd =
      framePool + MaxFrames * sizeof ( Frame );

Frame::Frame()
{
   name[ 0 ] = data[ 0 ] = '\0';
}

Frame::Frame( const char* n )
{
   strcpy( name, n );
   data[ 0 ] = '\0';
   print();
}

Frame::Frame( const char* n, const char* d )
{
   strcpy( name, n );
   strcpy( data, d );
   print();
}

void Frame::print()
{
   cout << name << " created." << endl;
}

void* Frame::operator new( size_t size )
{
   // allocating a new Frame?
   if ( size != sizeof ( Frame ) ) {
      cout << "!! ERROR -- not a Frame!."
            << endl;
      return 0;
   }
```

```
      // any storage left?
      if ( allFrames == ( Frame* ) poolEnd ) {
         cout << "No more storage for Frames."
              << endl;
         return 0;
      }

      // storage allocated yet?
      if ( !allFrames ) {
         allFrames = ( Frame* ) framePool;
         for ( int i = 0; i < MaxFrames - 1; i++ )
            allFrames[ i ].nextFrame = &allFrames[ i + 1 ];
         allFrames[ i ].nextFrame = ( Frame* ) poolEnd;
      }

      Frame* temp = allFrames; // current chunk
      allFrames = allFrames -> nextFrame; // next chunk
      return temp;
   }
```

A Frame has data member name, which we use to trace the program's execution. Data member data holds DataSize bytes to be transmitted in a data communications application. All storage for Frames comes from framePool, an array of unsigned char with size

```
MaxFrames * sizeof ( Frame )
```

Accordingly, framePool points to storage for up to MaxFrames objects of type Frame. The objects may be allocated one at a time

```
Frame* f1 = new Frame( "f1" ); // allocate one
Frame* f2 = new Frame( "f2" ); // allocate another
```

or as a Frame vector

```
// allocate a vector of three Frames
Frame* f1 = new Frame[ 3 ];
```

The allocation syntax for the overloaded new operator is the same as for the built-in new operator.

The class Frame has a static data member allFrames that points to framePool. The data member is static because there is only one storage pool shared by the whole class, rather than a storage pool for each individual Frame object (see Figure 6.6.1).

When a Frame object is created dynamically, the overloaded new operator allocates storage from framePool if any is still available. The first time new allocates storage from framePool, it breaks the storage into chunks

Frame::allFrames

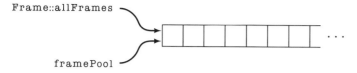

framePool

Figure 6.6.1 Storage pool for Frames.

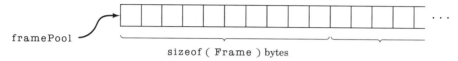

framePool

sizeof (Frame) bytes

Figure 6.6.2 Allocating from Frame storage pool.

(each chunk with `sizeof ( Frame )` bytes) so that the chunks then can be allocated one per **Frame** (see Figure 6.6.2):

```
// storage allocated yet?
if ( !allFrames ) {
   allFrames = ( Frame* ) framePool;
   for ( int i = 0; i < MaxFrames - 1; i++ )
      allFrames[ i ].nextFrame = &allFrames[ i + 1 ];
   allFrames[ i ].nextFrame = ( Frame* ) poolEnd;
}
```

Data member **nextFrame** points to the next available storage, if any, in **framePool**. After **MaxFrames** have been allocated, **nextFrame** points to **poolEnd**, which means that no more **Frames** can be allocated. The allocation itself occurs at the end of **new**:

```
Frame* temp = allFrames; // current chunk
allFrames = allFrames -> nextFrame; // next chunk
return temp;
```

The code slice

```
int main()
{
   Frame* f1 = new Frame( "f1" );
   Frame* f2 = new Frame( "f2" );
   ...
   Frame* f48 = new Frame( "f48" );
   Frame* f49 = new Frame( "f49" );
   ...
}
```

produces the output

```
f1 created.
f2 created.
   ...
```

```
f48 created.
No more storage for Frames.
```

because MaxFrames is currently set to 48.   □

Exercises

1. Assume that the **new** operator is overloaded for class C1 but not for class C2. Explain which **new** operator, C1::**new** or built-in **new**, is invoked in each case:

   ```
   C1* c1 = new C1;
   C2* c2 = new C2;
   int* i1 = new int;
   C1* cs = new C1[ 10 ];
   ```

2. Explain the error.

   ```
   void* C::new( int howmany )
   {
       ...
   }
   ```

3. Explain the error.

   ```
   void delete( char* ptr )
   {
       ...
   }
   ```

4. Explain the role of poolEnd in Example 6.6.3.

5. Is an overload of the **new** operator restricted to a single parameter?

6. Overload the **delete** operator for class Frame in Example 6.6.3. A delete operation should recover the storage so that it can be used to allocate yet another Frame.

Common Programming Errors

1. It is an error to overload these five operators:

```
.           // class member operator
.*          // class member dereference operator
::          // scope resolution operator
?:          // conditional operator
sizeof  // size in bytes operator
```

2. Except for memory management operators `new`, `delete`, and `delete[ ]`, an operator must either be overloaded as a method or have at least one class object among its arguments. For example,

```
// ***** ERROR: neither a method nor a
// function that takes a class argument
void operator+( const int num1, const int num2 )
{
  ...
}
```

has an error because the overloaded operator is not a method and does not have a class object among its arguments.

3. It is an error to overload `operator[ ]` except as a method.

4. It is an error to overload `operator()` except as a method.

5. It is an error to change an operator's arity when overloading it. For example,

```
// ***** ERROR: + must remain binary
Complex Complex::operator+( const Complex c1,
                            const Complex c2 )
{
  ...
}
```

contains an error because `operator+` must remain binary when overloaded. Recall that an expression such as

```
c3 = c2 + c1;   // c3, c2, and c1 are Complex
```

is shorthand for

```
c3 = c2.operator+( c1 );
```

The overloaded `Complex::operator+` therefore should take one argument, not two, to remain binary:

```
// ok -- + remains binary
Complex Complex::operator+( const c )
{
  . . .
}
```

6. It is an error to specify, in either a declaration or a definition, the return data type—even **void**—for a type conversion operator despite the fact that such an operator contains a **return** statement. For example,

```
// ***** ERROR: can't give return data type
char* String::operator const char*() const
{
   return str; // str is of type char*
}
```

7. It is an error to have the overloaded **new** operator return any value except **void***.

8. It is an error if the first argument to the overloaded **new** operator is not of type **size_t**. The overloaded operator may have additional arguments of any type, however.

9. It is an error to have the overloaded **delete** and **delete[ ]** operators return any value except **void**.

10. It is an error if the first argument to the overloaded operators **delete** or **delete[ ]** is not of type **void***. The overloaded operators may have additional arguments of any type, however.

Programming Exercises

6.1. Overload a unary operator for the **Deck** class (see Programming Exercise 3.3) whose invocation results in a **Deck**'s being shuffled. For example, if the bitwise complement operator ~ is overloaded, then the code slice

```
Deck d;
~d; // shuffle the Deck
```

shuffles d.

6.2. Overload the preincrement operator ++ and the predecrement operator -- for the **Spaceship** class (see Programming Exercise 3.13). The following code slice illustrates how the operators work:

```
// create a spaceship -- default velocity is zero
Spaceship s;
++s; // increment velocity by constant s.velUp
++s; // do it again
--s; // decrement velocity by constant s.velDown
```

6.3. Overload the binary operators +, -, and * as **Set** methods (see Programming Exercise 3.9). The following code slice illustrates how the operators work:

```
Set set1( a, b, c ); // set1 = {a,b,c}
Set set2( x, y );    // set2 = {b,x,y}
Set set3;            // set3 = {}
// compute union of set1 and set2
set3 = set1 + set2;  // set3 = {a,b,c,x,y}
// compute intersection of set1 and set2
set3 = set1 * set2;  // set3 = {b}
// computer difference of set1 and set2
set3 = set1 - set2;  // set3 = {a,c}
```

6.4. Overload the negation operator ! for the **String** class (see Section 4.1). A code slice such as

```
String s( "Tish Hinojosa" );
// convert uppercase to lowercase and
// lowercase to uppercase in s
!s;
```

has the effect of converting any uppercase character in **s** to a lowercase character and vice-versa. After the expression **!s** evaluates, **s.str** points to the character string

```
tISH hINOJOSA
```

An expression such as

```
!!s;  // double negate s
```

leaves **s** unchanged, as pairs of negations cancel each other out. Also overload the *unary* + and - operators for **Strings**. An expression such as

```
String s( "Kim" );
// convert to uppercase: KIM
+s;
```

converts any lowercase characters in **s** to uppercase. Similarly, the expression

```
String s( "Kim" );
// convert to lowercase: kim
-s;
```

converts any uppercase characters in **s** to lowercase.

6.5. Overload the + operator as a **LAN** method (see Programming Exercise 4.3). The code slice

```
LAN lan1;    // create one LAN
LAN lan2;    // create another
LAN lan3;    // create a third
lan3 = lan1 + lan2;
```

makes **lan3** a **LAN** that includes **lan1** and **lan2** as subLANs. A combined **LAN** includes all the nodes from the two or more LANs that it combines. However, its topology may differ from theirs because, for example, we might combine a *star* and a *bus* **LAN** into a new **LAN** with a hybrid topology.

6.6. The BST (binary search tree) class of Section 4.4 has a method **addNode** to add nodes to a BST. To add three nodes to a BST requires a code slice such as

```
BST bst;              // create a BST
bst.addNode( 'K' ); // add one node
bst.addNode( 'G' ); // add a second
bst.addNode( 'R' ); // add a third
```

Overload the function call operator () so that expressions such as

```
bst( "KGR" );   // add three nodes at once
bst( "MAQP" ); // add four more
```

adds nodes represented as characters in a string. The expression

```
bst( "" );     // remove all nodes
```

removes all nodes from the BST leaving an empty BST.

6.7. Provide a type conversion operator for BSTs (see Section 4.4) so that they can be passed to a string library function such as **strlen**. For example, in the code slice

```
BST bst;              // create a BST
bst( "KGRMAQP" ); // add 7 nodes
cout << "Node count for bst is "
     << strlen( bst ) << endl;
```

7 is printed to the standard output because **bst** has seven nodes. The second statement uses the overloaded function call operator as described in Programming Exercise 6.6.

6.8. Overload the relational operators <, <=, ==, >=, and > for the **Graph** class of Programming Exercise 4.9. If **g1** and **g2** are two **Graphs**, then the expression

```
g1 < g2
```

evaluates to *true* (1) if the total number of vertices and edges in **g1** is less than the total number of vertices and edges in **g2**. The other relational operators also should be overloaded to extend their built-in meanings to **Graphs**.

6.9. Overload the preincrement operator ++ and the predecrement operator -- for the **Spreadsheet** class (see Programming Exercise 4.8). Add a data member **currCell** to **Spreadsheet**, which points to the *current* or *active* cell in the **Spreadsheet**. A cell is current or active if the user is currently editing it. When the **Spreadsheet** is first opened, the current cell is the first cell. When the user is not actively editing the **Spreadsheet**, the current cell is the most recently edited cell or, in case no editing has been done, the first cell. The code slice

```
// create a Spreadsheet
Spreadsheet taxes;  // current cell is 1st
++taxes;            // current cell is 2nd
++taxes;            // current cell is 3rd
--taxes;            // current cell is 2nd
```

illustrates how the operators can be used to navigate the **Spreadsheet** one cell at a time. Also, overload the ! operator so that an expression such as

```
!taxes
```

has the effect of *computing* the **Spreadsheet**, which means computing the value of each cell in it.

6.10. Create a class hierarchy with **Int** as an abstract base class that has **Int1**, **Int2**, and **Int4** as derived types. **Int1** represents a signed integer in one byte, **Int2** represents a signed integer in two bytes, and **Int4** represents an unsigned integer in four bytes:

```
sizeof ( Int1 ) == 1
sizeof ( Int2 ) == 2
sizeof ( Int4 ) == 4
```

Assume further that your application must do its own memory management because, for example, it is part of an embedded system with very limited memory resources. When your application begins to run, it receives m bytes of memory (e.g., 64K bytes). The application then must do its own memory management. In particular, storage for integers must be dynamically allocated and freed. Overload the **new**, the **delete**, and the **delete[ ]** operators as **virtual** operator functions that manage allocation and release of storage for **Int1**, **Int2**, and **Int4**. The **new** operator should ensure that no more than m bytes of memory have been allocated.

Chapter 7

The C++ Input/Output Class Hierarchy

Input and output facilities are not part of the C++ language but instead are furnished through a class library. In this chapter, we explore this class library in detail.

The class hierarchy for C++'s input/output library is complex. We examine the hierarchy in detail for three reasons. First, this hierarchy illustrates the power available by combining polymorphism and multiple inheritance. Even programmers with no particular interest in the details of C++'s input/output hierarchy can learn important object-oriented design and coding lessons by attending to these details. Second, most C++ environments extend the language by providing class libraries (e.g., Microsoft Visual C++'s Foundation Classes, Borland C++'s ObjectWindows). Part of learning C++ is learning how to use class libraries so that time and energy are not wasted in recreating what is already available. Because the input/output class library is standard within C++, it is an excellent case study for the use of class libraries in general. Third, through inheritance a programmer can extend the input/output classes (see Section 7.6). Such extensions require a clear understanding of the details of the classes.

7.1   Overview

We begin by discussing the object-oriented design of the input/output class library. Object-oriented design begins by identifying objects and continues by defining the operations (methods) appropriate to the objects. In C++ input and output, a central object is the **stream**, which is a sequence of bytes (see Figure 7.1.1). Operations on a stream include **reading from** and **writing to** the stream. A clean design can be achieved by having a common base class `ios` for the two derived stream classes `istream`, the input stream class, and `ostream`, the output stream class (see Figure 7.1.2). The base class `ios` has members that the derived classes `istream` and `ostream` inherit. These inherited members are used to describe and to modify various stream attributes. Such attributes include the mode (e.g., whether the stream is opened for reading only or for both reading and writing); the format (e.g., the number of digits of floating-point precision); and the status of operations on the stream (e.g., whether end-of-file was encountered, whether the last operation failed). Class `ios` has data members to describe these attributes and methods to read, set, and clear the attribute flags.

Class `istream` adds methods for reading and moving around in the stream. Also, the right-shift operator `>>` is overloaded within `istream` for reading the built-in types. Similarly, `ostream` contains methods for writing and moving around in the stream. The left-shift operator `<<` is overloaded within `ostream` for writing the built-in types.

Class `iostream` is derived from both `istream` and `ostream` so that it inherits methods for both reading and writing a stream. Class `iostream` has

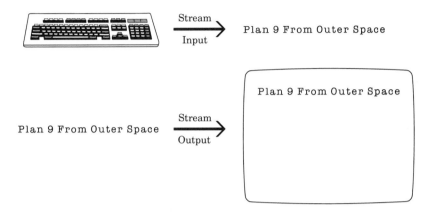

Figure 7.1.1 Stream input/output.

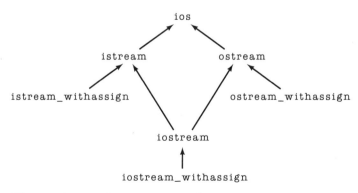

Figure 7.1.2 Basic stream classes.

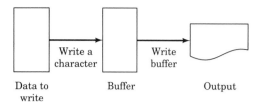

Figure 7.1.3 Buffered output.

no additional data members and, except for constructors and destructors, it has no additional methods either.

The classes

`istream_withassign`
`ostream_withassign`
`iostream_withassign`

are directly derived from `istream`, `ostream`, and `iostream`, respectively. As the names suggest, each overloads the assignment operator. The system defines the objects `cin`, which is a member of `istream_withassign`, and `cout` and `cerr`, which are members of `ostream_withassign`.

The C++ input/output class library provides for **buffered input/output**, in which data are not directly read or written but rather pass through intermediate storage (e.g., an array of `char`) called a **buffer**.

Example 7.1.1. Figure 7.1.3 depicts buffered output. When a request is received to write a character, the character is not written directly to the output but rather to the buffer. Periodically the buffer is written to the output. Writing the buffer is called **flushing** the buffer. In C++ a newline typically flushes the output buffer. □

A buffer is another essential object in the C++ class input/output library, and reading and writing the buffer are among the required operations. Various buffer classes (e.g., `filebuf`, the file buffer class, and `strstreambuf`, the character array buffer class) are derived from a common base class `streambuf` (see Figure 7.1.4). These derived classes serve as interfaces to the actual sources and destinations of input and output. The base class `streambuf` has methods (e.g., reading and writing the buffer) needed by both `filebuf` and `strstreambuf`, which `filebuf` and `strstreambuf` then obtain through inheritance. A buffer object is connected to class `ios` through a pointer-to-`streambuf` data member in `ios` (see Figure 7.1.4).

Class `streambuf` contains constructors and methods for creating an array of `char` or `unsigned char` to use as a buffer. In addition, it has methods for reading and writing the buffer and for moving around in the stream. These reading and writing methods are sometimes called *low-level input/output methods* because they provide direct access to the buffer. By contrast,

Figure 7.1.4 The C++ buffer classes.

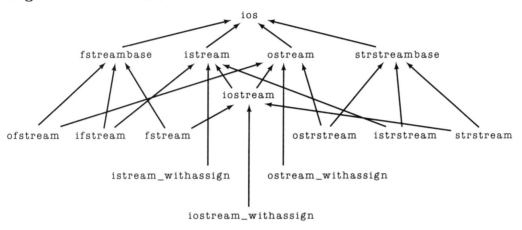

Figure 7.1.5 The C++ stream classes.

the methods in the classes **istream** and **ostream** are called *high-level input/output methods* because they access the stream indirectly—by making calls to the low-level methods in **streambuf**.

Class **streambuf** also contains the **virtual** methods **underflow**, which is responsible for dealing with an attempted read from an empty buffer, and **overflow**, which is responsible for dealing with an attempted write to a full buffer. A class derived from **streambuf** typically overrides **underflow** and **overflow** so that action appropriate to the specific source or destination is taken. For example, when the buffer is full, **overflow** might ignore new writes or return an error flag, or, if the destination is a file, it might flush the buffer.

The class **filebuf** contains constructors and methods for associating a **filebuf** object with a file, and the class **strstreambuf** contains constructors and methods for associating a **strstreambuf** object with a character array. Each overrides **underflow** and **overflow**.

One reason that the buffer class hierarchy (Figure 7.1.4) is distinct from the stream class hierarchy (Figure 7.1.5) is to separate the high-level and low-level input/output methods. If these hierarchies were combined into a single hierarchy, some class would necessarily contain both high-level and low-level input/output methods.

Two additional classes are derived from **ios**:

fstreambase strstreambase

(see Figure 7.1.5). These classes serve as base classes for derived classes that provide a high-level interface to file and character array input and output.

The class `fstreambase` contains a buffer member (a member of type `filebuf`). The base class `ios` is connected to this buffer object through a pointer (see Figure 7.1.4); in this way, `fstreambase` establishes a connection to a physical stream—a file. The class `fstreambase` provides constructors and methods for opening, attaching, and closing a file.

Class `ifstream` is derived from both `fstreambase` and `istream`; thus, it contains a file buffer object and methods for reading and moving around within the stream. Therefore `ifstream` provides high-level, indirect access to the file. Class `ifstream` also inherits from `fstreambase` methods for attaching and closing a file. It redefines the method `open` to assure that the file is opened in read mode.

Similarly, class `ofstream` is derived from both `fstreambase` and `ostream`; thus, it contains a file buffer object and methods for writing and moving around within the stream. Class `ofstream` also inherits from `fstreambase` methods for attaching and closing a file. It redefines the method `open` to assure that the file is opened in write mode.

Class `fstream` is derived from both `fstreambase` and `iostream`; thus, it contains a file buffer object and methods for reading, writing, and moving around within the stream. Class `fstream` also inherits from `fstreambase` methods for attaching and closing a file. It redefines the method `open` to remove any default protection.

The `strstream` classes (`strstreambase`, `ostrstream`, `istrstream`, and `strstream`), which read and write arrays of characters, are designed similarly to their `fstream` counterparts, which read and write files.

The class `strstreambase` contains a buffer member (a member of type `strstreambuf`). The base class `ios` is connected to this buffer object through a pointer (see Figure 7.1.4); in this way, `strstreambase` establishes a connection to a physical stream—an array of characters. The class `strstreambase` provides a constructor for establishing a connection with a character array.

Class `istrstream` is derived from both `strstreambase` and `istream`; thus, it contains an `strstreambuf` object and methods for reading and moving around within the buffer. Therefore `istrstream` provides high-level, indirect access to the character array.

Class `ostrstream` is derived from both `strstreambase` and `ostream`; thus, it contains an `strstreambuf` object and methods for writing and moving around within the buffer.

Class `strstream` is derived from both `strstreambase` and `iostream`; thus, it contains an `strstreambuf` object and methods for reading, writing, and moving around within the buffer.

The header file *iostream.h* declares the classes

ios
streambuf
istream
ostream
iostream
istream_withassign
ostream_withassign
iostream_withassign

the objects `cin`, `cout`, and `cerr`; and the manipulators `endl`, `ends`, `flush`, `dec`, `hex`, `oct`, and `ws`. The header file *fstream.h* `#include`s the file *iostream.h*, if it was not already included, and declares the classes

filebuf
fstreambase
ifstream
ofstream
fstream

The header file *strstream.h* `#include`s the file *iostream.h*, if it was not already included, and declares the classes

strstreambuf
strstreambase
istrstream
ostrstream
strstream

Figure 7.1.6 summarizes the classes and functionality given in this section. In the remainder of this chapter, we look at these classes in detail.

Exercises

---

1. Print the header files *iostream.h*, *fstream.h*, and *strstream.h*, and identify the data members and methods referred to in this section.

2. The C++ input/output class hierarchy assumes the stream model for input and output. Give an example of input or output for which some other model might be more suitable.

3. Argue that *any* input or output can be viewed as a stream.

4. Suggest how an input/output class hierarchy might be organized in the absence of multiple inheritance.

5. Why not replace class `ofstream` with a class derived from `ostream` and `filebuf`?

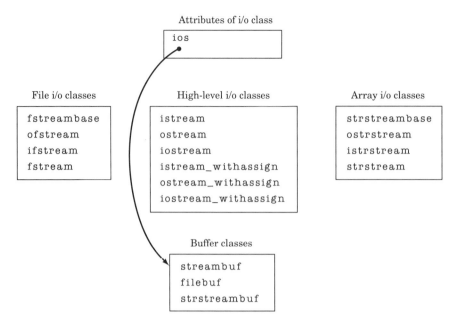

Figure 7.1.6 Summary of the C++ input/output class hierarchy.

7.2   The Class ios

In this section we look closely at the base input/output class **ios** (see Figure 7.1.5). The names used in this section are fairly standard across C++ systems, but the implementation is less standardized. Thus the reader should be able to use the flags and methods as described herein; the implementation should be considered merely as an example.

Class **ios** defines several **protected** integer members whose bits are used as flags. For example, the integer member **state** could be used to indicate the status of the stream: the first bit is set to indicate end-of-file; the second bit is set to indicate that the last input/output operation failed; and so on. The bits are named by using a **public enum**:

```
class ios {
public:
    ...
    enum io_state {
        goodbit  = 0x00,  // ok -- no bit is set
        eofbit   = 0x01,  // set = eof
        failbit  = 0x02,  // set = last i/o operation failed
        badbit   = 0x04,  // set = invalid operation
        hardfail = 0x80   // set = unrecoverable error
    };
    ...
};
```

Method	Returns
rdstate()	the stream state (state)
good()	nonzero if state is zero; otherwise, returns zero
eof()	nonzero if eofbit is set; otherwise, returns zero
fail()	nonzero if failbit is set; otherwise, returns zero
bad()	nonzero if badbit is set; otherwise, returns zero

Figure 7.2.1   Methods to access the status of the stream.

Because the *names* names are public, they can be used by the programmer. However, the programmer cannot directly access the integer member state containing the flags because this member is protected. Instead, ios furnishes public methods to access the status of the stream (see Figure 7.2.1).

Example 7.2.1. Because cin is a member of istream_withassign, a class inherited from ios, we may apply the methods of Figure 7.2.1 to cin. The statement

```
cur_state = cin.rdstate();
```

saves the current state for the standard input in cur_state.   □

Example 7.2.2. The code

```
int i;

do {
   cin >> i;
   if ( !cin.eof() )
      cout << i << endl;
} while ( !cin.eof() );
```

echoes integers in the standard input to the standard output, one per line. An attempted read beyond the end of the stream is required to set eofbit; thus, the following code that attempts to echo integers in the standard input to the standard output is *not* correct; an extra line is printed:

```
int i;

// ***** ERROR: extra line is printed
while ( !cin.eof() ) {
   cin >> i;
   cout << i < endl;
}
```

□

The member `clear` replaces the stream state with the value passed or 0 if no argument is passed.

Example 7.2.3. On many systems, a control character (e.g., control-D in UNIX, control-Z in MS-DOS or VAX/VMS) is interpreted as end-of-file. To receive additional input after an end-of-file signal from the standard input, some systems require the end-of-file flag to be cleared. The statement

```
cin.clear();
```

clears all of the standard input status flags, including the end-of-file flag. □

Class `ios` overloads the not operator `!` and provides a conversion from `ios` to `void*`. The declarations are

```
class ios {
public:
   ...
   operator void*();
   int operator!();
   ...
};
```

The `operator void*` converts `ios` to the pointer value zero if `state` is nonzero, and it converts `ios` to a nonzero pointer value if `state` is zero. Similarly, the overloaded not operator returns nonzero if `state` is nonzero, and it returns zero if `state` is zero.

Example 7.2.4. In the code

```
if ( cin ) { // standard input ok?
   // process input
}
```

if there is an error in the standard input, `state` is nonzero, so `cin` is converted to zero and we do not process input. If there is no error in the standard input, `state` is zero, so `cin` is converted to nonzero and we process the input.   □

Class `ios` declares an **enum** to give names to flag bits to indicate modes as shown in Figure 7.2.2. These flags are typically used in classes derived from `ios`.

Example 7.2.5. The class `ofstream` has a constructor whose first argument is a file name (see Section 7.5), and whose second argument is *or*ed with `ios::out` (to open the file for output) after which it becomes the initial mode. Thus

```
ofstream fout( "out.dat", ios::app );
```

Name	Purpose
`in`	Open for reading
`out`	Open for writing
`ate`	Open and move to end-of-stream
`app`	Open for appending
`trunc`	Discard stream if it already exists
`nocreate`	If stream does not exist, open fails
`noreplace`	If stream exists, open for output fails unless `ate` or `app` is set
`binary`	Open as a binary stream

Figure 7.2.2 Mode flags.

Name	Purpose
`beg`	Seek from the beginning
`cur`	Seek from the current position
`end`	Seek from the end

Figure 7.2.3 Seek flags.

creates an **ofstream** object associated with the file *out.dat*, which is opened for appending (writing at the end of the file). □

Class **ios** declares an **enum** to give names to flag bits to indicate how to seek (move) in the stream as shown in Figure 7.2.3. These flags are also typically used in classes derived from **ios** (see Section 7.3).

Example 7.2.6. The method **seekp** is defined in the output class **ostream** (see Section 7.3). One form of **seekp** has two arguments: the first is an offset, and the second is the direction. If **out** is an object in class **ostream**, the expression

```
out.seekp( 10, ios::cur )
```

moves the current position in the stream 10 bytes forward. □

Class **ios** declares an **enum** to give names to flag bits to indicate how to format the stream as shown in Figure 7.2.4. Also, **ios** furnishes methods to read, set, and clear the format flags (see Figure 7.2.5) and methods to read and change the field width, the fill character, and the number of digits of floating-point precision (see Figure 7.2.6).

Example 7.2.7. The statement

```
old_flags = cout.flags( ios::left
                      | ios::hex
```

Name	Purpose
skipws	Skip white space
left	Left-justify
right	Right-justify
internal	Padding after sign or base flag
dec	Decimal
oct	Octal
hex	Hexadecimal
showbase	Use base indicator on output
showpoint	Print trailing zeros in floating-point numbers
uppercase	Use uppercase letters on hex output
showpos	Use + with positive integers
scientific	Use scientific notation for floating-point numbers: `d.dddEdd`
fixed	Use fixed notation for floating-point numbers: `d.ddd`
unitbuf	Flush any stream after write
stdio	Flush standard output and standard error after write

Figure 7.2.4 Format flags.

```
                    | ios::showpoint
                    | ios::uppercase
                    | ios::fixed );
```

saves the old flags in `old_flags` and formats the standard output as left-justify output, print integers in hexadecimal, print trailing zeros, print hexadecimal output using uppercase letters, and print floating-point output as `dd.dddddd`.   □

Example 7.2.8. The code

```
old_fill = cout.fill( '0' );
// write to standard output
cout.fill( old_fill );
```

changes the fill character to zero and saves the old fill character in `old_fill`. After writing to the standard output, it restores the original fill character. The same effect could be obtained more easily by using manipulators (see Section 7.4).   □

Example 7.2.9. The method `setf`, with one argument, sets the specified format flags without changing the other flags. For example, the statement

```
cout.setf( ios::showbase );
```

Method	Purpose
flags()	Return a **long** that shows the format flags
flags(long)	Set the format flags to the **long** passed and return the old flags
setf(long)	Set specified flags and return the old flags
setf(ios::dec, ios::basefield)	Set integer base to decimal and return the old flags
setf(ios::oct, ios::basefield)	Set integer base to octal and return the old flags
setf(ios::hex, ios::basefield)	Set integer base to hex and return the old flags
setf(ios::left, ios::adjustfield)	Set left justification and return the old flags
setf(ios::right, ios::adjustfield)	Set right justification and return the old flags
setf(ios::internal, ios::adjustfield)	Put fill character between sign and value and return the old flags
setf(ios::scientific, ios::floatfield)	Set scientific notation and return the old flags
setf(ios::fixed, ios::floatfield)	Set fixed notation and return the old flags
setf(0, ios::floatfield)	Set default notation and return the old flags
unsetf(long)	Clear specified flags and return the old flags

Figure 7.2.5 Methods to read, set, and clear the format flags.

Method	Purpose
width()	Return the field width
width(int)	Change the field width and return the old width (the width reverts to 0 after the next number or string is written)
fill()	Return the fill character
fill(char)	Change the fill character and return the old fill character
precision()	Return the precision (number of digits of floating-point precision)
precision(int)	Change the precision and return the old precision

Figure 7.2.6 Methods to read and change the field width, the fill character, and the precision.

causes subsequent output to show the integer base; that is, octal integers
will be printed with a leading zero, hexadecimal integers will be printed
with a leading 0x, and decimal integers will be printed in the usual way.
The preceding statement is equivalent to

```
cout.flags( cout.flags() | ios::showbase );
```

□

Example 7.2.10. Example 7.2.9 shows how **setf** can be used to change
the format when only a single flag is involved. The situation is more complex
when several flags are involved. For example, to format integer output as
hexadecimal, the **hex** bit must be set and the **dec** and **oct** bits cleared.
To simplify changing the format when several flags are involved, **setf** can
take a second argument. For example, output can be formatted as decimal,
hexadecimal, or octal by using **basefield** as the second argument to **setf**.
The output from the following code

```
cout.setf( ios::hex, ios::basefield );
cout << "Hex: " << 168 << endl;
cout.setf( ios::oct, ios::basefield );
cout << "Octal: " << 168 << endl;
```

is

```
Hex: a8
Octal: 250
```

□

Example 7.2.11. We can modify the code of Example 7.2.10 so that the
output shows the base, and uppercase letters are used on hexadecimal output:

```
cout.setf( ios::showbase | ios::uppercase );
cout.setf( ios::hex, ios::basefield );
cout << "Hex: " << 168 << endl;
cout.setf( ios::oct, ios::basefield );
cout << "Octal: " << 168 << endl;
```

The output is now

```
Hex: 0XA8
Octal: 0250
```

□

Example 7.2.12. We can left- or right-justify output by using **adjustfield**
as the second argument to **setf**. The output from the following code

```
cout.width( 6 );
cout << -100 << endl; // default is right-justify

cout.width( 6 );
cout.setf( ios::left, ios::adjustfield );
cout << -100 << endl;

cout.width( 6 );
cout.setf( ios::right, ios::adjustfield );
cout << -100 << endl;

// width reverts to 0 (default)
cout.setf( ios::right, ios::adjustfield );
cout << -100 << endl;
```

is

```
  -100
-100
  -100
-100
```

In C++, if the output is larger than the width, the output is written anyway in a field whose width is equal to the width of the item to write. Thus, in the last line, the output is right-justified in a field of width four.

Another option that can be used with **adjustfield** is **internal**, which uses the fill character to pad between the sign and the value. For example, the output from the following code

```
cout.width( 6 );
cout.fill( '0' );
cout.setf( ios::internal, ios::adjustfield );
cout << -100 << endl;
```

is

```
-00100
```

□

Example 7.2.13. Floating-point output can be formatted in fixed or scientific notation by using **floatfield** as the second argument to **setf**. The output from the following code

```
const float log10_pi = .497149872;
cout.setf( ios::scientific, ios::floatfield );
cout << log10_pi << endl;
cout.setf( ios::fixed, ios::floatfield );
cout << log10_pi << endl;
```

on our system is

```
4.971499e-01
0.49715
```

On our system, the default precision (which can be changed using the method **precision**) is six. Thus, in the first line of output, six digits are printed to the right of the decimal point. Notice that the value is rounded. In the second line of output, the sixth digit to the right of the decimal point is zero and, by default, is not printed. (Trailing zeros can be printed by setting the **showpoint** flag.) Again, the value is rounded. □

Example 7.2.14. The method **unsetf** always takes only one argument. It clears the specified flags. For example, the statement

```
cin.unsetf( ios::skipws );
```

clears the **skipws** flag so that white space is *not* skipped. (The default is to skip white space.) □

The method **tie** in **ios** "ties" an input stream to an output stream.

Example 7.2.15. After the statements

```
istream in;
ostream out;
in.tie( out );
```

are executed, the streams **in** and **out** are tied, which means that the **ostream out** is flushed whenever an input operation is attempted on the **istream in**. The value of **in.tie(out)** is the stream to which **in** was previously tied. If **in** was not tied to a stream, the value is 0. When invoked with argument 0, **tie** breaks the tie, if any. When invoked with no argument

```
in.tie();
```

tie simply returns the stream to which **in** is tied, or 0 if **in** is not tied to a stream. □

Class **ios** contains a **static** member **sync_with_stdio** that synchronizes the C++ input/output with the standard C input/output functions. Anytime the C and C++ input/output libraries are intermixed, the method **sync_with_stdio** should be invoked

```
ios::sync_with_stdio();
```

before doing any input or output.

Exercises

In Exercises 1–4, assume that io_obj is an object in class ios.

1. Write an expression whose value is 1 if io_obj's eofbit is 1, and 0 if io_obj's eofbit is 0.

2. Write a statement that clears io_obj's eofbit and does not change any other status bit.

3. Explain how the expression !cin is evaluated in the code

   ```
   if ( !cin ) {
       ...
   }
   ```

4. Write a statement to create an object flout of type ofstream, where flout is associated with the file *data.dat*, which is opened as a binary file. Discard the file if it already exists.

5. Write a statement that moves the current position in the file associated with the object fout in class ostream 10 bytes from the end of the file.

6. Write a statement that formats the standard output as follows: skip white space, right justify, use decimal conversion, use + with positive integers, and use fixed notation for floating-point numbers.

7. Use the method setf to set the showpoint flag on the standard output.

8. Using only the method flags, set the showpoint flag on the standard output. Do not change any other format flag.

9. Use the method unsetf to clear the showpoint flag on the standard output.

10. Using only the method flags, clear the showpoint flag on the standard output. Do not change any other format flags.

11. Use the method setf to set the integer base to octal on the standard output.

12. Using only the method flags, set the oct flag, and clear the dec and hex flags on the standard output.

13. Use the method setf to restore the default notation for floating-point output on the standard output.

14. What is the output?

```
cout.setf( ios::showpos );
cout.setf( ios::left, ios::adjustfield );
cout.fill( 'X' );
cout.width( 6 );
cout << 66;
cout.width( 6 );
cout << 66 << 66 << 66 << endl;
```

15. What is the output?

```
cout.setf( ios::hex, ios::basefield );
cout.setf( ios::showbase | ios::uppercase );
cout.setf( ios::left, ios::adjustfield );
cout.fill( '$' );
cout.width( 6 );
cout << 66;
cout.width( 6 );
cout << 66 << 66 << 66 << endl;
```

16. What is the output?

```
cout.setf( ios::showpoint );
cout.setf( ios::left, ios::adjustfield );
cout.setf( ios::fixed, ios::floatfield );
cout.precision( 4 );
float x = 8.72;
cout.width( 8 );
cout << x;
cout.width( 8 );
cout << x << x << x << endl;
```

7.3   The High-Level Input/Output Classes

In this section we discuss the classes

```
                    istream
                    ostream
                    iostream
                    istream_withassign
                    ostream_withassign
                    iostream_withassign
```

which provide a high-level interface to input and output.

istream

The class `istream` is publicly derived from `ios`

```
class istream : virtual public ios {
   ...
};
```

and provides high-level methods for input streams.

The method **get** is overloaded and so can be invoked in various ways. When the version of **get** whose declaration is

```
istream& get( signed char* a, int m, char c = '\n' );
```

is invoked, characters are read from the stream into the array **a** until the character **c** (whose default value is '\n') is encountered, until end-of-stream, or until **m** - **1** characters have been read into **a**, whichever happens first. The character **c** is *not* placed in the array **a**, nor is it removed from the stream. The method **get** adds a null terminator '\0'. Notice that **get** never stores more than **m** characters in **a**. This version of **get** resembles the C function **fgets**. It is different from **fgets** in that **fgets** stores the newline terminator and removes it from the stream. The method **get** returns the (updated) stream that invoked it.

Example 7.3.1. The value returned by **get** may be used as a true/false condition to test for end-of-file:

```
while ( cin.get( a, 81 ) ) {
   // process line stored in a
   ...
}
```

The stream return value is converted to type **void***, which is zero on an error condition such as end-of-file, and nonzero, otherwise. □

Another version of **get** behaves exactly as the version described previously except that the first parameter has type **unsigned char***.

When the version of **get** whose declaration is

```
istream& get( signed char& c );
```

is invoked, the next character, white space or not, is read into the **char c**, and **get** returns the (updated) stream that invoked it.

Another version of **get** behaves exactly as the version described in the last paragraph except that the first parameter has type **unsigned char&**.

Example 7.3.2. The following code reads a line (defined as ending with a newline) and then checks to see whether the line read was too long to store:

```
const int line_len = 81;
char a[ line_len ], c;
cin.get( a, line_len );
cin.get( c );
```

```
if ( c != '\n' )
    cout << "Line too long." << endl;
```

□

When the version of **get** whose declaration is

```
int get();
```

is invoked, the next character in the stream, white space or not, is returned, or if no characters remain to be read, **get** returns EOF. This version of **get** resembles the C function **fgetc**.

When the version of **get** whose declaration is

```
istream& get( streambuf& buff, char = '\n' );
```

is invoked, characters are read from the stream into the **streambuf** object **buff** until the character c, whose default value is '\n', is encountered. The character c is *not* placed in **buff**, nor is it removed from the stream.

The method **read** whose declaration is

```
istream& read( signed char* a, int n );
```

works similarly to **get**, except that no terminator character such as '\n' is provided and no null terminator '\0' is placed in the array a. The method **read**, which is used to read binary data, returns the stream which invoked it. The method **gcount** can be used to obtain the number of characters actually read. The method **read** resembles the C function **fread**.

Another version of **read** behaves exactly as the version described in the last paragraph except that the first parameter has type **unsigned char***.

The method **peek** whose declaration is

```
int peek();
```

returns the next character from the stream but does not remove it from the stream. If no characters remain to be read, **peek** returns EOF.

The method **putback** whose declaration is

```
istream& putback( char c );
```

returns the character c to the stream. The method **putback** returns the stream which invoked it. It resembles the C function **ungetc**.

The method **ignore** whose declaration is

```
istream& ignore( int count = 1, int stop = EOF );
```

removes **count** characters from the stream or all characters from the stream up to **stop**, whichever comes first. The removed characters are not stored but simply discarded. The method **ignore** returns the stream which invoked it.

The method **gcount** whose declaration is

```
int gcount();
```

returns the number of characters last read.

There are separate stream position markers—one for input and one for output. The methods `seekg` and `tellg` set and read the position within the input stream (**g** in `seekg` stands for "get"). The output stream class `ostream` has methods `seekp` and `tellp` to set and read the position within the output stream (**p** in `seekp` and `tellp` stands for "put"). These methods resemble the C functions `fseek` and `ftell`.

There are two versions of `seekg`. The first, whose declaration is

```
istream& seekg( streamoff off, seek_dir dir );
```

moves the input stream position marker `off` bytes from `dir`, which must be one of the following: `beg` (from the beginning of the stream), `cur` (from the current position), or `end` (from the end of the stream). A `typedef` makes `streamoff` an actual type—typically, `long`. The method `seekg` returns the stream which invoked it. When this version of `seekg` is used with a file, the file should be opened as a binary file.

The method `tellg` whose declaration is

```
streampos tellg();
```

returns the location of the input stream position marker. A `typedef` makes `streampos` an actual type—typically `long`.

The version of `seekg` whose declaration is

```
istream& seekg( streampos pos );
```

sets the input stream position marker to location `pos` as returned by `tellg`. When this version of `seekg` is used with a file, it is *not* necessary to open the file as a binary file.

The class `istream` overloads the right-shift operator for formatted input of built-in types. A typical declaration is

```
istream& operator>>( int& );
```

Here an `int` is read into a variable passed by reference, after which the stream is returned.

Example 7.3.3. Because `operator>>` returns the stream, `>>` can be chained:

```
cin >> i >> j;
```

Because `>>` associates from the left, first the expression

```
cin >> i
```

is evaluated. An integer is read into `i` and the expression is replaced by its value, the updated stream. This updated stream then acts on `j`

```
cin >> j
```

and an integer is read into `j`.   □

Among the types handled by `>>` are

```
signed char*      unsigned short&
unsigned char*    unsigned int&
signed char&      unsigned long&
unsigned char&    float&
short&            double&
int&              long double&
long&
```

When `>>` is used for input, the default action is to skip white space, even for type `char` (unlike `scanf` in C).

Example 7.3.4. The type `char&` is used to read one character. For the input

```
x    y    z
```

the code

```
char c;

while ( cin >> c )
   cout << c;
cout << endl;
```

prints

```
xyz
```

since white space is skipped.   □

The type `char*` is used with `>>` to read a string. If the field width is zero (the default), white space is skipped, after which all non-white space characters up to the next white space character are read and stored. If the width is set to **n**, white space is skipped, after which all non-white space characters up to the next white space character, or **n** − 1 characters, whichever occurs first, are read and stored. In either case, a null terminator is added.

Example 7.3.5. The code

```
char a[ 80 ];
cin.width( 80 );
cin >> a;
```

avoids overflow in the array **a**.   □

The skip white space option can be disabled by clearing the `skipws` flag.

Example 7.3.6. The following code echoes the standard input to the standard output:

```
char c;

// clear skip white space flag
cin.unsetf( ios::skipws );

while ( cin >> c )
   cout << c;
cout << endl;
```

           □

For integer types, if the first non-white space character is not a digit or a sign, **failbit** is set and no further data can be read until **failbit** is cleared. Similarly, for floating-point types, if the first non-white space character is not a digit, a sign, or a decimal point, **failbit** is also set and no further data can be read until **failbit** is cleared.

Example 7.3.7. The following program accepts integer input and echoes it in hexadecimal. If the input is not an integer, a message is printed and the user is prompted to reenter the item:

```
#include <iostream.h>
#include <stdlib.h>

enum { false, true };

int main()
{
   int val, ok;
   char line[ 80 ], c;

   cout << hex;

   for ( ; ; ) {
      cout << "Enter an integer (negative to quit): "
           << flush;
      ok = true;
      cin >> val; // if val is illegal, state != 0
      if ( cin.rdstate() ) {
         cout << "Bad input. Redo." << endl;
         cin.clear(); // clear state so input can be read
         cin.get( line, 80 ); // read and dump bad input
         cin.get( c ); // read and dump '\n'
         ok = false;
      }
```

```
        if ( ok )
           if ( val < 0 )
              break;
           else
              cout << val << endl;
     }

     return EXIT_SUCCESS;
}
```

□

The operator >> can be overloaded for user-defined types.

Example 7.3.8. Given the declaration

```
struct String {
   char str[ 100 ];
   void store( char* );
};
```

we can overload >> to read a C string into a **String** object as follows:

```
istream& operator>>( istream& in, String& s )
{
   return in >> s.str;
}
```

The overloaded input operator could be used as

```
String s;
cin >> s;
```

The second statement

```
cin >> s;
```

is equivalent to

```
operator>>( cin, s );
```

□

Class **istream** has one constructor

```
istream( streambuf* );
```

which can be used to establish a connection to a buffer object.

ostream

The class **ostream** is publicly derived from **ios**:

```
class ostream : virtual public ios {
   ...
};
```

and provides high-level methods for output streams.

The method `put` whose declaration is

```
ostream& put( char );
```

writes the character passed to the output stream. The method `put` returns the (updated) stream which invoked it. It resembles the C function `fputc`.

Example 7.3.9. Given the definition

```
char c = '$';
```

the statements

```
cout << c;
```

and

```
cout.put( c );
```

are equivalent. □

The method `write` whose declaration is

```
ostream& write( const signed char* a, int m );
```

writes `m` characters from the array `a` to the output stream. The method `write`, which is used to write binary data, returns the stream which invoked it. It resembles the C function `fwrite`.

Another version of `write` behaves exactly as the version described in the last paragraph except that the first parameter has type `const unsigned char*`.

The methods `seekp` and `tellp` whose declarations are

```
ostream& seekp( streampos );
ostream& seekp( streamoff, seek_dir );
streampos tellp();
```

set and read the output stream file position marker. They behave similarly to their `istream` counterparts `seekg` and `tellg`.

When the version

```
ostream& seekp( streamoff, seek_dir );
```

is used with a file, the file should be opened as a binary file. The version

```
ostream& seekp( streampos );
```

should take as an argument a value returned by `tellp`. When this latter version is used with a file, it is *not* necessary to open the file as a binary file.

The method `flush` whose declaration is

```
ostream& flush();
```

flushes the buffer. The method **flush** returns the stream which invoked it. It resembles the C function **fflush**.

The class **ostream** overloads the left-shift operator for formatted output. A typical declaration is

```
ostream& operator<<( short );
```

Here a **short** is written, after which the stream is returned.

Among the types handled by << are

```
const signed char*      float
const unsigned char*    double
signed char             long double
unsigned char           unsigned short
short                   unsigned int
int                     unsigned long
long                    void*
```

Either version

```
ostream& operator<<( const signed char* );
ostream& operator<<( const unsigned char* );
```

writes a null-terminated string to the output stream.

The version

```
ostream& operator<<( void* );
```

writes the value of a pointer to the output stream.

Example 7.3.10. In our system, the code

```
float x = 146.25;
cout << "x = " << x << endl << "&x = "
     << ( void* ) &x << endl;
```

printed

```
x = 146.25
&x = 0xefffef90
```

□

The operator << can be overloaded for user-defined types.

Example 7.3.11. Given the declaration

```
struct String {
   char str[ 100 ];
   void store( char* );
};
```

we can overload << to write the string stored in a **String** object as follows:

```
ostream& operator<<( ostream& out, String& s )
{
    return out << s.str;
}
```

The overloaded output operator could be used as

```
String s;
s.store( "Friends of Bill\n" );
cout << s;
```

□

Class `ostream` also has one constructor

```
ostream( streambuf* );
```

which permits a connection to a buffer object.

iostream

Class `iostream` is publicly inherited from both `istream` and `ostream`. Its *entire* declaration is

```
class iostream : public istream, public ostream {
public:
    iostream( streambuf* );
    virtual ~iostream();
protected:
    iostream();
};
```

thus it provides high-level methods for input/output streams.

The withassign Classes

Class `istream_withassign` is publicly inherited from `istream`. Its entire declaration is

```
class istream_withassign : public istream {
public:
    istream_withassign();
    virtual ~istream_withassign();
    istream_withassign& operator=( istream& );
    istream_withassign& operator=( streambuf* );
};
```

The default constructor does no initialization. The overload of the assignment operator with parameter type `istream&` gets a buffer from the `istream` object passed to it and does a complete initialization. The overload of the assignment operator with parameter type `streambuf*` associates the `streambuf` object whose address is passed with the stream and does a complete initialization.

Similarly, `ostream_withassign` is publicly inherited from `ostream` and it adds an overload of the assignment operator; `iostream_withassign` is publicly inherited from `iostream` and it adds an overload of the assignment operator.

Exercises

---

1. Write a statement that reads the next 100 bytes from the standard input (white space or not) and stores them in the `char` array `a`.

2. Write a statement that reads and discards the next 100 bytes from the standard input (white space or not).

3. What is the output?

   ```
   cin.ignore( 50 );
   cout << cin.gcount() << endl;
   ```

   Assume that the standard input is `abcde` (with `e` as the last character). Tell which character would next be read after each sequence of statements in Exercises 4–8 is executed.

4. `cin.seekg( 1, ios::beg );`

5. `cin.seekg( -1, ios::end );`

6. `cin.seekg( 2 );`
   `cin.seekg( 1, ios::cur );`

7. `cin.seekg( -2, ios::end );`
   `cin.seekg( 1, ios::cur );`

8. `cin.seekg( 1, ios::beg );`
   `p = cin.tellp();`
   `cin.seekg( -2, ios::end );`
   `cin.seekg( p );`

9. Assume that a method `read` has been added to the zip code class of Section 3.4 and overload `>>` to read a zip code.

10. Write a code slice that reads strings, delimited by single quotes, from the standard input until end-of-file and stores the strings in a two-dimensional array of `char`. *Example*: If the input is

```
'Marty Kalin'    'Don Knuth'
```

Marty Kalin would be read and stored as the first string and **Don Knuth** would be read and stored as the second string. Assume that there are no errors in the input.

11. Write a code slice that reads lines (terminated by '**\n**') from the standard input and stores them in a two-dimensional array of **char**. Reading stops when a line containing only '**\n**' is encountered. This newline is removed from the standard input but is not stored. *Example*: If the input is

```
Marty Kalin
Don Knuth

Grace Slick
```

the strings **Marty Kalin** and **Don Knuth** would be read and stored. The file position marker would be on **G** in **Grace Slick**. Assume that the standard input begins with a nonblank line.

12. Write a statement to write 50 characters from the **char** array **a** to the standard output.

13. Overload **<<** to print a zip code for the zip code class of Section 3.4.

7.4 Manipulators

We introduced manipulators in Section 2.4; here, we look at them in detail.

A **manipulator** is a function that either directly or indirectly modifies a stream. For example, the system manipulator **hex** causes subsequent input or output to be hexadecimal. A manipulator is used with the overloaded input operator **>>** or the overloaded output operator **<<**. For example,

```
int i = 10;
cout << hex << i << endl;
```

prints the value 10 in hexadecimal.

Several manipulators are predefined (see Figure 7.4.1). To use predefined manipulators with no arguments (e.g., **endl**), include *iostream.h*. To use predefined manipulators with arguments (e.g., **setfill**), include *iomanip.h*.

Example 7.4.1. We can rewrite Example 7.2.11 in which the output shows the base, and uppercase letters are used on hexadecimal output:

```
cout << setiosflags( ios::showbase | ios::uppercase )
     << hex << "Hex: " << 168 << endl
     << oct << "Octal: " << 168 << endl;
```

$\square$

Manipulator	*Acts On*	*Purpose*
`endl`	`ostream`	Write newline and flush stream
`ends`	`ostream`	Write null terminator in string
`flush`	`ostream`	Flush output stream
`ws`	`istream`	Skip white space
`dec`	`ios`	Read or write integers in decimal
`oct`	`ios`	Read or write integers in octal
`hex`	`ios`	Read or write integers in hexadecimal
`setbase( int n )`	`ostream`	Set integer base to n (0 means default)
`setfill( int c )`	`ostream`	Set fill character to c
`setprecision( int n )`	`ios`	Set precision to n
`setw( int n )`	`ios`	Set field width to n
`setiosflags( long )`	`ios`	Set specified format bits
`resetiosflags( long )`	`ios`	Clear specified format bits

Figure 7.4.1 Manipulators.

We use the terminology *manipulator with no arguments* to refer to manipulators such as **hex** or **endl** because, *when used with << or >>*, these manipulators appear without arguments. Here is an example:

```
cout << endl;
```

In this example, the overloaded << operator invokes the manipulator **endl** and, at this time, **endl** *is passed an argument* and performs its modifications to the stream.

Consider how we might write the code to implement a manipulator such as **endl** with no arguments. Because **endl** modifies the output stream **ostream**, it should take an argument of type **ostream&** and return an argument of type **ostream&**. Now consider a statement such as

```
cout << endl;
```

where **endl** is referenced. The name of a function by itself is of type pointer to function; thus, **endl** is of type "pointer to a function with one argument of type **ostream&** that returns type **ostream&**." Because the statement

```
cout << endl;
```

is equivalent to

```
cout.operator<<( endl );
```

we need an overload of **operator<<** that takes this type of argument: "pointer to a function with one argument of type **ostream&** that returns type **ostream&**." Fortunately for our needs, class **ostream** contains the following version of the overloaded << operator:

```
ostream& ostream::operator<<( ostream& ( *f )( ostream& ) )
{
    return ( *f )( *this );
}
```

The argument **f** to **operator<<** is of type "pointer to a function with one argument of type **ostream&** that returns type **ostream&**." In practice, **f** is a pointer to a manipulator. The method **operator<<** simply invokes the manipulator to which **f** points.

Example 7.4.2. The manipulator **endl** might be written as

```
ostream& endl( ostream& os )
{
    os << '\n';
    return os.flush();
}
```

When the statement

```
cout << endl;
```

is executed, **operator<<** is invoked as

```
cout.operator<<( endl );
```

The body of **operator<<**

```
return ( *f )( *this );
```

is equivalent to

```
return endl( cout );
```

which in turn is equivalent to

```
cout << '\n';
return cout.flush();
```

$\square$

Using the technique illustrated in Example 7.4.2, it is possible to write our own manipulators.

Example 7.4.3. The manipulator

```
ostream& bell( ostream& os )
{
    return os << "\a";
}
```

rings the bell. It could be used as

```
cout << bell;
```

□

Consider writing a manipulator that takes an argument. Suppose, for example, that we want a manipulator `bell( n )` that rings the bell n times. Such a manipulator could be invoked as

```
cout << bell( 10 );
```

Because the function call operator has greater precedence than `<<`, when this statement executes, the function `bell` is invoked with argument 10, after which `operator<<` is invoked as

```
operator<<( cout, val );
```

where *val* is the value returned by `bell`.

So that the compiler can unambiguously choose the correct version of `operator<<` to invoke, the type of the value returned by `bell` must be different from the type of argument expected by all of the other versions of `operator<<`. The trick is to define a class for use with manipulators and to have a manipulator return an object in this class. The returned object is then responsible for invoking some function that actually modifies the stream. We illustrate with the `bell` example.

The argument to the manipulator `bell` is of type `int`, but other manipulators might have different types of arguments. For this reason, the class for use with manipulators is a parameterized class; the parameter type matches the type of the argument to the manipulator.[†] The templates for these classes are declared in *iomanip.h*. We illustrate how to write a manipulator that takes an argument by writing the manipulator `bell( n )` that rings the bell n times.

Example 7.4.4. We use the following template from *iomanip.h* that facilitates writing one-argument manipulators:

```
template< class Typ > class OMANIP {
    Typ n;
    ostream& ( *f )( ostream&, Typ );
public:
    OMANIP( ostream& ( *f1 )( ostream&, Typ ), Typ n1 )
        : f( f1 ), n( n1 ) { }
    friend ostream& operator<<( ostream& os, OMANIP& oman )
        { return ( *oman.f )( os, oman.n ); }
};
```

The parameterized type `Typ` describes the type of the manipulator's argument. In our case, the type is `int`.

[†]Some older versions of C++ may use macros rather than a parameterized class.

The constructor has two parameters: the first `f1` is a pointer to a secondary function that actually modifies the stream, and the second `n1` is the argument to `*f1`. The constructor simply initializes the private members to the arguments passed to it. The **friend** function `operator<<` invokes the function that modifies the stream.

We can write the secondary bell ringer function as

```
ostream& bell_ringer( ostream& os, int n )
{
   for ( int i = 0; i < n; i++ )
      os << "\a";

   return os;
}
```

and the `bell` manipulator as

```
OMANIP< int > bell( int n )
{
   return OMANIP< int >( bell_ringer, n );
}
```

The `bell` manipulator can be invoked as

```
cout << bell( 10 );
```

which is equivalent to

```
operator<<( cout, bell( 10 ) );
```

Because `cout` is a type derived from **ostream** and `bell` returns type `OMANIP< int >`, the correct version of `<<` is invoked (i.e., the **friend** version in class `OMANIP< int >` that takes such an argument).

When the expression

```
OMANIP< int >( bell_ringer, n )
```

in `bell` is evaluated, the constructor for `OMANIP< int >` is invoked, and an object *temp* of type `OMANIP< int >` comes into existence. The constructor initializes `f` to `bell_ringer` and `n` to 10. The function `bell` then returns *temp*, which becomes the second argument to `operator<<`.

When `operator<<` executes with arguments `cout` and *temp*, it in effect returns

```
bell_ringer( cout, 10 )
```

The bell is rung 10 times and the updated `cout` is returned.   □

Although our examples in this section have dealt with **ostream**, exactly the same techniques can be used to write manipulators for **ios** and **istream**. The templates

```
SMANIP< class Typ >
```

for use with `ios`, and

IMANIP< class Typ >

for use with `istream`, are supplied in *iomanip.h.*

Exercises

---

1. Write a statement to clear the **showpoint** flag on **cout**. Use a manipulator.

2. Write a statement to set the fill character on **cout** to '0'. Use a manipulator.

3. Provide an implementation of the manipulator **ws**.

4. Provide an implementation of the manipulator **hex**. *Hint*: This manipulator takes an **ios&** argument and returns type **ios&**.

5. Write a manipulator **scien** that sets scientific notation for floating-point numbers on **ostream**.

6. Write a manipulator **tab** that writes a tab in **ostream**.

7. Provide an implementation of the manipulator **setfill**.

8. Provide an implementation of the manipulator **resetiosflags**.

9. Write a manipulator **setoff(streamoff n)** that sets the file position marker in **istream** to n.

10. Write a manipulator **skipline(int n)** that writes n newlines to **ostream** and then flushes the stream.

11. Explain the difference between a manipulator and a method.

7.5   The File Input/Output Classes

The classes

```
fstreambase
ofstream
ifstream
fstream
```

are declared in *fstream.h*. They provide a high-level interface to file input and output. The header file *fstream.h* includes *iostream.h*, if the latter was not already included.

fstreambase

The class `fstreambase` is publicly inherited from `ios`:

```
class fstreambase : virtual public ios {
    ...
};
```

Its constructors, destructor, and methods contain code for associating files with `fstreambase` objects.

Class `fstreambase` serves as a base class for the file input/output classes `ofstream`, `ifstream`, and `fstream`, which are the classes typically used by a programmer to manipulate files. Each of `ofstream`, `ifstream`, and `fstream` is also derived from the corresponding `stream` class (`ostream`, `istream`, or `iostream`) and, so, has methods for associating files with `ofstream`, `ifstream`, or `fstream` objects as well as methods for moving around in files and for reading or writing files.

The derived classes `ofstream`, `ifstream`, and `fstream` contain constructors, destructors, and methods with behavior similar to those in `fstreambase`. Indeed, the definitions of the constructors, destructors, and methods in these derived classes typically contain calls to the corresponding constructors, destructors, and methods in `fstreambase`, where the actual implementation takes place. Because of the similarity of the constructors, destructors, and methods in `fstreambase` and the derived classes, we give examples only for the derived classes.

The default constructor whose declaration is

```
fstreambase();
```

is used when an `fstreambase` object is created, but a file is not attached to the object.

The constructor whose declaration is

```
fstreambase( const char* filename,
             int mode,
             int prt = filebuf::openprot );
```

is used to associate an `fstreambase` object with the file `filename`, which is opened in mode `mode`. The mode is described by *or*ing mode bits defined in `ios` (see Figure 7.2.2). The static member `openprot` is declared in class `filebuf`; it provides default protection when a file is opened. This constructor provides a system defined buffer.

Among other things, the destructor

```
~fstreambase();
```

closes the file, if any, attached to an **fstreambase** object.

The method **open**

```
void open( const char* filename,
           int mode,
           int prt = filebuf::openprot );
```

is used to open the file **filename** in mode **mode** and associate it with an already existing **fstreambase** object.

The method **close**

```
void close();
```

closes the file, if any, attached to the **fstreambase** object.

ofstream

The class **ofstream** is publicly inherited from **fstreambase** and **ostream**:

```
class ofstream : public fstreambase, public ostream {
    ...
};
```

It contains constructors, a destructor, and methods to associate output files with **ofstream** objects. The class **ofstream** inherits methods from **ostream** to write and move within files.

The default constructor whose declaration is

```
ofstream();
```

is used when an **ofstream** object is created, but a file is not attached to the object.

The constructor whose declaration is

```
ofstream( const char* filename,
          int mode = ios::out,
          int prt = filebuf::openprot );
```

is used to associate an **ofstream** object with the file **filename**, which is opened in mode **mode**. The default mode is output. If a mode is specified, it is automatically *or*ed by the constructor with **ios::out**.

Example 7.5.1. The statement

```
ofstream fout( "data.out" );
```

opens the file *data.out* for output and creates an **ofstream** object **fout** associated with this file.   □

Recall (see Section 7.2) that an **ios** object can be used as a condition in a statement. Since **ofstream** is indirectly derived from **ios**, an **ofstream** object can be used as a condition.

Example 7.5.2. The code

```
ofstream fout( "data.out" );
if ( !fout )
   cerr << "Can't open data.out\n";
```

attempts to open the file *data.out* for output. If the file cannot be opened, an error message is written to the standard error.   □

Typically the constructor whose declaration is

```
ofstream( const char* filename,
          int mode = ios::out,
          int prt = filebuf::openprot );
```

is implemented by simply invoking the corresponding constructor in the base class **fstreambase**:

```
ofstream::ofstream( const char* filename,
                    int mode = ios::out,
                    int prt = filebuf::openprot ) :
   fstreambase( filename, mode | ios::out, prt )
{
}
```

Among other things, the destructor

```
~ofstream();
```

closes the file, if any, attached to an **ofstream** object.

The method **open**

```
void open( const char* filename,
           int mode = ios::out,
           int prt = filebuf::openprot );
```

is redefined in **ofstream** so that the file **filename** is opened in mode **mode** and associated with an already existing **ofstream** object. The default mode is output. If a mode is specified, it is automatically *or*ed with **ios::out**.

Example 7.5.3.   The code

```
ofstream fout;
fout.open( "data.out" );
```

has the same effect as that of Example 7.5.1. The file *data.out* is opened for output and the **ofstream** object **fout** is associated with this file.   □

The method **close**, which is inherited from **fstreambase**, closes the file, if any, attached to the **ofstream** object.

Example 7.5.4.   The file *data.dat* associated with the **ofstream** object **fout** of Example 7.5.3 may be closed with the statement

```
fout.close();
```

ifstream

The class `ifstream` is publicly inherited from `fstreambase` and `istream`:

```
class ifstream : public fstreambase, public istream {
   ...
};
```

It contains constructors, a destructor, and methods to associate input files with `ifstream` objects. The class `ifstream` inherits methods from `istream` to read and move within files.

The default constructor whose declaration is

```
ifstream();
```

is used when an `ifstream` object is created, but a file is not attached to the object.

The constructor whose declaration is

```
ifstream( const char* filename,
          int mode = ios::in,
          int prt = filebuf::openprot );
```

is used to associate an `ifstream` object with the file `filename`, which is opened in mode **mode**. The default mode is input. If a mode is specified, it is automatically *or*ed by the constructor with `ios::in`.

Example 7.5.5. The statement

```
ifstream fin( "data.in" );
```

opens the file *data.in* for input and creates an `ifstream` object `fin` associated with this file.   □

Among other things, the destructor

```
~ifstream();
```

closes the file, if any, attached to an `ifstream` object.

The method **open**

```
void open( const char* filename,
           int mode = ios::in,
           int prt = filebuf::openprot );
```

is redefined in `ifstream` so that the file `filename` is opened in mode **mode** and associated with an already existing `ifstream` object. The default mode is input. If a mode is specified, it is automatically *or*ed with `ios::in`.

Example 7.5.6. The code

```
ifstream fin;
fin.open( "data.in" );
```

has the same effect as that of Example 7.5.5. The file *data.in* is opened for
input and the `ifstream` object `fin` is associated with this file. □

The method `close`, which is inherited from `fstreambase`, closes the file,
if any, attached to the `ofstream` object.

Example 7.5.7. The following program copies one file to another. The
files, whose names are supplied on the command line, are opened in binary
mode so that the program performs a byte-for-byte copy.

```
#include <stdlib.h>
#include <fstream.h>

int main( int argc, char** argv )
{
   ifstream fin( argv[ 1 ], ios::binary );
   if ( !fin ) {
      cerr << "Can't open " << argv[ 1 ] << endl;
      return EXIT_FAILURE;
   }

   ofstream fout( argv[ 2 ], ios::binary );
   if ( !fout ) {
      cerr << "Can't open " << argv[ 2 ] << endl;
      return EXIT_FAILURE;
   }

   char c;
   while ( fin.get( c ) )
      fout.put( c );

   return EXIT_SUCCESS;
}
```

□

fstream

The class `fstream` is publicly inherited from `fstreambase` and `iostream`:

```
class fstream : public fstreambase, public iostream {
   ...
};
```

It contains constructors, a destructor, and methods to associate input/out-
put files with `fstream` objects. The class `fstream` inherits methods from
`iostream` to read, write, and move within files.

The default constructor whose declaration is

```
fstream();
```

is used when an **fstream** object is created but a file is not attached to the object.

The constructor whose declaration is

```
fstream( const char* filename,
         int mode,
         int prt = filebuf::openprot );
```

is used to associate an **fstream** object with the file **filename**, which is opened in mode **mode**. The mode must be specified since no default value is supplied.

Example 7.5.8. The statement

```
fstream finout( "data.dat", ios::in | ios::out );
```

opens the file *data.dat* for input and output, and creates an **fstream** object **finout** associated with this file.   □

Among other things, the destructor

```
~fstream();
```

closes the file, if any, attached to an **fstream** object.

The method **open**

```
void open( const char* filename,
           int mode,
           int prt = filebuf::openprot );
```

is redefined in **fstream** so that the file **filename** is opened in mode **mode** and associated with an already existing **fstream** object. The mode must be specified since no default value is supplied.

Example 7.5.9. The code

```
fstream finout;
finout.open( "data.dat", ios::in | ios::out );
```

has the same effect as that of Example 7.5.8. The file *data.dat* is opened for input and output, and the **fstream** object **finout** is associated with this file.   □

The method **close**, which is inherited from **fstreambase**, closes the file, if any, attached to the **fstream** object.

The next section gives a major example involving the class **fstream**.

Exercises

---

1. Write two statements. The first statement creates an **ifstream** object **fin**. The second statement opens the file *weather.in* and associates it with **fin**.

2. Write two statements. The first statement creates an **ofstream** object **fout**. The second statement opens the file *news.out* for appending and associates it with **fout**.

3. Write one statement that creates an **fstream** object **finout** associated with the binary file *stars.dat*, which is opened for input and output. The open should fail if the file does not exist.

4. Since we could open a file for input and output with the statement

   ```
   ifstream finout( "data.dat", ios::out );
   ```

   why do we need class **fstream**?

5. The following code attempts to open the file *data.dat* for input, do some processing, close it, reopen it for output, and then do more processing. What is the error?

   ```
   // open file for reading
   ifstream f( "data.dat" );
   // process
   f.close();
   // open file for writing
   ofstream f( "data.dat" );
   // process
   ```

6. Correct the error in Exercise 5.

7. Write a complete program that copies files in the order listed on the command line (the first file—the executable—is skipped) to the standard output. Files that cannot be opened for reading are ignored. (This program is similar to the UNIX utility **cat**.)

7.6 Sample Application: A Random Access File Class

Problem _____

A **random access file** is a file in which we can access records in any order whatsoever and not necessarily in physical order. We implement a random access file class that allows the user to create and use a random access file. In particular, the user can add a record, find a record, or remove a record.

In our implementation, the data read and written are *binary data*, so that *any* kind of data can be stored and retrieved from the file. The user can directly manipulate the binary data, or a class could be created as an interface to the binary data.

Sample Input/Output

The following sample input/output shows the random access file class in action. We first create a new file. Although the random access file class allows records and keys of any size, the records here are five bytes long to simplify the example. The first three bytes make up the key. User input is underlined.

```
New file (Y/N)? y

[A]dd
[F]ind
[R]emove
[Q]uit? a
Which record to add? 125xx
Record added

[A]dd
[F]ind
[R]emove
[Q]uit? f
Key? 125
Record found: 125xx

[A]dd
[F]ind
[R]emove
[Q]uit? f
Key? 130
Record not found

[A]dd
[F]ind
[R]emove
[Q]uit? r
Key? 125
Record removed
```

File   *Header...* T150aaF   T167bb...
                     ↑   ↑   ↑   ↑
Byte   0   256 262   268
Relative address   0   1   2

Figure 7.6.1 A relative file.

```
[A]dd
[F]ind
[R]emove
[Q]uit? f
Key? 125
Record not found

[A]dd
[F]ind
[R]emove
[Q]uit? q
```

Solution

We use a **relative file**, that is, a file in which a record's **relative address** (as opposed to its *physical* address) is its position in the file: first, second, ... Given a key, we can translate it into a relative address. Once we have the relative address, we can quickly determine approximately where the record is located in the file and then access it directly. A relative file is thus analogous to an array. Just as each of the array's elements has a position relative to the first, so each element in a relative file has a position relative to the first.

The records in a relative file are stored contiguously following the file header, whose purpose we will explain later. The first byte of a record, which is not part of the logical record, holds a status flag that indicates whether a record is stored (T for "taken"), whether a record was stored but deleted (D for "deleted"), or whether a record was never stored (F for "free"). The remaining bytes store the key and the rest of the record. If, as in the sample input/output, the logical records are five bytes, the file appears as in Figure 7.6.1, assuming a 256-byte header.

To access a record, we define a **hash function** h that, given a key, produces a relative storage address:

$$h(\ key\ ) = \text{Record's relative address}$$

Although there are many different ways to define hash functions, our implementation uses the division-remainder method. We define the hash function

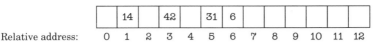

Relative address: 0   1   2   3   4   5   6   7   8   9   10 11 12

Figure 7.6.2 Inserting in a relative file.

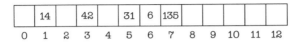

Relative address: 0   1   2   3   4   5   6   7   8   9   10 11 12

Figure 7.6.3 Resolving a collision in a relative file.

h by the rule

$$h(\ key\ ) = key\ \%\ divisor$$

where the modulus operator % yields the remainder after dividing *key* by *divisor*. For example, if *key* is 134 and *divisor* is 13, the record's relative address is 4. If *divisor* is n, the relative addresses range from 0 through $n - 1$.

When two distinct keys hash to the same relative storage address, we say that a **collision** occurs. For example, if our hash function is

$$h(\ key\ ) = key\ \%\ 13$$

we have

$$h(\ 134\ ) = 4 = h(\ 147\ )$$

There is a collision: The keys 134 and 147 map to the same relative address.

Any hashing system must provide a **collision resolution policy**—a way of handling collisions. Our collision resolution policy is called **linear probing**. When a collision occurs, we simply move to the next highest relative address (with the first record position assumed to follow the last record position). For example, if we insert the keys 42, 6, 31, and 14 in the relative file with relative addresses 0 through 12 using the hash function $h(\ key\ ) = key\ \%\ 13$, we obtain the situation shown in Figure 7.6.2. Now suppose that we insert the key 135. Because

$$h(\ 135\ ) = 5 = h(\ 31\ )$$

a collision occurs. Using linear probing, we insert 135 in the next highest unoccupied spot, 7. We obtain the situation shown in Figure 7.6.3.

Divisors should be chosen to minimize collisions. Research and experience show that divisors with no small prime factors do reasonably well at avoiding collisions. Avoiding collisions requires more than a good divisor, however. As more and more records are added to a relative file, collisions become more likely. A file's **load factor**, defined as

$$\text{load factor} = \frac{\text{number of records in file}}{\text{file's maximum capacity}}$$

is the percentage of occupied cells. Research and experience show that a relative file's load factor should not exceed 70 to 80 percent.

To delete a record, we mark it D (deleted) rather than physically delete it.

When we search for a record with a given key k, we first hash to relative address $addr = k \% divisor$, where $divisor$ is the number of slots in the file. If the record at relative address $addr$ has status T (taken), we check whether this record has key k. If so, the search terminates successfully; otherwise, we continue the search by checking the record at relative address

$$(addr + 1) \% divisor$$

If the record at relative address $addr$ has status F (free), the search terminates unsuccessfully since, if the record were present, we would have found it before reaching the free slot. If the record at relative address $addr$ has status D (deleted), we must continue the search by checking the record at relative address

$$(addr + 1) \% divisor$$

since the record we are searching for may have been inserted before the record at address $addr$ was deleted and would thus be found after further probing.

Distinguishing between free and deleted slots usually allows us to terminate the search for a nonexistent record before searching the entire file.

C++ Implementation

```
#include <stdio.h>
#include <fstream.h>
#include <string.h>
#include <stdlib.h>
#include <ctype.h>

const int header_size = 256;
const char Taken = 'T';
const char Free = 'F';
const char Deleted = 'D';
const int Success = 1;
const int Fail = 0;

class frandom : public fstream {
protected:
    int isopen; // 1 if file is open, else 0
    long slots;
    long record_size; // includes 1-byte flag
```

```
        long key_size;
        long total_bytes;
        long no_records; // no of records stored
        long loc_address; // computed by locate
        char* buffer; // holds one record
        char* stored_key; // holds one key
        long get_address( const char* );
        int locate( const char* );
    public:
        frandom();
        frandom( const char* ); // open existing file
        frandom( const char*, int, int, int ); // open new file
        ~frandom();
        void open( const char* ); // open existing file
        void open( const char*, int, int, int ); // open new file
        void close();
        long get_slots() { return slots; }
        long get_record_size() { return record_size; }
        long get_key_size() { return key_size; }
        long get_total_bytes() { return total_bytes; }
        long get_no_records() { return no_records; }
        int add_record( const char* );
        int find_record( char* );
        int remove_record( const char* );
    };


    frandom::~frandom()
    {
        if ( isopen ) {
            delete [ ] stored_key;
            delete [ ] buffer;
            char buff[ header_size ];
            for ( int i = 0; i < header_size; i++ )
                buff[ i ] = ' ';
            sprintf( buff, "%ld %ld %ld %ld",
                    slots, record_size,
                    key_size, no_records );
            seekp( 0, ios::beg );
            write( buff, header_size );
        }
    }
```

```
frandom::frandom() : fstream()
{
   buffer = stored_key = 0;
   slots = record_size = key_size = 0;
   total_bytes = no_records = 0;
   isopen = fstreambase::rdbuf() -> is_open();
}

frandom::frandom( const char* filename ) : fstream()
{
   buffer = stored_key = 0;

   fstream::open( filename,
                  ios::in |
                  ios::out |
                  ios::binary |
                  ios::nocreate );

   isopen = fstreambase::rdbuf() -> is_open();

   if ( isopen ) {
      char buff[ header_size ];
      read( buff, header_size );
      sscanf( buff, "%ld%ld%ld%ld",
              &slots, &record_size, &key_size,
              &no_records );
      total_bytes = slots * record_size + header_size;
      // get_address needs \0
      stored_key = new char [ key_size + 1 ];
      buffer = new char [ record_size ];
   }
}

frandom::frandom( const char* filename,
                  int sl,
                  int actual_record_size,
                  int ks ) : fstream()
{
   buffer = stored_key = 0;
   fstream::open( filename,
                  ios::in |
                  ios::out |
                  ios::binary |
                  ios::noreplace );
```

```
        isopen = fstreambase::rdbuf() -> is_open();

    if ( isopen ) {
        char buff[ header_size ];
        slots = sl;
        record_size = actual_record_size + 1;
        key_size = ks;
        total_bytes = slots * record_size + header_size;
        no_records = 0;
        // get_address needs \0
        stored_key = new char [ key_size + 1 ];
        for ( int i = 0; i < header_size; i++ )
            buff[ i ] = ' ';
        sprintf( buff, "%ld %ld %ld %ld",
                    slots, record_size,
                    key_size, no_records );
        write( buff, header_size );
        buffer = new char [ record_size ];
        for ( i = 1; i < record_size; i++ )
            buffer[ i ] = ' ';
        buffer[ 0 ] = Free;
        for ( i = 0; i < slots; i++ )
            write( buffer, record_size );
    }
}


// hash function
long frandom::get_address( const char* key )
{
    memcpy( stored_key, key, key_size );
    stored_key[ key_size ] = '\0';
    return ( atol( stored_key ) % slots )
            * record_size + header_size;
}


// locate searches for a record with the specified key.
// If successful, locate returns 1.
// If unsuccessful, locate returns 0.
// locate sets data member loc_address to the address
// of the record if the record is found. This
// address can be then used by find_record
// or remove_record.
//
```

```
// If the record is not found, locate sets loc_address
// to the first D or F slot encountered in its search
// for the record. This address can be used by add_record.
// If there is no D or F slot (full file), locate sets
// loc_address to the hash address of key.
int frandom::locate( const char* key )
{
   // address = current offset in file
   // start_address = hash offset in file
   // unocc_address = first D slot in file
   //               = start_address, if no D slot
   long address, start_address, unocc_address;

   // delete_flag = Fail, if no D slot is found
   //             = Success, if D slot is found
   int delete_flag = Fail;

   address = get_address( key );
   unocc_address = start_address = address;
   do {
      seekg( address, ios::beg );
      switch( get() ) {
      case Deleted:
         if ( !delete_flag ) {
            unocc_address = address;
            delete_flag = Success;
         }
         break;
      case Free:
         loc_address = delete_flag ? unocc_address : address;
         return Fail;
      case Taken:
         seekg( address + 1, ios::beg );
         read( stored_key, key_size );
         if ( memcmp( key, stored_key, key_size ) == 0 ) {
            loc_address = address;
            return Success;
         }
         break;
      }
      address += record_size;
      if ( address >= total_bytes )
         address = header_size;
   } while ( address != start_address );
```

```
    loc_address = unocc_address;
    return Fail;
}

int frandom::add_record( const char* record )
{
    if ( no_records >= slots || locate( record ) )
        return Fail;

    seekp( loc_address, ios::beg );
    write( &Taken, 1 );
    write( record, record_size - 1 );
    no_records++;
    return Success;
}

int frandom::find_record( char* record )
{
    if ( locate( record ) ) {
        seekg( loc_address + 1, ios::beg );
        read( record, record_size - 1 );
        return Success;
    }
    else
        return Fail;
}

int frandom::remove_record( const char* key )
{
    if ( locate( key ) ) {
        --no_records;
        seekp( loc_address, ios::beg );
        write( &Deleted, 1 );
        return Success;
    }
    else
        return Fail;
}

void frandom::open( const char* filename )
{
    fstream::open( filename,
                   ios::in |
```

```
                                     ios::out |
                                     ios::binary |
                                     ios::nocreate );

        int open_fl = fstreambase::rdbuf() -> is_open();

        if ( open_fl ) {
            isopen = open_fl;
            char buff[ header_size ];
            read( buff, header_size );
            sscanf( buff, "%ld%ld%ld%ld",
                    &slots, &record_size, &key_size,
                    &no_records );
            total_bytes = slots * record_size + header_size;
            // get_address needs \0
            stored_key = new char [ key_size + 1 ];
            buffer = new char [ record_size ];
        }
    }

    void frandom::open( const char* filename,
                        int sl,
                        int actual_record_size,
                        int ks )
    {
        fstream::open( filename,
                       ios::in |
                       ios::out |
                       ios::binary |
                       ios::noreplace );

        int open_fl = fstreambase::rdbuf() -> is_open();

        if ( open_fl ) {
            isopen = open_fl;
            char buff[ header_size ];
            slots = sl;
            record_size = actual_record_size + 1;
            key_size = ks;
            total_bytes = slots * record_size + header_size;
            no_records = 0;
            // get_address needs \0
            stored_key = new char [ key_size + 1 ];
```

```
      for ( int i = 0; i < header_size; i++ )
         buff[ i ] = ' ';
      sprintf( buff, "%ld %ld %ld %ld",
               slots, record_size,
               key_size, no_records );
      write( buff, header_size );
      buffer = new char [ record_size ];
      for ( i = 1; i < record_size; i++ )
         buffer[ i ] = ' ';
      buffer[ 0 ] = Free;
      for ( i = 0; i < slots; i++ )
         write( buffer, record_size );
   }
}

void frandom::close()
{
   if ( isopen ) {
      delete [ ] stored_key;
      delete [ ] buffer;
      char buff[ header_size ];
      for ( int i = 0; i < header_size; i++ )
         buff[ i ] = ' ';
      sprintf( buff, "%ld %ld %ld %ld",
               slots, record_size,
               key_size, no_records );
      seekp( 0, ios::beg );
      write( buff, header_size );
      fstreambase::close();
   }
}

int main()
{
   char b[ 10 ], c;

   frandom finout;

   cout << "New file (Y/N)? " << flush;
   cin >> c;
   if ( toupper( c ) == 'Y' ) {
      finout.open( "data.dat", 15, 5, 3 );
      if ( !finout ) {
         cerr << "Couldn't open file" << endl;
```

```
            return EXIT_FAILURE;
        }
    }
    else {
        finout.open( "data.dat" );
        if ( !finout ) {
            cerr << "Couldn't open file" << endl;
            return EXIT_FAILURE;
        }
    }

    do {
        cout << "\n\n[A]dd\n[F]ind\n[R]emove\n[Q]uit? " << flush;
        cin >> c;
        switch ( toupper( c ) ) {
        case 'A':
            cout << "Which record to add? " << flush;
            cin >> b;
            if ( finout.add_record( b ) )
                cout << "Record added" << endl;
            else
                cout << "Record not added" << endl;
            break;
        case 'F':
            cout << "Key? " << flush;
            cin >> b;
            if ( finout.find_record( b ) ) {
                b[ 5 ] = '\0';
                cout << "Record found: " << b << endl;
            }
            else
                cout << "Record not found" << endl;
            break;
        case 'R':
            cout << "Key? " << flush;
            cin >> b;
            if ( finout.remove_record( b ) )
                cout << "Record removed" << endl;
            else
                cout << "Record not removed" << endl;
            break;
        case 'Q':
            break;
```

Member	Purpose
`isopen`	1, if file is open; 0, if file is closed.
`slots`	Number of slots.
`record_size`	Actual record size + 1 (for flag).
`key_size`	Size of key.
`total_bytes`	`slots * record_size`
`no_records`	Number of records stored.
`loc_address`	Set by method `locate`. `loc_address` is where a record was found or where a record can be stored.
`buffer`	Storage for one record.
`stored_key`	Storage for one key plus null terminator.

Figure 7.6.4 Data members of `frandom`.

```
            default:
                cout << "Illegal choice" << endl;
                break;
            }
        } while ( toupper( c ) != 'Q' );

        return EXIT_SUCCESS;
    }
```

Discussion ⎯⎯⎯⎯⎯⎯⎯⎯⎯⎯⎯⎯⎯⎯⎯⎯⎯⎯⎯⎯⎯⎯⎯⎯⎯

We derive our random access file class from the library input/output file class `fstream`:

```
    class frandom : public fstream {
        ...
    };
```

We provide constructors and a destructor, with behavior similar to those in the base class `fstream`, for associating a random access file with an `frandom` object. We also provide methods for associating a random access file with an already existing `frandom` object; for adding, finding, and removing records; and for obtaining information about the file (e.g., the number of slots, the record size, etc.).

The data members of `frandom` and their purposes are listed in Figure 7.6.4. The first 256 bytes of the file are reserved as a *header* for the file. The values of `slots`, `record_size`, `key_size`, and `no_records`, in this order, are stored in the file header.

The default constructor

```
frandom::frandom() : fstream()
{
    ...
}
```

invokes the base class constructor, initializes certain members to zero, and
sets the `isopen` flag:

```
isopen = fstreambase::rdbuf() -> is_open();
```

The member `rdbuf` in `fstreambase` returns a pointer to a buffer object. The
buffer class contains the method `is_open` that returns 1 if the file is open,
or 0 if the file is not open. The default constructor does not associate a file
with an `frandom` object. If an `frandom` object is created with the default
constructor, the method `open` could be used to open a file and associate it
with the `frandom` object.

The constructor

```
frandom::frandom( const char* filename,
                  int sl,
                  int actual_record_size,
                  int ks ) : fstream()
{
    ...
}
```

creates an `frandom` object and associates the new file `filename` with it.

After invoking the base class default constructor and initializing `buffer`
and `stored_key`, the file is opened using the method `open` from `fstream`:

```
fstream::open( filename,
               ios::in |
               ios::out |
               ios::binary |
               ios::noreplace );
```

The file is opened as a binary file for input and output, thus allowing any
kind of data to be read and written. The flag

```
ios::noreplace
```

causes `open` to fail if the file exists, unless **ate** or **app** is set, which is not the
case here. Thus the file is successfully opened only if it is a new file.

The next statement initializes `is_open`

```
isopen = fstreambase::rdbuf() -> is_open();
```

just as in the default constructor.

If the file is opened

```
if ( isopen ) {
```

we initialize data members, allocate storage, write the file header, and initialize the file.

We first allocate storage for the header

```
char buff[ header_size ];
```

and initialize `slots`, `record_size`, `key_size`, `total_bytes`, and `no_records`. We then allocate storage for the key:

```
stored_key = new char [ key_size + 1 ];
```

Next we place the text for the header in `buff` and then write the header to the file:

```
for ( int i = 0; i < header_size; i++ )
   buff[ i ] = ' ';
sprintf( buff, "%ld %ld %ld %ld",
         slots, record_size,
         key_size, no_records );
write( buff, header_size );
```

We then create storage for a record and write `slots` Free records to the file:

```
buffer = new char [ record_size ];
for ( i = 1; i < record_size; i++ )
   buffer[ i ] = ' ';
buffer[ 0 ] = Free;
for ( i = 0; i < slots; i++ )
   write( buffer, record_size );
```

We use the methods `read` and `write` throughout since their purpose is to read and write binary data.

The constructor

```
frandom::frandom( const char* filename ) : fstream()
{
   ...
}
```

creates an `frandom` object and associates an existing file `filename` with it.

After invoking the base class default constructor and initializing `buffer` and `stored_key`, the file is opened using the method `open` from `fstream`:

```
fstream::open( filename,
               ios::in |
               ios::out |
               ios::binary |
               ios::nocreate );
```

The file is opened as a binary file for input and output. The flag

```
ios::nocreate
```

causes **open** to fail if the file does not exist. Thus the file is successfully opened only if it is an existing file.

The next statement initializes **is_open** as in the other two constructors.

If the file is opened, we create storage for the header, read the header, initialize **slots**, **record_size**, **key_size**, **total_bytes**, and **no_records**:

```
char buff[ header_size ];
read( buff, header_size );
sscanf( buff, "%ld%ld%ld%ld",
        &slots, &record_size, &key_size,
        &no_records );
total_bytes = slots * record_size + header_size;
```

We conclude by creating storage for a key and a record:

```
stored_key = new char [ key_size + 1 ];
buffer = new char [ record_size ];
```

The two versions of **open** work similarly to the two preceding constructors. Each associates a file with an existing **frandom** object.

The destructor checks whether a file is open. If a file is open, it **deletes** the dynamically allocated storage for the key and record and writes an updated header to the file:

```
if ( isopen ) {
   delete [ ] stored_key;
   delete [ ] buffer;
   char buff[ header_size ];
   for ( int i = 0; i < header_size; i++ )
      buff[ i ] = ' ';
   sprintf( buff, "%ld %ld %ld %ld",
            slots, record_size,
            key_size, no_records );
   seekp( 0, ios::beg );
   write( buff, header_size );
}
```

The file is closed when the destructor executes since the destructor implicitly calls the base class (**fstream**) destructor, which closes the file.

The method **close** works similarly to the destructor. It adds a call to **fstreambase**'s method **close** to close the file:

```
fstreambase::close();
```

The **protected** method **locate** is used to search for a record. It is used by the **public** methods **add_record**, **find_record**, and **remove_record**.

First **locate** initializes **delete_flag** to **Fail**:

```
int delete_flag = Fail;
```

The flag `delete_flag` is reset to `Success` if `locate` encounters a D (delete) slot. A D slot could be used by **add_record** to store a record.

Next `locate` calls the hash function `get_address`:

```
address = get_address( key );
```

This value is then copied into `unocc_address` and `start_address`:

```
unocc_address = start_address = address;
```

The value of `start_address` is never changed. It is used to check whether all slots in the file have been examined and to terminate the loop if all slots have been examined:

```
do {
    ...
} while ( address != start_address );
```

The variable `unocc_address` is used to save the first occurrence of a D slot.

In the loop, `locate` seeks to `address`

```
seekg( address, ios::beg );
```

and reads the first byte

```
switch( get() ) {
```

If this slot is D and this is the first occurrence of a D slot, the address of this slot is saved and `delete_flag` is changed to `Success`:

```
case Deleted:
    if ( !delete_flag ) {
        unocc_address = address;
        delete_flag = Success;
    }
    break;
```

and the search continues.

If this slot is F (free), `loc_address` is set to the first occurrence of an F or D slot

```
case Free:
    loc_address = delete_flag ? unocc_address : address;
    return Fail;
```

and `Fail` is returned to signal an unsuccessful search. If `locate` was called by **add_record**, **add_record** will insert the new record at address `loc_address`.

If this slot is T (taken), `locate` reads the record and checks whether it is has the desired key:

```
case Taken:
    seekg( address + 1, ios::beg );
    read( stored_key, key_size );
    if ( memcmp( key, stored_key, key_size ) == 0 ) {
```

```
            loc_address = address;
            return Success;
         }
         break;
```

If the key matches, `loc_address` is set to the address of the record and `Success` is returned to signal a successful search. If `locate` was called by `find_record`, `find_record` will store the record at address `loc_address`. If `locate` was called by `delete_record`, `delete_record` will change the flag to D at address `loc_address`.

If the record was not found and an F slot did not terminate the search, `address` is updated to the next slot and the search continues:

```
   address += record_size;
   if ( address >= total_bytes )
      address = header_size;
```

If all the slots are searched, `loc_address` is set to `unocc_address`, and `locate` returns `Fail`.

The method **add_record** checks whether all slots are filled and, if so, it returns `Fail`; it also returns `Fail` if there is already a record stored with the given key:

```
   if ( no_record >= slots || locate( record ) )
      return Fail;
```

Duplicate keys are not allowed.

If `locate` cannot find a record with the given key, **add_record** stores the record at `loc_address` (computed by `locate`), updates `no_records`, and returns `Success`:

```
   seekp( loc_address, ios::beg );
   write( &Taken, 1 );
   write( record, record_size - 1 );
   no_records++;
   return Success;
```

The method **find_record** calls `locate`. If `locate` finds the record, **find_record** copies it at the address passed and returns `Success`; otherwise, **find_record** simply returns `Fail`:

```
   if ( locate( record ) ) {
      seekg( loc_address + 1, ios::beg );
      read( record, record_size - 1 );
      return Success;
   }
   else
      return Fail;
```

The method `remove_record` calls `locate`. If `locate` finds the record, `remove_record` updates `no_records`, flags the record as D, and returns `Success`; otherwise, `remove_record` simply returns `Fail`:

```
if ( locate( key ) ) {
   --no_records;
   seekp( loc_address, ios::beg );
   write( &Deleted, 1 );
   return Success;
}
else
   return Fail;
```

The function **main** creates an **frandom** object (using the default constructor):

```
frandom finout;
```

The user is then asked whether a new or existing file is to be opened:

```
cout << "New file (Y/N)? " << flush;
```

If a new file is to be opened, the version of **open** for new files is invoked. An attempt is made to open the new file *data.dat* with 15 slots, 5-byte records, and 3-byte keys:

```
finout.open( "data.dat", 15, 5, 3 );
```

If the file cannot be opened, a message is printed and the program is terminated:

```
if ( !finout ) {
   cerr << "Couldn't open file" << endl;
   exit( EXIT_FAILURE );
}
```

(Recall that this version of **open** was written so that opening the file would fail if it already exists.)

If an existing file is to be opened, the version of **open** for existing files is invoked. An attempt is made to open the existing file *data.dat*:

```
finout.open( "data.dat" );
```

As in the previous code, if the file cannot be opened, a message is printed and the program is terminated. (Recall that this version of **open** was written so that opening the file would fail if it did not already exist.) A loop then allows the user to repeatedly add, find, or remove records.

7.7   The Character Array Input/Output Classes

The classes

```
strstreambase
ostrstream
istrstream
strstream
```

are declared in *strstream.h*. They provide a high-level interface to character array input and output in much the same way that their counterparts, the **fstream** classes, provide a high-level interface to file input and output. The header file *strstream.h* includes *iostream.h*, if it was not already included.

strstreambase

The class **strstreambase** is publicly inherited from **ios**:

```
class strstreambase: virtual public ios {
    ...
};
```

It serves as a base class for the character array input/output classes **ostrstream**, **istrstream**, and **strstream**, which are the classes used by a programmer to manipulate character arrays. Each of **ostrstream**, **istrstream**, and **strstream** is also derived from the corresponding **stream** class (**ostream**, **istream**, or **iostream**) and, so, has methods for moving around in character arrays and for reading and writing character arrays. The derived classes provide constructors for associating user-defined character arrays or system-defined (dynamic) character arrays with objects in these derived classes.

The only public member in **strstreambase** is **rdbuf**. Its declaration is

```
strstreambuf* rdbuf();
```

The method returns a pointer to the **strstreambuf** buffer object associated with the **strstreambase** object.

Class **strstreambase** has a **protected** constructor that contains code for associating a user-specified character array buffer with an **strstream** object. A second **protected** (default) constructor permits the system to dynamically allocate the character array buffer. Class **strstreambase** also contains a **protected** destructor that, among other things, deallocates any dynamically allocated storage. These **protected** constructors and destructor are typically invoked by **public** constructors, destructors, and methods in derived classes.

ostrstream

The class **ostrstream** is used to write formatted output to character arrays. It performs somewhat the same functionality as the C function **sprintf**.

The entire declaration of the class **ostrstream** is

```
class ostrstream : public strstreambase, public ostream {
public:
   ostrstream( char* buff,
               int len,
               int mode = ios::out );
   ostrstream();
   ~ostrstream();
   char* str();
   int pcount();
};
```

Its constructors and destructor make calls to the **protected** constructors and destructor in **strstreambase** to allocate and deallocate character array buffers. It inherits **public** methods from **ostream** to write and move within character arrays.

The default constructor is used when an **ostrstream** object is created but a character array is not attached to the object. In this case, the system uses its own dynamically created character array buffer.

Example 7.7.1. The statement

```
ostrstream sout;
```

defines the **ostrstream** object **sout**. Output is written to a system-generated, dynamic character array.   □

The constructor whose declaration is

```
ostrstream( char* buff,
            int len,
            int mode = ios::out );
```

is used to associate an **ostrstream** object with the user-specified character array **buff** of length **len**. The character array is opened in mode **mode**. The default mode is output. If **mode** is **ios::app** (append) or **ios::ate** (at end), a null terminator '\0' must occur in the array and the file position marker is placed at this null terminator.

Example 7.7.2. The statement

```
char name[ 10 ];
ostrstream sout( name, 10 );
```

opens the character array **name** for output and creates an **ostrstream** object **sout** associated with this character array.   □

Example 7.7.3. A safer version of the code of Example 7.7.2 is

```
char name[ 10 ];
ostrstream sout( name, sizeof ( name ) );
```

because, if we change the size of the array **name**, the definition is automatically updated to the new size. □

The method **pcount** returns the number of characters currently stored in the character array.

Example 7.7.4. The output from the code

```
ostrstream sout;
sout << "Godzilla vs. the Bionic Monster" << ends;
cout << sout.pcount() << endl;
```

is 32.

The manipulator **ends** writes a null terminator to the output. Notice that the null terminator is included in the count 32. The statement

```
sout << "Godzilla vs. the Bionic Monster";
```

does *not* append a null terminator. □

The method **str** returns the address of the character array buffer. If the buffer has been allocated by the system, the user is now responsible for deallocating it.

Example 7.7.5. The output from the code

```
int i = 6;
ostrstream sout;
sout << "Santa Claus Conquers " << i << " Martians" << ends;
char* ptr = sout.str();
cout << ptr << endl;
delete [ ] ptr;
```

is

```
Santa Claus Conquers 6 Martians
```

After writing to the standard output, the storage for the character array buffer is deallocated. □

istrstream

The class **istrstream** is used to read formatted input into character arrays. It performs somewhat the same functionality as the C function **sscanf**.

The entire declaration of the class **istrstream** is

```
class istrstream : public strstreambase, public istream {
public:
    istrstream( char* buff );
```

```
    istrstream( char* buff, int len );
    ~istrstream();
};
```

It inherits `public` methods from `istream` to read and move within character arrays. Notice that no default constructor is supplied; the user *must* specify the character array to read.

The constructor whose declaration is

```
istrstream( char* buff );
```

is used to associate an `istrstream` object with the user-specified character array `buff`. In this case, a null terminator marks the end of the data, and this null terminator itself is never read. Here, `buff` is an ordinary null-terminated C string.

Example 7.7.6. The output from the code

```
float x;
char* s = "37.805";
istrstream sin( s );
if ( sin >> x )
    cout << "Input succeeded. x = " << x << endl;
else
    cout << "Input failed." << endl;
if ( sin >> x )
    cout << "Input succeeded. x = " << x << endl;
else
    cout << "Input failed." << endl;
```

is

```
Input succeeded. x = 37.805
Input failed.
```

The first time the expression

```
sin >> x
```

is evaluated, the `istrstream` object `sin` reads 37.805 from the character array to which `s` points into the `float` variable `x`. Because the stream position marker is now at the null terminator, the next attempt to read from `s` fails. □

The constructor

```
istrstream( char* buff, int len );
```

is used to associate an `istrstream` object with the user-specified, `len`-byte, character array `buff`. In this case, the byte at index `len` $- 1$ marks the end of the data.

Example 7.7.7. The output from the code

```
    char c, s[ 5 ];
    int i;
    for ( i = 0, c = 'a'; i < 5; i++, c++ )
        s[ i ] = c;
    istrstream sin( s, sizeof ( s ) );
    while ( sin >> c )
        cout << "Input succeeded. c = " << c << endl;
    cout << "at end of array" << endl;
```

is

```
    Input succeeded. c = a
    Input succeeded. c = b
    Input succeeded. c = c
    Input succeeded. c = d
    Input succeeded. c = e
    at end of array
```

☐

strstream

The class **strstream** is used to read and write formatted input and output
in character arrays.

The entire declaration of the class **strstream** is

```
class strstream : public strstreambase, public iostream {
public:
    strstream();
    strstream( char* buff, int len, int mode );
    ~strstream();
    char* str();
};
```

It inherits **public** methods from **iostream** to read, write, and move within
character arrays.

The default constructor is used when an **strstream** object is created but
a character array is not attached to the object. As for class **ostrstream**,
the system uses its own dynamically created character array buffer.

The constructor whose declaration is

```
    strstream( char* buff, int len, int mode );
```

is used to associate an **strstream** object with the user-specified character
array **buff** of length **len**. The character array is opened in mode **mode**. If
mode is **ios::app** (append) or **ios::ate** (at end), a null terminator '\0'
must occur in the array and the stream position marker is placed at this null
terminator.

Example 7.7.8. The statements

```
char name[ 80 ];
strcpy( name, "Hercules" );
strstream sinout( name, sizeof ( name ),
                  ios::in | ios::out | ios::ate );
```

open the character array `name` for input and output and create an `strstream` object `sinout` associated with this character array. Initially reading and writing occur at byte 8, where the null terminator following *Hercules* is stored.   □

The method `str` behaves exactly like the method with the same name in `ostrstream`.

Exercises

---

1. Rewrite the code of Example 7.7.5 replacing the system-generated character buffer with a user-defined character buffer.

2. Use an `ostrstream` object to convert a `long` value to a character string.

3. Use an `istrstream` object to convert a character string that represents a `long double` value to type `long double`.

4. A character array contains

   ```
   s "..." "..."
   ```

   Use an appropriate object from this section to place the characters between the first pair of double quotes in the character array `first` and the characters between the second pair of double quotes in the character array `second`.

7.8   Sample Application: A High-Level Copy Function

Problem _____

Write a function that copies from an arbitrary `istream` object to an arbitrary `ostream` object.

Solution _____

We copy character by character using the overloaded `>>` and `<<` operators. We must be careful to change the default from "skip white space" to "do

not skip white space," because we want to copy all of the characters—white
space or not. Before returning from the function, we restore the format flags.
After presenting the C++ implementation, we give several examples using
classes discussed in this chapter.

C++ Implementation

```cpp
#include <iostream.h>

// copy from istream to ostream
void copy( istream& in, ostream& out )
{
   char c;
   long fl;

   // don't skip white space
   // save old flags in fl to restore at end
   fl = in.unsetf( ios::skipws );

   while ( in >> c )
      out << c;

   // restore flags
   in.flags( fl );
}
```

Discussion

We present several **main** programs to show how **copy** can be used to copy
one object to another when the objects are in classes derived from **istream**
and **ostream**.

The following code copies the standard input to the standard output:

```cpp
#include <iostream.h>
#include <stdlib.h>

void copy( istream&, ostream& );

int main()
{
   copy( cin, cout );

   return EXIT_SUCCESS;
}
```

The next code copies from the file *data.in* to the file *data.out*:

```
#include <fstream.h>
#include <stdlib.h>

void copy( istream&, ostream& );

int main()
{
   ifstream fin( "data.in" );
   ofstream fout( "data.out" );

   copy( fin, fout );

   return EXIT_SUCCESS;
}
```

The next code copies a character array to a character array and then writes to the standard output to confirm the copy:

```
#include <strstream.h>
#include <stdlib.h>

void copy( istream&, ostream& );

int main()
{
   char buff[ 30 ];
   istrstream sin( "Junior G-Men of the Air" );
   ostrstream sout( buff, sizeof ( buff ) );

   copy( sin, sout );
   sout << ends;
   cout << buff << endl;

   return EXIT_SUCCESS;
}
```

Notice that it is necessary to append a null terminator because the null terminator is not copied by the copy function.

Our last example copies an array to the file *data.out*:

```
#include <fstream.h>
#include <strstream.h>
#include <stdlib.h>

void copy( istream&, ostream& );
```

```
int main()
{
    istrstream sin( "Junior G-Men of the Air" );
    ofstream fout( "data.out" );

    copy( sin, fout );

    return EXIT_SUCCESS;
}
```

Exercises

1. Write a **main** function that copies a file to an array.

2. Write a **main** function that copies an array to the standard output.

3. Write a **main** function that copies a file to the standard error.

4. Write a high-level copy function that converts each lowercase character to an uppercase character and passes non-lowercase characters unchanged.

5. Write a high-level copy function that replaces each tab character by the appropriate number of spaces. The copy function should have a third parameter that describes the tab setting (e.g., if this parameter is 3, the tabs are set at columns $4, 7, 10, \ldots$, where column 1 is the first column).

7.9   The Buffer Classes

The classes

streambuf

filebuf

strstreambuf

provide support for the programmer to manipulate buffers. Class **streambuf** is declared in *iostream.h*; class **filebuf** is declared in *fstream.h*; and class **strstreambuf** is declared in *strstream.h*. Class **streambuf** provides constructors and methods for setting up character arrays to use as buffers, for moving around in buffers, and for reading from and writing to buffers. Class **filebuf**, which is derived from **streambuf**, provides buffered access to files. Class **strstreambuf**, which is also derived from **streambuf**, provides access to character arrays. The high-level classes discussed previously in this chapter make use of these buffer classes (recall that class **ios** contains a pointer to a buffer object) and provide a transparent user interface to the buffer classes. For this reason, many programmers never directly use these buffer classes.

Each object in a buffer class uses a character array as a buffer. We refer to this array as a *character buffer* and the classes or objects themselves as *buffer classes* or *buffer objects*.

streambuf

Class `streambuf` is the base buffer class. The default constructor creates a `streambuf` object without assigning a character buffer. The constructor whose declaration is

```
streambuf( char* buff, int len );
```

creates a `streambuf` object, which uses the `len`-byte array `buff` as a character buffer.

The methods

```
streambuf* setbuf( signed char* buff, int len );
streambuf* setbuf( unsigned char* buff, int len );
```

associate a `streambuf` object, created with the default constructor, with the `len`-byte array `buff`, which serves as the character buffer.

The method

```
int in_avail();
```

returns the number of characters remaining in the input character buffer and the method

```
int out_avail();
```

returns the number of characters remaining in the output character buffer.

The method

```
int sbumpc();
```

returns the current character in the input character buffer and advances the buffer position marker, which designates the character to read or write, one byte. If `sbumpc` fails (e.g., we are at the end of the file), it returns `EOF`. This low-level method resembles the high-level method `get` in class `istream`.

The method

```
int sgetc();
```

returns the next character in the character buffer. The buffer position marker is unchanged. If `sgetc` fails, it returns `EOF`. This low-level method resembles the high-level method `peek` in class `istream`.

The method

```
int sgetn( char* store, int n );
```

returns the next `n` characters from the character buffer and stores them in `store`. It returns the number of characters actually retrieved. The buffer position marker is moved the number of bytes retrieved. This low-level method resembles the high-level method **read** in class **istream**.

The method

```
int snextc();
```

advances the buffer position marker one byte and returns the character in the character buffer. If **snextc** fails, it returns **EOF**.

The method

```
int sputbackc( char c );
```

returns the character **c** to the character buffer. The value returned by **sputbackc** is **EOF** on error. This low-level method resembles the high-level method **putback** in class **istream**.

The method

```
int sputc( int c );
```

writes the character **c** to the output character buffer. It returns **EOF** on error. This low-level method resembles the high-level method **put** in class **ostream**.

The method

```
int sputn( const char* store, int n );
```

writes **n** characters, beginning at address **store**, into the character buffer. It returns the number of characters actually placed into the character buffer. This low-level method resembles the high-level method **write** in class **ostream**.

The method

```
void stossc();
```

advances the buffer position marker one byte.

The method

```
streampos seekoff( streamoff off,
                   ios::seek_dir dir,
                   int pt = ( ios::in | ios::out ) );
```

moves the input or output stream position marker (or both) **off** bytes from **dir**, which must be one of the following: **beg** (from the beginning of the stream), **cur** (from the current position), or **end** (from the end of the stream). If **pt** is **ios::in**, the input marker is moved; if **pt** is **ios::out**, the output marker is moved; and if **pt** is **ios::in | ios::out**, both markers are moved.

The method

```
streampos seekpos( streampos off,
                   int pt = ( ios::in | ios::out ) );
```

moves the input or output stream position marker (or both) to position **off**. As in method **seekoff**, the second argument determines which markers are moved. The low-level methods **seekoff** and **seekpos** resemble the high-level methods **seekg** and **seekp** in classes **istream** and **ostream**.

We defer examples to the next subsections, which consider the derived classes **filebuf** and **strstreambuf**, as it is these classes that provide the facilities for associating buffer objects with files and character arrays.

filebuf

The class **filebuf** is publicly inherited from **streambuf**:

```
class filebuf : public streambuf {
    . . .
};
```

It provides buffered access to files.

The default constructor creates a **filebuf** object that is not associated with any file.

The method **open**

```
filebuf* open( const char* filename,
               int mode,
               int pr = filebuf::openprot );
```

opens the file **filename** in mode **mode** and associates it with the **filebuf** object. The file receives default protection **openprot** if a protection is not specified.

Example 7.9.1. The code

```
filebuf fin;
fin.open( "data.in", ios::in )
```

creates the **filebuf** object **fin**. It then opens the file *data.in* for input and associates this file with the object **fin**.   □

The method **setbuf**

```
streambuf* setbuf( char* b, int len );
```

establishes the array **b** as the character buffer for the **filebuf** object.

Example 7.9.2. The code

```
filebuf fout;
char b[ 256 ];
fout.setbuf( b, sizeof ( b ) );
fout.open( "data.out", ios::out );
```

creates the **filebuf** object **fout**. It next establishes the array **b** as the character buffer for **fout**. It then opens the file *data.out* for output and associates this file with the object **fout**. Output to *data.out* takes place through the buffer b.   □

In Example 7.9.1, the system supplies a character buffer because none was specified. In Example 7.9.2, if the last two lines are interchanged

```
filebuf fout;
char b[ 256 ];
fout.open( "data.out", ios::out )
fout.setbuf( b, sizeof ( b ) );
```

the system supplies its own character buffer. The statement

```
fout.open( "data.out", ios::out )
```

establishes a system-defined character buffer and the next statement

```
fout.setbuf( b, sizeof ( b ) );
```

is, in effect, ignored.

Example 7.9.3. The following program copies file *data.in* to *data.out*:

```
#include <fstream.h>
#include <stdlib.h>

const int buffsize = 256;

int main()
{
   char inbuff[ buffsize ], outbuff[ buffsize ];
   filebuf fin, fout;
   int c;

   fin.setbuf( inbuff, sizeof ( inbuff ) );
   fin.open( "data.in", ios::in );

   fout.setbuf( outbuff, sizeof ( outbuff ) );
   fout.open( "data.out", ios::out );

   c = fin.sgetc();

   while ( c != EOF ) {
      fout.sputc( c );
      c = fin.snextc();
   }

   return EXIT_SUCCESS;
}
```

After setting up the character buffers `inbuff` and `outbuff` and opening the files, we read a character from the input character buffer `inbuff`, but the input buffer position marker does not move:

```
c = fin.sgetc();
```

If we are not at the end of the file, we enter the body of the **while** loop. We write one character to the output character buffer **outbuff** and move one byte in the input character buffer and return that character:

```
fout.sputc( c );
c = fin.snextc();
```

We continue until all of the characters have been read from the input file. □

The method

```
filebuf* close();
```

closes the file associated with the **filebuf** object and flushes the character buffer. The destructor also closes the file and flushes the character buffer.

Example 7.9.4. When the program of Example 7.9.3 terminates, the destructor is automatically called for **fin** and **fout**. The destructor closes the files. The destructor for **fout** flushes the output character buffer; that is, data still in the output character buffer but not yet written to the file is now written to the file.   □

The methods **overflow** and **underflow** take action when the character buffer is full or empty. The method

```
int overflow( int stop = EOF );
```

flushes the character buffer. More precisely, it writes all the data in the character buffer, up to but not including **stop**, to the destination file.
   The method

```
int underflow();
```

reads data from the source file into the character buffer.

Example 7.9.5. In this example, we look more closely at what happens when the code of Example 7.9.3 executes. For the purposes of illustration, we assume that **buffsize** is 8, rather than 256.
   When we first execute

```
c = fin.sgetc();
```

the input character buffer is empty, so method **underflow** is invoked and the input character buffer is filled (see Figure 7.9.1).
   Next we execute

```
fout.sputc( c );
```

and c is written to the output character buffer (see Figure 7.9.2). We then execute

```
c = fin.snextc();
```

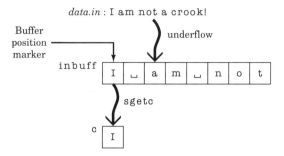

Figure 7.9.1 Result of invoking `fin.sgetc()`.

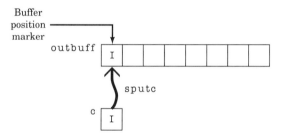

Figure 7.9.2 First call of `fout.sputc( c )`.

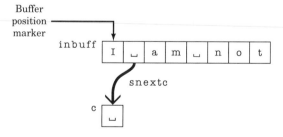

Figure 7.9.3 First call of `fin.snextc()`.

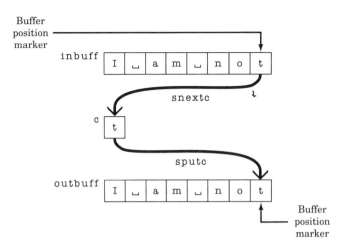

Figure 7.9.4 Full buffers.

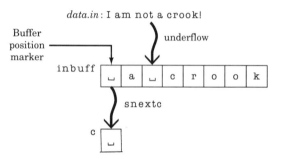

Figure 7.9.5 Refilling the input buffer the first time.

and the next character in the input character buffer is read (see Figure 7.9.3).
Figure 7.9.4 shows the situation somewhat later—just after we execute

```
fout.sputc( c );
```

for the eighth time. At this point, both the input and output character
buffers are full. When we next execute

```
c = fin.snextc();
```

no characters are available in the input character buffer, so method **underflow** is invoked and the input character buffer is refilled (see Figure 7.9.5).
Next we execute

```
fout.sputc( c );
```

Since the output character buffer is full, the method **overflow** is invoked
and the output character buffer is flushed (see Figure 7.9.6).
Figure 7.9.7 shows the situation when the statement

```
c = fin.snextc();
```

is executed and the last character ! is read; underflow again occurs. Next

```
fout.sputc( c );
```

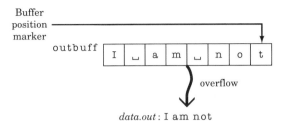

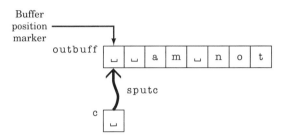

Figure 7.9.6 Flushing the output buffer the first time.

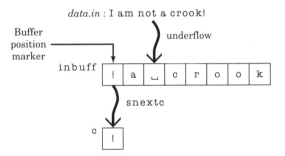

Figure 7.9.7 Refilling the input buffer the last time.

is executed; overflow occurs and the output character buffer is flushed (see Figure 7.9.8).

When we next execute

```
c = fin.snextc();
```

since we are at the end of the file, `snextc` returns `EOF` and the `while` loop terminates. When the program terminates and the destructor for `fout` is called, the output character buffer is flushed and the last character (!) is written to the file *data.out* (see Figure 7.9.9).

If the program terminated without the destructor for `fout` being called, the output character buffer would not be flushed the last time and *data.out* would contain

```
I am not a crook
```

For example, the destructor would *not* be called if the program terminated with a call to `exit`:

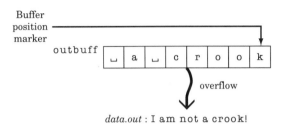

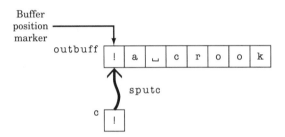

Figure 7.9.8 Flushing the output buffer the second time.

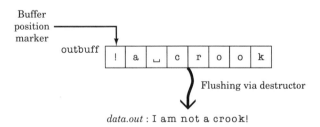

Figure 7.9.9 The result of the destructor flushing the output buffer.

```
int main()
{
   ...
   while ( c != EOF ) {
      fout.sputc( c );
      c = fin.snextc();
   }
   exit( EXIT_SUCCESS );
}
```

□

The method

```
int is_open();
```

returns nonzero if the file is open and zero if the file is not open.

The method **seekoff** behaves exactly like the method with the same name in **streambuf**.

strstreambuf

The class **strstreambuf** is publicly inherited from **streambuf**:

```
class strstreambuf : public streambuf {
   ...
};
```

It provides access to character buffers.

The default constructor creates an **strstreambuf** object that uses dynamic storage allocation; that is, the character buffer is allocated as needed. Similarly, the constructor

```
strstreambuf( int n );
```

creates an **strstreambuf** object that uses dynamic storage allocation beginning with a character buffer of n bytes. (If necessary, the buffer is expanded.) Dynamic buffers are useful for output.

Each of the constructors

```
strstreambuf( signed char* b,
              int len,
              signed char* s = 0 );
strstreambuf( unsigned char* b,
              int len,
              unsigned char* s = 0 );
```

creates an **strstreambuf** object that uses the static len-byte character buffer b. Static buffers are useful for input.

Example 7.9.6. The following program modifies the file-copying program of Example 7.9.3. This program uses **strstreambuf** objects to copy an array.

The program prints the contents of the destination array `outbuff` to confirm that the input array `inbuff` was copied.

```
#include <strstream.h>
#include <string.h>
#include <stdlib.h>

int main()
{
   char inbuff[ ] = "Magical Mystery Tour",
        outbuff[ 25 ];

   strstreambuf sin( inbuff, strlen( inbuff ) );
   strstreambuf sout( outbuff, sizeof ( outbuff ) );
   int c;

   c = sin.sgetc();

   while ( c != EOF ) {
      sout.sputc( c );
      c = sin.snextc();
   }

   for ( int i = 0; i < strlen( inbuff ); i++ )
      cout << outbuff[ i ];
   cout << endl;

   return EXIT_SUCCESS;
}
```

$\square$

The method

```
void freeze( int flag = 1 );
```

with a nonzero argument, freezes the output—no more characters can be written to the character buffer. With argument zero, the output is unfrozen.

The methods **seekoff** and **str** behave exactly like the methods with the same names in **streambuf**.

The methods **overflow** and **underflow** take action appropriate to the type of character buffers defined—dynamic or static.

Exercises

1. Write statements that open the file *balance.dat* for input and output, associate it with the `filebuf` object `finout`, and use a 256-byte user-supplied character buffer.

2. Using class `filebuf`, write a complete program that copies files in the order listed on the command line (the first file—the executable—is skipped) to the standard output. Files that cannot be opened for reading are ignored.

3. Rewrite Example 7.9.3. Change `buffsize` to 8 and print the contents of `inbuff` and `outbuff` at various points so that the process of reading and writing the character buffers is clarified.

4. Use class `strstreambuf` to write a function `hi_to_lo` that receives a null-terminated array of `char` and changes each uppercase letter to lowercase. (Non-uppercase letters are unchanged.)

5. The C++ class library has separate classes `istream` and `ostream` for high-level input and output. Why do you think that the C++ designers declared a single buffer class `streambuf` for *both* input and output?

Common Programming Errors

1. It is an error to attempt to use any of the input/output classes

```
ios
streambuf
istream
ostream
iostream
istream_withassign
ostream_withassign
iostream_withassign
```

or any of the system manipulators with no parameters (e.g., `endl`) without including at least one of the header files *iostream.h*, *fstream.h*, or *strstream.h*.

2. It is an error to attempt to use any of the file input/output classes

```
filebuf
fstreambase
ifstream
ofstream
fstream
```

without including the header file *fstream.h.*

3. It is an error to attempt to use any of the character array input/output classes

```
strstreambuf
strstreambase
istrstream
ostrstream
strstream
```

without including the header file *strstream.h.*

4. It is an error to attempt to use any of the system manipulators with parameters (e.g., **setfill**) without including the header file *iomanip.h.*

5. If the programmer writes a manipulator without parameters using the method of Section 7.4, the header file *iostream.h* must be included.

6. If the programmer writes a manipulator with parameters using the method of Section 7.4, the header file *iomanip.h* must be included.

7. The flag **eofbit** in class **ios** is set by attempting to read beyond the end of the file. Simply reading the last byte does *not* set **eofbit**. For this reason, the following code that attempts to echo integers in the standard input to the standard output is incorrect; an extra line is printed:

```
int i;

// ***** ERROR: extra line is printed
while ( !cin.eof() ) {
   cin >> i;
   cout << i << endl;
}
```

A correct version is

```
int i;

do {
   cin >> i;
```

```
        if ( !cin.eof() )
            cout << i << endl;
    } while ( !cin.eof() );
```

8. The method **flags** with one argument in class **ios** sets the format flags to the value passed, whereas method **setf**, also in class **ios**, sets *specified* flags without changing the other flags. For example,

```
    cout.flags( ios::showpoint );
```

sets the flag that causes subsequent floating-point numbers to be printed with trailing zeros and *clears all other format flags*. The statement

```
    cout.setf( ios::showpoint );
```

also sets the flag that causes subsequent floating-point numbers to be printed with trailing zeros but does *not* modify any other format flag. In many applications, **setf** is more useful than **flags**.

9. Do not assume that after an output statement is executed, all format attributes revert to their default status. Except for the field width, which can be changed using method **width** in class **ios** or the manipulator **setw**, format attributes remain in effect until modified, even through multiple statements. For example, the output from the following code

```
    cout << hex << setw( 8 ) << endl;
    cout << 200 << endl;
    cout << 200 << endl;
```

is

```
        c8
    c8
```

In the second line of output, the integer is still written in hexadecimal, but the field width reverts to zero.

10. When the versions of methods **seekg** and **seekp** whose declarations are

```
    istream& seekg( streamoff, seek_dir );
    ostream& seekp( streamoff, seek_dir );
```

are used with files, the files should be opened as **binary** files. These methods may not work properly if they are used with files which were not opened in **binary** mode.

When the versions of methods **seekg** and **seekp** whose declarations are

```
    istream& seekg( streampos );
    ostream& seekp( streampos );
```

are used with files, the files can be opened as `binary` or non-`binary` files. The argument should be a value returned by `tellg` (for `seekg`) or `tellp` (for `seekp`).

11. When the overloaded operator `>>` is used to read a character, the default action is to skip white space. Do *not* assume (as in C) that the next character, white space or not, is read.

12. When the overloaded operator `>>` is used to read a string and the field width is set to n $\neq$ 0, do *not* assume that the next n characters, white space or not, are read and stored. The default action is to skip white space and then read and store all non-white space characters up to the next white space character, or n $-$ 1 characters, whichever occurs first. A null terminator is always added. As examples, if the standard input is

    ␣␣␣`Pepper`

    the code

    ```
    char a[ 10 ];
    cin >> setw( 6 ) >> a;
    ```

    reads and stores

    `Peppe`

    followed by `'\0'` in the array `a`. If the standard input is

    ␣␣␣`Dr␣Pepper`

    the code

    ```
    char a[ 10 ];
    cin >> setw( 6 ) >> a;
    ```

    reads and stores

    `Dr`

    followed by `'\0'` in the array `a`.

13. When overloading `>>` for input, the first argument should be of type `istream&` and the second argument should be the user-defined type. The return type should be `istream&`. The type `istream&` is necessary to correctly update the `istream` object passed.

14. When overloading `<<` for output, the first argument should be of type `ostream&` and the second argument should be the user-defined type. The return type should be `ostream&`. The type `ostream&` is necessary to correctly update the `ostream` object passed.

15. The code for a manipulator *must* return the modified stream. For this reason,

```
void bell( ostream& os )
{
   // ***** ERROR: Must return the stream
   os << "\a";
}
```

is an error. A correct version is

```
ostream& bell( ostream& os )
{
   return os << "\a";
}
```

16. It is an error to omit the mode when opening a file and associating it with an **fstream** object

```
fstream fio;
```

```
// ***** ERROR: No mode
fio.open( "payroll.dat" );
```

since no default mode is supplied. The mode can be omitted for **ifstream** and **ofstream** objects; the default mode for an **ifstream** object is input, and the default mode for an **ofstream** object is output.

17. It is an error to fail to supply a character buffer when an **istrstream** object is created. (The buffer supplied contains the input.) The programmer may or may not supply a character buffer when an **ostrstream** object is created. If the programmer does not supply a character buffer for the output, the system supplies a dynamic character buffer.

18. When a string is output by an **ostrstream** object using the **<<** operator, a null terminator is *not* added to the output. For this reason

```
ostrstream s;
s << "Wow";
char* p = s.str();
// ***** ERROR: No null terminator
cout << p;
```

The error can be corrected by replacing the line

```
s << "Wow";
```

by

```
s << "Wow" << ends;
```

19. The method `sgetc` in class `streambuf` returns the next character in the character buffer but does *not* change the buffer position marker. For this reason,

```
filebuf fin, fout;
...
// ***** ERROR: Infinite loop
while ( ( c = fin.sgetc() ) != EOF )
   fout.sputc( c );
```

is an infinite loop. See Example 7.9.3 for a correct version.

20. When supplying a buffer for file input/output, set the buffer *before* opening the file:

```
// Uses programmer-supplied buffer b
filebuf fout;
char b[ 256 ];
fout.setbuf( b, 256 );
fout.open( "winnings.dat", ios::out );
```

If the last two lines are reversed, the programmer's buffer `b` is ignored:

```
// Uses system-supplied buffer
filebuf fout;
char b[ 256 ];
fout.open( "winnings.dat", ios::out );
fout.setbuf( b, 256 );
```

21. The output file character buffer is *not* flushed if the file is not closed. The file may be closed by using the method `close` or passively by the destructor.

22. The programmer *must* supply a character buffer for input to an `strstreambuf` object. The programmer may or may not supply a character buffer for output from an `strstreambuf` object. If the programmer does not supply a character buffer for output from an `strstreambuf` object, the system supplies a dynamic character buffer.

Programming Exercises

7.1. Modify the random access file class of Section 7.6 in the following manner. Add another field to the header, which flags the file as a random access file, by writing **RA** in the first two bytes of the header. When an existing file is opened, this flag is checked. If the file is the wrong type, it is closed and an error condition is set.

7.2. Provide implementations of **flags**, **setf**, and **unsetf** (see Section 7.2).

7.3. Write an **IMANIP** template (see Section 7.4).

7.4. Derive a **sequential file** class from **fstream** (see Section 7.6).

7.5. Derive an **indexed file** class from **fstream** (see Section 7.6). The underlying data structure should be a **B-tree** [see, e.g., L. Nyhoff and S. Leestma, *Data Structures and Program Design in Pascal*, 2nd ed., (New York: Macmillan, 1992)]. The indexed file class should allow the following operations:

- Direct access to a record through the key.

- Sequential reads.

- Adding, deleting, or updating records.

7.6. Develop a class that serves as an interface to the **frandom** class of Section 7.6. The class should contain a pointer to another class that describes a record. The record must contain a member of type **char***, which serves as the key.

7.7. Install assertions in the **frandom** class (see Section 7.6).

7.8. Write a high-level (in the sense of Section 7.8) encryption function based on Huffman codes [see, e.g., L. Nyhoff and S. Leestma, *Data Structures and Program Design in Pascal*, 2nd ed., (New York: Macmillan, 1992)].

7.9. Rewrite the **frandom** class (see Section 7.6) using buffer classes directly.

7.10. Derive a class **scrn_out** from **ostream** that provides output in specified colors to specified parts of the screen.

Chapter 8

Advanced Topics

In this final chapter, we discuss several advanced topics. Exception handling is a recent addition to C++ and lets the programmer deal with certain error conditions. Run-time type identification and namespaces are even more recent additions to C++. Run-time type identification allows type conversions that are checked at run-time, provides an operator that describes the run-time type of an object, and allows the user to extend run-time type identification beyond that provided in the language. Namespaces provide a way to distinguish among identical global names. Since these features have been recently added to the language, they may not be generally supported by existing C++ compilers.

We briefly introduce some other important object-oriented languages: Smalltalk, Eiffel, and Objective C. We conclude by discussing several new issues involving the object-oriented paradigm.

8.1   Exception Handling

An **exception** is a run-time error caused by some abnormal condition, for example, an out-of-bounds array index. In C++, it is possible for a function f to define conditions that identify exceptions. Another function g that calls f can, optionally, elect to test whether the exceptions defined by f occur while the program executes. Further, g can provide its own handlers to deal with these exceptions should they occur. We illustrate with an example.

Example 8.1.1. The following code

```
class string {
   char* s;
public:
   enum { minSize = 1, maxSize = 1000 };
   string();
   string( int );
   ...
};

string::string( int size )
{
   // define "out of bounds" exception and throw it
   if ( size < minSize || size > maxSize )
      throw( size );
   s = new char[ size ];
   // define "out of memory" exception and throw it
   if ( s == 0 )
      throw( "Out of Memory" );
}
   ...
```

```
void f( int n )
{
   try {
      string str( n );
   }

   // handlers provided in case
   //    string str( n );
   // fails
   catch( char* errMsg )
   {
      cerr << errMsg << endl;
      abort();
   }

   catch( int k )
   {
      cerr << "Out of range error: " << k << endl;
      f( string::maxSize );
   }

   // The code for f which logically follows the statement
   //    string str( n );
   // goes here. This code will be executed immediately
   // after
   //    string str( n );
   // if no exception is raised. If an exception was
   // raised, this code will be executed after
   // the exception that occurred has been handled.
   // If the exception was not handled, the program
   // will terminate.
}
```

illustrates the C++ technique for defining and handling exceptions.

Code to detect an exception can be included in a function in which the exception might occur. For example, the constructor

```
string::string( int )
```

contains the line

```
if ( size < minSize || size > maxSize )
```

that checks for an out-of-bounds argument to the constructor. If the out-of-bounds exception occurs, it can be thrown by using the **throw** operator:

```
throw( size );
```

(`throw` is a keyword.) The `throw` operator requests action from a handler to cope with the exception.

A function that uses the constructor

```
string::string( int )
```

and is willing to handle exceptions defined by the constructor must indicate this willingness by placing the code in which an out-of-bounds exception might occur in a `try` block. (`try` is a keyword.) In our example, the function `f` is willing to handle an out-of-bounds argument to the constructor so it includes the `try` block

```
try {
    string str( n );
}
```

When this `try` block is executed and no exception occurs, execution continues with the code that follows the `catch` blocks. (`catch` is a keyword.) If `n` is out of bounds, the exception is thrown because of the statement

```
throw( size );
```

in the constructor. The exception is caught by the `catch` block whose argument type matches that of the thrower. Since `size`, the `throw` argument, is of type `int`, the exception is caught by the `catch` block

```
catch( int k )
{
    cerr << "Out of range error: " << k << endl;
    f( string::maxSize );
}
```

whose argument is of type `int`. An error message is printed and then execution of `f` is restarted with the argument `string::maxSize`.

When the `try` block is executed and the out-of-memory exception occurs, the exception is thrown because of the statement

```
throw( "Out of Memory" );
```

in the constructor. The exception is caught by the `catch` block whose argument type matches that of the thrower. Since the argument

```
"Out of Memory"
```

is of type `char*`, the exception is caught by the `catch` block

```
catch( char* errMsg )
{
    cerr << errMsg << endl;
    abort();
}
```

whose argument is of type `char*`. An error message is printed and then the library function `abort`, which terminates the program, is invoked. □

An exception may be rethrown by using the statement

`throw;`

Example 8.1.2. In the code

```
void f()
{
   try {
      ...
   }
   catch( int i )
   {
      if ( ... )
         ...
      else
         throw;
   }
}

void g()
{
   try {
      f();
   }
   catch( int k )
   {
      ...
   }
   ...
}
```

g calls f, which is in a **try** block. When f executes, if an **int** exception is raised in f's **try** block, f's handler

```
catch( int i )
{
   if ( ... )
      ...
   else
      throw;
}
```

is invoked. If the condition in the **if** statement is false, the exception is rethrown. Since f now terminates and returns to g, the rethrown exception is now handed off to g's handler:

```
catch( int k )
{
    ...
}
```

                     □

    If a function throws an exception and no handler is defined, the function **terminate** whose declaration is

```
void terminate();
```

is automatically invoked. The default action of **terminate** is to call **abort**, but this default action can be changed by using the function **set_terminate** whose declaration is

```
typedef void( *PFV )();
PFV set_terminate( PFV );
```

In this case, **terminate** invokes the function specified in the most recent call of **set_terminate**.

    A function may specify exceptions that it may throw. For example, the declaration

```
void f() throw( t1, t2, t3 );
```

states that **f** may throw exceptions of type **t1**, **t2**, and **t3**, exceptions derived from these types if the type is a class, and *no* others. The function **f** does *not* guarantee that it *will* throw these exceptions—only that it *may* throw these exceptions. When no types are listed in the **throw** expression

```
void f() throw( );
```

f cannot throw any exception. When the **throw** statement is missing in the declaration (as in Example 8.1.1), an exception of any type can be thrown.

    An attempt to throw an exception not in the **throw** list (if present) is an error and results in a call of the library function **unexpected** whose declaration is

```
void unexpected();
```

The default action of **unexpected** is to call **terminate**, but this default action can be changed by using the function **set_unexpected** whose declaration is

```
typedef void( *PFV )();
PFV set_unexpected( PFV );
```

In this case, **unexpected** invokes the function specified in the most recent call of **set_unexpected**.

Assertions, discussed in Section 3.8, provide another means of dealing with exceptions. Preconditions, postconditions, and class invariants are introduced that *must* be satisfied in order for the code to be correct. If a precondition, postcondition, or class invariant fails, the code is incorrect and so the program terminates with a message. One problem with assertions is that they do not permit the program to attempt to recover from the violation and continue executing.

Standard C through the header file *signal.h* provides yet another method of dealing with certain kinds of exceptions [see, e.g., R. Johnsonbaugh and M. Kalin: *Applications Programming in ANSI C*, 3rd ed., (New York: Macmillan, 1995), Appendix F]. Signals can be used to handle exceptions such as keyboard interrupts that are external to the program (such exceptions are called *asynchronous exceptions*). The C++ exception handling mechanism handles only exceptions that result from executing the C++ code itself (such exceptions are called *synchronous exceptions*).

Exercises

1. What will happen in Example 8.1.1 if the lines

```
catch( int k )
{
    cerr << "Out of range error: " << k << endl;
    f( string::maxSize );
}
```

are removed from the function f and f is invoked with argument 2000?

2. What will happen in Example 8.1.1 if the constructor is changed to

```
string::string( int size ) throw( char* )
{
    ...
}
```

and the function f is invoked with argument 2000?

8.2 Run-Time Type Identification

Run-time type identification provides mechanisms to permit type conversions that are checked at run-time, to determine the type of an object at run-time, and to allow the user to extend the run-time type identification provided by C++.

The `dynamic_cast` Operator

C++ provides the `dynamic_cast` operator to perform safe type conversions at run-time for classes with virtual functions. The operator is invoked as

```
dynamic_cast< T* >( p )
```

where p is a pointer and T is a type. If p points to an object of type T or to an object in a class derived from T, the value of the expression is p and the type is T*. If p does not point to an object of type T or to an object in a class derived from T, the value of the expression is zero. The action of the dynamic cast operator is twofold: it determines whether the conversion of p to T* is valid and, if it is valid, it performs the conversion. Thus the dynamic cast operator is a safe method of performing casts. Its principal use is to a perform safe cast from a base class to a derived class.

Example 8.2.1. Given the declarations

```
class Book {
public:
   virtual void print_title();
};


class Textbook : public Book {
public:
   void print_title();
   virtual void print_level();
};


class Paperback : public Book {
public:
   void print_title();
};
```

the dynamic cast operator can be used to print appropriate information about an arbitrary book:

```
void print_book_info( Book* book_ptr )
{
   Textbook* ptr = dynamic_cast< Textbook* >( book_ptr );

   if ( ptr ) { // used if book_ptr points to Textbook
      ptr -> print_title();
      ptr -> print_level();
   }
   else // used if book_ptr does not point to a Textbook
      book_ptr -> print_title();
}
```

In the function `print_book_info`, if at run-time the pointer `book_ptr` points to a `Textbook` object, the dynamic cast operation

```
Textbook* ptr = dynamic_cast< Textbook* >( book_ptr );
```

succeeds and the address of the `Textbook` object is stored in `ptr`. In this case, the methods of class `Textbook` are used to print information about the `Textbook`:

```
ptr -> print_title();
ptr -> print_level();
```

If, on the other hand, at run-time the pointer `book_ptr` does not point to a `Textbook` object, the dynamic cast operation fails and zero is stored in `ptr`. In this case, the `virtual` method `print_title` is used:

```
book_ptr -> print_title();
```

□

Example 8.2.2. A dynamic cast expression can also be used as a condition. For example, the function `print_book_info` can be rewritten as:

```
void print_book_info( Book* book_ptr )
{
   if ( Textbook* ptr
           = dynamic_cast< Textbook* >( book_ptr ) ) {
      ptr -> print_title();
      ptr -> print_level();
   }
   else
      book_ptr -> print_title();
}
```

□

An alternative to the technique of Example 8.2.1 is to change the declaration of the classes and simply use polymorphism.

Example 8.2.3. We revise the code of Example 8.2.1 to use polymorphism to achieve the same effect:

```
class Book {
public:
   virtual void print_title();
   virtual void print_level();
};

class Textbook : public Book {
public:
```

```
   void print_title();
   void print_level();
};

class Paperback : public Book {
public:
   void print_title();
   void print_level();
};

void print_book_info( Book* book_ptr )
{
   book_ptr -> print_title();
   book_ptr -> print_level();
}
```

□

The code of Example 8.2.3 is cleaner than that of Example 8.2.1 and is preferable. In Example 8.2.3, the use of **virtual** functions automatically takes care of the details of determining which versions of **print_title** and **print_level** to use. If, however, the programmer cannot modify the classes, the technique of Example 8.2.1 may be the only safe way to obtain the desired result.

The typeid Operator

The **typeid** operator returns a reference to an object in the library class **Type_info** that describes the run-time type of an object. When using the **typeid** operator, the header file *Type_info.h* must be included.

The **typeid** operator is invoked as

   typeid(*typename*)

or

   typeid(*expression*)

If the operand of the **typeid** operator is the type *typename*, **typeid** returns a reference to a **Type_info** object that represents *typename*. If the operand of the **typeid** operator is the expression *expression*, **typeid** returns a reference to a **Type_info** object that represents the *expression*'s type. The programmer need not know the details of the return type to use the **typeid** operator to compare types, as the following examples illustrate.

Example 8.2.4. The **typeid** operator can be used with built-in types and operators. Figure 8.2.1, which assumes the definitions

```
float x;
long val;
```

Expression	Value
typeid(x) == typeid(float)	True
typeid(x) == typeid(double)	False
typeid(x) == typeid(float*)	False
typeid(val) == typeid(long)	True
typeid(val) == typeid(short)	False
typeid(5280) == typeid(int)	True
typeid(9.218836E-9L) == typeid(long double)	True

Figure 8.2.1 Using the `typeid` operator to test run-time built-in types.

Expression	Value
typeid(book_ptr) == typeid(Book*)	True
typeid(book_ptr) == typeid(Book)	False
typeid(*book_ptr) == typeid(Book)	False
typeid(book_ptr) == typeid(Textbook*)	False
typeid(book_ptr) == typeid(Textbook)	False
typeid(*book_ptr) == typeid(Textbook)	True

Figure 8.2.2 Using the `typeid` operator to test run-time class types.

shows the values of several expressions that use the `typeid` operator. □

Example 8.2.5. Figure 8.2.2, which assumes the declarations of Example 8.2.1 and the definition

```
Book* book_ptr = new Textbook;
```

shows the values of several expressions that use the `typeid` operator.
The value of the expression

```
typeid( book_ptr )
```

represents the type (Book*) *declared* for `book_ptr`, *not* the type of object (Textbook) to which `book_ptr` points. For this reason, the first expression is true, but the second, fourth, and fifth expressions are false.
The value of the expression

```
typeid( *book_ptr )
```

represents the type of object (**Textbook**) to which `book_ptr` points. For this reason, the third expression is false, but the last expression is true. □

The programmer can extend the run-time type identification provided by the system by deriving classes from the standard class **Type_info**.

Exercises

---

1. Explain how `print_book_info` in Example 8.2.1 executes when invoked as

   ```
   Book* bptr = new Book;
   print_book_info( bptr );
   ```

2. Explain how `print_book_info` in Example 8.2.1 executes when invoked as

   ```
   Book* bptr = new Textbook;
   print_book_info( bptr );
   ```

3. Explain how `print_book_info` in Example 8.2.1 executes when invoked as

   ```
   Book* bptr = new Paperback;
   print_book_info( ptr );
   ```

   Give the value of each expression in Exercises 4–27. Assume the declarations of Example 8.2.1 and the statements

   ```
   double* dptr;
   short i;
   char student[ 100 ][ 80 ];
   Book* bptr = new Book;
   ```

4. `typeid( 2.0 ) == typeid( float )`

5. `typeid( 2.0 ) == typeid( double )`

6. `typeid( 6972u ) == typeid( int )`

7. `typeid( 6972u ) == typeid( unsigned int )`

8. `typeid( 6972u ) == typeid( unsigned )`

9. `typeid( dptr ) == typeid( double )`

10. `typeid( dptr ) == typeid( double* )`

11. `typeid( *dptr ) == typeid( double )`

12. `typeid( *dptr ) == typeid( double* )`

13. `typeid( i ) == typeid( short )`

14. `typeid( ( int ) i ) == typeid( int )`

15. `typeid( i ) == typeid( int )`

16. `typeid( student ) == typeid( char )`

17. `typeid( student ) == typeid( char* )`

18. `typeid( student ) == typeid( char** )`

19. `typeid( *student ) == typeid( char )`

20. `typeid( *student ) == typeid( char* )`

21. `typeid( *student ) == typeid( char** )`

22. `typeid( bptr ) == typeid( Book* )`

23. `typeid( bptr ) == typeid( Book )`

24. `typeid( bptr ) == typeid( Textbook* )`

25. `typeid( bptr ) == typeid( Textbook )`

26. `typeid( *bptr ) == typeid( Book )`

27. `typeid( *bptr ) == typeid( Textbook )`

8.3   Namespaces

C++ uses **namespaces** to distinguish among identical global names. Without namespaces, a programmer could not directly use two libraries each of which contains identical global names.

Example 8.3.1. Suppose that two libraries each contain a toplevel function named `clr_screen`. To use namespaces to resolve the ambiguity, the libraries, say `lib1` and `lib2`, put the global declarations in namespaces: the library `lib1` contains the code

```
namespace lib1 {
    void clr_screen();
    ...
}
```

and the library `lib2` contains the code

```
namespace lib2 {
    void clr_screen();
    ...
}
```

(Any global declarations or definitions can be placed into a namespace.)   □

The programmer may refer to namespace members in several ways.

Example 8.3.2. Given the namespaces of Example 8.3.1, the programmer can reference lib1's `clr_screen` as

```
lib1::clr_screen()
```

and lib2's `clr_screen` as

```
lib2::clr_screen()
```

Since continually appending a namespace to an identifier can clutter a program, the programmer can also write

```
using lib1::clr_screen;
```

which means that after this line, the reference

```
clr_screen()
```

is to lib1's `clr_screen`.   □

The line

```
using lib1::clr_screen;
```

is equivalent to declaring a variable named `clr_screen`. Any reference thereafter to `clr_screen` within the scope of the declaration is to `clr_screen` in lib1's namespace. If the declaration is in a block, the identifier `clr_screen` is known only within the block; otherwise, the identifier is known to the end of the file.

Example 8.3.3. The code

```
namespace lib3 {
    char fname[ 100 ];
}

void printname()
{
    char fname[ 500 ];
    using lib3::fname; // ***** ERROR: fname ambiguous
    ...
}
```

contains an error since `printname` contains two declarations of `fname`.   □

The programmer can make all of the declarations in lib1's namespace available by writing

```
using lib1;
```

After this line, all references to names in `lib1`'s namespace are resolved in favor of `lib1`.

Namespaces were very recently added to C++. Some of the details of the semantics are yet to be resolved.

Exercises

---

1. Given

   ```
   namespace kalin_software {
      class string {
         char item[ 100 ];
         int len;
      public:
         void store( char* );
         char* get();
      };
   }
   ```

   and

   ```
   namespace jbaugh_software {
      class string {
         char item[ 100 ];
      public:
         void store( char* );
         char* get();
      };
   }
   ```

   write code that creates an object k of type `string` from `kalin_software` and an object j of type `string` from `jbaugh_software`.

2. Given the code of Exercise 1, an object k of type `string` from `kalin_software`, and an object j of type `string` from `jbaugh_software`, write code that stores the string `Hi, Mom` in k and in j.

8.4 Other Object-Oriented Languages

Many languages support object-oriented programming. Some such as Smalltalk and Eiffel were developed specifically as object-oriented languages. Others such as C++ and Objective C are extensions of existing non-object-oriented languages.

Smalltalk

Smalltalk, developed at Xerox PARC, is a "pure" object-oriented language in the sense that everything is an object, all action is via message passing, and all binding is dynamic. Implementations of Smalltalk vary and Smalltalk code is typically nonportable. For example, some versions of Smalltalk support multiple inheritance whereas others support only single inheritance. Variables are untyped and so may reference any object. (Internally, variables are simply pointers.) As a result, there is no need for generics and there is no type checking. Every Smalltalk system provides a rich class hierarchy.

Smalltalk usually includes a window-based, interactive development platform that is tightly interwoven with the language. This platform usually has an interactive debugger and a "browser," which permits the programmer to inspect code and examine existing classes. Smalltalk is typically translated into an intermediate language, which is then interpreted. The disadvantage of an interpreted, pure object-oriented language on a highly interactive platform is that execution is often quite slow. We next give some examples of Smalltalk code.

Smalltalk has *unary*, *binary*, and *keyword messages*. The statement

```
x := 9 sqrt.
```

furnishes an example of a unary message. The `sqrt` message is passed to the *object* 9. (Everything in Smalltalk is an object—including numbers.) The effect is to return the object 3, which is then copied into x. The assignment operator is :=. A period marks the end of a statement, except that a period at the end of the last statement is optional.

Binary messages are used for (binary) arithmetic operations as, for example,

```
x := 2 + 5.
```

Although the syntax is the same as C++, the meaning is quite different. Here the + message, with argument object 5, is passed to the object 2. The effect is to return the object 7, which is then copied into x.

The statement

```
a := b max: c.
```

is an example of a keyword message, in which a keyword followed by a colon precedes each argument. Here the argument c, which is preceded by the keyword max and a colon, is passed to object b. Object b computes the maximum of itself and c and returns this maximum value, which is then copied into a. Equivalent C++ statements are

```
a = max( b, c );
```

or

```
a = b.max( c );
```

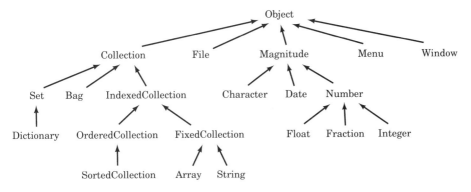

Figure 8.4.1 Part of the Smalltalk class hierarchy.

if **b** is an object.

The syntax for keyword messages with more than one argument is quite different from C++. For example, the message **between:and:** takes two arguments as indicated by the two colons. If the object has a value between the two arguments, **between:and:** returns **True**; otherwise, it returns **False**. For example, the statement

```
x := y between: a and: b.
```

sets **x** to **True**, if **y** is between **a** and **b**, and to **False** otherwise. Equivalent C++ statements are

```
x = between( y, a, b );
```

or

```
x = y.between( a, b );
```

if **y** is an object.

Smalltalk has one base class **Object** from which all other classes are directly or indirectly derived. A partial tree of a typical class library is shown in Figure 8.4.1. Notice that characters, integers, and so on are indeed classes, as are strings, sets, and arrays.

Since an array is an object, a method called **at:** must be used to access data in the array. The counterpart of the C++ statement

```
x = a[ i ];
```

in Smalltalk is

```
x := a at: i.
```

The assignment operator simply copies a pointer. For example, the statements

```
str1 := 'Cool, Beavis'.
str2 := str1.
```

point **str1** and **str2** to the same string object (see Figure 8.4.2). The operator **=** tests whether two variables (pointers) reference equal objects.

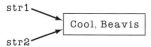

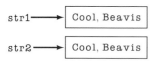

Figure 8.4.2 The assignment operator `str1 := str2`.

Figure 8.4.3 Equal, but distinct, objects.

The operator `==` tests whether two variables (pointers) contain the same address. Thus after the two previous statements execute, the conditions

        str1 = str2
        str1 == str2

are both true. For the situation in Figure 8.4.3, the condition

        str1 = str2

is true, but the condition

        str1 == str2

is false.

Since Smalltalk is typeless, the version of a method to be invoked is determined by the kind of object that is being referenced. In other words, all binding is done at run-time and polymorphism is automatic. For example, the method `at:` can be applied to an array object to obtain the item at a specified index or to a string object to obtain the character at a specified index.

Smalltalk has *instance methods* and *class methods*. An instance method, which is like an ordinary method in C++, applies to an object. In the preceding examples, all methods are instance methods. A class method, on the other hand, applies to a class. An example of a class method is the *method* **new**, which is the counterpart of the C++ *operator* **new**. Method **new** is defined in class **Object** (see Figure 8.4.1) and thus is inherited by any class indirectly derived from **Object**. For example, if **Complex** is a class indirectly derived from **Object**,

        c := new Complex.

passes the message **new** to the class **Complex**. The effect is to create a **Complex** object and return its address, which is then copied into c. No **delete** method is furnished since it is unnecessary; Smalltalk provides automatic garbage collection.

In Smalltalk, every class except **Object** is a subclass of some existing class. When a new hierarchy is constructed, it is customary to make the top class a subclass of the library class **Object**. The class declaration

```
Object subclass: #Complex
    instanceVariableNames: 'real imag'
    classVariableNames: ''
    poolDictionaries: ''
```

declares the class `Complex` as a subclass of `Object`. The pound sign signifies that `Complex` is a symbol (identifier). Single quotes delimit the names in the declaration; thus, `Complex` has two data members, `real` and `imag`, and no class variable names and no pool dictionaries. (A discussion of the last two items is beyond the scope of this brief introduction.) Data members are always private.

Methods, which are always public, are tied to the class through the user interface and do not appear directly as part of the class declaration. The code for the method `initialize:i:` to initialize a `Complex` object might be written as

```
initialize: re i: im
    real := re.
    imag := im
```

Notice that `initialize:i:` is the name of the method and `re` and `im` are parameters. To obtain a `Complex` object `C` and initialize it with values 2 and -4.86, we could write

```
C := Complex new.
C initialize: 2 i: -4.86.
```

References on Smalltalk are: A. Goldberg and D. Robson, *Smalltalk-80: The Language*, (Reading, Mass.: Addison-Wesley, 1989) and W. LaLonde and J. Pugh, *Inside Smalltalk*, (Englewood Cliffs, N.J.: Prentice Hall, 1990).

Eiffel

Eiffel was developed by Bertrand Meyer [see B. Meyer, *Object-oriented Software Construction*, (Englewood Cliffs, N.J.: Prentice Hall, 1988)]. Its design embodies Meyer's view of proper principles of software design including modularity, reusability, object-oriented techniques, and correctness. Our comments apply to Eiffel, version 2.3.

Eiffel is a typed, object-oriented language. The types available are *simple types*—INTEGER, REAL, CHARACTER, and BOOLEAN—and classes. Arrays, strings, sets, and the like, are classes. An INTEGER, REAL, or CHARACTER variable is similar to its `int`, `float`, or `char` counterpart in C++. A BOOLEAN variable can take on only the values `true` or `false`. A class variable is a pointer. All action is via message passing. Every Eiffel system provides a rich class hierarchy.

In Eiffel, `:=` is the assignment operator. When used with simple types, the value is copied. When used with classes, the address is copied. We illustrate the difference.

Variables `i` and `j` of type INTEGER are declared as

Figure 8.4.4 Copying values in Eiffel.

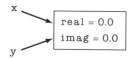

Figure 8.4.5 Copying addresses in Eiffel.

    `i, j: INTEGER`

Storage is reserved for two integers and `i` and `j` refer to this storage. The instruction

    `i := 3`

copies the value 3 to the storage named `i`. The instruction

    `j := i`

then copies `i`'s value to `j` (see Figure 8.4.4).

    Variables `x` and `y` of type `COMPLEX`, where `COMPLEX` is a class, are declared as

    `x, y: COMPLEX`

Storage is reserved for two pointers, but no `COMPLEX` objects are created. To obtain a `COMPLEX` object and point `x` to it, we would write

    `x.Create`

A `Create` method is provided by Eiffel although it can be overridden. The instruction

    `y := x`

then copies the address of the object so that both `x` and `y` point to the object (see Figure 8.4.5).

    The `Clone` method

    `y.Clone(x)`

creates a copy of the object referenced by `x` and stores the address of the object in `y` (see Figure 8.4.6).

    The equality test (=) compares the values of simple types and the addresses of objects for class types. For the situations in Figures 8.4.4 and 8.4.5, the expression

    `x = y`

is true, but for the situations in Figures 8.4.6 and 8.4.7, the expression

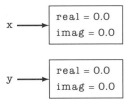

Figure 8.4.6 Cloning an object in Eiffel.

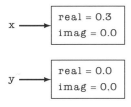

Figure 8.4.7 Unequal addresses and unequal objects.

```
x = y
```

is false.

The `Equal` method tests whether the data members of objects are equal. For the situations in Figures 8.4.5 and 8.4.6, the expression

```
x.Equal(y)
```

is true, but for the situation in Figure 8.4.7, the expression

```
x.Equal(y)
```

is false.

As in C++, the dot notation is used to pass a message to an object. After declaring `z` to be type `COMPLEX` and associating `z` with a `COMPLEX` object, we could invoke the method `init` with arguments `-4` and `26.9` for the object `z` by writing

```
z.init( -4, 26.9 )
```

Class `COMPLEX` could be written as

```
class COMPLEX export
    init
feature
    real, imag: REAL;
    init( re: REAL, im REAL ) is
        -- initialize the real and imaginary parts
      do
        real := re;
        imag := im
      end -- init
end -- class COMPLEX
```

Two dashes introduce a comment, which extends to the end of the line. Semi-colons serve as statement separators. The data members and methods listed in the `export` section are available outside the class (`export` is like `public` in C++). Data members and methods not listed in the `export` section are not available outside the class hierarchy; they are like `protected` members in C++. All data members and methods are specified in the `feature` section. Methods are distinguished from data members by the `is-do-end` syntax.

Eiffel includes preconditions, postconditions, and class invariants as part of the language. A precondition is signaled by the keyword `require` and a postcondition is signaled by the keyword `ensure`:

```
class C export
   ...
feature
   ...
   f( ... ) is
   require
      -- preconditions for f
   do
      ...
   ensure
      -- postconditions for f
   end;
   ...
end
```

A class invariant is signaled by the keyword `invariant`:

```
class C export
   ...
feature
   ...
invariant
   -- class invariants
end
```

At compile time, the programmer can elect to check no assertions, to check preconditions only, or to check all assertions. If an assertion to be checked is false at run-time, the program is terminated and an error message is printed.

Eiffel also has automatic garbage collection, generic classes, exception handling (much like that in C++), and multiple inheritance. Polymorphism is the default in Eiffel, so there is no need for a "virtual" flag as in C++.

Objective C

Objective C, like C++, is an extension of C that includes object-oriented features. Brad Cox, Productivity Products International, developed Objective

C [see B. Cox, *Object-Oriented Programming: An Evolutionary Approach*, (Reading, Mass.: Addison-Wesley, 1986)].

Objective C can be described as C combined with Smalltalk. The C subset is essentially the same as standard C. We describe the Smalltalk subset of Objective C.

As in Smalltalk itself, the Smalltalk subset of Objective C is typeless. Variables used to reference objects are declared as generic type id. An id variable can reference *any* object. Binding is done at run-time; thus, polymorphism is automatic and there is no need for a "virtual" flag as in C++. For id variables, the assignment operator copies addresses as in Smalltalk. There is a copy method

```
x = [ y copy ];
```

which makes a copy of the object referenced by y. As shown, messages passed to objects, such as the copy message passed to y, must be enclosed in brackets [ ].

All classes are directly or indirectly derived from the class Object. All data members are private; thus, outside a class, methods must be used to access the data. The syntax for methods is that of Smalltalk. For example, the statement

```
[ C initialize: 2 i: -4.86 ];
```

passes a message to object C to invoke the method initialize:i: with arguments 2 and -4.86.

Objective C has *instance methods* (like Smalltalk's instance methods), which are preceded by a minus sign, and *factory methods* (like Smalltalk's class methods), which are preceded by a plus sign. The code

```
@interface Complex : Object
{
   double real;
   double imag;
}

- ( void ) initialize: ( double ) re i: ( double ) im;
@end
```

declares the class Complex as a subclass of the class Object. As shown, a class declaration is delimited by @interface and @end and is said to belong to the interface description part of the code. Data members, enclosed in braces, are followed by declarations of the methods. Class Complex has one instance method, initialize:i, with parameters re and im each of type double. The code to implement method initialize:i could be written

```
@implementation Complex
- ( void ) initialize: ( double ) re i: ( double ) im
{
   real = re;
   imag = im;
}
@end
```

As shown, code to implement the methods is delimited by `@implementation` and `@end` and is said to belong to the implementation part of the code.

The **new** method is used to dynamically create an object

```
Complex z;
z = [ Complex new ];
```

and the **free** method is used to free a dynamically allocated object

```
[ Complex free ];
```

There is no automatic garbage collection in Objective C.

Other Languages

Other languages that include support for object-oriented programming are

- Object Pascal, QuickPascal, Turbo Pascal, Actor

  - Each extends Pascal to include object-oriented features. Quick-Pascal is an implementation of Object Pascal. L. Telser, "Object Pascal Report," (Santa Clara, Calif.: Apple Computer, 1985), describes Object Pascal, and N. Shammas, *Object-Oriented Programming with QuickPascal*, (New York: Wiley, 1990), describes QuickPascal. Turbo Pascal is described in the programming guide that accompanies the product from Borland International, Scotts Valley, Calif. Actor is described in the *Actor Language Manual*, (Evanston, Ill.: The Whitewater Group, 1987).

- Simula

  - An object-oriented extension of Algol 60 [see B. Kirkerud, *Object-Oriented Programming with Simula*, (Reading, Mass.: Addison-Wesley, 1989)], which is considered to be the first object-oriented language. Simula is a general-purpose language, but, as its name suggests, it includes support for simulations.

- CLOS (Common Lisp Object System)

  - An object-oriented extension of Lisp [see S. E. Keene, *Object-Oriented Programming in Common Lisp*, (Reading, Mass.: Addison-Wesley, 1989)].

Exercises

---

1. Compare the advantages and disadvantages of the object-oriented languages C++, Smalltalk, Eiffel, and Objective C.

2. Report on another object-oriented language such as Simula or CLOS.

8.5 New Issues

In this section we discuss some current topics and future directions.

Concurrency

Concurrency refers to the concurrent execution of two or more processes. A real-time system in a factory consisting of many processors monitoring equipment provides an example of concurrency. Some languages (e.g., Ada) provide support for concurrency directly within the language. Languages (e.g., C and C++) that do not directly support concurrency rely on system calls (e.g., `fork` and `join` in UNIX) to handle concurrent processes.

There is considerable interest and research into integrating support for concurrency into object-oriented languages and using the object-oriented paradigm to provide a coherent concurrency model [see, e.g., Proceedings of the ACM SIGPLAN Workshop on Object-Based Concurrent Programming, April 1989, *SIGPLAN Notices*, 24 (4)]. One idea is to consider a process to be an object. Certain objects are *active* (executing) whereas others are *inactive* (not executing). The objects communicate through message passing for synchronization.

Persistence

An object is **persistent** if after creation it exists until destroyed even if the program terminates. In C++, objects are *not* persistent; after a C++ program terminates, all objects are automatically destroyed either by destructors or by the system. Some object-oriented languages provide classes that provide support for persistent objects. Eiffel, for example, provides the class STORABLE with methods `store` and `retrieve` to store permanently and retrieve objects. Persistence is major issue in object-oriented databases.

Object-Oriented Databases

The major database model is the *relational model*. The basic structure within a relational database is a *table* (see Figure 8.5.1). Records correspond to rows, and columns describe attributes of the records. Operators on a relational database manipulate the tables (e.g., store a table, retrieve a table, combine tables).

ID Number	Name	Position	Age
22012	Johnsonbaugh	c	22
93831	Glover	of	24
90015	Kalin	ss	33
06682	Krueger	3b	38
58199	Battey	p	18
84341	Cage	c	30
01180	Homer	1b	37
26710	Score	p	22
61049	Epp	of	30
39826	Singleton	2b	31

Figure 8.5.1 A table in a relational database.

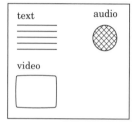

Figure 8.5.2 An object in an object-oriented database.

In an **object-oriented database**, tables are replaced by arbitrary objects (see Figure 8.5.2), which offer the user of the database considerably more flexibility. Persistence is an issue in object-oriented databases since a stored object must remain in existence even if the program is not executing.

Operations on tables in a relational database are well understood and can be implemented efficiently. A challenge in developing object-oriented databases is to optimize the operations on the objects so the performance is acceptable. Optimization is more difficult when tables are replaced by objects since tables, by definition, are of a very special type, whereas objects are perfectly general.

Future Directions

We speculate that *object* will be ubiquitous in computer science. Writing code in the traditional sense will be replaced by modifying and specializing existing classes through the use of inheritance and generics. These modified classes will then be organized into the desired system. Programmers will necessarily deal with more abstract, larger building blocks. The distinction among programs, files, databases, and so on, will be blurred as the components become simply "objects." Objects will also form the basis of many theoretical models. (The example of objects modeling processes was previously mentioned.)

The trend toward the replacement of large mainframe computers with networks of small but powerful desktop machines will continue. The highly productive nature of these systems will result, in part, from the application of object-oriented technology.

Even with these changes in the creation of systems, it will still be necessary for programmers to have a detailed knowledge of the underlying object-oriented language in order to deal with the available tools and to understand and modify existing classes. Programming will be on a higher, more abstract level; it will become more challenging and even more of an intellectual endeavor. It will involve not just "coding," but also the use of advanced, formal design techniques. A more sophisticated education of programmers will be required. Efficient software production will become a reality even as fewer programmers do the work that many did with older technologies.

Because of the impact of the object-oriented paradigm on the development of software, object-oriented languages and object-oriented design methods will be found throughout the curriculum. (This is already beginning at many institutions.) C++ will replace C. Object-oriented techniques will start with the introductory course. "Data structures" will become "abstract data types." An exciting future awaits educators and software developers.

Appendix A

ASCII Table

Table A.1 ASCII Codes

Decimal	Hexadecimal	Octal	Standard Function
0	00	000	NUL (Null)
1	01	001	SOH (Start of heading)
2	02	002	STX (Start of text)
3	03	003	ETX (End of text)
4	04	004	EOT (End of transmission)
5	05	005	ENQ (Enquiry)
6	06	006	ACK (Acknowledge)
7	07	007	BEL (Ring bell)
8	08	010	BS (Backspace)
9	09	011	HT (Horizontal tab)
10	0A	012	LF (Line feed)
11	0B	013	VT (Vertical tab)
12	0C	014	FF (Form feed)
13	0D	015	CR (Carriage return)
14	0E	016	SO (Shift out)
15	0F	017	SI (Shift in)
16	10	020	DLE (Data link escape)
17	11	021	DC1 (Device control 1)
18	12	022	DC2 (Device control 2)
19	13	023	DC3 (Device control 3)
20	14	024	DC4 (Device control 4)

Table A.1 ASCII Codes (Continued)

Decimal	Hexadecimal	Octal	Standard Function
21	15	025	NAK (Negative acknowledge)
22	16	026	SYN (Synchronous idle)
23	17	027	ETB (End of transmission block)
24	18	030	CAN (Cancel)
25	19	031	EM (End of medium)
26	1A	032	SUB (Substitute)
27	1B	033	ESC (Escape)
28	1C	034	FS (File separator)
29	1D	035	GS (Group separator)
30	1E	036	RS (Record separator)
31	1F	037	US (Unit separator)
32	20	040	SP (Space)
33	21	041	!
34	22	042	"
35	23	043	#
36	24	044	$
37	25	045	%
38	26	046	&
39	27	047	' (Single quote)
40	28	050	(
41	29	051	)
42	2A	052	*
43	2B	053	+
44	2C	054	, (Comma)
45	2D	055	- (Hyphen)
46	2E	056	.
47	2F	057	/
48	30	060	0
49	31	061	1
50	32	062	2
51	33	063	3
52	34	064	4
53	35	065	5
54	36	066	6
55	37	067	7
56	38	070	8
57	39	071	9
58	3A	072	:
59	3B	073	;
60	3C	074	<
61	3D	075	=
62	3E	076	>

Table A.1 ASCII Codes (Continued)

Decimal	Hexadecimal	Octal	Standard Function
63	3F	077	?
64	40	100	@
65	41	101	A
66	42	102	B
67	43	103	C
68	44	104	D
69	45	105	E
70	46	106	F
71	47	107	G
72	48	110	H
73	49	111	I
74	4A	112	J
75	4B	113	K
76	4C	114	L
77	4D	115	M
78	4E	116	N
79	4F	117	O
80	50	120	P
81	51	121	Q
82	52	122	R
83	53	123	S
84	54	124	T
85	55	125	U
86	56	126	V
87	57	127	W
88	58	130	X
89	59	131	Y
90	5A	132	Z
91	5B	133	[
92	5C	134	\
93	5D	135	]
94	5E	136	^
95	5F	137	_ (Underscore)
96	60	140	' (Grave accent)
97	61	141	a
98	62	142	b
99	63	143	c
100	64	144	d
101	65	145	e
102	66	146	f
103	67	147	g
104	68	150	h

Table A.1 ASCII Codes (Continued)

Decimal	Hexadecimal	Octal	Standard Function
105	69	151	i
106	6A	152	j
107	6B	153	k
108	6C	154	l
109	6D	155	m
110	6E	156	n
111	6F	157	o
112	70	160	p
113	71	161	q
114	72	162	r
115	73	163	s
116	74	164	t
117	75	165	u
118	76	166	v
119	77	167	w
120	78	170	x
121	79	171	y
122	7A	172	z
123	7B	173	{
124	7C	174	|
125	7D	175	}
126	7E	176	~
127	7F	177	DEL (Delete)

Appendix B

Selected C++ Functions

Before summarizing in detail several useful library functions and class methods, we shall briefly describe each. The following lists group the functions by type:

Math Functions

abs	Absolute value of an int	floor	Floor
acos	Arccosine	labs	Absolute value of a long
asin	Arcsine	log	$\log_e x$
atan	Arctangent	log10	$\log_{10} x$
atof	Convert string to double	pow	x^y
atoi	Convert string to int	rand	Generate a random integer
atol	Convert string to long	sin	Sine
ceil	Ceiling	sinh	Hyperbolic sine
cos	Cosine	sqrt	Square root
cosh	Hyperbolic cosine	srand	Seed the random number generator
exp	e^x	tan	Tangent
fabs	Absolute value of a double	tanh	Hyperbolic tangent

ANSI C Input/Output Functions

fclose	Close a file	getc	Read a character
fgetc	Read a character	getchar	Read a character
fgets	Read a string	gets	Read a string
fopen	Open a file	printf	Write formatted output
fprintf	Write formatted output	putc	Write a character
fputc	Write a character	putchar	Write a character
fputs	Write a string	puts	Write a string
fread	Read binary data	rewind	Move to beginning of file
fscanf	Read formatted input	scanf	Read formatted input
fseek	Move within a file	sprintf	Write formatted output
ftell	Find position within a file	sscanf	Read formatted input
fwrite	Write binary data	ungetc	Return a character to a buffer

Input/Output Class Methods

bad	Signal whether badbit is set	put	Write character
clear	Replace or clear stream state	putback	Return character to stream
close	Close a file	rdbuf	Return pointer to buffer
eof	Signal end-of-file	rdstate	Return stream state
fail	Signal whether failbit is set	read	Read binary data
fill	Change the fill character	seekg	Move within input stream
flags	Change and/or return format flags	seekp	Move within output stream
flush	Flush buffer	setf	Set specified format flags
gcount	Return number of characters read	str	Return character buffer
get	Read characters and strings	sync_with_stdio	Synchronize C++ and C input/output
good	Signal whether state is good	tellg	Return position within input stream
ignore	Discard characters	tellp	Return position within output stream
open	Open a file	tie	Tie an input stream to an output stream
pcount	Return number of characters stored	unsetf	Clear specified format flags
peek	Return next character	width	Change field width
precision	Change the precision	write	Write binary data

Type and Conversion Functions

atof	Convert string to `double`	islower	Lowercase character?
atoi	Convert string to `int`	isprint	Printable character?
atol	Convert string to `long`	ispunct	Punctuation character?
isalnum	Alphanumeric?	isspace	Space character?
isalpha	Alphabetic character?	isupper	Uppercase character?
iscntrl	Control character?	isxdigit	Hexadecimal character?
isdigit	Decimal digit?	tolower	Convert from uppercase to lowercase
isgraph	Nonblank, printable character?	toupper	Convert from lowercase to uppercase

String Functions

memchr	Find leftmost character in object	strlen	Length of string
memcmp	Compare objects	strncat	Concatenate strings
memcpy	Copy object	strncmp	Compare strings
memmove	Copy object	strncpy	Copy string
strcat	Concatenate strings	strpbrk	First break character
strchr	Find leftmost character in string	strrchr	Find rightmost character in string
strcmp	Compare strings	strspn	Span
strcpy	Copy string	strstr	Find substring
strcspn	Complement of span		

Miscellaneous Functions

abort	Cause abnormal program termination	set_unexpected	Specify function for `unexpected` to call
bsearch	Binary search	signal	Invoke a function to handle a signal
clearerr	Clear end-of-file and error indicators	system	Execute a command
difftime	Compute difference between times	terminate	End because of exception handling error
exit	Terminate program	time	Find time
qsort	Quicksort	unexpected	Called when illegal `throw` specification
set_terminate	Specify function for `terminate` to call		

We now list the functions and class methods alphabetically. Class methods are designated as such and the class to which each belongs is specified. Each description consists of the file to include (when the *Working Paper* so specifies), the function's declaration, and a few sentences that describe what the function does. All character codes are given in ASCII. When we write **string**, it is the address of (pointer to) a sequence of null-terminated, contiguous **chars**.

abort

```
#include <stdlib.h>
void abort();
```

Causes abnormal program termination. The status "unsuccessful termination" is returned to the invoking process.

abs

```
#include <stdlib.h>
int abs( int integer );
```

Returns the absolute value of `integer`. See also `fabs` and `labs`.

acos

```
#include <math.h>
double acos( double real );
```

Returns the arccosine (in radians) of `real`. The value returned is between 0 and π.

asin

```
#include <math.h>
double asin( double real );
```

Returns the arcsine (in radians) of `real`. The value returned is between $-\frac{\pi}{2}$ and $\frac{\pi}{2}$.

atan

```
#include <math.h>
double atan( double real );
```

Returns the arctangent (in radians) of `real`. The value returned is between $-\frac{\pi}{2}$ and $\frac{\pi}{2}$.

atof

```
#include <stdlib.h>
double atof( const char *string );
```

Converts a real number, represented as `string`, to `double`. Returns the converted number; `string` consists of optional tabs and spaces followed by an optional sign followed by digits followed by an optional decimal point followed by an optional exponent. The optional exponent is `e` or `E` followed by an integer. See also `atoi` and `atol`.

atoi

```
#include <stdlib.h>
int atoi( const char *string );
```

Converts an integer, represented as **string**, to **int**. Returns the converted number; **string** consists of optional tabs and spaces followed by an optional sign followed by digits. See also **atof** and **atol**.

atol

```
#include <stdlib.h>
long atol( const char *string );
```

Converts an integer, represented as **string**, to **long**. Returns the converted number; **string** consists of optional tabs and spaces followed by an optional sign followed by digits. See also **atof** and **atoi**.

bad

```
#include <iostream.h>
int ios::bad();
```

Returns nonzero if **badbit** is set; otherwise, returns zero.

bsearch

```
#include <stdlib.h>
void *bsearch( const void *key,
               void *start,
               size_t no_elts,
               size_t size_elt,
               int ( *cmp ) ( const void *, const void * ) );
```

Searches for ***key** in a sorted array of size **no_elts** whose initial cell is at address **start**. The parameter **size_elt** is the size in bytes of one cell of the array. The parameter **cmp** is a pointer to a function that compares ***key** and an element in the array and returns an integer to signal the result of the comparison. The first argument to the comparison function ***cmp** is **key** and the second is a pointer to an item in the array. The value of the expression ***cmp(*first, *second)** is negative if ***first** precedes ***second** in the sorted order; ***cmp(*first, *second)** is zero if ***first** is equal to ***second**; and ***cmp(*first, *second)** is positive if ***first** follows ***second** in the sorted order. If ***key** is in the array, bsearch returns a pointer to a cell containing ***key**; if ***key** is not in the array, bsearch returns NULL.

ceil

```
#include <math.h>
double ceil( double real );
```

Returns the least integer (as a `double`) greater than or equal to `real`.

clear

```
#include <iostream.h>
void ios::clear( int st = 0 );
```

Changes stream state to `st`.

clearerr

```
#include <stdio.h>
void clearerr( FILE *file_pointer );
```

Clears the end-of-file and error indicators in the file referenced by `file_point-er`.

close

```
#include <fstream.h>
void fstreambase::close();
```

Closes the file, if any, attached to the object.

cos

```
#include <math.h>
double cos( double real );
```

Returns the cosine of `real`; `real` must be in radians.

cosh

```
#include <math.h>
double cosh( double real );
```

Returns the hyperbolic cosine of `real`.

difftime

```
#include <time.h>
double difftime( time_t end, time_t begin );
```

Returns the difference ($end - begin$), in seconds, between the times `end` and `begin`. See also `time`.

eof

```
#include <iostream.h>
int ios::eof();
```

Returns nonzero if **eofbit** is set; otherwise, returns zero.

exit

```
#include <stdlib.h>
void exit( int status_value );
```

Terminates the program and sends the value **status_value** to the invoking process (operating system, another program, etc.). The constants **EXIT_SUC-CESS** and **EXIT_FAILURE**, defined in *stdlib.h*, may be used as arguments to **exit** to indicate successful or unsuccessful termination. The function **exit** flushes all buffers and closes all open files.

exp

```
#include <math.h>
double exp( double real );
```

Returns e^{real}, where e (2.71828...) is the base of the natural logarithm. See also **pow**.

fabs

```
#include <math.h>
double fabs( double real );
```

Returns the absolute value of **real**. See also **abs** and **labs**.

fail

```
#include <iostream.h>
int ios::fail();
```

Returns nonzero if **failbit** is set; otherwise, returns zero.

fclose

```
#include <stdio.h>
int fclose( FILE *file_pointer );
```

Closes the file referenced by **file_pointer**. Flushes all buffers. If successful, **fclose** returns 0; otherwise, it returns EOF.

fgetc

```
#include <stdio.h>
int fgetc( FILE *file_pointer );
```

Returns the next character from the file referenced by `file_pointer`, or if the end of the file is reached or an error occurs, it returns EOF. Equivalent to the function `getc`. See also `getc`, `getchar`, and `ungetc`.

fgets

```
#include <stdio.h>
char *fgets( char *storage, int max_line,
             FILE *file_pointer );
```

Reads the next line from the file referenced by `file_pointer` and stores it at address `storage`. The "next line" consists of

The next `max_line` − 1 characters.

or

All characters up to and including the next newline character.

or

All characters up to the end of the file.

whichever is shortest. If at least one character is stored, `fgets` adds a terminating null '\0' to the end of the line. Notice that `fgets` stores the newline character if it was read, and that `fgets` never stores more than `max_line` characters (including newline and '\0'). If no characters are stored or an error occurs, `fgets` returns NULL; otherwise, `fgets` returns the address `storage`. See also `gets`.

fill

```
#include <iostream.h>
char ios::fill();
char ios::fill( char fill_char );
```

The first version returns the current fill character. The second version changes the fill character to `fill_char` and returns the old fill character.

flags

```
#include <iostream.h>
long ios::flags();
long ios::flags( long new_flags );
```

The first version returns the current format flags. The second version changes the format flags to `new_flags` and returns the old flags.

floor

```
#include <math.h>
double floor( double real );
```

Returns the greatest integer (as a **double**) less than or equal to **real**.

flush

```
#include <iostream.h>
ostream& ostream::flush();
```

Flushes the output buffer and returns the updated stream.

fopen

```
#include <stdio.h>
FILE *fopen( const char *string, const char *mode );
```

Opens the file whose name is pointed to by **string**. In addition, **fopen** returns the address of a structure that allows access to the file, or in case of error, it returns NULL. The pointer returned can be used in subsequent input/output calls involving functions such as **fread** and **fprintf**.

If **mode** is **"r"** and the file exists, the file is opened as a text file for reading. Reading commences at the beginning of the file. If the file does not exist, **fopen** returns NULL.

If **mode** is **"w"**, the file is opened as a text file for writing. A new (initially empty) file is created whether the file exists or not.

If **mode** is **"a"**, the file is opened as a text file for appending (writing at the end of the file). If the file does not exist, it is created.

If **mode** is **"r+"** and the file exists, the file is opened as a text file for reading and writing. Reading and writing commence at the beginning of the file. If the file does not exist, **fopen** returns NULL.

If **mode** is **"w+"**, the file is opened as a text file for reading and writing. A new (initially empty) file is created whether the file exists or not.

If **mode** is **"a+"**, the file is opened as a text file for reading and writing. Reading and writing commence at the end of the file. If the file does not exist, it is created.

The modes **"ab"**, **"rb"**, and **"wb"** have the same effect as **"a"**, **"r"**, and **"w"** except that the file is opened as a binary file. The modes **"ab+"**, **"rb+"**, and **"wb+"** have the same effect as **"a+"**, **"r+"**, and **"w+"** except that the file is opened as a binary file. The mode **"ab+"**, **"rb+"**, or **"wb+"** may be written **"a+b"**, **"r+b"**, or **"w+b"**, respectively.

fprintf

```
#include <stdio.h>
int  fprintf( FILE *file_pointer, const char *string,... );
```

Writes formatted output to the file referenced by `file_pointer`. The parameter `string` points to characters to be copied to the output, as well as format specifications for the following arguments. The function `fprintf` returns the number of characters written, or in case of error, it returns a negative number. See also `printf` and `sprintf`.

fputc

```
#include <stdio.h>
int fputc( int character, FILE *file_pointer );
```

Writes `character` to the file referenced by `file_pointer`. In addition, `fputc` returns the character written, or in case of error, it returns EOF. Equivalent to the function `putc`. See also `putc` and `putchar`.

fputs

```
#include <stdio.h>
int fputs( const char *string, FILE *file_pointer );
```

Writes `string` to the file referenced by `file_pointer`. The function `fputs` does *not* add a newline or copy the null terminator to the output. If successful, `fputs` returns a nonnegative value; in case of error, it returns EOF. See also `puts`.

fread

```
#include <stdio.h>
size_t fread( void *storage, size_t size,
              size_t count, FILE *file_pointer );
```

Reads up to `count` items, each of `size` bytes, from the file referenced by `file_pointer`. The items are stored in memory, beginning at address `storage`. The function `fread` returns the number of items (*not* bytes) read.

fscanf

```
#include <stdio.h>
int fscanf( FILE *file_pointer, const char *string,... );
```

Reads formatted input from the file referenced by `file_pointer`. The converted data are stored at addresses given by the arguments that follow `string`, which contains the format specifications for the data read. If the end of the file is reached before any conversion, `fscanf` returns EOF; otherwise, it returns the number of items read and stored. See also `scanf` and `sscanf`.

fseek

```
#include <stdio.h>
int fseek( FILE *file_pointer, long offset, int base );
```

Repositions the file position marker in the file referenced by `file_pointer`. In a binary file, `fseek` repositions the file position marker `offset` bytes from the beginning of the file (if `base` is equal to SEEK_SET), from the current position of the file position marker (if `base` is equal to SEEK_CUR), or from the end of the file (if `base` is equal to SEEK_END). In a text file, `base` must be equal to SEEK_SET and `offset` must be either zero (in which case the file position marker is moved to the beginning of the file) or a value returned previously by `ftell` (in which case the file position marker is moved to a previously saved position). If successful, `fseek` returns 0; otherwise, it returns a nonzero value. See also `ftell` and `rewind`.

ftell

```
#include <stdio.h>
long ftell( FILE *file_pointer );
```

Returns the location of the file position marker in the file referenced by `file_pointer`, or in case of error, it returns -1. If the file is a binary file, the location is measured in bytes from the beginning of the file. If the file is a text file, the value returned by `ftell` is useful only as an argument to `fseek`. See also `fseek`.

fwrite

```
#include <stdio.h>
size_t fwrite( const void *storage, size_t size,
               size_t count, FILE *file_pointer );
```

Writes `count` items from address `storage` (unless an error occurs), each of `size` bytes, to the file referenced by `file_pointer`. Returns the number of items written.

gcount

```
#include <iostream.h>
int istream::gcount();
```

Returns the number of characters last read.

get

```
#include <iostream.h>
istream& istream::get( signed char* buff,
                       int n,
                       char stop = '\n' );
istream& istream::get( unsigned char* buff,
                       int n,
                       char stop = '\n' );
istream& istream::get( signed char& c );
istream& istream::get( unsigned char& c );
istream& istream::get( streambuf& sbuff, char stop = '\n' );
int istream::get();
```

In the first two versions, characters are read from the steam into the array
buff until the character stop, whose default value is '\n', is encountered,
until end-of-stream, or until n - 1 characters have been read into buff,
whichever happens first. The character stop is *not* placed in the array buff,
nor is it removed from the stream. The method get adds a null terminator
'\0'.

In the third and fourth versions, the next character, white space or not,
is read into c.

In the fifth version, characters are read from the stream into the streambuf object sbuff until the character stop, whose default value is '\n', is
encountered. The character stop is *not* placed into sbuff, nor is it removed
from the stream.

In all but the last version, get returns the updated stream.

In the last version, the next character, white space or not, is returned,
or if no characters remain to be read, get returns EOF.

getc

```
#include <stdio.h>
int getc( FILE *file_pointer );
```

The function getc is equivalent to fgetc, except that getc is usually implemented as a macro. The function getc returns the next character from
the file referenced by file_pointer, or if the end of the file is reached or an
error occurs, it returns EOF. See also fgetc, getchar, and ungetc.

getchar

```
#include <stdio.h>
int getchar( void );
```

Returns the next character from the standard input, or if the end of the
file is reached or an error occurs, it returns EOF. See also fgetc, getc, and
ungetc.

gets

```
#include <stdio.h>
char *gets( char *storage );
```

Reads the next line from the standard input. The "next line" consists of all characters up to and including the next newline character or the end of the file, whichever comes first. If at least one character is read, **gets** stores at address **storage** all characters read except the newline that is discarded and adds a terminating null to the end of the line. Notice that **gets** never stores a newline character. If no characters are stored or an error occurs, **gets** returns **NULL**; otherwise, **gets** returns the address **storage**. See also **fgets**.

good

```
#include <iostream.h>
int ios::good();
```

Returns nonzero if **state** is zero; otherwise, returns zero.

ignore

```
#include <iostream.h>
istream& ignore( int count = 1, int stop = EOF );
```

Removes **count** characters from the stream, or all characters from the stream up to **stop**, whichever comes first. The removed characters are not stored, but discarded. Returns the updated stream.

isalnum

```
#include <ctype.h>
int isalnum( int character );
```

Returns a nonzero integer if **character** is an alphanumeric character ('a' through 'z', 'A' through 'Z', or '0' through '9'); otherwise, it returns 0.

isalpha

```
#include <ctype.h>
int isalpha( int character );
```

Returns a nonzero integer if **character** is an alphabetic character ('a' through 'z' or 'A' through 'Z'); otherwise, it returns 0.

iscntrl

```
#include <ctype.h>
int iscntrl( int character );
```

Returns a nonzero integer if `character` is a control character (integer value decimal 127 or less than decimal 32); otherwise, it returns 0.

isdigit

```
#include <ctype.h>
int isdigit( int character );
```

Returns a nonzero integer if `character` is a decimal digit ('0' through '9'); otherwise, it returns 0.

isgraph

```
#include <ctype.h>
int isgraph( int character );
```

Returns a nonzero integer if `character` is a nonblank printing character (integer value greater than or equal to decimal 33 and less than or equal to decimal 126); otherwise, it returns 0.

islower

```
#include <ctype.h>
int islower( int character );
```

Returns a nonzero integer if `character` is a lowercase character ('a' through 'z'); otherwise, it returns 0.

isprint

```
#include <ctype.h>
int isprint( int character );
```

Returns a nonzero integer if `character` is a printable character (integer value greater than or equal to decimal 32 and less than or equal to decimal 126); otherwise, it returns 0.

ispunct

```
#include <ctype.h>
int ispunct( int character );
```

Returns a nonzero integer if `character` is a punctuation character (integer value decimal 127 or integer value less than decimal 33); otherwise, it returns 0.

isspace

```
#include <ctype.h>
int isspace( int character );
```

Returns a nonzero integer if **character** is a space character (space, tab, carriage return, form feed, vertical tab, or newline—decimal 32 or greater than decimal 8 and less than decimal 14); otherwise, it returns 0.

isupper

```
#include <ctype.h>
int isupper( int character );
```

Returns a nonzero integer if **character** is an uppercase character ('A' through 'Z'); otherwise, it returns 0.

isxdigit

```
#include <ctype.h>
int isxdigit( int character );
```

Returns a nonzero integer if **character** is a hexadecimal digit ('0' through '9', 'a' through 'f', or 'A' through 'F'); otherwise, it returns 0.

labs

```
#include <stdlib.h>
long labs( long integer );
```

Returns the absolute value of **integer**. See also **abs** and **fabs**.

log

```
#include <math.h>
double log( double real );
```

Returns the natural logarithm (log to the base e) of **real**.

log10

```
#include <math.h>
double log10( double real );
```

Returns the logarithm to the base 10 of **real**.

memchr

```
#include <string.h>
void *memchr( const void *block, int character, size_t numb );
```

Returns the address of the first occurrence of `character` in the first `numb` bytes of the object at address `block`, or if `character` does not appear in the first `numb` bytes of the object, it returns `NULL`. On some systems, `memchr` may execute faster than `strchr`. See also `strchr` and `strrchr`.

memcmp

```
#include <string.h>
int memcmp( const void *block1,
            const void *block2,
            size_t numb );
```

Compares the first `numb` bytes of the object at address `block1` with the first `numb` bytes of the object at address `block2`. Returns a negative integer if the item at `block1` is less than the item at `block2`. Returns zero if the item at `block1` is equal to the item at `block2`. Returns a positive integer if the item at `block1` is greater than the item at `block2`. On some systems, `memcmp` may execute faster than `strncmp`. See also `strcmp` and `strncmp`.

memcpy

```
#include <string.h>
void *memcpy( void *block1, const void *block2, size_t numb );
```

Copies the first `numb` bytes of the object at address `block2` into the object at address `block1` and returns `block1`. The copy may not work if the objects overlap. On some systems, `memcpy` may execute faster than `memmove` and `strncpy`. See also `memmove`, `strcpy`, and `strncpy`.

memmove

```
#include <string.h>
void *memmove( void *block1, const void *block2, size_t numb );
```

Copies the first `numb` bytes of the object at address `block2` into the object at address `block1` and returns `block1`. The objects are allowed to overlap. On some systems, `memmove` may execute faster than `strncpy`. See also `memcpy`, `strcpy`, and `strncpy`.

open

```
#include <fstream.h>
void fstreambase::open( const char* filename,
                        int mode,
                        int ptr = filebuf::openprot );
void ofstream::open( const char* filename,
                     int mode = ios::out,
                     int ptr = filebuf::openprot );
void ifstream::open( const char* filename,
                     int mode = ios::in,
                     int ptr = filebuf::openprot );
void fstream::open( const char* filename,
                    int mode,
                    int ptr = filebuf::openprot );
```

Opens the file **filename** in mode **mode** with protection **ptr** and associates it with an already existing object.

pcount

```
#include <strstream.h>
int ostrstream::pcount();
```

Returns the number of characters currently stored in the character array.

peek

```
#include <iostream.h>
int istream::peek();
```

Returns, but does not remove, the next character from the stream. If no characters remain to be read, it returns **EOF**.

pow

```
#include <math.h>
double pow( double real1, double real2 );
```

Returns $real1^{real2}$. An error occurs if **real1** is negative and **real2** is not an integer. See also **exp**.

precision

```
#include <iostream.h>
int ios::precision();
int ios::precision( int new_prec );
```

The first version returns the current precision. The second version changes the precision to **new_prec** and returns the old precision.

printf

```
#include <stdio.h>
int printf( const char *string,... );
```

Writes formatted output to the standard output. The parameter `string` points to characters to be copied to the output, as well as format specifications for the following arguments. The function `printf` returns the number of characters written, or in case of error, it returns a negative number. See also `fprintf` and `sprintf`.

put

```
#include <iostream.h>
ostream& ostream::put( char c );
```

Writes `c` to the output stream and returns the updated stream.

putback

```
#include <iostream.h>
istream& istream::putback( char c );
```

Puts the character `c` back into the stream and returns the updated stream.

putc

```
#include <stdio.h>
int putc( int character, FILE *file_pointer );
```

The function `putc` is equivalent to `fputc`, except that `putc` is usually implemented as a macro. The function `putc` writes `character` to the file referenced by `file_pointer`. In addition, `putc` returns the character written, or in case of error, it returns EOF. See also `fputc` and `putchar`.

putchar

```
#include <stdio.h>
int putchar( int character );
```

Writes `character` to the standard output. In addition, `putchar` returns the character written, or in case of error, it returns EOF. See also `fputc` and `putc`.

puts

```
#include <stdio.h>
int puts( const char *string );
```

Writes `string` followed by a newline to the standard output. The function `puts` does *not* copy the null terminator to the output. If successful, `puts` returns a nonnegative value; in case of error, it returns EOF. See also `fputs`.

qsort

```
#include <stdlib.h>
void qsort( void *start, size_t no_elts, size_t size_elt,
            int ( *cmp ) ( const void *, const void * ) );
```

Sorts an array of size `no_elts` whose initial cell is at address `start`. The parameter `size_elt` is the size of one cell of the array in bytes. The parameter `cmp` is a pointer to a function that compares two elements whose data type is the same as that of the array and returns an integer to signal the result of the comparison. The arguments to the comparison function `*cmp` are pointers to the two items to be compared. The value of the expression `*cmp( *first, *second )` is negative if `*first` precedes `*second` in the sorted order; `*cmp( *first, *second )` is zero if `*first` is equal to `*second`; and `*cmp( *first, *second )` is positive if `*first` follows `*second` in the sorted order.

rand

```
#include <stdlib.h>
int rand( void );
```

Returns a pseudorandom integer in the range 0 to `RAND_MAX` (a constant defined in *stdlib.h*). See also **srand**.

rdbuf

```
#include <strstream.h>
strstreambuf* strstreambase::rdbuf();
```

Returns a pointer to the **strstreambuf** buffer object associated with the **strstreambase** object.

rdstate

```
#include <iostream.h>
int ios::rdstate();
```

Returns the stream state (**state**).

read

```
#include <iostream.h>
istream& read( signed char* buff, int n );
istream& read( unsigned char* buff, int n );
```

Reads n characters into **buff** and returns the updated stream.

rewind

```
#include <stdio.h>
void rewind( FILE *file_pointer );
```

Repositions the file position marker in the file referenced by `file_pointer` to the beginning of the file. See also `fseek`.

scanf

```
#include <stdio.h>
int scanf( const char *string,... );
```

Reads formatted input from the standard input. The converted data are stored at addresses given by the arguments that follow `string`, which contains the format specifications for the data read. If the end of the file is reached before any conversion, `scanf` returns EOF; otherwise, it returns the number of items read and stored. See also `fscanf` and `sscanf`.

seekg

```
#include <iostream.h>
istream& istream::seekg( streamoff off, seek_dir dir );
istream& istream::seekg( streampos pos );
```

The first version moves the input stream position marker `off` bytes from `dir`, which must be one of: `beg` (from the beginning of the stream), `cur` (from the current position), or `end` (from the end of the stream). The second version sets the input stream position marker to location `pos`, which should be a value returned by `tellg`. Returns the updated stream.

seekp

```
#include <iostream.h>
ostream& ostream::seekp( streamoff off, seek_dir dir );
ostream& ostream::seekp( streampos pos );
```

The first version moves the output stream position marker `off` bytes from `dir`, which must be one of: `beg` (from the beginning of the stream), `cur` (from the current position), or `end` (from the end of the stream). The second version sets the output stream position marker to location `pos`, which should be a value returned by `tellp`. Returns the updated stream.

setf

```
#include <iostream.h>
long ios::setf( long spec_flags );
long ios::setf( long spec_flags, long field );
```

The first version sets specified format flags `spec_flags`. In the second version, `field` must be one of

ios::basefield, ios::adjustfield, floatfield

If field is ios::basefield, spec_flags must be ios::dec (set integer base to decimal), ios::oct (set integer base to octal), or ios::hex (set integer base to hexadecimal). If field is ios::adjustfield, spec_flags must be ios::left (set left justification), ios::right (set right justification), or ios::internal (put fill character between sign and value). If field is ios::floatfield, spec_flags must be ios::scientific (set scientific notation), ios::fixed (set fixed notation), or zero (set default notation). In every case, setf returns the old format flags.

set_terminate

```
typedef void( *PFV )();
PFV set_terminate( PFV );
```

A function for terminate to invoke may be specified by passing to set_terminate a pointer to the function for terminate to invoke. In this case, set_terminate returns a pointer to the function previously specified. If no function is specified by set_terminate, terminate invokes abort.

set_unexpected

```
typedef void( *PFV )();
PFV set_unexpected( PFV );
```

A function for unexpected to invoke may be specified by passing to set_unexpected a pointer to the function for unexpected to invoke. In this case, set_unexpected returns a pointer to the function previously specified. If no function is specified by set_unexpected, unexpected invokes terminate.

signal

```
#include <signal.h>
void ( *signal( int sig, void ( *handler ) ( int ) ) )( int );
```

Catches a signal and invokes a function to handle the signal. If the request can be handled, signal returns the value of handler for the previous call to signal for the given sig; otherwise, it returns SIG_ERR.

sin

```
#include <math.h>
double sin( double real );
```

Returns the sine of real, which must be in radians.

sinh

```
#include <math.h>
double sinh( double real );
```

Returns the hyperbolic sine of **real**.

sprintf

```
#include <stdio.h>
int sprintf( char *storage, const char *string,... );
```

Writes formatted output to memory beginning at address **storage**. **sprintf** adds a null terminator to the end of the output. The parameter **string** points to characters to be copied, as well as format specifications for the following arguments. The function **sprintf** returns the number of characters written (not counting the added null terminator), or in case of error, it returns a negative number. See also **fprintf** and **printf**.

sqrt

```
#include <math.h>
double sqrt( double real );
```

Returns the square root of **real**.

srand

```
#include <stdlib.h>
void srand( unsigned int seed );
```

Seeds the random number generator. Calling **srand** with **seed** equal to 1 is equivalent to calling the random number function **rand** without first invoking **srand**. See also **rand**.

sscanf

```
#include <stdio.h>
int sscanf( const char *string1, const char *string2,... );
```

Reads formatted input from **string1**. The converted data are stored at addresses given by the arguments that follow **string2**, which contains the format specifications for the data read. If the end of **string1** is reached before any conversion, **sscanf** returns EOF; otherwise, it returns the number of items read and stored. See also **fscanf** and **scanf**.

str

```
#include <strstream.h>
char* ostrstream::str();
char* strstream::str();
```

Returns a pointer to the character array buffer. If the buffer was allocated by the system, the user is now responsible for deallocating it.

strcat

```
#include <string.h>
char *strcat( char *string1, const char *string2 );
```

Copies string2 to the end of string1. Returns string1 (the address of the first string). See also strncat.

strchr

```
#include <string.h>
char *strchr( const char *string, int character );
```

Returns the address of the first occurrence of character in string, or if character does not occur in string, it returns NULL. See also strrchr, strstr, and memchr.

strcmp

```
#include <string.h>
int strcmp( const char *string1, const char *string2 );
```

Returns a negative integer if string1 is (lexicographically) less than string2. Returns 0 if string1 is equal to string2. Returns a positive integer if string1 is greater than string2. See also strncmp and memcmp.

strcpy

```
#include <string.h>
char *strcpy( char *string1, const char *string2 );
```

Copies string2 to string1. Returns string1 (the address of the first string). See also strncpy, memcpy, and memmove.

strcspn

```
#include <string.h>
size_t strcspn( const char *string1, const char *string2 );
```

Returns the number of consecutive characters in string1, beginning with the first, that do not occur anywhere in string2. See also strspn.

strlen

```
#include <string.h>
size_t strlen( const char *string );
```

Returns the length of `string` (not counting the null terminator).

strncat

```
#include <string.h>
char *strncat( char *string1, const char *string2,
               size_t max_len );
```

Copies `string2` or `max_len` characters from `string2`, whichever is shorter, to the end of `string1`. In either case, a terminating null is placed at the end. Returns `string1` (the address of the first string). See also `strcat`.

strncmp

```
#include <string.h>
int strncmp( const char *string1,
             const char *string2, size_t max_len );
```

Let **s** denote the string obtained by choosing `string2` or `max_len` characters from `string2`, whichever is shorter. Returns a negative integer if `string1` is (lexicographically) less than **s**. Returns 0 if `string1` is equal to **s**. Returns a positive integer if `string1` is greater than **s**. See also `strcmp` and `memcmp`.

strncpy

```
#include <string.h>
char *strncpy( char *string1, const char *string2,
               size_t max_len );
```

Copies exactly `max_len` characters (counting the null terminator '\0') from `string2` to `string1`. If the length of `string2` is less than `max_len`, null terminators are used to fill `string1`. The resulting string is *not* not null terminated if the length of `string2` is greater than or equal to `max_len`. Returns `string1` (the address of the first string). See also `strcpy`, `memcpy`, and `memmove`.

strpbrk

```
#include <string.h>
char *strpbrk( const char *string1, const char *string2 );
```

Returns the address of the first character in `string1` that occurs anywhere in `string2`, or if no character in `string1` is also in `string2`, it returns `NULL`.

strrchr

```
#include <string.h>
char *strrchr( const char *string, int character );
```

Returns the address of the last occurrence of **character** in **string**, or if **character** does not occur in **string**, it returns NULL. See also **strchr**, **strstr**, and **memchr**.

strspn

```
#include <string.h>
size_t strspn( const char *string1, const char *string2 );
```

Returns the number of consecutive characters in **string1**, beginning with the first, that occur somewhere in **string2**. See also **strcspn**.

strstr

```
#include <string.h>
char *strstr( const char *string1, const char *string2 );
```

Returns the address of the first occurrence in **string1** of **string2**, or NULL if **string2** is not a substring of **string1**. See also **strchr** and **strrchr**.

sync_with_stdio

```
#include <iostream.h>
static void ios::sync_with_stdio();
```

Synchronizes the C++ input/output with the standard C input/output functions. Anytime the C and C++ input/output libraries are intermixed, the method **sync_with_stdio** should be invoked before doing any input or output.

system

```
#include <stdlib.h>
int system( const char *string );
```

Executes the command **string**. The value returned is implementation dependent. (The value returned usually indicates the exit status of the command executed.)

tan

```
#include <math.h>
double tan( double real );
```

Returns the tangent of **real**, which must be in radians.

tanh

```
#include <math.h>
double tanh( double real );
```

Returns the hyperbolic tangent of **real**.

tellg

```
#include <iostream.h>
streampos istream::tellg();
```

Returns the location of the input stream position marker.

tellp

```
#include <iostream.h>
streampos ostream::tellp();
```

Returns the location of the output stream position marker.

terminate

```
void terminate();
```

The function **terminate** is called when there is an error in the exception handling mechanism (e.g., a handler is missing for a thrown exception). The function **terminate**, in turn, calls the function most recently specified by **set_terminate**. If no function was specified by **set_terminate**, **terminate** calls **abort**.

tie

```
#include <iostream.h>
ostream* ios::tie( ostream* out );
ostream* ios::tie();
```

In the first version, **out** is tied to the (input) stream object, on which **tie** is invoked. If **out** is zero, **tie** breaks the tie, if any. In either case, **tie** returns the output stream to which the (input) stream object was previously tied or, if the stream object was not tied to an output stream, it returns zero.

In the second version, **tie** returns the stream to which the (input) object is tied, or zero, if it is not tied to an output stream.

time

```
#include <time.h>
time_t time( time_t *storage );
```

Returns the time (typically measured in seconds elapsed since midnight, January 1, 1970 GMT). If **storage** is not equal to **NULL**, **time** stores the current time at address **storage**. See also **difftime**.

tolower

```
#include <ctype.h>
int tolower( int character );
```

Converts `character` from uppercase to lowercase and returns the converted value. If `character` is not `'A'` through `'Z'`, `tolower` returns `character`.

toupper

```
#include <ctype.h>
int toupper( int character );
```

Converts `character` from lowercase to uppercase and returns the converted value. If `character` is not `'a'` through `'z'`, `toupper` returns `character`.

unexpected

```
void unexpected();
```

When a function throws an exception not specified in its **throw** specification, `unexpected` is called. The function `unexpected`, in turn, calls the function most recently specified by `set_unexpected`. If no function was specified by `set_unexpected`, `unexpected` calls `terminate`.

ungetc

```
#include <stdio.h>
int ungetc( int c, FILE *file_pointer );
```

Writes `c` to the buffer of the file referenced by `file_pointer` (opposite of `getc`). If `c` is equal to `EOF`, the buffer is unchanged. If successful, `ungetc` returns `c`; otherwise, it returns `EOF`. See also `fgetc`, `getc`, and `getchar`.

unsetf

```
#include <iostream.h>
long ios::unsetf( long spec_flags );
```

Clears specified flags `spec_flags` and returns old flags.

width

```
#include <iostream.h>
int ios::width();
int ios::width( int new_width );
```

The first version returns the field width. The second version changes the field width to `new_width` and returns the old field width.

`write`

```
#include <iostream.h>
ostream& ostream::write( const signed char* buff, int n );
ostream& ostream::write( const unsigned char* buff, int n );
```

Writes n characters from the array `buff` to the output stream. Returns the updated stream.

Appendix C

UNIX

UNIX provides utilities, such as **make**, to aid program development in C++, and C++ programs have straightforward access to the UNIX run-time libraries and system calls. This appendix serves as an introduction to UNIX, but you should consult your user's manual for your particular system.

On-line Help

man

UNIX systems usually furnish an on-line UNIX manual with clarification of its commands. For example, the command **man** ("manual")

    % man cp

asks the system to display to the standard output the manual pages on the cp command. (We are using % as the system prompt.) The **man** command also may be used with benign self-reference. The command

    % man man

asks the system to display information about the **man** command itself. If you want more information about the commands discussed in this appendix, you may find it convenient to use the **man** command.

Producing Executable C++ Programs Under UNIX

When C++ source code is submitted to a C++ compiler, the preprocessor first reads one or more source files, processes these files in accordance with directives such as **#define** and **#include**, and produces one or more output files that are then ready for the compilation. After the preprocessor produces its files, the C++ compiler takes as input one or more preprocessed files and produces as output the same number of object modules. (Some compilers may produce additional intermediate files. For example the AT&T **cfront** compiler translates C++ source files to a C source files, which are then compiled.) In the final stage, the linker takes as input one or more object modules and produces as output a single load module. Only the load module is executable. To run a C++ program under UNIX is to execute a load module.

In this appendix, we describe the GNU project C++ compiler, which is commonly available on UNIX systems. Other compilers, such as the AT&T **cfront** compiler, are also supported under UNIX, and work similarly to the GNU C++ compiler, although there are some differences. You should check the specific details of the compiler on your system.

The GNU C++ compiler provides a single command **g++** to accomplish all of the stages of translation. Suppose that the program **ROBOT** has its component functions spread among three files: *main.C, sensors.C*, and *plans.C*. (The GNU C++ compiler requires that the C++ source code files have the extension *.C, .cc,* or *.cxx.*) If we invoke the command **g++** and reference the files *main.C, sensors.C*, and *plans.C*,

```
% g++ main.C sensors.C plans.C
```

a single load module is produced. (The files can be listed in any order.) The object modules produced along the way, *main.o, sensors.o*, and *plans.o*, are deleted automatically once the load module has been produced. Each object module receives a *.o* extension by default. The load module is named *a.out* by default. To execute the load module, the user enters its name

```
% a.out
```

at the system prompt. This simple method of producing a load module requires that the **g++** command reference files that contain, among them, the entire program. Of course, **#include** directives may be used to access functions or macros from both standard and user-created files and libraries.

The second way of producing a load module from source code involves separate compilation. Suppose that we want to compile each source file in the **ROBOT** program after it is written. After completing the file *plans.C*, we can compile it separately by issuing the command

```
% g++ -c plans.C
```

The -c ("compile" only) flag specifies that an object module, rather than a load module, should be produced as output. In this case, the object module is named *plans.o*. After separately compiling each of *main.C*, *sensors.C*, and *plans.C*, we have the object modules *main.o*, *sensors.o*, and *plans.o*. These object modules can then be linked by issuing the command

```
% g++ main.o plans.o sensors.o
```

The load module is named *a.out*. The **g++** command can be invoked with any mix of *.C* and *.o* files. For example, the command

```
% g++ main.C plans.o sensors.C
```

produces a load module from the source files *main.C* and *sensors.C* and the object module *plans.o*. The load module is again named *a.out*.

The **g++** command allows several options including:

Option	Meaning
-c	Compile separately, producing an object module rather than a load module.
-lm	Load referenced modules from the mathematics library.
-o *name*	Name the resulting load module *name* instead of *a.out*, the default.
-w	Suppress warning messages.
-E	Have the preprocessor, but not the compiler, pass over the file and print the result to the standard output.
-O	Use the optimizer.

The flags may be used in combination. For example, the command

```
% g++ -o robot -w -O main.C plans.o sensors.o
```

directs the compiler to produce a load module from the files *main.C*, *plans.o*, and *sensors.o*; to give the load module the name *robot*; to suppress warning messages; and to use the optimizer. The flags can occur in any order, but the **g++** command must come first, and the file names must follow the flags.

Directories and Paths

UNIX has a hierarchical directory structure. The root directory, whose identifier is the character /, has no parent directory but may have any number of child directories or subdirectories. Any child directory has exactly one parent directory and none or more child directories. Figure D.1 depicts a directory structure with the root directory and various subdirectories.

A file resides in a directory. Its **full path name** lists the names of directories from the root down to the directory in which the file resides. For example,

/users/fred/robotplans.C

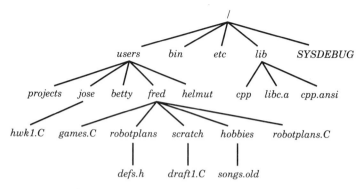

Figure C.1 UNIX directory structure.

is the full path name of the file *robotplans.C*, which resides in the child directory *fred* whose parent directory is *users*, which in turn is a child directory of root (see Figure D.1). A **working directory** is the directory in which you currently find yourself. For example, after you have just logged onto the system, you may find that your working directory is */users/fred*. We next consider some UNIX commands for navigating its directory structure.

pwd, cd

The command **pwd** ("print working directory") displays the working directory. For example, if the working directory is */users/fred/robotplans*, then

    % pwd

displays

    /users/fred/robotplans

The command **cd** ("change directory") changes the working directory. For example, if the working directory is */users/fred/robotplans*, then

    % cd roughdraft

changes the working directory to */users/fred/robotplans/roughdraft*, assuming that *roughdraft* is a child directory of */users/fred/robotplans*. The command

    % cd /users/fred/robotplans/roughdraft

has the same effect regardless of what the working directory is, as the command specifies the full path name.

mkdir, rmdir

Directories may be created with the **mkdir** ("make directory") command and destroyed with the **rmdir** ("remove directory") command. If the working directory is */users/fred*, the command

    % mkdir scratch

creates a child directory whose full path name is */users/fred/scratch.* The command

```
% mkdir /users/fred/scratch
```

would accomplish the same thing regardless of the working directory, assuming that the directory */users/fred/scratch* did not already exist because it is an error to create a directory that already exists. The command

```
% rmdir /users/fred/scratch
```

removes the directory */users/fred/scratch* if the directory contains no files, including subdirectories of its own. (Technically, a UNIX directory is a special kind of file.)

rm

Files may be removed with the **rm** ("remove") command. The command

```
% rm /users/fred/scratch/draft1.C
```

removes the file *draft1.C* from the directory */users/fred/scratch.* The more dangerous command

```
% rm /users/fred/scratch/*
```

removes all files, but not subdirectories, from */users/fred/scratch.* The star * is a wildcard character that matches any file name that is not itself a subdirectory name. The extremely powerful and comparably dangerous command

```
% rm -r /users/fred
```

removes all files in */users/fred*—including all files and subdirectories that have */users/fred* in their full path name. For example the command would remove all files from */users/fred/scratch,* */users/fred/goodstuff,* and */users/fred/robotplans*—and apply the **rmdir** command to these subdirectories in the process. The -r in the command stands for "recursive" to suggest that the **rm** command works its way down the subdirectories starting at the specified directory.

ls, cat, pr, lp, more

UNIX provides various commands for displaying files, finding files, finding contents of files, and copying or moving files. The command **ls** ("list") lists files in the working directory, except those such as *.profile* or *.login* whose names begin with a period. The command

```
% ls -a
```

lists all such files, including those such as *.profile* whose names do begin with a period. The **ls** command also can be used with the wildcard character and with full path names. For example, the command

```
% ls /users/fred/robotplans/*.h
```

lists all files with a *.h* extension in the subdirectory */users/fred/robotplans*, whatever the working directory may be.

The command `cat` ("concatenate")

```
% cat walk.C talk.C chew_gum.C
```

displays to the standard output the contents of files *walk. C*, *talk. C*, and *chew_gum. C* if these files reside in the working directory. Again, `cat` may specify the full path name, as in

```
% cat /users/fred/robotplans/defs.h
```

The `pr` ("print") command behaves similarly to the `cat` command, except that it does some formatting. For example, `pr` breaks the displayed text into numbered pages, whereas `cat` does not. Either command may be used with wildcard characters as, for example, in the command

```
% pr /users/fred/robotplans/*.h
```

which formats and displays the contents of all files with a *.h* extension in the specified directory.

If we `cat` or `pr` a file that has too many lines to be displayed all at once, UNIX simply displays the lines without pausing so that the top lines cannot be seen when the bottom ones are finally displayed. A solution is to use the `more` command, which stops after displaying as many lines as will fit on the display. An example is

```
% more /users/fred/scratch/draft1.C
```

After the screen fills, to advance one line, the user hits *Return*; to advance one full screen, the user hits the space bar.

The command `lp` ("line printer") sends a designated file to the line printer. For example, the command

```
% lp /users/fred/robotplans/defs.h
```

requests that the file */users/fred/robotplans/defs.h* be printed. Later in this appendix we explain how the `pr` and `lp` commands may be combined.

grep, find

The command `grep` ("grab regular expression") can be used to search a file for a pattern, and the command `find` ("find") can be used to find a file. Suppose, for example, that we want to find all occurrences of the pattern

```
misanthrope
```

in any file with a *.txt* extension in the working directory. The command

```
% grep misanthrope *.txt
```

does the job by displaying to the standard output any line in the file that contains the pattern `misanthrope`. If the pattern contains white space, it should be enclosed in single quotation marks. For example, the command

```
% grep 'My Blue Heaven' /users/fred/hobbies/songs.old
```

searches the file */users/fred/hobbies/songs.old* for the pattern

```
My Blue Heaven
```

and displays to the standard output any lines containing this pattern.

The **find** command can be used to locate a file. Suppose, for example, that we want to find the file *plans.C.* We are not sure in which directory it resides but suspect that the directory begins */users.* The command

```
% find /users -name plans.C -print
```

asks UNIX to search for the file named *plans.C,* starting at the directory */users,* and to print the file's full path name if it is found. (On some systems the -print option may not be required.) The search begins at directory */users* and descends through all subdirectories.

cp, mv

UNIX has commands to copy and move files. The command **cp** ("copy") makes a copy of a specified file, whereas the command **mv** ("move") moves a specified file. For example, the command

```
% cp /users/fred/games.C /tmp/hide.C
```

copies the file */users/fred/games.C* to the file */tmp/hide.C.* If the latter file does not already exists, UNIX creates it; if it does exist, UNIX overwrites the previous contents with */users/fred/games.C.* Accordingly, **cp** should be used with caution.

The command

```
% mv /users/fred/games.C newgames.C
```

moves the file */users/fred/games.C* to the file *newgames.C* in the working directory. Again, UNIX creates *newgames.C* if it does not exist already and overwrites it otherwise. After the **mv** command, the file */users/fred/games.C* ceases to exist; after the **cp** command, */users/fred/games.C* continues to exist.

The make Utility

Suppose that you are working on a large program that has many component functions. You could put all the functions in a single file and simply recompile the entire file every time you add a new function, correct an error, or make any other changes; but if you make only a minor change to the file, it will become tedious to have to recompile the entire file. On the other hand, if you divide the functions among various files and then make changes to only a few files, you must remember exactly which files to recompile; then you have to link all the object modules to produce a load module.

The UNIX **make** utility (also available in Turbo C++ and Borland C++) addresses just this problem. It allows you to divide a program's component functions among various files. Whenever you alter a file, it takes note of the fact and recompiles only the altered file. It then links the resulting object module with the others to produce an executable program. We clarify this process with a short example.

Suppose that you have a program that computes your taxes and has the following modules:

Module	Sketch of Its Role
globals.h	Definitions of macros; referenced in all functions.
defs.h	Definitions used only in *expenses.C*.
taxes	The load module (executable program).
main.C	Invokes income and expenses.
income.C	Computes income.
expenses.C	Computes expenses.

To use the **make** utility, we first create a file called *makefile*, which looks like

```
taxes: main.o income.o expenses.o
   g++ -o taxes main.o income.o expenses.o
main.o: globals.h main.C
   g++ -c main.C
income.o: globals.h income.C
   g++ -c income.C
expenses.o: globals.h defs.h expenses.C
   g++ -c expenses.C
```

The file has two types of commands. The unindented commands, such as

```
taxes: main.o income.o expenses.o
```

are *dependency descriptions*. A dependency description shows which modules depend on other modules in the sense that certain modules are needed to produce another module. This particular dependency description shows that the (load) module *taxes* depends on the object modules *main.o*, *income.o*, and *expenses.o*. The indented commands, such as

```
g++ -o taxes main.o income.o expenses.o
```

are *compile-link descriptions*. A compile-link description shows what needs to be compiled and/or linked to obtain the required module. This particular compile-link description shows the command that links *main.o*, *income.o*, and *expenses.o* to obtain *taxes*. Our example *makefile* also shows that *main.o* depends on *globals.h* and *main.C*; *income.o* depends on *globals.h* and *income.C*; and *expenses.o* depends on *globals.h*, *defs.h*, and *expenses.C*. Furthermore, we obtain *main.o* by compiling *main.C*; we obtain *income.o* by compiling *income.C*; and we obtain *expenses.o* by compiling *expenses.C*.

On most UNIX systems, a dependency description must begin in column 1 of *makefile*, and the entire description must occur on a single line. The compile-link description occurs on its own line but on most systems must begin with a tab character.

Once *makefile* has been built, we invoke the **make** utility by entering

% make

at the command level. If nothing needs to be done, the system responds

'taxes' is up to date

Otherwise, the utility recompiles and links any modules that have been changed since the last invocation of **make**. In our example, any change to *globals.h* would result in the recompilation and relinking of all modules. By contrast, a change to *main.C* would result only in the recompilation of the module *main.C* and the relinking of *main.o* with the other object modules.

The **make** utility compiles all files with the **-O** option for optimization. On most UNIX systems, the **make** command itself can be invoked with various options. For example, the command

% make -f spaceSystem

invokes the **make** utility, but the utility uses the file *spaceSystem* instead of the file *makefile*.

Redirection and Pipes

In UNIX, the standard input may be redirected using **<** and the standard output may be redirected using **>**. Suppose, for example, that we have an executable program *stock_tips* that reads from the standard input, processes the data read, and then writes to the standard output. The UNIX command

% stock_tips < market.dat

causes *stock_tips* to read from the file *market.dat* instead of from the standard input. The standard input has been redirected. The command

% stock_tips > tips.dat

causes *stock_tips* to write to the file *tips.dat* instead of to the standard output. The standard output has been redirected. The command

% stock_tips < market.dat > tips.dat

causes *stock_tips* to read from the file *market.dat* instead of from the standard input and to write to the file *tips.dat* instead of to the standard output. Both the standard input and the standard output have been redirected.

UNIX also supports the *pipe*, a utility through which one program's output becomes another program's input. For example, suppose that we have an executable program *report_tips* that can generate a report from the output of *stock_tips*. We could combine the programs by executing the following UNIX commands:

```
% stock_tips > temp.dat
% report_tips < temp.dat
```

stock_tips reads from the standard input and writes to *temp.dat*, after which *report_tips* reads from *temp.dat* and writes to the standard output. A pipe accomplishes the same result, but more conveniently:

```
% stock_tips | report_tips
```

The vertical bar | designates a pipe. *stock_tips* pipes its output into *report_tips*, which then writes to the standard output.

A *pipeline* may be built out of individual pipes. Suppose that we want the input to *stock_tips* to be sorted before it is formatted by *report_tips* and written to the standard output and that we have a program *sort_tips* that does the sorting. We could build a pipeline as follows:

```
% stock_tips | sort_tips | report_tips
```

The input to *stock_tips* is the standard input. Because of the first pipe, the output of *stock_tips* is the input to *sort_tips*. Because of the second pipe, the output of *sort_tips* is the input to *report_tips*, and *report_tips* writes to the standard output.

Pipes can be combined with redirection. The following command is the same as the preceding command except that the report is written to the file *report.dat*:

```
% stock_tips | sort_tips | report_tips > report.dat
```

Pipes may be combined with various other commands in quite powerful ways. Consider the pr, lp, more, and man commands discussed earlier. To format the file */users/fred/robotplans/defs.h* and print it, we pipe the output of pr to lp:

```
% pr /users/fred/robotplans/defs.h | lp
```

Similarly, to format the file */users/project/large.C* and display it a screen at a time, we pipe the output of pr to more:

```
% pr /users/project/large.C | more
```

As a final example, suppose that we want a printed copy of the UNIX manual pages on the command grep. The command

```
% man grep | lp
```

redirects the output of man to lp, which gives us a printed copy. UNIX encourages its users to become pipers.

Run-Time Libraries

System header files such as *math.h* usually contain function declarations in addition to macros and **typedef**s. For example, the header file *math.h* includes declarations such as

```
extern double pow( double, double );
extern double floor( double );
extern double ceil( double );
```

because C++ requires that all functions have prototype declarations. The system typically provides the functions themselves as object modules collected in a run-time library, that is, a library of functions that an applications program can access at run time but for which the source code is not available. For example, the functions declared in *math.h* are available in most UNIX systems in the run-time library *libm.a*. To access the functions in this library, an applications program typically must be linked explicitly with this library. This can be done by using the **-lm** option in the **g++** command. For instance, if we wrote statistics functions that needed mathematics functions such as **pow**, **floor**, and **ceil**, and placed these functions in the file *stats.C*, our **g++** command might look like

```
% g++ -c stats.C -lm
```

The **-lm** option in the command directs the linker to the library named *libm.a*. If the **g++** command succeeds, the object module produced, *stats.o*, contains not only the functions defined in *stats.C* but also any functions in *libm.a*, such as **pow**, invoked in *stats.C*.

In general, run-time libraries have names of the pattern *libNAME.a*, where *NAME* identifies the particular library. To take a second example, most UNIX implementations provide a library named *libcurses.a*, which contains functions for screen management and basic graphics. This library, too, can be linked through the **-l** option in the **g++** command:

```
% g++ -c cusses_with_curses.C -lcurses
```

In the two preceding examples, the **-l** option does not give the full path name for the library because UNIX searches one or more default directories to find a specified library. Many run-time libraries, such as *libm.a* and *libcurses.a*, reside in the directory */usr/lib*.

Programmers often find it useful to build run-time libraries of their own, thereby allowing the component functions to be shared among many different applications programs. It is common for each such library to have its own header file that contains declarations for the functions implemented in the library. The library and the header file could be located in any directory, but it is convenient to place them in default directories so that their full path names need not be given in **#include** directives or **-l** options. The C++ preprocessor, when encountering an **#include** directive with a header

file name in angle brackets, searches one or more default directories for the
header file. A familiar example is

```
#include <string.h>
```

Many system header files, such as *string.h*, reside in the directory
/usr/include. If our header files reside in a default directory, angle brackets may be used in the corresponding **#include** directive. If our run-time
library's name follows the pattern *libNAME.a* and resides in a default directory the **-l** option in the **g++** command need not give the library's full path
name. We illustrate with a short example that assumes that */usr/include*
is a default directory for header files and that */usr/lib* is a default directory
for run-time libraries.

Suppose that we want to build a library of statistical functions for use
in a variety of applications programs. We create a header file

$$/usr/include/stats.h$$

which contains function declarations such as

```
// median of n doubles
extern double median( double nums[ ], int n );

// mean of n doubles
extern double mean( double nums[ ], int n );

// variance of n doubles
extern double var( double nums[ ], int n, double mean );
```

An applications program now can **#include** our header file with the directive

```
#include <stats.h>
```

Definitions for our statistical functions, which invoke mathematics functions
such as **pow** and **floor**, reside in the file *stats.C*. Accordingly, we compile
stats.C with the **-lm** option:

```
% g++ -c stats.C -lm
```

The object module produced, *stats.o*, contains our functions and ones from
the mathematics library. Next, we use the object module to create a run-
time library named, say, *libstats.a* and we move *libstats.a* to a default library
directory such as */usr/lib*. (On most UNIX systems, a run-time library is
created from one or more object modules by using the **ld** commands with
specified flags.) An applications program that needs to access our run-time
library should have the **#include** directive for *stats.h* in the appropriate
source files and should use the **-l** option in the **g++** command:

```
% g++ -o small_lies source.C -lstats
```

Note that the application sees no distinction between our run-time library and one furnished by a UNIX system.

Appendix D

Borland C++

This appendix summarizes the commands for compiling, linking, and running a C++ program in Borland C++. Borland C++ provides two different ways to compile programs. The first way is to issue UNIX-like instructions from the command line, and the second way is to use a windows-like environment that includes a compiler, linker, editor, and debugger. We discuss each method in turn.

The Command Line Compiler

We first discuss the situation in which the entire program resides in one file, say *convert.cpp*. (Borland C++ files typically use the extension *.cpp*.) To compile and link the program, we issue the command

```
C> bcc convert.cpp
```

(We assume that C> is the system prompt.) The executable file is named *convert.exe*. To run the program, we type

```
C> convert
```

To compile and link multiple source modules that make up a program, we proceed as follows. Suppose that the program comprises the modules *series.cpp*, *sum.cpp*, and *transform.cpp*. To compile and link the three modules from the command line, we issue the command

```
C> bcc series.cpp sum.cpp transform.cpp
```

The name of the load module produced, *series.exe*, is derived from the first file listed. To run the program, we type

```
C> series
```

It is also possible to compile each file individually and then link the resulting object files. In this case, we issue the commands

```
C> bcc -c series.cpp
C> bcc -c sum.cpp
C> bcc -c transform.cpp
```

At this point, we have the object modules *series.obj*, *sum.obj*, and *transform.obj*. To link these object modules and produce the load module *series.exe*, we issue the command

```
C> bcc series.obj sum.obj transform.obj
```

The Integrated Environment

Borland C++ also provides an integrated environment, which is a menu-driven system that includes a compiler, linker, editor, and debugger. From DOS, the integrated environment is invoked by issuing the command

```
C> bc
```

or from within windows, the user clicks on the Borland C++ icon. In either case, the user is presented with a screen divided into two windows—a window at the top to edit a file and a window at the bottom for messages (see Figure D.1). In addition, a menu is given at the top of the screen and a reference line is given at the bottom. A menu item can be selected by using a mouse to click on the desired item. Alternatively, a main menu item can be selected by pressing *Alt* and the identifying letter of the desired item simultaneously, and pop-up menu items can be selected by pressing the indicated letter. For example, to select the compile option on the main menu, press *Alt-c*, and to select the make option on the compile pop-up menu, type *m*.

To create a program that resides in the file *convert.cpp*, select *File* on the main menu, and then select *Open* on the file pop-up menu. In the box provided, type *convert.cpp*, the name of the file to edit, and hit *Return*. At this point, Borland C++ transfers control to the editor and the screen will be that shown in Figure D.1. Type in the program. Figure D.2 summarizes some of the most commonly used editor commands.

After typing in the program, to compile, link, and run it, select *Run* on the main menu, and then select *Run* on the run pop-up menu. Borland C++ tries to compile and link the program and, if successful, it then runs the program. When the program is run, the screen clears, the program executes, and control is returned to the Borland C++ screen. To view the previous screen in which the program was run, hit *Alt-F5*. To return from the program screen to the Borland C++ screen, hit any key.

If an error is detected by the compiler or linker, a message will be displayed in a special window that gives information about the compilation and linking process. To correct the errors, first leave the compiler by hitting any

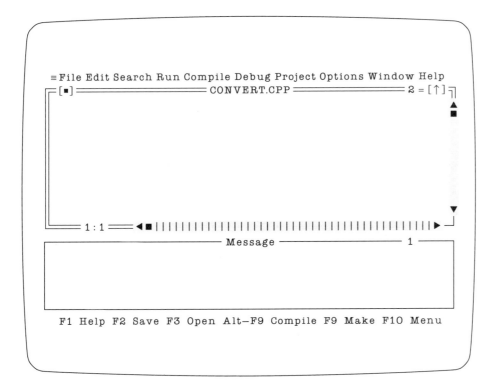

≡File Edit Search Run Compile Debug Project Options Window Help

Figure D.1 Borland C++ integrated environment screen.

key. To correct the first error, hit *Return*. You will automatically be placed into the editor, and the cursor will be at the position in the file that caused the error message to be generated. You can now correct this error.

To correct the next error, click on *Next Msg* at the bottom of the screen or hit *Alt-F8*; either moves the cursor to the line that caused the next error message. Since you remain in the editor, the next error can immediately be corrected. Clicking on *Prev Msg* or hitting *Alt-F7* moves to the previous error, and clicking on *Next Msg* or hitting *Alt-F8* moves to the next error. After correcting all the errors, the program can be rerun by selecting *Run* on the main menu and then selecting *Run* on the run pop-up menu.

To save the editor file, select *File* on the main menu and then *Save* on the file pop-up menu, or hit *F2*. To leave any pop-up menu, hit *Esc*. To leave the integrated environment and return to windows or DOS, select *File* on the main menu and then *Quit* on the file pop-up menu, or type *Alt-x*.

When the *convert* program is successfully compiled and linked, the executable file *convert.exe* is created. This file can be run from the MS-DOS command line by typing

```
C> convert
```

To compile, link, and run a C++ program divided among two or more source files in the integrated environment, we first use the editor to create the

Cursor Movement

Movement	Command
Character left	Left arrow
Character right	Right arrow
Line up	Up arrow
Line down	Down arrow
Word left	Ctrl-a
Word right	Ctrl-f
Start of line	Home
End of line	End
Page up	PgUp
Page down	PgDn
Beginning of file	Ctrl-qr
End of file	Ctrl-qc

Insert/Delete

Action	Command
Insert mode on/off	Ins
Delete character	Del
Del char left	Backspace
Del word right	Ctrl-t
Delete line	Ctrl-y

Find/Replace/Block Commands

Action	Command
Find	Ctrl-qf
Find/replace	Ctrl-qa
Begin block	Ctrl-kb
End block	Ctrl-kk
Copy block	Ctrl-kc
Delete block	Ctrl-ky
Hide/display block	Ctrl-kh
Move block	Ctrl-kv

Figure D.2   Commands for the Borland C++ editor.

files, say *series.cpp*, *sum.cpp*, and *transform.cpp*. We then create a "project" that tells Borland C++ the names of the files that make up the program. To open a project, select *Project* on the main menu and then select *Open* on the project pop-up menu. In the space provided, type the name of the project. In this example, we might select the name *series*. At this point, the message window at the bottom of the screen is replaced by the project window. To add files to the project, select *Project* on the main menu and then select *Add* on the project pop-up menu. A window pops up into which the names of the files that make up the project can be entered. Type in the file names *series.cpp*, *sum.cpp*, and *transform.cpp*, and terminate each with *Return*. After each file name is entered, it is also displayed in the project window. After all the files are added, hit *Esc* to leave the add pop-up window. To compile the program, select *Compile* on the main menu. Then in the compile pop-up window, select *Make*. Borland C++ tries to compile and link all files in the project into an executable file. Errors are flagged and corrected, as described previously. After the files are successfully compiled and linked, hit *Return* to leave the compile message window. To run the program, select *Run* on the main menu, then select the *Run* option on the run pop-up window.

When the program is successfully compiled and linked, the executable file *series.exe*, whose name is derived from the project name *series*, is created. This file can be run from the MS-DOS command line by typing

```
C> series
```

Hints and Solutions to Odd-Numbered Exercises

Section 1.1

1. Films, directors, stars.

3. The toplevel function *main* would invoke functions such as *prompt_user*, *get_response*, and *find_film*. A function such as *find_film* would invoke functions such as *open_file*, *close_file*, and *display_films*.

5. Useful objects include pages, sections, paragraphs, and headers. The toplevel function *main* would invoke functions such as *write_chap_opener*, *put_page_no*, and *write_sec_opener*.

7. When code that has been carefully designed and tested is reused, the reused version will perform as reliably as the original. Since object-oriented design provides a cleaner separation of the components, maintenance—being easier—will also be more reliable.

Section 1.2

1. Other methods might support standard operations on strings such as concatenation, substring extraction, copying, and string comparison.

3. Method `store` should copy the characters passed into the array `data` and set `len` to the length of the string. Method `length` should simply return `len`.

5.
```
class stack {
    int data[ 100 ];
    int top;
```

```
public:
    void init();
    void push( int );
    int pop();
};
```

Method `init` would be invoked to set up an empty stack by initializing `top` to −1. Method `push` would increment `top` and then store the value passed in `data[ top ]`. Method `pop` would copy the value in `data[ top ]`, decrement `top`, and then return the saved value.

7.
```
s.push( 10 );
s_arr[ 8 ].pop();
```

Section 1.3

1.
```
class book {
    char title[ 100 ];
    char author[ 100 ];
    long id_number;
public:
    void store_title( char* );
    void store_author( char* );
    void store_id_number( long );
};
```

3.
```
class person {
public:
    char name[ 100 ];
    char address[ 100 ];
};
```

Derive a class `book_borrower` from `book` and `person` and add a flag to indicate whether the person has borrowed the book.

5.   Multiple inheritance can simplify the construction of new classes. For example, if there is a class to handle input and a class to handle output, we can derive an input/output class from these two using multiple inheritance. If only single inheritance is available, we would have to derive the input/output class from either the input class (and add the output members) or the output class (and add the input members), which is awkward and requires repeating code. A disadvantage of multiple inheritance is that it adds considerable complexity to the language.

Section 1.4

1.
```
book* book_array[ 50 ];
    ...
```

```
    for ( i = 0; i < 50; i++ )
       book_array[ i ] -> print();
```

3. The following code shows one solution in C. The idea is to store pointers to the various drawing functions in the array.

```
void draw_circle( void );
void draw_box( void );

typedef void ( *DRAW_PTR )( void );

DRAW_PTR composite_fig[ 100 ];

/* Initialize composite_fig. For example,

      composite_fig[ 0 ] = draw_circle;
      composite_fig[ 1 ] = draw_box;

   etc.
*/

for ( i = 0; i < 100; i++ )
   composite_fig[ i ]();
```

Section 2.1

1. `good_jobs job1, job2;`

3. `string s1, s2;`

5. This statement is erroneous since it is illegal to change the values in the storage to which p points.

7. This statement is erroneous since it is illegal to change the value of p.

9. Legal

11.
```
// This program reads up to 100 floats from the
// standard input, computes the average of the numbers
// read, and then prints each number and its absolute
// difference from the average.

// The statement
//
//    return EXIT_SUCCESS;
//
// is explained in Section 2.2.
```

```c
#include <stdio.h>
#include <math.h>
#include <stdlib.h>

// can handle at most max numbers
const int max = 100;

int main()
{
   float sum, x, a[ max ];
   int count;

   count = 0;
   sum = 0.0;
   while ( count < max )
      if ( scanf( "%f", &x ) != EOF ) {
         a[ count++ ] = x;
         sum += x;
      }
      else
         break;

   if ( count == 0 ) {
      printf( "No numbers read\n" );
      return EXIT_SUCCESS;
   }

   const float average = sum / count;

   printf( "%10s  |x - average|\n", "x" );
   // fabs returns the absolute value as a
   // double so needs a cast to float
   for ( int i = 0; i < count; i++ )
      printf( "%10f  %f\n", a[ i ],
              ( float ) fabs( a[ i ] - average ) );

   return EXIT_SUCCESS;
}
```

Section 2.2

1.   `void move_arm( int, float, float );`

3.   Portable

5. Portable

7. Portable

9. x = 5, y = -12

11. x = 4, y = -11

13.
```
int* new_index_C( const int a[ ], const int i )
{
    return &a[ i - 1 ];
}
```
The first line would be rewritten as

```
val = *new_index_C( a, 8 );
```

The second line would be rewritten as

```
*new_index_C( a, 8 ) = -16;
```

15.
```
void print( string& str )
{
    printf( "%s\n", str.s );
}
```

17. Function **print** promises not to modify the structure to which **fp** points; however, **print** then passes **fp** to **fprintf** which *does* modify the structure to which **fp** points. The error can be corrected by omitting the modifier **const** in **print**'s header.

Section 2.3

1. 18 4

3. `delete dbl_ptr;`

5. `delete[ ] str;`

7. Add the statement

```
if ( current == 0 )
    return 0;
```

after the statement

```
current = first = new elephant;
```

9. `ptr = &odometer::miles;`

11.   `od2.*ptr = 15004;`

13.   `p = &od1;`

15.   `void ( odometer::* f_ptr )( long );`

17.   `( od1.*f_ptr )( 69402 );`

Section 2.4

1.   `cin >> i >> x >> str;`

3.   The program will go into an infinite loop since the newline will never be read and discarded.

Section 3.1

1.   Both data members and methods are **private** by default.

3.
```
union Sample {
private:
    int x;
    float y;
    char c;
public:
    void msg( char* );
};
```

5.
```
class Dilemma {
    enum Horn { Horn1, Horn2 };
    char horn1[ 100 ];
    char horn2[ 200 ];
public:
    int horn_crushed( Horn );
    void resolve_peacefully();
};
```

7.   In the class created with the keyword **struct**, all data members and methods are **public** by default. In the class created with the keyword **class**, all data members and methods are **private** by default.

9.
```
Dilemma d1; // create a Dilemma object
...             // manipulate it
// invoke d1's horn_crushed method
d1.horn_crushed( Horn1 );
```

11.
```
class Employee {
    enum Gender { Female, Male };
    char lname[ 25 ]; // last name
```

```
      char fname[ 25 ]; // first name
      char addr[ 100 ]; // address
      char dept[ 4 ];   // department
      float sal;        // base salary
      float bonus;      // yearly
      int age;          // in years
      int gender;
   public:
      void read_basics();
      void write_basics();
      float compute_taxes();
      void compute_raise( float raise );
      int years_in_service();
      void downsize();
   };
```

13. Yes.

15. Yes, but a class typically has methods.

17. A class declaration must end with a semicolon. The correct declaration is:

```
class C {
public:
   void write();
}; // must end in semicolon
```

19. No.

Section 3.2

1.
```
// return top item without popping
char Stack::view_top()
{
   if ( empty() )
      return EmptyFlag;
   else
      return items[ top ];
}
```

3. Reasons for: By having **full** and **empty** as **private** methods, we practice information hiding: the user can be spared details that are not essential to Stack manipulation. Methods **push** and **pop**, which do belong to the public interface, are sufficient for basic Stack manipulation. Reasons against: By having **full** and **empty** as **public** methods, we would give

the programmer greater flexibility. In certain applications, it may be convenient for the user to test `Stack` status directly through calls to `full` and `empty`.

5.
```
// substitute new for old on the Stack
void Stack::stack_sub( char c, char s )
{
    for ( int i = 0; i <= top; i++ )
        if ( items[ i ] == c )
            items[ i ] = s;
}
```

Section 3.3

1. No.

3.
```
// declaration for Mystery destructor
Mystery::~Mystery();
```

5. Constructors for the same class must differ in either the number or the data type(s) of their arguments. `C` has two constructors that expect a single `char*` argument.

7. Yes.

9. No, constructors should be `public` because they typically are invoked by the compiler wherever a class object is created.

11. A `C` constructor cannot take an argument of type `C`. However, a `C` constructor can take a `C` *reference* as an argument:

```
class C {
    int x;
    ...
public:
    C( C& ); // ok
    ...
};
```

13. No.

15. A constructor must not return a value, not even `void`.

17. The destructor automatically frees the storage to which `ptr` points whenever a `C` object is destroyed.

19. One.

21. A const data member must be initialized in a constructor's header. The correct version is:

```
// y must be initialized in header
// x could be initialized in header
// or in body
C( int a1, float a2 ) : y( a2 ) { x = a1; }
```

Section 3.4

1.
```
void ZipC::shorten()
{
    if ( strlen( ptr ) == MinZip )
        return;
    char temp[ BigZip + 1 ];
    // save original
    strcpy( temp, code );
    delete[ ] code;
    // shorten
    code = new char[ MinZip + 1 ];
    strncpy( code, temp, MinZip );
    code[ MinZip ] = '\0';
}
```

3.
```
// extract 5-digit ZipC and
// store in return_val, which invoker provides
void ZipC::getMainZip( char* return_val )
{
    strncpy( return_val, code, MinZip );
    return_val[ MinZip ] = '\0';
}
```

Section 3.5

1. The definition's header should be

```
int Dict::operator>( const Dict d ) const
```

instead of

```
int Dict::>( const Dict d ) const
```

3.
```
// sample use of Dict::operator> using
// method syntax, where d1 and d2 are
// two dictionary objects
if ( d1.operator>( d2 ) )
    ...
```

5. Because the comma operator is binary, it could be overloaded to extend arithmetic or relational operators to a class. For example, `operator,` might be used as an exponentiation operator for an `Integer` class.

7.
```
class C {
    char* string;
    float floater;
    ...
public:
    int operator==( const C ) const;
};

int C::operator==( const C arg ) const
{
    return floater == arg.floater &&
           strcmp( string, arg.string );
}
```

9. The member operator may not be overloaded.

Section 3.6

1.
```
Complex Complex::operator+=( const Complex c )
{
    return Complex( real += c.real,
                    imag += c.img );
}
```

3.
```
Complex Complex::operator/=( const Complex c )
{
    // Assumes divide operator already overloaded.

    // Note that we return a Complex and
    // and that current object is updated.

    return *this = *this / c;
}
```

5. The `const` in the parameter list indicates that the the parameter is to be read only. The `const` after the parameter list indicates that the object's data members (`real` and `imag`) are to be read only.

7.
```
Complex c1( 9.9, 8.8 );
Complex c2( 3.3, 4.4 );
Complex c3;
```

```
c3 = c1.operator-( c2 ); // method syntax
c3 = c1 - c2;            // operator syntax
```

Section 3.7

1. Any function, including **main**, may be a **friend**. Here is a sample.

   ```
   class C {
      . . .
      friend int main( int, char*[ ] );
   };
   ```

3. The principle of information hiding encourages the programmer to hide a class's internal representation (i.e., its data members) from all functions *except* the class's own methods; and **friend** functions violate this principle.

5. One obvious example is an overloaded operator such as **operator+**. A code slice such as

   ```
   Complex c1( 1.1, 2.2 );
   Complex c2;

   c2 = 99.9 + c1; // illegal if operator+ is a method
   ```

   is legal if **operator+** is overloaded as a **friend** to **Complex** but not if it is overloaded as a method. If **operator+** is overloaded as a method, then the first operand (in this case, **99.9**) must be a **Complex** object because its method is being invoked.

7. There are two errors:

   ```
   c3 = c1.operator+( c2 ); // method syntax!
   c3 = +( c2, c1 ); // should be c3 = operator+( c2, c1 )
   ```

Section 3.8

1.
   ```
   #include <stdio.h>
   #include <iostream.h>
   #include <string.h>
   #include <assert.h>

   const int MinZip = 5;
   const int BigZip = 10;
   const int MaxZip = 32;
   const int InitChar = '?';
   ```

```
const int Hyphen = '-';
const int SuffixLen = 4;

class ZipC {
   char* code;
public:
   ZipC();
   ZipC( const char* );
   ZipC( const unsigned long );
   ~ZipC();
   void write() { cout << code << endl; }
   void expand( const char* );
};

#define ZipC_inv ( strlen( code ) <= MaxZip )

ZipC::ZipC()
{
   code = new char[ MinZip + 1 ];
   for ( int i = 0; i < MinZip; i++ )
      code[ i ] = InitChar;
   code[ i ] = '\0';
   assert( strlen( code ) == MinZip && ZipC_inv );
}

ZipC::ZipC( const char* zipstr )
{
   int len = ( strlen( zipstr ) <= MaxZip )
      ? strlen( zipstr ) : MaxZip;
   code = new char[ len + 1 ];
   strncpy( code, zipstr, len );
   code[ len ] = '\0';
   assert( strlen( code ) <= MaxZip && strlen( code ) <= len
         && ZipC_inv );
}

ZipC::ZipC( const unsigned long zipnum )
{
   char buffer[ BigZip + 1 ];
   sprintf( buffer, "%0*ld", MinZip, zipnum );
   buffer[ MinZip ] = '\0';
   code = new char[ strlen( buffer ) + 1 ];
   strcpy( code, buffer );
```

```
   assert( strlen( code ) <= strlen( buffer )
           && strlen( code ) == MinZip && ZipC_inv );
}

ZipC::~ZipC()
{
   delete[ ] code;
}

void ZipC::expand( const char* suffix )
{
   assert( strlen( code ) == MinZip
           && strlen( suffix ) == SuffixLen && ZipC_inv );
   char temp[ BigZip + 1 ];
   char previous[ MinZip + 1 ];

   strcpy( previous, code );
   delete[ ] code;
   code = new char[ BigZip + 1 ];
   sprintf( code, "%s%c%s", previous, Hyphen, suffix );
   assert( strlen( code ) <= BigZip
           && strlen( code ) == MinZip + SuffixLen + 1
           && ZipC_inv );
}
```

Section 3.9

1. The class is C< class Typ > not C. The correct code is

```
template< class Typ >
C< class Typ >::C()
{
   ...
}
```

3. Stack< String*, 2000 > s;

5.
```
template< class Typ >
class Stack {
   int FullStack;
   enum { EmptyStack = -1 };
   Typ *items;
   int top;
public:
   Stack( int );
```

```
    ~Stack();
    void push( Typ );
    Typ pop();
    int empty();
    int full();
};

template< class Typ >
Stack< Typ >::Stack( int size = 100 )
{
    items = new Typ[ FullStack = size ];
    top = EmptyStack;
}

template< class Typ >
Stack< Typ >::~Stack()
{
    delete[ ] items;
}

template< class Typ >
void Stack< Typ >::push( Typ c )
{
    items[ ++top ] = c;
}

template< class Typ >
Typ Stack< Typ >::pop()
{
    return items[ top-- ];
}

template< class Typ >
int Stack< Typ >::full()
{
    return top + 1 == FullStack;
}

template< class Typ >
int Stack< Typ >::empty()
{
    return top == EmptyStack;
}
```

```
7.    Stack< Complex* > s( 1000 );
```

Section 4.1

```
1.    String s1;           // default
      String s2( 1000 );   // convert
      String s3( "fred" ); // convert
      String s4( s3 );     // copy
```

3.   Consider the code slice

```
class C {
  char* name;
public:
  C( char* n )
  {
    name = new char[ strlen( n ) + 1 ];
    strcpy( name, n );
  }
  ...
};

C c1( "bar" );
C c2( c1 );
```

The compiler's copy constructor does a member-by-member assignment, which means that `c1.name` and `c2.name` point to the *same* cells. What we probably want is for the two pointers to point to *different* cells that store the *same* chars.

```
5.    const int MaxStrLen = 80;

      // write String to standard output
      // with a terminating newline
      int String::write()
      {
         puts( str );
         putc( '\n' );
         return strlen( str );
      }

      // write String to specified file
      int String::write( FILE* outfile )
      {
         if ( !outfile )
            return WriteFail;
```

```
        fputs( str, outfile );
        fputc( '\n', outfile );
        return strlen( str );
    }

    // read String from standard input
    int String::read()
    {
        gets( str );

        return len = strlen( str );
    }

    // read String from designated file
    int String::read( FILE* infile )
    {
      · if ( !infile )
            return ReadFail;
        else {
            fgets( str, MaxStrLen, infile );
            return len = strlen( str );
        }
    }
```

7.  ```
    void String::substitute( const char c )
    {
        for ( int i = 0; i < len; i++ )
            str[ i ] = c;
    }
    ```

9.  ```
    int String::operator!=( const String s ) const
    {
        return strcmp( str, s.str ) != 0;
    }
    ```

11. Variable `compare_op` is a pointer to a `String` function or function operator that returns an `int` and expects a single `const` argument of type `String`.

13. ```
    // take ErrorsIO out of class declaration
    enum ErrorsIO { ReadFail, WriteFail };
    class String {

        ...

    };
    ```
    ```

15. There is a function call. Recall that `compare_op` points to either `operator>` or `operator<`, which are overloaded as `String` methods. So

```
( a[ j ].*compare_op )( a[ next ] );
```

invokes one of `a[ j ]`'s methods, either `operator<` or `operator>`, on argument `a[ next ]`. Note that each of the overloaded operators expects a *single* argument of type `String`.

17. Data member `str` points to a `char` *vector*, i.e., to a sequence of `char` cells rather than to a single, standalone `char` cell. Therefore, the storage is freed with `delete[ ]` rather than with `delete`.

19. `String*`, i.e., pointer to `String`

21. `this` cannot be the target in an assignment expression.

23. The `const` in the parameter list means that the `String` argument is read only. The `const` to the right of the parameter list means that the object whose `operator+` method is invoked is read only.

Section 4.2

1.
```
String s1;        // default
String s2 = s1;  // copy
String s3;        // default
s3 = s1;          // assignment
String s4( "glory days by bs" ); // convert
String s5;        // default
s5 = s4;          // assignment
String s6 = s5;  // copy
String s7 = String( "judy blue eyes" ); // convert
```

3. A `String` vector (i.e., contiguous `Strings` allocated through the **new** operator) cannot be given initial values. All `Strings` in the vector are initialized through the default constructor.

5. Yes.

7. The compiler's overload of the assignment operator uses member-by-member assignments and the `String` class contains a pointer `str`. In a code slice such as

```
String s1( "foo" );
String s2;
s2 = s1;
```

we want `s1.str` and `s2.str` to point to *different* cells that hold the same chars. The compiler's assignment operator would result in the two `str` data members pointing to the *same* vector.

9. The overloaded assignment operator first invokes the `delete[ ]` operator to free the storage to which `str` *currently* points. The operator next allocates new storage sufficient to hold the chars to which parameter `strarg` points. Finally, the operator uses `strcpy`—which expects a null-terminated array of char—to copy `strarg` into `str`. If we allowed a `String` to be assigned to itself in a code slice such as

```
String s1( "jean" );
s1 = s1;
```

then `s1.str` would *not* point to a null-terminated array of char when `strcpy` is invoked. The almost inevitable result is an access violation.

11. It is hard to imagine such a situation. The rule of thumb for writing your own copy constructor and assignment operator is the same: You should do so if the data members include a pointer.

13. No. Call by reference involves a *pointer* to an object, not a copy of the object. Therefore, the copy constructor is not needed in call by reference.

15. Even if the compiler provided a default overload of `operator!=`, the overloaded operator would use member-by-member tests for equality. In a code slice such as

```
String s1( "foo" );
String s2( "foo" );
if ( s1 != s2 )
   ...
```

we presumably want the `if` test to *fail* even though `s1.str` and `s2.str` point to different cells because the cells to which they point contain the same chars.

Section 4.3

1.
```
class C1 {
   ...
};
class C2 {
   friend C1;
   ...
};
```

```
class C3 {
  friend C2;
  ...
};
```

3. No.

5. No. By making A a **friend** to B, we do not thereby make B a **friend** to A.

Section 4.4

1. Yes.

3.
```
void BST::postorder()
{
  postorderAux( root );
}

void BST::postorderAux( Node* n )
{
  // if current subtree is empty,
  // return as there are no nodes
  // to traverse in it
  if ( n -> empty() )
    return;

  postorderAux( n -> lc );   // traverse left subtree
  postorderAux( n -> rc );   // traverse right subtree
  n -> write();              // visit Node
}
```

5. If a method is not part of a class's public interface, then the method should be **private**. For example, if method M1 is part of a functional decomposition of method M, then it makes sense for M1 to be **private** because M1 clearly is not part of the class's public interface. In different terms, a method should be **private** when the only functions that invoke it are other methods or **friend** functions.

7. The default constructor has the assignment statement

```
root = tree = new Node;
```

as its body.

9. The BST method **addNodeAux** accesses the **Node** data members **val**, **lc**, and **rc**.

11.   `BST bst;  // create a BST`

Section 4.5

1.   The only thing that needs to be changed is method `stackNodesAux`:

```
// preorder traversal
void IterBST::stackNodesAux( Node* n )
{
   if ( n -> empty() )
     return;

   nodeStack[ nextNode++ ] = n;
   stackNodesAux( n -> lc );
   stackNodesAux( n -> rc );
}
```

3.   `IterBST` methods need to access `root` and `count` in `BST` and `lc` and `rc` in `Node`.

5.   Neither `Node` nor `BST` methods access any `IterBST` data members or methods.

7.
```
Node* IterBST::getNextNode()
{
   if ( nextNode >= nodeCount )
     return 0;
   Node* retval = nodeStack[ nextNode ];
   nextNode++;
   return retval;
}
```

Section 4.6

1.   No, a `static` data member must be defined outside all blocks.

3.   A `static` data member must not be defined inside a block. In this example, `X::sX` is defined inside `main`'s body.

5.   A `static` data member must be defined *without* the keyword `static`.

7.   Yes.

9.   A `friend` function has access to *all* data members in a class, whereas a `static` method has access only to `static` data members in a class.

11.   No. A destructor belongs to a *specific* object in a class, not to the class as a whole.

13. A `static` data member is tied to a particular class, whereas a global variable is not. Further, a `static` data member is `private` by default, which promotes information hiding.

Section 5.1

1.

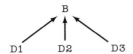

3.

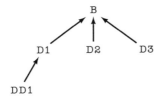

5. A superclass is called a base class in C++. A subclass is called a derived class in C++.

7.

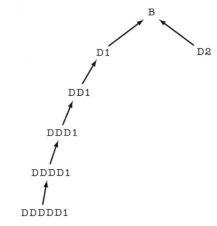

B has directly derived classes D1 and D2. B has indirectly derived classes DD1, DDD1, DDDD1, and DDDDD1.

9. The error is

```
y = x;
```

because **x** is accessible only within class **A**.

11. The error is

```
ptr -> f1 = 3.14;
```

because `f1` is `protected`, not `public`, in `A`. Therefore, `f1` cannot be accessed by a nonmethod or a nonfriend such as `main`.

13.
```
class B {
    ...
};

class D : public B {
    ...
};
```

15.
```
R
↑
Q
↑
P
```

17. A `protected` data member or method is accessible only within a class hierarchy, whereas a `public` data member or method is globally accessible. Accordingly, a `protected` data member or method exemplifies information hiding, a guiding principle of object-oriented programming.

19. The two references to `b1.f1` in `main` are illegal. Because inheritance from `A` to `B` is `private`, the `protected` data member `f1` in `A` becomes `private` in `B`; and a `private` data member is accessible only by methods or `friends`—and `main` is neither. The error would remain even if the inheritance from `A` to `B` were `protected` or `public` because an inherited `protected` member cannot become globally accessible (i.e., `public`) in a derived class.

21. The error is

```
b1.x = 8;
```

Since `x` is `protected` in B, it is not accessible outside B.

23.
```
num1 = n1;
num2 = n2;
num3 = n3;
```

25. The error is

```
a.x = 1;
```

in `B::f2`. The `x` inherited from `A` is accessible in `B`, which means that the reference to `x` in method `f1` is a reference to `B::x` and is therefore legal.

However, the data member `a.x` is *not* accessible in B because `a` is an A object but not a B object. Therefore, the reference to `a.x` in method `f2` is illegal.

Section 5.2

1. D's constructor must explicitly invoke B's parameterized constructor because B does *not* have a default constructor.

3.
```
#include <iostream.h>
class A {
    int dummy;
public:
    A() { cout << "A::A" << endl; }
};

class B : public A {
    int dummy;
public:
    B() : A() { cout << "B::B" << endl; }
};

class C : public B {
    int dummy;
public:
    C() : B() { cout << "C::C" << endl; }
};

A a1;
B b1, b2;
C c1, c2, c3;
```

5. No.

7. Yes. Here is an example:

```
class B { // base class
  int x;
};

class D : public B { derived class
public:
    D() { cout << "D::D" << endl; }
};

D d; // D::D fires
```

9. A derived class is a specialization of a base class. The base class constructor is used to take care of initialization, etc., for the part of the object that comes from the base class.

Section 5.3

1. Desktop is a derived class with respect to Computer but a base class with respect to WS and PC.

3.
```
// Desktop machines comprise workstations and
// personal computers.
class Desktop : public Computer {
   enum { True = 1, False = 0 };
protected:
   int superscalar;    // True or False
   Desktop( float al,  // arith-logic
            float c,    // control
            float m,    // memory
            float io,   // io
            float t,    // ct
            char* n,    // name
            float l,    // lower bound
            float u )   // upper bound
      : Computer( al, c, m, io, t, n, l, u ) { }
};
```

5. A good place to get current data on PC technology is from magazines such as *Byte* and *PC Magazine*. Vendor catalogs also contain extensive technical information.

7. No, an improvement in throughput does not automatically bring an improvement in response time. Suppose that job *J* takes 10 seconds to run on machine *M*. *M*'s response time when running *J* is 10 and its throughput is one *J* every 10 seconds. Now suppose that *M*'s vendor upgrades it by giving the machine parallel processing capability: *M* now can run two *J*s concurrently, but its response time per job does not change. So *M*'s response time with respect to *J* is still 10. However, *M*'s throughput has doubled as it can complete two *J*s every 10 seconds. In sum, *M*'s throughput with respect to *J* has doubled but its response time is unchanged.

9. When object workstation is created as a WS object, its constructor WS is invoked. However, the WS constructor invokes the Desktop constructor *before* executing its own body. The Desktop constructor, in turn, invokes the Computer constructor before executing its own body. So the logical order of constructor firing is Computer, then Desktop, then WS.

11.
```
class Test {
    float rt; // response time in nanoseconds
    float mips;
    void results( Computer c, BMark b );
public:
    Test( Computer c, BMark b );
    void setMips( float m ) { mips = m; }
};
```

Section 5.4

1. A!

3. Z!

5. Since no method is `virtual`, compile-time binding is in effect. Because `ptr` is of type `A*`, `ptr` binds to `A::f`. The statement

```
ptr -> f();
```

invokes `A`'s `f`. The statement

```
ptr -> Z::f();
```

therefore contains an error. For the statement to be correct, `Z` would have to be a base class for `A`.

7. Compile-time binding.

9. A virtual function must be a method.

11. An abstract class is a class to which objects cannot belong directly. An object can belong only indirectly to an abstract class by belonging directly to a class derived from the abstract class.

```
class Abstract {
    virtual void f() = 0;
};

class Derived : public Abstract {
    ...
};

// ***** ERROR: can't belong directly
// to Abstract
Abstract abs;
Derived der; // ok
```

13. In C++, we create an abstract class by declaring a pure `virtual` function in the class declaration.

15. Yes.

17. The keyword `virtual` may not appear in the `virtual` function's definition if the definition occurs outside the class declaration.

Section 5.5

1. BST still needs to access `Node`'s data members `lc` and `rc`.

3. BST method `traverse` is a pure `virtual` function.

5. No, the keyword occurs as part of the method's *declaration*.

7.
```
void PostBST::postorderAux( Node* n )
{
    if ( n -> empty() )
        return;
    postorderAux( n -> lc );
    postorderAux( n -> rc );
    n -> write();
}
```

9. The `PreBST` default and copy constructors simply invoke the BST default and copy constructors to do their work. Therefore, the `PreBST` versions have empty function bodies.

11. In the original version, the programmer determines the type of tree traversal (e.g., inorder) by *explicitly* invoking the `inorder` method on a BST. In the revised version, the object determines the sort of traversal appropriate to it. For example, a `preorder` traversal is appropriate to a `PreBST` object. The `virtual` method `traverse` is invoked on any BST object because the object itself then determines which version of the `virtual` function is appropriate to it. This is polymorphism at work. The original version has no polymorphism.

Section 5.6

1.
```
X::X
Y::Y
X::X
Y::Y
Z::Z
Z::~Z
Y::~Y
X::~X
```

```
         Y::~Y
         X::~X
```

3. Z() and ~Z().

5. No, and a derived class destructor typically does *not* invoke a base class destructor even if one exists.

7. In the class hierarchy

```
class A {
    int* ptrA;
public:
    A() { ptrA = new int[ 1000 ]; }
};

class B : public A {
    int* ptrB;
public:
    B() { ptrB = new int[ 1000 ]; }
};
```

there should be a **virtual** destructor because constructors for **A** and **B** dynamically allocate *separate* storage. If a program using this hierarchy should dynamically allocate, say, a **B**, then a **virtual** destructor would prevent the creation of garbage.

9. If (1) constructors for a base and derived class dynamically allocate separate storage and (2) the program dynamically allocates a class object from the hierarchy, then the hierarchy should have a **virtual** destructor.

Section 5.7

1. Single inheritance is used to specialize or refine a class, whereas multiple inheritance is used to combine classes.

3. R has four data members: **x** and **y** inherited from **P**, and **a** and **b** inherited from **Q**.

5.
```
void R::assign( int xx, int yy, int aa, int bb )
{
    x = xx; y = yy;
    a = aa; b = bb;
}
```

7. Two: one via **B1** and one via **B2**.

Section 6.1

1. The member operator . may not be overloaded.

3. The logical *or* operator || must be overloaded as a *binary* operator, which means that there should be a single argument instead of three arguments.

5.
```
class C {
    int x;
    int y;
public:
    // sample overload of && as friend
    friend int operator&&( C a1, C a2 )
    {
        if ( a1 <= 0 || a2 <= 0 )
            return 0;
        return a1 == a2;
    }
};
```

7.
```
class C {
    int x;
    int y;
public:
    // sample overload of + as friend
    friend int operator+( C a1, C a2 )
    {
        return a1 * a1 + a2 * a2;
    }
};
```

9. No, the ->* operator may be overloaded.

11. Yes, with the exception of the memory management operators new, delete, and delete[ ].

13. The sizeof operator already works on any data type, built-in or user-defined. It is hard to imagine a need to overload such a basic operator in the language.

15.
```
class C {
    int x;
    int y;
```

```
public:
    // sample overload of ,
    friend int operator,( C a1, C a2 )
    {
        return a1.x;
    }
};
```

Section 6.2

1.
```
void Matrix::dump()
{
    for ( int i = 0; i < side * side; i++ )
        cout << cells[ i ] << endl;
}
```

3.
```
void Matrix::copy( Matrix& m )
{
    // same size?
    if ( m.side != side )
        return;

    // copy
    for ( int i = 0; i < side * side; i++ )
        cells[ i ] = m.cells[ i ];
}
```

5. If `Matrix::operator()` returned an `int` value rather than an `int` reference, then a `Matrix` object could not be the *target* (i.e., left-hand side) of an assignment operation.

7. No, because `OverflowFlag` itself can be the target of an assignment operation and thus have its value reset.

9. Any other choice would be contrived or illegal. For example, we cannot use `operator[ ]` because in an expression such as

```
Matrix m;
m[ 3, 4 ]; // ***** ERROR: [ ] is unary
```

`operator[ ]` requires a single argument.

Section 6.3

1. We describe the changes. `Entry` no longer requires a default constructor to initialize `word` and `def` to empty strings because the `String` class's default constructor already handles this task. Methods `add`, `write`, and `match` must be adjusted to handle `String` rather than `char*` data members.

3.   `DictIter` references `private Dict` data members `count` and `entries`.

5.   The first pair of parentheses identifies the operator, i.e., `operator()`. The second pair is the argument list, which is empty.

7.   The function call operator `()` may take zero or more arguments, which makes it very flexible.

9.
```
// append d to w's definition in dictionary
void Dict::append( char* w, char* d )
{
    if ( !strlen( d ) ) // nothing to append
        return;

    int i = 0;
    while ( i < count )
        if ( entries[ i ].match( w ) )
            // any room?
            if ( strlen( entries[ i ].def +
                    strlen( d ) < MaxDef ) ) {
                strcat( entries[ i ].def, d );
                break;
            }
        else
            i++;
}
```

Section 6.4

1.   A type conversion operator must not have a return value in its definition.

3.   The first `const` signals that code outside the `String` class should not modify the storage to which `str` points. The second `const` signals that the type conversion operator does not change this storage.

5.   The compiler determines from context the type of value required for an operation. For instance, the `if` condition

```
String s( "alicia" );
if ( strlen( s ) )
    ...
```

invokes `strlen`, which expects a `char*` rather than a `String` argument. Therefore, the compiler invokes the `String` to `char*` type conversion operator, if one is defined.

7. The compiler rather than the programmer typically invokes a type conversion operator; and, in writing a type conversion operator, the programmer may not have anticipated all contexts in which compiler will invoke the operator. This can lead to subtle bugs.

Section 6.5

1. `FileRef`'s overload of `operator=` and its type conversion operator (from a `FileRef` to a `char`) both reference `File`'s `fptr private` data member.

3. The overloaded `operator=` returns a `FileRef` *reference* (i.e., a `FileRef&`) rather than a pointer to a `FileRef` (i.e., a `FileRef*`). Therefore, the return value is `*this` rather than `this`.

5. Implementation details are split between `File` and `FileRef` roughly as follows: `File` handles the high-level details, whereas `FileRef` handles the low-level details. In a code slice such as

```
File f( "out.dat" );
f[ 0 ] = 'Z';
```

the subscript operator is implemented as a `File` method precisely to allow the user to manipulate a `File` as if it were an array. The user needs to know that the array syntax

```
f[ 0 ] = ...;
```

is now legal for `Files`. The user does not need to understand how the assignment operator is working (e.g., that it does an `fseek` into a `File`), or even whether the assignment operator is built-in or overloaded. Accordingly, these details are hidden from the user within class `FileRef`.

7. The overloaded assignment operator comes into play during writes but not during reads. During reads, the type conversion operator (`FileRef` to `char`) comes into play.

9. In a an expression such as

```
f[ 0 ] = 'Z' // f is a File object
```

`f`'s overloaded subscript operator is invoked. But `f`'s overloaded assignment operator is *not* at work. Instead, the subscript operator returns a `FileRef` object so that *this* object's assignment operator can be invoked. We need a `FileRef` object because the assignment operator is overloaded as a `FileRef` method, not as a `File` method.

Section 6.6

1.
```
C1* c1 = new C1;         // C1's new
C2* c2 = new C2;         // built-in new
int* i1 = new int;       // built-in new
C1* cs = new C1[ 10 ];   // C1's new
```

3. If `delete` is overloaded, its first argument must be of type `void*`.

5. No.

Section 7.1

3. Any data set can ultimately be encoded as a string of bits and so is a stream.

5. If `ofstream` were derived from `ostream` and `filebuf` it would contain both high-level and low-level input/output methods. The intent of the original design was to separate the high-level and low-level methods into different classes.

Section 7.2

1. `io_obj.rdstate() & ios::eofbit`

3. The not operator (`!`) is overloaded so that the value of the expression `!cin` is converted to a pointer. (If the pointer value is `NULL` the expression is false; otherwise, the expression is true.)

5. `fout.seekp( -10, ios::end );`

7. `cout.setf( ios::showpoint );`

9. `cout.unsetf( ios::showpoint );`

11. `cout.setf( ios::oct, ios::basefield );`

13. `cout.setf( 0, ios::floatfield );`

15. `0X42$$0X42$$0X420X42`

Section 7.3

1. `cin.read( a, 100);`

3. 50

5. e

7. e

9.
```cpp
istream& operator>>( istream& in, ZipCode& z )
{
    return in >> z.read();
}
```

11.
```cpp
char a[ MAX_NO_STRINGS ][ MAX_STR_SIZE ];

while ( cin.peek() != '\n' ) {
    cin.get( a[ i++ ], MAX_STR_SIZE );
    cin.get(); // discard newline
}
cin.get(); // discard newline
```

13.
```cpp
ostream& operator<<( ostream& out, ZipCode& z )
{
    return out << z.write();
}
```

Section 7.4

1.
```cpp
cout << resetiosflags( ios::showpoint );
```

3.
```cpp
istream& ws( istream& is )
{
    is.setf( ios::skipws );  return is;
}
```

5.
```cpp
ostream& scien( ostream& os )
{
    os.setf( ios::scientific, ios::floatfield );  return os;
}
```

7.
```cpp
ostream& set_filler( ostream& os, int c )
{
    os.fill( c );
    return os;
}
OMANIP< int > setfill( int c )
{
    return OMANIP< int >( set_filler, c );
}
```

9.
```cpp
istream& seto( istream& is, streamoff n )
{
    is.seekg( n, ios::beg );
    return is;
}
```

```
IMANIP< streamoff > setoff( streamoff n )
{
    return IMANIP< streamoff >( seto, n );
}
```

11. A manipulator is a *toplevel* function that "manipulates" an object in a class using the overloaded input (>>) or output (<<) operator. A manipulator can be added without modifying the class. A method is part of a class. It too can manipulate an object using the overloaded input or output operator in the class to which it belongs; however, adding such a method means modifying the class, which may not be convenient or even possible if the class is provided by a library.

Section 7.5

1.  ```
    ifstream fin;
    fin.open( "weather.in" );
    ```

3.  ```
    fstream finout( "stars.dat", ios::in
                                 | ios::out
                                 | ios::nocreate );
    ```

5. It is illegal to have two definitions of the same variable in the same scope.

7.  ```
    #include <fstream.h>
    #include <stdlib.h>

    int main( int c, char** argv )
    {
        char c;
        ifstream fin;

        for ( int i = 1; i < c; i++ ) {
            fin.open( argv[ i ], ios::binary );
            if ( fin )
                while ( fin.get( c ) )
                    cout.put( c );
            fin.close();
        }

        return EXIT_SUCCESS;
    }
    ```
    ```

Section 7.7

1.  ```cpp
    char buff[ 100 ];
    int i = 6;
    ostrstream( buff, sizeof ( buff ) );
    sout << "Santa Claus Conquers " << i << " Martians" << ends;
    cout << buff << endl;
    ```

3.  ```cpp
    // s is a character string that represents a long double
    long double x;
    istrstream sin( s );
    sin >> x;
    ```

Section 7.8

1.  ```cpp
    #include <fstream.h>
    #include <strstream.h>
    #include <stdlib.h>

    int main()
    {
        char buff[ 10000 ];
        ifstream fin( "data.in" );
        ostrstream sout( buff, sizeof ( buff ) );

        copy( fin, sout );

        return EXIT_SUCCESS;
    }
    ```

3.  ```cpp
    #include <fstream.h>
    #include <stdlib.h>

    int main()
    {
        ifstream fin( "data.in" );

        copy( fin, cerr );

        return EXIT_SUCCESS;
    }
    ```

5.  ```cpp
    void copy( istream& in, ostream& out, int tabsize )
    {
        char c;
        long fl;
    ```
    ```

```
int i;

fl = in.unsetf( ios::skipws );
int c, count = 0, i, numb;

while ( in >> c )
   if ( c == '\t' ) {
      numb = tabsize - ( count % tabsize );
      for ( i = 0; i < numb; i++ )
         out << ' ';
      count += numb;
   }
   else {
      count++;
      out << c;
      if ( c == '\n' )
         count = 0;
   }

in.flags( fl );
}
```

Section 7.9

1.
```
char buff[ 256 ];
filebuf finout;
finout( buff, sizeof ( buff ) );
finout.open( "balance.dat", ios::in | ios::out );
```

5. An abstract buffer is simply storage that can *always* be written to or read from; the buffer classes reflect this abstract characterization. Also, the buffer classes are low-level classes that service the high-level classes and so are typically not accessed directly by the programmer. For this reason, there is no overriding need to provide a logical separation of the input and output methods. Finally, providing input/output buffer classes rather than separate input buffer classes, output buffer classes, and input/output buffer classes simplifies the declaration of the high-level input/output classes. Class ios contains a pointer to a buffer class that can then be used for either input or output or both by the various input classes, output classes, and input/output classes derived from ios.

Section 8.1

1. Since no handler is defined, the system function terminate will be invoked.

Section 8.2

1. Since **bptr** points to a **Book**, the code

   ```
   ptr -> print_title();
   ptr -> print_level();
   ```

   is executed.

3. Since **bptr** points to a **Paperback**, the code

   ```
   ptr -> print_title();
   ```

   is executed.

5. True

7. True

9. False

11. True

13. True

15. False

17. False

19. False

21. False

23. False

25. False

27. False

Section 8.3

1.
   ```
   kalin_software::string k;
   jbaugh_software::string j;
   ```

Index